# EZHICHIGEYANG
## *Ojibwe Word List*

**AUTHORS**
Nancy Jones (Ogimaawigwanebiik)
Gordon Jourdain (Maajiigwaneyaash)
Rose Tainter (Zhaangweshi)

**EDITORS**
Anton Treuer (Waagosh)
Keller Paap (Waawaakeyaash)

ISBN 978-1-257-04392-7

Produced, printed, and sold by Waadookodaading Ojibwe Immersion Charter School. Orders may be placed with the form printed the back of this book or at www.waadookodaading.org, www.lulu.com, or www.amazon.com. Cover design by Jordyn Flaada. Pictured on cover are Isaac, Elias, and Evan Treuer. Photographs by Anton Treuer and John Swartz.

For more information on the immersion school, grants, and orders, contact Waadookodaading Ojibwe Immersion Charter School, PO Box 860, Hayward, WI, 54843. For information on the editorial process or entries, contact Anton Treuer, 112 American Indian Resource Center #21, Bemidji State University, 1500 Birchmont Drive NE, Bemidji, MN 56601. Research and work sessions for this dictionary were conducted as part of a cooperative venture between Waadookodaading Ojibwe Immersion Charter School, Lac Courte Oreilles Ojibwe Community College, and Bemidji State University.

www.waadookodaading.org
www.lco.edu
www.bemidjistate.edu/airc/

The publication and working sessions for this project were funded by a grant to Bemidji State University from the *Minnesota History & Culture Grant Program*, supported by the Minnesota Clean Water, Land, and Legacy Amendment, a grant to Lac Courte Oreilles Ojibwe Community College from the *USDA National Institute of Food and Agriculture*, and a grant to Waadookodaading Ojibwe Immersion Charter Schools from the *Administration for Native Americans* (grant #90NL044702). Keller Paap and Anton Treuer both had time made available to work on this project through support from the *Bush Leadership Fellows Program*. Anton Treuer had additional support from the *American Philosophical Society Sabbatical Fellows Program*, the *American Philosophical Society Benjamin Franklin Research Grants Program,* and the *John Simon Guggenheim Foundation*.

# EZHICHIGEYANG
*Ojibwe Word List*

## CONTENTS

# EZHICHIGEYANG
*Ojibwe Word List*

## PREFACE
Anton Treuer

### Language Crisis

Language and culture loss are among the biggest concerns today in Ojibwe country. There are now fewer than 1,000 Ojibwe speakers living in the United States.[1] There are thousands more speakers of Ojibwe in Canada. However, even there, language loss is becoming readily apparent in many communities. Nancy Jones (Nigigoonsiminikaaning First Nation) estimates that there are 12 fluent speakers in her home community, and perhaps 6 at Koochiching First Nation. The entire Treaty Three area in Canada acknowledges an ongoing language crisis.

There is a growing desire among Ojibwe people in Minnesota and Wisconsin to stabilize and revitalize the Ojibwe language. Hoping to do what the Maori and Native Hawaiians have done for their languages, Ojibwe language immersion schools have been working for several years to share the language with young Ojibwe people in a total immersion environment. Many collegiate programs and community education efforts have also tried to do more of their teaching in an immersion environment.

Immersion schools thrive on content-based education. They teach science while harvesting rice, mathematics while playing the traditional Ojibwe moccasin game. Yet the fledgling immersion efforts already undertaken for Ojibwe today are profoundly challenging for schools with Ojibwe immersion mandates and

---

[1] Anton Treuer, *Ojibwe in Minnesota* (St. Paul: Minnesota Historical Society Press, 2010) 74-75.

---

required instruction of all state-mandated curriculum with limited resource materials available in print. Even many fluent speakers are not well versed in techniques for making bulrush mats, or the nomenclature of a #6 conibear trap. In order to better document and equip immersion schools and others with the traditional vocabulary needed to teach netting and wigwam building, a trio of brilliant Ojibwe speakers came together with a team of language learners, teachers, and scholars to document *ezhichigeyang* (what we do).

## Degosijigejig (Contributors)
In addition to the authors and editors, many other people made major contributions to this work. John Nichols spell-checked most of the entries and double-checked them with Nancy Jones, Gordon Jourdain, Rose Tainter, and Eugene Stillday. Word lists previously developed with other speakers were sometimes discussed to see if they matched the dialects represented in this book. Sometimes, entries from those word lists were included if they added to the work. Furthermore, many people attended the hands-on working sessions where we built a wigwam and brainstormed terminology. Participants included: Lisa LaRonge, Michael DeMarr, Jason Schlender, Lucia Bonacci, Brian McGinnis, David Bisonette, Michelle Haskins, Alex Decoteau, Monique Paulson, Sean Fahrlander, Brooke Ammann, Esther Kingfisher, and Brian Kingfisher. Major contributors not present for the working sessions included: John Nichols, Archie Mosay, Earl Otchingwanigan (Nyholm), Anna Gibbs, Leonard Moose, and Leona Wakonabo.

## Attribution of Entries
Because this dictionary and other vocabulary publications often involve speakers from many different dialects, it is critical to properly attribute the words documented to their speakers. We used first and last initial in parentheses as follows for contributors to this work:

Nancy Jones (NJ)                    Nigigoonsiminikaaning (Ontario)

| | |
|---|---|
| Gordon Jourdain (GJ) | Lac La Croix (Ontario) |
| Rose Tainter (RT) | Red Lake (Ponemah) |
| Anton Treuer (AT) | Leech Lake (Bena) |
| Keller Paap (KP) | Red Cliff (Wisconsin) |
| Leona Wakonabo (LW) | Leech Lake (Inger) |
| Marlene Stately (MS) | Leech Lake (Ball Club) |
| Eugene Stillday (ES) | Red Lake (Ponemah) |
| Anna Gibbs (AG) | Red Lake (Ponemah) |
| Rosemarie DeBungie (RD) | Red Lake (Ponemah) |
| Lisa LaRonge (LL) | Lac Courte Oreilles (Wisconsin) |
| Archie Mosay (AM) | St. Croix (Wisconsin) |
| Jason Schlender (JS) | Lac Courte Oreilles (Wisconsin) |
| Brian McGinnis (BM) | Curve Lake (Ontario) |
| Earl Otchingwanigan [Nyholm] (EO) | Crystal Falls (Michigan) |
| James Clark (JC) | Mille Lacs (Lake Lena) |
| Thomas Stillday (TS) | Red Lake (Ponemah) |
| Geraldine Howard (GH) | Leech Lake (Inger) |
| Lawrence Leonard Moose (LM) | Mille Lacs (Lake Lena) |

**Multi-dialect Process**

In two separate sessions, all of the authors, editors, and other participants met on the Lac Courte Oreilles reservation to build wigwams and to discuss procedures for harvesting fish in the Ojibwe custom. In addition to the hands-on work, we met in group to brainstorm traditional terminology. The fluent speakers were free to digress on tangents, which is why terms for dinosaurs and other parts of the language worked their way into dictionary. The participants were very careful to include all entries no matter how divergent the dialects were so that all speakers had voice. There was no attempt to standardize the language. On the contrary, difference of dialect and view were all documented with equal care. Some dialect issues are significant. We simply wrote the words the way speakers said them and noted who said them.

The words were directly entered into computers while the group was in session and projected onto a LCD screen for all participants to edit. Most entries were directly corrected, edited, or cast in variants with no attempt to standardize the dialects represented, but rather to capture all of their nuances. Even a simple conjugation such as *gibakite'waa*, meaning "you are hitting someone," took tremendous care to capture dialect variance. All contributors agreed on the meaning of the word and it's conjugation in this form, but upon further solicitation it became clear that each one of them had a different command form: *bakite'wi* for Nancy Jones, *bakite'o* for Gordon Jourdain, and *bakite'* for Rose Tainter. This was a common issue for many entries. The multi-dialect process requires substantial time with each contributor. The written work in progress and under constant view for editing was a huge part of the project's success. Any mistakes in data entry remain those of Anton Treuer and Keller Paap, who did most of the typing and formal editing of entries.

Once lists were generated in group, edited by Treuer and Paap, and presented again to the speakers who generated those lists, they were read, proofread, re-edited, and finalized. Several drafts were edited after the initial meetings as well. John Nichols checked most entries as discussed above. Anton Treuer checked entries again with Nancy Jones, Gordon Jourdain, and Rose Tainter. Nancy Jones, Gordon Jourdain, and other speakers responded to e-mails and phone calls about specific glosses and spellings as well. What is presented below is the final word list.

Ojibwe does not function like English. As a result, English noun-based word lists do not translate well into Ojibwe. Rather, the speakers did what comes naturally in Ojibwe—they talked about things, and used verbs to do that. Many of the nouns on these lists are presented as participles (verb-based nouns, noun-like verbs). However, the discussion also generated massive amounts of sentences, examples, and discussion. We included some example sentences in the citations. Additional pertinent and useful example sentences, applications, and cultural information are appended to the back of the word list. It is the sincere wish of the entire team that all of this material will be used, distributed, shared, taught, and incorporated into dictionaries and other publications (with proper credit given to these authors).

*Ezhichigeyang* is not a final product, but rather just the beginning of a massive undertaking to expand usage of the Ojibwe language and maintain its vibrancy. It is a starting point, not an end point. We need to have many more workshops and publications like this to help teachers of the language fill holes in their knowledge, curricula, and resources for the betterment of the language and the instruction of Ojibwe youth.

The entire team for the vocabulary project is deeply indebted to many people for their support, help, knowledge, and patience with this project. Michael DeMarr and Cathy Begay did much of the grant administration and logistical preparation for the work sessions. Several elders who were not present are cited in this work because their words were specifically queried or remembered by participants. Grant acknowledgements are listed on the copyright page.

## Orthography

The entire team for the vocabulary project has endorsed, approved of, and worked with the double-vowel orthography. All participants agree that the writing system is not the critical focus of instruction, but rather the spoken word. The writing system is just a tool. Amazingly, nobody once fought over, questioned, or doubted the validity of the system itself, but simply expended all energies on the work, enabling maximum productivity.

C.E. Fiero adapted the double-vowel orthography to Ojibwe in the 1950s, with additional writing conventions and refinements added by John D. Nichols and Earl Otchingwanigan (Nyholm) in the 1970s. Although some discussion of the format follows here, it is not comprehensive; and students of the language are recommended to John D. Nichols and Earl Nyholm (Otchingwanigan), *A Concise Dictionary of Minnesota Ojibwe* (Minneapolis: University of Minnesota Press, 1995) for more information on the writing system.

The double-vowel is the most consistent and precise of all the available options. It is not without problems, however. Sometimes the sound *o* is pronounced as *o* and sometimes sounds more like *wa*. Thus some speakers insist that "top of the hill" is *ogidaaki* and others insist that it is *wagidaaki*. The same is true for *waabigon* and *waabigwan* and many other words. The sounds *i* and *a* are also difficult to discern. These distinctions are difficult to discern, even for first speakers of the language. It almost seems like we need two more vowels to capture the nuances and eliminate inconsistencies. Again, we wrote words how the first speakers said them and spelled them, aware of these issues.

Ojibwe-English entires are alphabetized according to the Ojibwe double-vowel alphabet:

a, aa, b, ch, d, e, g, h, ', i, ii, j, k, m, n, o, oo, p,
s, sh, t, w, y, z, zh

Thus, *abi* comes before *aanakwad* because the double-vowel *aa* is considered a single vowel, voiced by a single sound. The letter *a* comes after the letter *aa*. Bear this in mind as you search for entries. The glossary follows the Ojibwe alphabet, not English. Also, many Ojibwe words take numerous conjugated forms, some of which differ significantly from the head word forms which are sequenced here. This is a word list, not a grammar book, and thus there is not sufficient space to provide a detailed grammatical analysis here. Students are recommended to refer to the *Oshkaabewis Native Journal*, Vol. 4, No. 1, 121-38, Vol. 4, No. 2, 61-108, *Oshkaabewis Native Journal*, Vol. 6, Nos. 1-2, 137-174, and *Our Ojibwe Grammar* by James Clark and Rick Greszcyk for pedagogical double-vowel grammar material. All material printed in the *Oshkaabewis Native Journal* is now available for free download on the internet at *bemidjistate.edu/airc/oshkaabewis*.

The gloss format employed here follows the Nichols and Nyholm (Otchingwanigan) system. Ojibwe-English entries begin with an Ojibwe head word. With the exception of preverbs and prenouns, which attach to verbs, all head words are complete Ojibwe words. The head word is followed by a class code, and abbreviation of the word class, identifying the type of word. The code is followed by the gloss, which approximates as closely as possible the English equivalent of the head word. A basic entry looks like this:

omaa   *pc*   here
/      |      \
(head word) (class code)   (gloss)

Plural noun forms and alternate spellings of certain words are also provided with many of the entries. For example:

**manoominii**   *na*   Menomini Indian; *pl* **manoominiig**; *also* **omanoominii**
/     /          |         \        \
(head word)   (class code)    (gloss)    (plural form)     (alternate reference)

Some of the verb entries also include a word stem immediately after the head word. This is done for the relatively small number of verbs for which the word stem is not a complete sentence or command. For example:

**waabandiwag** /**waabandi-**/   *vai*   they see one another
/         /       \          \
(head word)    (word stem)    (class code)     (gloss)

The only head words presented here which are not complete words are preverbs and prenouns. Some *vta* entries use the *n* for certain conjugations and the letter *zh* for other inflections of that same word. Letters that fall in this pattern are written just how they are used in the texts (*n* or *zh*), but the glossary notes that letter in the word stem as *N*. For example:

**miizh** /**miiN-**/ *vta* give something to someone

All Ojibwe nouns and verbs are differentiated by gender as animate or inanimate. A list of class codes and Ojibwe word classes follows here:

---

| Code | Word Class | Definition |
|---|---|---|
| *na* | animate noun | animate gendered noun |
| *nad* | dependent animate noun | animate gendered noun that must be possessed |
| *na-pt* | animate participle | animate gendered noun-like verb |
| *ni* | inanimate noun | inanimate gendered noun |
| *nid* | dependent inanimate noun | inanimate gendered noun that must be possessed |
| *ni-pt* | inanimate participle | inanimate gendered noun-like verb |
| *nm* | number | number |
| *pc* | particle | particle (can function as adverb, exclamation, or conjunction) |
| *pn* | prenoun | prefix attached to nouns (functions as adjective) |
| *pr* | pronoun | pronoun |
| *pv* | preverb | prefix attached to verbs (functions as adverb) |
| *vai* | animate intransitive verb | verb with no object and a subject of the animate gender |
| *vai+o* | animate intransitive verb plus object | verb with a subject of the animate gender and object (animate or inanimate) which inflects like a traditional *vai* |
| *vii* | inanimate intransitive verb | verb with no object and subject of the inanimate gender |
| *vta* | transitive animate verb | verb with a subject and object of the animate gender |
| *vti* | transitive inanimate verb | verb with a subject of the animate gender and object of the inanimate gender |

The codes used here are consistent with those employed by Nichols and Nyholm (Otchingwanigan) in *A Concise Dictionary of Minnesota Ojibwe*. The codes for *pv*, *vti*, and *vai* are further divided into subclasses by Nichols and Nyholm (Otchingwanigan). There are some differences in conjugation patterns within class codes. The subclasses of these word types primarily denote further differentiations in inflection patterns, not class description. Those differences, while significant, are relatively minor. Thus, this word list does not distinguish between them. Students of the language are encouraged to refer to the grammar references mentioned above for further analysis of inflection patterns.

Since hyphens (-) are used to separate preverbs and prenouns from the main forms they attach to, the equal sign (=) symbol is used to break up words that span more than one line. Entries in this dictionary have been carefully checked with Nancy Jones, Gordon Jourdain, and Rose Tainter. Mistakes in glossing and spelling words, however, are entirely those of the editors.

# OJIBWE-ENGLISH

# A

abaasindekeboozazhaan *ni* suntan oil (NJ)

abanzh *ni* lodge pole; *pl* abanzhiin (NJ, GJ)

abanzhiiwaatig *ni* lodge pole; *pl* abanzhiiwaatigoon (GJ)

abwaanaak *ni* roasting stick; *pl* abwaanaakoon (NJ, GJ)

abwebiigaskatigwe *vai* have a sweaty forehead (GJ)

abwebiigazhe *vai* have sweaty skin, have sweaty body (NJ, GJ)

abwenagizhiinsi *vai* roast wieners over a fire (NJ)

achigaazo *vai* be put somewhere (RT)

adikamebinidis *ni* whitefish pipes; *ni* adikamebinidisiin (NJ, GJ)

adikameg *na* whitefish; *pl* adikamegwag (RT, NJ, GJ)

adikamegoons *na* herring; *pl* adikamegoonsag (GJ)

adiman *ni* snowshoe binding; *pl* adimanan (NJ)

adiswi /adisw-/ *vta* dye s.o. (NJ); *also* adiso /adisw-/ *vta* dye s.o. (GJ); *also* adis /adisw-/ *vta* dye s.o. (RT)

adisigan *ni* dye; *pl* adisiganan (RT, NJ, GJ)

adiso *vai* ripen (RT)

adite *vii* ripen (RT)

agawaate *vii* be a shadow (RT, NJ)

agawaateshkaa *vii* be shade, be a shadow (RT, NJ)

agaamiigin *pc* the next page (NJ, GJ)

agawaate'odizo *vai+o* shade one's self with s.t. [*example*: Babaamaajimoo-mazina'igan agawaate'odizon. = Shade youself with an umbrella.] (NJ)

agigokaawin *ni* headcold (RT, NJ, GJ)

agikokaa *vai* have a headcold (RT, NJ, GJ)

agogwaade *vii* sewn on, up against s.t. (as in ends of birch bark lodge coverings) (NJ, GJ)

agoke *vii* attach, adhere, be stuck onto s.t. (RT, NJ, GJ)

agonjidoon *vti* soak s.t. (GJ); *also* agwanjidoon *vti* soak s.t. (RT, NJ)

agonjiwasin *na* anchor rock (weight); *pl* agonjiwasiniig (NJ, GJ)

agonjiwinaagan *ni* net float; *pl* agonjiwinaaganan (GJ); *also* agwinjiwinaagan; *pl* agwinjiwinaaganan (NJ); *also* agoonjoonaagan; *pl* agoonjoonaaganan (JC); *also* angooji-onaagan; *pl* angooji-onaaganan (RT)

agonjiwinaaganens *ni* bobber; *pl* agonjiwinaaganensan (GJ)

**agoodakikwaanaak** *ni* kettle hanger (as in planted kettle hanger); *pl* **agoodakikwaanaakoon** (NJ, GJ)

**agoodasabaanaak** *ni* net drying rack; *pl* **agoodasabaanaakoon** (RT, NJ, GJ)

**agoodasabii** *vai* hang nets (NJ)

**agoodisabii** *vai* hang nets (GJ)

**agoojiganaak** *ni* hanger for fire; *pl* **agoojiganaakoon** (RT, NJ, GJ)

**agoojiganeyaab** *ni* clothesline; *pl* **agoojiganeyaabiin** (RT, NJ, GJ)

**agoonjoonaagan** *ni* floater; *pl* **agoonjoonaaganan** (JC)

**agoozimakakii** *na* boreal chorus frog (type of tree frog); *pl* **agoozimakakiig** (NJ, GJ); *also* **obiibaagimakakii**; *pl* **obiibaagimakakiig** (NJ)

**agoskodin** *vii* freeze to the ice (as in a net) (NJ, GJ)

**agwaaba'iwe** *vai* get off water to safety, seek shelter (NJ, GJ)

**agwaanaadan** *vti* empty s.t. (NJ, GJ)

**agwaanaaso** *vai* empty the canoe (NJ, GJ)

**agwaashim** *vta* take s.o. out of the canoe (NJ, GJ)

**agwaawaanaak** *ni* A-frame pointed smokehouse; *pl* **agwaawaanaakoon** (NJ, GJ)

**agwaawaanaakoons** *ni* smoking rack stick; *pl* **agwaawaanaakoonsan** (NJ, GJ)

**agwaawe** *vai* curing meat/fish by smoking (NJ)

**agwaawen** *vta* cure s.o. by smoking (NJ)

**agwana'an** *vti* cover s.t. (NJ, GJ)

**agwanjidoon** *vti* soak s.t. (RT, NJ); *also* **agonjidoon** (GJ)

**agwaskodin** *vii* freeze to the ice (as in a net) (NJ, GJ)

**agwaayaashkaa** *vii* tide comes in (NJ, GJ)

**agwinjiwinaagan** *ni* net float; *pl* **agwinjiwinaaganan** (NJ); *also* **agonjiwinaagan**; *pl* **agonjiwinaaganan** (GJ); *also* **agoonjoonaagan**; *pl* **agoonjoonaaganan** (JC); *also* **angooji-onaagan**; *pl* **angooji-onaaganan** (RT)

**akakanzhewaakizo** *vai* burn to a state of charcoal (NJ)

**akamaw** *vta* wait for s.o., anticipate s.o. (RT, NJ, GJ)

**akandamaw** *vta* lie in wait for s.o. (RT, NJ, GJ)

**akandiikan** *ni* buoy (for net or navigation); *pl* **akandiikanan** (RT, NJ, GJ)

**akandoowin** *ni* blind (RT, NJ, GJ)

**akawaabam** *vta* wait for s.o. to come into view (RT, NJ, GJ)

**akawadabi** *vai* sit dozing off, spacing out vacuously (RT, NJ, GJ)

**akikaandag** *na* jack pine; *pl* **akikaandagoog** (RT, NJ, GJ)

**akongoshi** *vai* be very sleepy (GJ, NJ)

**akoweba'o** /akoweba'w-/ *vta* push s.o. aside (GJ); *also* **ikoweba'wi** /ikoweba'w-/ (NJ); *also* **ikoweba'** /ikoweba'w-/ (RT)

**akwa'waa** *vai* spear through the ice (dark house) (RT)

**akwa'we** *vai* spear through the ice (dark house) (NJ, GJ)

**Akwa'wewin** *place* Chief Lake, Wisconsin (JS)

**akwaandawe-boonii** *vai* taking off to land at a higher location (NJ, GJ)

**akwaate** *vii* light shines a certain distance or length of time (RT, NJ, GJ)

**akwiindimaa** *vii* be a certain depth (water) (RT, NJ, GJ)

**amaniso** *vai* be frightened of the unseen (LM)

**amikob** *ni* beaver pond; *pl* **amikobiin**; *loc* **amikobiing** (NJ, GJ)

**amikobiigaa** *vii* forming of a beaver lake or pond (NJ); *also* **amikobiikaa** (GJ)

**amikwaabid** *ni* beaver tooth; *pl* **amikwaabidan** (RT, NJ, GJ)

**anama'ewi-giizhikwagad** *vii* be a week (RT)

**anaakan** *ni* woven mat; *pl* **anaakanan** (RT, NJ, GJ)

**anaakanike** *vai* make mats, rugs (RT, NJ, GJ)

**anaamakamig** *pc* underground (RT)

**anaamibag** *pc* under the lily pads (RT)

**anaamiindim** *pc* under water (NJ, GJ)

**anaamikaa** *vii* be underneath (RT)

**anaamikwam** *pc* under the ice (RT, NJ, GJ)

**anaamininj** *pc* under the palm (NJ)

**anaamizid** *pc* under the foot, underneath (RT, NJ, GJ)

**anaamizigoneyaab** *ni* ice netting string (with pole); *pl* **anaamizigoneyaabiin** (NJ, GJ)

**anaamizigoneyaabii** *vai* put net string under ice (NJ, GJ)

**anaamizigoneyaatig** *ni* anchor pole for ice netting; *pl* **anaamizigoneyaatigoon** (NJ, GJ)

**anaamizigosabii** *vai* set net under the ice (RT, NJ, GJ)

**anaamizigwam** *pc* under the ice (RT, NJ, GJ)

**anaamizigwaneyaatig** *ni* slider push-pole for setting net under ice; *pl* **anaamizigwaneyaatigoon** (NJ, GJ)

**anda-ningaapoono** *vai* eat off the bush (ES, RT)

**andawaabi** *vai* be on lookout (RT)

**andawanagekwe** *vai* look for, search for bark (RT, NJ, GJ)

**andawendaagwad** *vii* be wanted (RT)

**andawendam** *vai* want, desire, wish (RT, NJ, GJ)

**andawenjigan** *ni* objective; *pl* **andawenjiganan** (RT, NJ, GJ); *also* **nandawenjigan** (LM)

**andidaagan** *ni* ghost bowl (ES)

**ando-gikinoo'amaagozi** *vai* go to school (NJ)

**ando-mazitam** *vai2* be emotionally oversensitive, easy to offend, looking for fault (NJ, GJ)

**ando-ningaapoono** *vai* eat off the bush (NJ)

**ando-zhooshkozideshimo** *vai* go dancing (NJ, GJ)

**andobigiwe** *vai* go after pitch (NJ, GJ)

**andojiibike** *vai* harvest roots (NJ, GJ)

**andowiigobii** *vai* searching for basswood (NJ, GJ)

**andozhaangweshiwe** *vai* go after mink (NJ, GJ)

**andoobii** vai get a drink from somewhere (NJ, GJ)

**angooji-onaagan** *ni* net float; *pl* **angooji-onaaganan** (RT); *also* **agonjiwinaagan**; *pl* **agonjiwinaaganan** (GJ); *also* **agwinjiwinaagan**; *pl* **agwinjiwinaaganan** (NJ); *also* **agoonjoonaagan**; *pl* **agoonjoonaaganan** (JC)

**ani-aanjigin** *vii* reproduce (RT)

**aniibiishanjige-makwa** *na* koala bear *pl* **aniibiishanjige-makwag** (RT, NJ, GJ)

**animaanimad** *vii* wind goes onward, wind goes out (RT, NJ, GJ)

**animaashkaa** *vii* tide goes out (RT, NJ, GJ)

**animaasige** *vai* wane (as in moon phase) (JC)

**animikogaabawi** *vai* stand with back facing (RT, NJ, GJ)

**animikogaabawitaadiwag /animikogaabawitaadi-/** *vai* they stand back-to-back (RT, NJ, GJ)

**animikogaabawitaw** *vai* stand with back facing s.o. (RT, NJ, GJ)

**animikoshin** *vai* lie with back facing up (RT, NJ, GJ)

**animweweshka'am** *vai2* paddle or pole away making noise from reeds brushing against canoe (NJ, GJ)

**anit** *ni* spear; *pl* **anitiin** (RT, NJ, GJ)

**anwaabiisaa** *vii* be a calm after raining (NJ, GJ)

**anweshim** *vta* make s.o. rest [*example*: Nindanweshimigoo. = I am being made to rest. *cultural note*: High wind or rain that forces one to rest on a journey may be taken as a sign that it's not wise to try to beat the weather.] (NJ, GJ)

**anwi** *ni* bullet, moccasin game bullet, or marble; *pl* **anwiin** (RT, NJ, GJ)

**anzanz** *ni* seaweed; *pl* **anzanziin** (RT, NJ, GJ)

**apakwaan** *ni* covering; *pl* **apakwaanan** (GJ)

**apakwe** *vai* cover things, roof (NJ, GJ)

**apakweshkway** *na* cattail mat; cattail; *pl* **apakweshkwayag**; *also* **nabagashk** (NJ)

**apashkwebiigininjiishin** *vai* get a blister on one's hand, finger (NJ, GJ)

**apashkwebiigizideshin** *vai* get a blister on one's foot (NJ, GJ)

**apigwaajigan** *ni* sewn covering reinforcement tab (as on birch bark lodge coverings) (NJ, GJ)

**apigwaason** *ni* reinforcing tab on end of birch bark roll or basket (as a wide strip placed inside out on the end creating a double layer); *pl* **apigwaasonan** (GJ)

**apikaadan** *vti* braid s.t. (NJ, GJ)

**apikaade** *vii* be braided (NJ, GJ)

**apikaazh** /apikaaN-/ *vta* braid s.o.'s hair (NJ, GJ)

**apikaazo** *vai* be braided, wears braids (NJ, GJ)

**apikan** *ni* braid, braided tump line, shoulder strap; *pl* **apikanan** (NJ, GJ)

**apishkaamon** *ni* mat for the bottom of a canoe; *pl* **apishkaamonan** (NJ, GJ)

**apisijigan** *ni* protective mat; *pl* **apisijiganan** (NJ, GJ)

**apisin** *vii* lie as a protective layer (NJ, GJ)

**apiigishin** *vai* lay as a protective layer (as in a trivet or pot holder) (RT, NJ, GJ)

**apiigisidoon** *vti* put it on s.t. (as in hot plate) (RT, NJ, GJ)

**apiigisijigan** *ni* layer or sheet; *pl* **apiigisijiganan** (RT, NJ, GJ)

**apiigisijiganekonaye** *vai* wear a layer of clothing (NJ, GJ)

**apiigisin** *vii* lay as a protective layer (as in a trivet or pot holder) (RT, NJ, GJ)

**apiitadezi** *vai* be a certain width, be a certain dimension of mesh (as in a net) (NJ, GJ)

**apiitani** *vai* weigh a certain amount, be a certain weight (NJ)

**apiitashkizi** *vai* be a certain size mesh (as in a net) (NJ, GJ)

**asaawens** *na* perch; *pl* **asaawensag** (RT, NJ, GJ)

**asabii-biiwabikoons** *ni* wire mesh, screen (RT, NJ, GJ)

**asabikaanaak** *ni* twine spindle; *pl* **asabikaanaakoon** (NJ, GJ)

**asabike** *vai* make nets (RT, NJ, GJ)

**asabikewaatig** *ni* net making stick; *pl* **asabikewaatigoon** (RT, NJ, GJ)

**asabikeyaab** *ni* net string; *pl* **asabikeyaabiin** (NJ)

**asamiko-** *pv* at the bottom of the lake (NJ, GJ)

**Asamikowiishiwi-zaaga'igan** *place* Beaver House Lake (in Quetico Park) (GJ)

**asamikozhiwe** *vai* swims on the bottom of the lake (GJ)

**asamishkoodoon** *vti* sink s.t. by weighting it down (GJ)

**asanii** *vii* won't peel easily (as in dry birch bark, basswood fiber) (GJ)

**asanjigo** *vai+o* store things (RT)

**asemaakandan** *vti* offer tobacco to s.t. (NJ)

**asemaakande** *vii* tobacco is offered to it (NJ)

**ashawaabam** *vai* wait for s.o. to appear, be on lookout for s.o. (NJ, GJ)

**ashawaamiwe** *vai* lie in wait for fish (spearing) in open water or ice (NJ, GJ)

**ashawebii'igaade** *vii* be italicized (GJ)

**ashawi-zagimeweke** *vai* make smudge to chase off mosquitoes (NJ, GJ)

**ashidaako-gibinewen** *vta* pin s.o. against the wall by choke-hold (GJ)

**ashidaakobizh** /**ashidaakobiN-**/ *vta* pin s.o. against the wall (GJ)

**ashidaakoshkaw** *vta* pin s.o. against something wooden (as in wall or floor) (GJ)

**ashishawe-bajiishkaa** *vii* be a three-sided pyramid (NJ, GJ)

**ashishawe-zhaabonigan** *ni* glovers needle, three-sided needle; *pl* **ashishawe-zhaaboniganan** (NJ, GJ)

**ashishaweyaa** *vii* be a triangular prism (NJ, GJ)

**ashidakamig** *pc* against the ground (GJ)

**ashidakamigishkaw** *vta* hold down, pin down s.o. by verbal or with body (GJ, NJ)

**ashidakamigwem** *vta* hold s.o. in place by speech (GJ)

**ashidakamigwewem** *vta* hold s.o. in place by repeated speech (GJ)

**ashkamegoke** *vai* work on raw fish (NJ); *also* **ashkimegoke** (GJ)

**ashkibag** *ni* green leaf; *pl* **ashkibagoon** (RT)

**ashkibagokaa** *vii* be many green leaves (RT)

**ashkidaawani** *vai* open one's mouth wide (NJ, GJ)

**ashkikomaan** *ni* lead (metal); *pl* **ashkikomaanan** (RT, NJ, GJ)

**ashkimaazh** /**ashkimaaN-**/ *vta* lace s.o. (as in a snowshoe) (NJ)

**ashkimaneyaab** *ni* snowshoe lacing; *pl* **ashkimaneyaabiin** (NJ)

**ashkimegoke** *vai* work on raw fish (GJ); *also* **ashkamegoke** (NJ)

**asho'ige** *vai* accidentally chase things off (GJ); *also* **ashwaa'ige** (GJ); *also* **ashwa'ige** (NJ); *also* **ozha'ige** (NJ)

**ashoodakamig** *pc* against the ground (NJ, GJ)

**ashoodakamigishkaw** *vta* pin s.o. down with foot or body against ground, submit so. (GJ)

**ashwa'ige** *vai* accidentally chase things off (NJ); *also* **asho'ige** *vai* accidentally chase things off (GJ); *also* **ashwaa'ige** (GJ); *also* **ozha'ige** (NJ)

**ashwabi** *vai* sit in wait (NJ, GJ)

**ashwaa'ige** *vai* accidentally chase things off (GJ); *also* **asho'ige** (GJ); *also* **ashwa'ige** (NJ); *also* **ozha'ige** (NJ)

**asigibii'iganens** *ni* number; *pl* **asigibii'iganensan** (NJ)

**asigiginjigemaagan** *ni* fact family number; *pl* **asigiginjigemaaganag** (GJ); **inawendangibii'igan**; *pl* **inawendangibii'iganan** (RT, NJ, GJ); *also* **inawendibii'igan**; *pl* **inawendibii'iganan** (RT, NJ, GJ)

**asigobaan** *ni* processed basswood fiber (RT, NJ, GJ)

**asinaab** *na* net sinker (below each net float) made from rocks; *pl* **asinaabiig** (NJ, GJ)

**ataagib** *ni* algae (RT, NJ, GJ)

**atoominesigan** *ni* silo; *pl* **atoominesiganan**; *loc* **atoominesiganing** (RT)

**awasigaabawitaadiwag** /awasigaabawitaadi-/ *vai* they stand back-to-back (NJ, GJ)

**awasigamig** *pc* the next room (RT, NJ, GJ); *also* **awasisag** (GJ)

**aweniban** *pc* gone! (RT, NJ, GJ)

**ayate** *vii* just sitting there (NJ, GJ)

**ayekomanji'o** *vai* be tired (NJ)

**ayiite** *pc* insufficient (NJ); *also* **aayiide** (GJ)

**ayinaabi** *vai* keep one's eyes open (RT, NJ, GJ)

**ayinaate** *vii* shine in a certain way or color (RT, NJ, GJ)

**ayinanjige** *vai* have a special, certain diet (RT)

**ayinigokwaa** *vii* be a certain size, be a certain dimension (RT)

**ayizhinaagwad** *vii* be a certain size (RT)

**azhashkiiwaagamin** *vii* be murky water, be muddy water (NJ, GJ)

**azhashkiiyaamikaa** *vii* be a muddy bottom (as in a lake or pond) (RT)

**azhe-mayaawibidoon** *vti* turn s.t. upright, upright s.t. (NJ, GJ)

**azhe-miinobijige** *vai* upright things, pull things straight (NJ, GJ)

**azhiwaasin** *vii* get dull (NJ)

# AA

**aabajitamaagoowizi** *vai+o* rely upon things, make use of things (NJ)

**aabawaanimad** *vii* be a warm wind (RT, NJ, GJ)

**aabawaasige** *vai* shine warmly (RT, NJ, GJ)

**aabiding wekwaagindaasowin** *ni* one million (NJ, GJ)

**aabitanakakeyaa** *vii* a shoe is worn on the wrong foot (NJ) [*example:* Aabitanakakeyaawan. = Two left-footed/right-footed shoes are worn.]; *also* **aapidanakakeyaa** (GJ)

**aabitanakakezi** *vai* a mitten or glove is worn on the wrong hand (NJ) [*example*: Aabitanakakeziwag. = Two left-handed or right-handed gloves or mittens are worn.]; *also* **aapidanakakezi** (GJ)

**aaboojiigisin** *vii* be turned inside out (cloth-like) (NJ, GJ)

**aadaagoneshin** *vai* have a hard time going through snow [*cultural note*: indicates a deep snowy winter to come] (NJ, GJ)

**aadakiise** *vii* get stuck in the mud in the water (NJ, GJ)

**aadikwe'ige** *vai* stabilize, control (as in a paddle or pole on the bottom) (GJ)

**aadwaa'am** *vta* travel with s.o. (by boat or car) (GJ)

**Aadwaa'amoog** *name* Orion's Belt (constellation) (GJ)

**aagawaate** *vii* be a shadow (GJ)

**aagawaateshkaa** *vii* be shade, be a shadow (GJ)

**aajibijigan** *ni* gaff hook; *pl* **aajibijiganan** (GJ)

**aajisaga'igan** *ni* room divider; *pl* **aajisaga'iganan** (RT); *also* **aajisaginigan** (GJ)

**aamanoozo** *vai* be in rut (RT, NJ, GJ)

**aami** *vai* spawn (RT, NJ, GJ)

**aamiiwaagamin** *vii* be spawn water (NJ, GJ)

**aamimaagwad** *vii* smells of spawn (NJ, GJ)

**aanawendan** *vti* reject s.t. (as in food offered to s.o., as in being picky) (NJ, GJ)

**aandaate** *vii* light changes (RT, NJ, GJ)

**aandakiiwin** *ni* changing season; *pl* **aandakiiwinan** (RT, NJ)

**aandanjige** *vai* change diet (RT, NJ, GJ)

**aanikawiganinjaan** *ni* wrist; *pl* **aanikawiganinjaanan** (RT, NJ); *also* **aanikawiganeninjaan** (GJ)

**aanikebii'igan** *ni* hyphen (–) (JC)

**aanikebii'ige** *vai* hyphenate (JC)

**aanikekonesesijigan** *ni* web link; *pl* **aanikekonesesijiganan** (NJ, GJ)

**aanikoogwaade** *vii* be sewn on in succession, in a linear fashion (RT, NJ, GJ)

**aanikoogwaajigan** *ni* sewn on extension; *pl* **aanikoogwaajiganan** (NJ, GJ)

**aanikoowaaginan** *vti* bend together joining (as in lodge poles) (NJ, GJ)

**aanikwaaginan** *vti* bend together (as in lodge poles) (NJ)

**aanji-baabisapidoon** *vti* retighten (NJ, GJ)

**aanji-boonii** *vai* hop to a new perch (RT, NJ, GJ)

**aanjibo** *vai* change weight, grow in weight (as a child) (NJ, GJ)

**aanjigin** *vii* change while growing, grow into s.t. else (RT)

**aanjinaagwad** *vii* change appearance, look different (RT, NJ, GJ)

**aanjiigin** *vii* be changed by hand (hide or sheet) (GJ)

**aapidapide** *vii* be knotted to the point of being impossible to untie (NJ, GJ)

**aapidapidoon** *vti* knot s.t. to point of being unable to untie (NJ, GJ)

**aapijigaazo** *vai* gone in hiding (RT, NJ, GJ)

**aaswaakogaabawi** *vai* stand leaning up against s.t. (NJ, GJ)

**aatawe-boodaadan** *vti* blow s.t. out (lamp) (RT, NJ, GJ)

**aate'ishkodawewidaabaan** *na* firetruck; *pl* **aate'ishkodawewidaabaanag** (RT, NJ); *also* **aatawe'ishkodawewidaabaan** (GJ)

**aayaazhawi-bakite'amaadiwag** /aayaazhawi-bakite'amaadi-/ *vai+o* they hit s.t. back-and-forth to one another [*example:* Aayaazhawi-bakite'amaadiwag bikwaakwad. = They are hitting the ball to one another.] (NJ, GJ)

**aayaazhawi-basikamaadiwag** /aayaazhawi-basikamaadi-/ *vai+o* they kick s.t. back-and-forth to one another [*example:* Aayaazhawi-basikamaadiwag bikwaakwad. = They are kicking the ball to one another.] (NJ, GJ)

**aayaazhawi-boonii** *vai* hop from one branch to another (NJ, GJ)

**aayaazhawi-webinamaadiwag** /aayaazhawi-webinamaadi-/ *vai+o* they throw s.t. back-and-forth to one another [*example:* Aayaazhawi-webinamaadiwag bikwaakwad. = They are throwing the ball to one another.] (NJ, GJ)

**aayiide** *pc* insufficient (GJ); *also* **ayiite** (NJ)

**aazhaanzhenan** *vti* turn s.t. down (as in a kerosene lantern) (RT, NJ); *also* **ondaazhenan** (GJ)

**aazhawaasin** *vii* blows across (RT)

**aazhawagaakobizo** *vai* drive across ice (NJ, GJ)

**aazhawikonesesijigan** *ni* web link; *pl* **aazhawikonesesijiganan** (RT, NJ, GJ)

**aazhigijishin** *vai* lie on one's back (RT, NJ, GJ)

**aazhookana** *ni* cross road, intersection; *loc* **aazhookanaang** (RT, NJ, GJ)

# B, C

**babakeyaate** *vii* light separates (RT, NJ, GJ)

**babaa-debam** *vta* go around catching s.o. (as in a bird catching bugs) (RT)

**babaamaandawe** *vai* climb around (RT)

**babaamiwijigaade** *vii* be carried, taken around (RT)

**babaamaajimo** *vai, vii* tell news (RT, NJ, GJ)

**babigwaanag** *na* flint stone; *pl* **babigwaanagoog** (RT, NJ); *also* **biiwaanag** (GJ)

**babiiwizhenhyi** *vai* be small in stature (NJ)

**babinezi** *vai* decay (as in a tree becoming rotten) (GJ)

**badagwanidiye'o** *vai* cover one's hind end (NJ, GJ)

**badagwanidiyegoojigan** *ni* butt flap; *pl* **badagwanidiyegoojiganan** (NJ, GJ)

**badagwanishkiinzhigwe'o** *vai* cover one's eyes (NJ, GJ)

**badagwanitawage'o** *vai* cover one's ears (NJ, GJ)

**badakakiisin** *vii* stuck in, anchored in (NJ, GJ)

**badakakiiwebinigaade** *vii* anchor is thrown in (NJ, GJ)

**badakamigisidoon** *vti* plant s.t. in the ground (RT, NJ, GJ)

**bagakaabi** *vai* see clearly (RT, NJ, GJ)

**bagakaate** *vii* be bright light (RT, NJ, GJ)

**bagaki-ozaawizi** *vai* be the color of deer in the spring and summer (NJ)

**bagakitaagod** *vii* sound sharp, have a piercing sound; *also* **bagakitaagwad** (NJ, GJ)

**bagakitam** *vai* hear clearly (NJ)

**bagamaanimad** *vii* wind comes up, gets windy (RT, NJ, GJ)

**bagamaate** *vii* light arrives in a certain place, light is captured in a certain place (RT)

**bagamijiwan** *vii* water arrives in a certain place (RT)

**bagaskibiigishin** *vai* break the surface of water (as a beaver hitting water with tail) (NJ, GJ)

**bagaskindibe** *vai* strike (in moccasin game), smack on the head (NJ, GJ)

**bagaskindibe'wi** /bagaskindibe'w-/ *vta* strike s.o. on the head (NJ); *also* **bagaskindibe'o** /bagaskindibe'w-/ (GJ); *also* **bagaskindibe'** /bagaskindibe'w-/ (RT)

**bagesaan** *na* bagese game piece; *pl* **bagesaanag** (NJ)

**bagesaan** *na* plum; *pl* **bagesaanag** (RT, NJ, GJ)

**bagese** *na* bagese game (GJ)

**bagese** *vai* play bagese game (GJ)

**bagesewinaagan** *ni* bagese game bowl (GJ)

**bagidanaamo** *vai* breathe, exhale (RT, NJ, GJ)

**bagonebiiwan** *vii* there is a pool of water on the ice from a hole (NJ, GJ)

**bagonezigwaa** *vii* current cuts a hole in ice (RT, NJ, GJ)

**bagonezigojiwan** *vii* current cuts the ice (GJ)

**bagonib** *pc* an air hole through the ice (created by current or vortex) (NJ, GJ)

**bagwa'an** *vti* patch s.t. (NJ, GJ)

**bagwa'ige** *vai* patch things (NJ, GJ)

**bagwaawanib** *ni* hole in the ice caused by air (as in from a beaver disturbing the lake bottom); *pl* **bagwaawanibiin** (NJ, GJ)

**bagwaawanibii** *vii* there is a hole in the ice (NJ, GJ)

**bagwaji-** *pv* wild (RT)

**bajiba'am** *vai* break through and sink down in the snow, as when walking on crusty snow (NJ)

**bajibashkobii'am** *vai* break through and sink down in the snow, as when walking on slushy snow [*morphological note:* "bii" pertains to water in this snow term] (NJ)

**bajibashkobiigibizo** *vai* break through and sink down in the snow, as when driving on slushy snow (NJ)

**bajiishka'ogaan** *ni* pointed lodge (conical); *pl* **bajiishka'ogaanan** (NJ, GJ)

**bajiishkibag** *ni* cactus; *pl* **bajiishkibagoon** (RT)

**bakaaninaagane** *vai* use different dishes (as in when a girl on first menses, or anytime on menses) (RT, NJ, GJ)

**bakinaagewin** *ni* goal; *pl* **bakinaagewinan**; *also* **mizhodamowin** *ni* goal; *pl* **mizhodamowinan** (RT, NJ, GJ)

**bakite'igaage** *vai+o* use s.t. for a hammer, use s.t. to hit [*example*: Waagaakwadoon bakite'igaagen. = Use the hatchet as a hammer.] (NJ)

**bakitewe** *vii* make a hammering sound (RT, NJ, GJ)

**bakiwebishkaw** break s.o. (as a fish in a net) (NJ, GJ)

**bakobiigwaashkwani** *vai* leap into the water (RT)

**bakwadaasin** *vii* be pulled up by the wind (NJ, GJ)

**bakwadanabakweyaasin** *vii* roof ripped off by the wind (of a house) (NJ, GJ)

**bakwadanabakweyaashi** *vai* have one's roof ripped off by the wind (NJ, GJ)

**bakwanii** *vii* peels easy (as in birch bark, basswood fiber) (NJ, GJ)

**bakwekode** *vii* be notched (as in nettle strings) (NJ, GJ)

**Bakwewaang** *place* where the thunder beings touched down, New Post, WI (on Lac Courte Oreilles Reservation); *also* **Bakweweyaang** (GJ)

**bakweweyaa** *vii* rumble (NJ, GJ)

**Bakweweyaang** *place* where the thunder beings touched down, New Post, WI (on Lac Courte Oreilles Reservation); *also* **Bakwewaang** (GJ)

**bakweyaabika'o** *vai* put a groove in rock (as in to attach an anchor line) (NJ, GJ)

**bakweyaandagaasin** *vii* be broken off in the wind (as in a pine bough) (NJ, GJ)

**bakwezhiganaabiins** *na* pasta, spaghetti; *pl* **bakwezhiganaabiinsag** (RT)

**bakwezhiganashk** *ni* wheat; *pl* **bakwezhiganashkoon** (RT)

**bakwezhiganikaan** *na* pie; *pl* **bakwezhiganikaanag** (NJ)

**bakwezhiganikewigamig** *ni* bakery; *pl* **bakwezhiganikewigamigooon**; *loc* **bakwezhiganikewigamigong** (RT)

**bakwezhiganimin** *na* grain; *pl* **bakwezhiganiminag** (RT)

**bangibiisaanishi** *vai* be caught in a light rain (NJ, GJ)

**bangisinamaa** *vai* caught in inclement weather (NJ, GJ)

**bapakiteshka'igaade** *vii* be hit repeatedly (as in wheat being struck repeatedly by a combine) (RT)

**bapasangwaabam** *vta* blink eyes at s.o. repeatedly [*example*: Gego bapasangwaabamaaken awiiya. = Don't keep blinking your eyes at anyone. *cultural note*: Considered extremely rude and offensive to repeatedly blink at someone.] (NJ, GJ)

**bapasangwaabi** *vai* blink one's eyes repeatedly (NJ, GJ)

**bapashkwaa** *vii* be tundra (RT)

**basaakobijigan** *ni* tree spring noose trap; *pl* **basaakobijiganan** (NJ, GJ)

**basangwaabi** *vai* close one's eyes, blink (RT, NJ, GJ)

**bashagaakwa'an** *vti* scrape s.t. (as in bark off a tree) (RT); *also*
 **bishagaakwa'an** (GJ)
**bashagam** *vta* dehusk s.o. with one's teeth (as in a squirrel to an acorn)
 (RT); *also* **bishagam** (GJ)
**bashkobijigaade** *vii* be pulled out, be weeded, be removed from
 somewhere (RT)
**bashkobijige** *vai* pull out plants, weed (RT)
**bashkoga'ige** *vai* make a clear cut, log by cutting all trees in an area (NJ,
 GJ)
**bashkwadikwane'ige** *vai* knock branches or limbs off a tree (NJ, GJ)
**bashkwatigwanezhwi /bashkwatigwanezhw-/** *vta* limb s.o. (tree) using
 s.t. (like an ax, knife) (NJ)
**basiindaamikane** *vai* have a dimpled chin (NJ, GJ)
**basiingwe** *vai* have a dimple (RT, NJ, GJ)
**basikawaadam** *vai* play soccer (NJ)
**basikawaadan** *vti* kick s.t. (NJ)
**basitebijigan** *ni* slingshot; *pl* **basitebijiganan** (NJ, GJ)
**baswewe** *vai* echo (RT, NJ, GJ)
**baswewe** *vii* echo (RT, NJ, GJ)
**bawa'am** *vai* knock rice (RT, NJ, GJ)
**bawa'an** *vti* knock s.t. (as in rice) (RT, NJ, GJ)
**bawa'igaade** *vii* be knocked (as in rice) (RT, NJ, GJ)
**bawega'am** *vai* brush off (RT)
**bazagodenaniwe** *ni* have a sticky tongue (as in a frog) (RT)
**bazigwa'o** *vai* take off in flight (RT, NJ, GJ)
**baabagonagekwe** *vai* peel bark (in sheet, not string, as in birch bark)
 (RT, NJ, GJ)
**baabagonige** *vai* peel bark (RT, NJ, GJ)
**baabagose** *vii* peels easily (as in when bark pops off tree on its own)
 (NJ, GJ)
**baabisapidoon** *vti* tighten s.t. down (NJ, GJ)
**baakibidoon** *vii* break s.t. open (as in a dam) (RT, NJ, GJ)
**baakibiigibidoon** *vti* loosen dam to make partial leak (not break entirely)
 [*cultural note*: this is a common technique for setting beaver
 traps] (NJ, GJ)
**baakibiise** *vii* dam breaks open by itself (NJ, GJ)
**baakibiishkaa** *vii* be an opening (as in a dam opening) (NJ, GJ)
**baakiiginan** *vti* open s.t. (sheet-like) (RT, NJ, GJ)
**baakindenamaw** *vta* open (s.t.) for s.o. (RT, NJ, GJ)

**baakindenan** *vti* open s.t. (as in a cloth door) (RT, NJ, GJ)

**baakishkaa** *vii* open up lengthwise (as in a metal sinker) (GJ)

**baanizhaawe** *vai* cut fish into strips, fillet (NJ, GJ)

**baapise** *vai* laugh suddenly (NJ)

**baashkaawanwe'o** *vai* hatch (NJ)

**baashkiinad** *vii* thrive (RT)

**baashkiino** *vai* thrive, be prolific (as in a baby boom) (RT, NJ, GJ)

**baashkijiinesijigan** *ni* smudge to ward off mosquitoes; *pl*
      **baashkijiinesijiganan** (NJ, GJ)

**baashkijiinesin** *vii* continuous smoke (NJ, GJ)

**baashkiminasigan** *ni* marmalade, jam, jelly (NJ); *pl*
      **baashkiminasiganan**; *also* **baashkominisigan** (RT)

**baasikamigishkaa** *vii* ground cracks, be a fault line (NJ, GJ)

**baaskobiigishkaa** *vii* be a broken blister (NJ, GJ)

**baataniinoonikesi** *na* octopus; *pl* **baataniinoonikesiwag** (RT, NJ, GJ)

**baate** *vii* be dry (RT)

**baatekamigaa** *vii* be a desert (RT)

**bebinewang** *vii-prt* powder; *pl* **bebinewangin** (RT, NJ, GJ)

**bebinezid bakwezhigan** *vai-prt* flour (RT, NJ, GJ)

**bedaakogomo** *vai* paddle slowly (implies floating) (NJ, GJ)

**bedakwaandaweshiinh** *na* sloth; *pl* **bedakwaandaweshiinyag** (RT)

**bedakwazhiwe** *vai* paddle slowly (implies forced movement) (NJ, GJ)

**bedowe** *vii* have a soft voice (low and slow) (NJ, GJ)

**bejitaagod** *vii* sound slow (as in a fog horn) (NJ); *also* **bejitaagwad**

**bejitaagozi** *vai* slow sounding call (as in a bird call) (NJ, GJ)

**bemiging** *vii-prt* vine, plant (as in one that grows along the ground); *pl*
      **bemigingin** (RT)

**bemisemagak** *vii-prt* airplane; *pl* **bemisemagakin** (RT, NJ, GJ)

**bengwadaawangaa** *vii* be dry sand (NJ, GJ)

**bepeshizi-bebezhigooganzhii** *na* zebra; *pl* **bepeshizi-**
      **bebezhigooganzhiig** (NJ)

**beshiga'an** *vti* chop a slit in s.t. (as in bark) (NJ, GJ)

**bezikaa** *vai* go slow, be late [*example*: Ningii-ondami'aa wenji-
      bezikaayaang. = I'm the reason we are late. *example*: Hay'
      onzaam gibezikaamin, aazha gii-kiba'igaade. = Shoot, we're too
      late, it's already closed. *example*: Wiikaa ningii-koshkoz wenji-
      bezikaayaan. = I got up too late, which is why I'm late.] (NJ)

**bi-andogiba'ige** *vai* come to repair dam (as in a beaver) (NJ, GJ)

**bi-bakwewe** *vai* come rumbling (like thunderbird) (GJ)

**bibagadin** *vii* be thin (as in ice) (NJ, GJ)

**bibine-bakwezhiganiigin** *na* tortilla; *pl* **bibine-bakwezhiganiiginag** (RT)

**bibinewan** *vii* fine, powdery (RT, NJ, GJ)

**bibinezi** *vai* be fine, powdery (RT, NJ, GJ)

**biboonishi** *vai* spend the winter somewhere (RT)

**bida'am** *vai* get caught in a net (NJ)

**bigishkigamizige** *vai* break things up by boiling (NJ, GJ)

**bigishkaabid** *ni* molar; *pl* **bigishkaabidan** (RT)

**bigishkaabide** *vai* have molars (RT)

**bigishkandan** *vti* grind s.t. in one's mouth (RT)

**bigishkanjige** *vai* grind, eat by grinding (RT)

**bigishkigamide** *vii* breaks up while boiling (NJ, GJ)

**bigishkigamizwi** /**bigishkigamizw-**/ *vta* break s.o. up by boiling (NJ); *also* **bigishkigamizo** /**bigishkigamizw-**/ (GJ)

**bigishkigamizan** *vti* break s.t. up by boiling (NJ, GJ)

**bijiinag** *pc* for the first time, just now [*example*: Mii bijiinag gii-izhichigeyaan. = This is the first time I did this. *example*: Mii bijiinag wii-wiisiniyaang. = We're going to eat just now, we're just eating now (apologetic way of saying, because we were late in getting up).] (NJ, GJ)

**bikwaakwadotaawag** /**bikwaakwadotaa**/ *vai* they are balled up (ducks, geese, bugs) [*conjugation note*: requires multiple actors to make sense even though this is not a reflexive verb] (NJ, GJ)

**bikwaakwadwaanawe** *vai* have clubs (as in a dinosaur) (NJ)

**bikwadaawangisin** *vii* be a sand hill, be an ant hill (NJ, GJ)

**bima'igan** *ni* counting stick for moccasin game; *pl* **bima'iganan** (GJ)

**bimaaboojige** *vai* float logs (NJ, GJ)

**bimaadad** *vii* live (RT)

**bimaakobide** *vii* be held out across by a stick (as in lodge runners parallel to the ground) (GJ)

**bimaakobijigan** *ni* stick for holding s.t. across; *pl* **bimaakobijiganan** (GJ)

**bimaasimoono** *vai* sail along, sail by (NJ, GJ)

**bimaasin** *vii* float, travel on the air or wind (RT)

**bimakwazhiwe** *vai* paddling, swimming underwater (NJ, GJ)

**bimi-zaagikwegomo** *vai* head sticks out while floating by (NJ, GJ)

**bimibide** *vii* be running, be moving, be in use (as in something motorized) (NJ)

**bimidaabiiga'ige** *vai* weave (NJ)

**bimidaakobijigan** *ni* cross pole; *pl* **bimidaakobijiganan** (NJ, GJ)

**bimidaawangibatoo** *vai* run on sand (NJ, GJ)

**bimidaawangii** *vai* trudge through sand (NJ, GJ)

**bimigin** *vii* grow along (RT)

**bimijizide-miikanaake** *vai* make trail sideways (NJ, GJ)

**bimijizideshimo** *vai* dance sideways (NJ, GJ)

**biminige** *vai* portage a canoe (NJ, GJ)

**bimiskwa'oozo** *vai* he is tangled (as a fish in the net) (NJ, GJ)

**bimoode** *vai* slither, crawl (RT, NJ, GJ)

**bimoojiganaak** *ni* aiming stick (for moccasin game); *pl*
    **bimoojiganaakoon** (GJ)

**bimoomigoodaabaan** *na* bus; *pl* **bimoomigoodaabaanag** (RT, NJ, GJ)

**bimweweshka'am** *vai2* make noise while paddling or poling from reeds
    brushing against canoe (NJ, GJ)

**binaakwii** *vai* lose leaves (as in a tree in autumn) (RT)

**binawanise** *vii* precipitate (cross between snow and rain but misty-like,
    tiny particles of precipitation) (NJ)

**binigan** *ni* vinegar (RT)

**biniskosabii** *vai* soften nets (RT)

**bishagam** *vta* dehusk s.o. with one's teeth (as in a squirrel to an acorn)
    (GJ); *also* **bashagam** (RT)

**bishagaakobidoon** *vti* peel s.t. (as in bark) by hand (RT, NJ, GJ)

**bishagaakobijige** *vai* peeling bark (string of fiber) by hand (as in peeling
    basswood) (RT, NJ, GJ)

**bishagaakobizh /bishagaakobiN-/** *vta* peel s.o. by hand (as in a tree)
    (RT, NJ, GJ)

**bishagaakwa'an** *vti* scrape s.t. (as in bark off a tree) (GJ); *also*
    **bashagaakwa'an** (RT)

**bishigendaagwad** *vii* be magnificent (RT)

**bishigonige** *vai* miss and drop things (NJ)

**biskaabikada'an** *vti* bend s.t. (metal-like) down with a tool (as in
    bending over a protruding nail) (NJ)

**biskaakonese** *vii* ignite, spark (RT, NJ, GJ)

**biskada'an** *vti* bend s.t. down (NJ)

**bizaakwaa** *vii* be weedy, full of sticks (GJ)

**bizini** *vai* be dusty, be dirty (NJ); *also* get something in one's eye (GJ)

**bizishigwaa** *vii* be empty (NJ); *also* **bizhishigwaa** (RT)

**biibaaginamewe** *vai* announce the coming of sturgeon spawn (as in gray tree frog) [*cultural note*: this particular tree frog sound is only heard at the start of the sturgeon spawn and is different from the characteristic call of other tree frogs] (NJ)

**biidaadodan** *vti* come and tell about s.t. (RT, NJ, GJ)

**biidaajimo** *vai* come tell about things (RT, NJ, GJ)

**biidaashkaa** *vii* waves or tide roll in (RT, NJ, GJ)

**biidaasige** *vai* wax (as in cycle of the moon) (JC)

**biidakwazhiwe** *vai* come paddling (RT, NJ, GJ)

**biigijiisag** *na* rotten wood (still standing); *pl* **biigijiisagoog** (GJ)

**biigijiisag** *ni* rotten wood (downed); *pl* **biigijiisagoon** (GJ)

**biigijiisagaatig** *ni* rotten wood; *pl* **biigijiisagaatigoon** (GJ)

**biigijiisagowi** *vai* be a decayed tree (standing) (GJ)

**biigijiisagowan** *vii* be rotten (as in wood) (GJ)

**biigijiisagwaatig** *ni* rotten wood; *pl* **biigijiisagwaatigoon** (NJ)

**biigojiwan** *vii* erodes (from water flowing), erosion (RT)

**biigwaagime** *vai* have broken snowshoes (lacing or wood) (NJ, GJ)

**biigwawe** *vai* bushy (RT, NJ, GJ)

**biijimaam** *vta* smell s.o. (RT, NJ, GJ)

**biijimaandan** *vti* smell s.t., sense s.t. by smell (RT, NJ, GJ)

**biijimaanjige** *vai* smell, have a sense of smell, sense or identify things by smell (RT, NJ, GJ)

**biijimaate** *vii* smell issues forth, aroma emanates (RT, NJ, GJ)

**biijimanjitoon** *vti* feel s.t. all around (by touch), sense by touch s.t. all around (as in a foot soaking in warm water) (RT, NJ, GJ)

**biijipijigaage** *vai* taste, sense things by taste (NJ, GJ)

**biijipidan** *vti* taste s.t., sense s.t. by taste (RT, NJ, GJ)

**biijipogwad** *vii* have a certain taste, come to have a certain taste (RT, NJ, GJ)

**biima'igan** *ni* screwdriver; *pl* **biima'iganan** (RT, NJ, GJ)

**biimaakwa'ige** *vai* wring out twisting with stick (NJ, GJ)

**biimisko-onagizhiikaanens** *ni* cavataapi pasta, *pl* **biimisko-onagizhiikaanensan** (RT, NJ, GJ)

**biimiskozhiganens** *ni* fusilli (pasta), *pl* **biimiskozhiganensan** (RT, NJ, GJ)

**biimiskwa'igan** *ni* screwdriver; *pl* **biimiskwa'iganan** (RT, NJ, GJ)

**biinaagamin** *vii* be clean water (RT, NJ, GJ)

**biinda'agoo** *vai* get caught in a net (RT, NJ, GJ)

**biinda'am** *vai2* get caught in a net (RT, GJ); *also* **biinda'ozo** (LW); *also* **bida'am** (NJ); *also* **biinda'agoo** (RT, NJ, GJ)

**biinichigemagad** *vii* it cleans (RT, NJ, GJ)

**biinji-boodaadan** *vti* blow in s.t. (RT, NJ, GJ)

**biinji-boodaajige** *vai* blow in things (RT, NJ, GJ)

**biinjiboonaagan** *ni* fish trap; *pl* **biinjiboonaaganan** (NJ, GJ)

**Biinjiboonaaganing** *place* the shoot between Three Mile and Woseley Lake (in Quetico Park) (GJ)

**biinjidiyeshkozo** *vai* shoot s.o. right in the rectum (NJ, GJ)

**biinjiweba'amaw** *vta* score a point on s.o. [*example*: Gigii-biinjiweba'amawin. = I scored on you.] (GJ)

**biinjiweba'ige** *vai* score, score a goal, score a point (as in soccer or lacrosse) [*example*: Ningii-biinjiweba'ige. = I scored a point.] (GJ)

**biisiboojigaazo** *vai* be ground up, be granulated (RT)

**biisiboojigewigamig** *ni* grist mill; *pl* **biisiboojigewigamigoon**; *loc* **biisiboojigewigamigong** (RT)

**biisiga'igaade** *vii* be chopped into small pieces (as in wood) (NJ, GJ)

**biisiwebinige** vai make syncopated beat for moccasin game song (GJ)

**biitawinagekobijige** *vai* thin out layers of bark (as in basswood), shape basswood fiber to size (NJ, GJ)

**biitewegani-ozhibii'igan** *ni* foam letter; *pl* **biitewegani-ozhibii'iganan** (RT)

**biitewegani-ozhibii'iganaaboo** *ni* ink (RT, NJ, GJ)

**biitoobiigibijige** *vai* peel in layers (RT, NJ, GJ)

**biitoobiiyaa** vii the lakes are one after another (RT, NJ, GJ)

**biitoobijigaade** *vii* be peeled in layers (RT, NJ, GJ)

**biitooskibiigadin** *vii* ice shelf freezes (NJ, GJ)

**biitooskibiiyaa** *vii* be an ice shelf (NJ, GJ)

**biitooskobiig** *pc* slush water (NJ, GJ)

**biitooskobiigaa** *vii* be water under snow, be slush (NJ, GJ)

**biitooskobiigaaboo** *ni* slush water; *pl* **biitooshkobiigaaboon** (NJ, GJ)

**biiwaanag** *na* flint stone; *pl* **biiwaanag** (GJ); *also* **babigwaanag** (NJ)

**biiwaanagoons** *na* arrowhead; *pl* **biiwaanagoonsag** (NJ, GJ)

**biiyiijimaandam** *vai* feel by smell (NJ)

**biiyiijimaandan** *vti* feel s.t. by smell (NJ)

**biiyiijimanjitoon** *vti* feel s.t. by touch (NJ)

**biiyiijipidan** *vti* feel s.t. by taste (NJ)

**boodawaadan** *vti* make a fire in s.t. (RT, NJ, GJ)

**boodawaage** *vai+o* make a fire with s.t. (RT, NJ, GJ)

**boodawaan** *ni* fireplace; *pl* **boodawaanan** (RT, NJ, GJ)

**boodawaanakik** *na* fire kettle; *pl* **boodawaanakikoog** (RT, NJ, GJ)

**boodawaanidizo** *vai* build fire to warm oneself (NJ, GJ)

**boodawaazh** /**boodawaaN-**/ *vta* build a fire for s.o. (RT, NJ); *also* **boodawaazho** /**boodawaaN-**/ GJ)

**boodawaazo** *vai* build fire for warming (RT, GJ)

**boogidi-apikweshimon** *ni* whoopee cushion; *pl* **boogidi-apikweshimonan** (NJ)

**boogijibizh** /**boogijibiN-**/ *vta* squeeze s.o. to point of flatulence (RT, NJ, GJ)

**boogijidan** *vti* fart on s.t. (RT, NJ, GJ)

**boojidiyeshin** *vai* fall or sit on s.t. causing anal penetration (GJ)

**bookaagonebizo** *vai* dive into the snow (NJ, GJ)

**bookizigwajiwan** *vii* current cuts the ice (GJ)

**bookizigwaa** *vii* be an air hole, be a current hole in ice (GJ)

**bookoganaandan** *vti* break s.t. by applying pressure, snap s.t. off (NJ, GJ)

**bookose** *vii* break (as in a sapling stick being bent for a hide stretching frame) (NJ)

**bookozhigaazo** *vai* be cut in half (NJ)

**bookwaashi** *vai* broken off half way up by the wind (NJ, GJ)

**boome** *vai* be safe (RT)

**boonakajigan** *ni* boat anchor; *pl* **boonakajiganan** (NJ, GJ)

**boonam** *vai2* lay an egg (RT, NJ, GJ)

**boonikamigizi** *vai* stop doing certain activities, refrain from doing special activities (as when in mourning) (RT, NJ, GJ)

**boonii** *vai, vii* land, perch (RT, NJ, GJ)

**boozininjaan** *ni* lotion; *pl* **boozininjaanan** (NJ)

**boozitaaso** *vai* load up (RT, NJ, GJ)

**bwaanawi-ishkodawe** *vai* be unable to make a fire (RT, NJ, GJ)

**chi-doodooshaaboo** *ni* cheese (RT)

**chi-gitigaan** *ni* farm; *pl* **chi-gitigaanan** (RT)

# D

**dabasi-ayaa** *vii* be low (as in on the ground or floor) (RT)

**dabinoo'ige** *vai* seek shelter (RT)

**dadaatabose** *vai* walk fast (RT, NJ, GJ)

**dadiibaabandamaazo** *vai* make sure one is aware of weather  (NJ, GJ)

**dagobidoon** *vti* attach s.t. to an object (GJ)

**dagosidoon** *vti* contribute to s.t., add s.t. in (RT, NJ, GJ)

**dagosijige** *vai* contribute, add to things (RT, NJ, GJ)

**daji'** *vai* make s.o. late, run s.o. out of time

**dajise** *vai* have insufficient time to do s.t. [*example*: Ningii-tajise ji-gii-andawaabandamaan. = I didn't have time to go pick it up.] (NJ, GJ)

**dakaagamisin** *vii* it cools (as in a liquid) (RT)

**dakaanimad** *vii* be a cold wind (RT, NJ, GJ)

**dakibiigaji** *vai* be cold from being wet (rained on, sweaty) (NJ, GJ)

**dakigamisin** *vii* it cools (as in a liquid) (NJ)

**dako-dibikad** *vii* be a short night (RT, NJ, GJ)

**dako-giizhigad** *vii*  be a short day (RT, NJ, GJ)

**dakogin** *vii* grow to a small stature (RT)

**dakokii** *vai+o* step on things (RT, NJ, GJ)

**dakonjigaans** *ni* pliers, vice grip; *pl* **dakonjigaansan** (NJ, GJ); *also* **dakwanjigaans** (RT)

**dakwanjige** *vai* bite and put in one's mouth (RT); *also* perform oral sex (TS)

**dakwaasige** *vai* be short day, sun shines for a short period of time (as in short winter days) (RT)

**dakwiindimaa** *vii* be shallow (a short depth of water) (RT, NJ, GJ)

**damoo'am** *vai* slap one's tail on the water (as in a beaver) (NJ)

**danaami** *vai* spawn in a certain place (RT, NJ, GJ)

**danachiishkise** *vii* split along the grain (as in bark) (GJ)

**danakone** *vii* burn in certain place (RT, NJ, GJ)

**dasin** *vii* be a certain number (RT, NJ, GJ)

**dasoonidizo** *vai* trap oneself (RT, NJ, GJ)

**dasosagoons** *pc* era, a certain extent of time (RT)

**gidaatabose** *vai* walk fast (NJ)

**dawaa** *vii*  be sufficient room, space (RT)

**dawaasin** *vii*  be sufficient room, space (RT)

**dawate** *vii* be sufficient time (RT)

**dawi-ayaa** *vii* be sufficient time, space (GJ)

**dawise** *vai* have sufficient or spare time (GJ, NJ)

**dawisidoon** *vti* leave a space (RT, NJ, GJ)

**dazhe** *vai* build a nest in a certain place (RT)

**dazhigi** *vai* grow in a certain place (RT)

**dazhigin** *vii* grow in a certain place (RT)

**dazhimikwewe** *vai* talk about women (RT, NJ, GJ)

**daashkibiigibijige** *vai* peel into long strips (GJ)

**daashkibiigobijige** *vai* peel into long strips (NJ)

**daashkibiiwadabiigobijige** *vai* split roots [*cultural note*: typically done with jack pine or black spruce to prepare heavy sewing fiber] (NJ, GJ)

**daashkiga'an** *vti* split s.t. into pieces lengthwise using a tool (GJ)

**daashkizhigaazo** *vai* be cut in half lengthwise, be slit (GJ)

**daataagwaagoneshkige** *vai* pack trail with snowshoes or shoes (NJ, GJ)

**debakiikozhiwe** *vai* swim down to the bottom (touching), make contact with the bottom (GJ)

**debakiise** *vai* jump in and hands or feet touch the bottom (GJ)

**debakiishkige** *vai* stand and touch the bottom (GJ)

**debam** *vta* catch s.o. in the mouth (RT)

**debanendan** *vti* have a sufficiently large mouth to bite s.t. [*lexicon note*: from discussion of the size of a bagidaabaan, an item for ice fishing] (NJ)

**debashkine** *vai* be covered; *also* fit inside (NJ)

**debaasin** *vii* be sufficient wind (as from a fan) (RT, NJ, GJ)

**debibizh** /**debibiN-**/ *vta* catch, grab, or grasp s.o. (RT, NJ, GJ)

**debinaagozi** *vai* be seen at a distance (ES)

**debinaak** *pc* any old way, just barely sufficient (RT, NJ, GJ)

**debise** *vii* be sufficient, be enough (RT)

**debitan** *vti* hear s.t. clearly, identify the type or direction of a sound of s.t. (NJ, GJ)

**debizigwaa** *vii* be sufficiently thick (as in the ice) (NJ, GJ)

**debwewenjige** *vai* be heard chewing from a distance (NJ, GJ)

**debweweshka'am** *vai* make noise paddling or poling from reeds sliding on a canoe (NJ, GJ)

**dedeb** *expression* it's a good thing, it's fortunate (NJ, GJ) [*example*: Dedeb igo gaa-wiisiniyaan zhebaa. = It's a good thing I ate this morning. *example*: Dedeb igo gaa-agwana'aman daa-gii-tibaabaawan. = It's is a good thing you covered them they would have gotten damp.]

**degosijiged** *na-prt* contributor; *pl* **degosijigejig** (KP)

**desaa** *vii* be flat as in a shelf, be level (NJ, GJ)

**desaakwa'iganaak** *ni* smoking shelf, storage shelf; *pl* **desaakwa'iganaakoon** (NJ, GJ)

**desabi** *vai* straddle, sit straddling (RT, NJ, GJ)

**det** *expression* shocking (ES)

**detebaa'angose** *vii* float up (as in beaver dam) (NJ)

**detebaa'angose** *vai* float up (as in ice) (NJ, GJ)

**detebaa'agonji-gibide'ebizon** *ni* personal floatation device, life jacket (NJ, GJ)

**detesabi-booniimagad** *vii* skip landing, land by bouncing on the water (as in duck or float plane) (NJ, GJ)

**detibiseg** *vii-prt* tires, wheels; *pl* **detibisegin** (RT, NJ, GJ)

**diba'amaazo** *vai* pay one's self (RT, NJ, GJ)

**diba'amaazowin** *ni* tax; *pl* **diba'amaazowinan** (RT, NJ, GJ)

**dibaabiishkoojiganeyaa** *vii* be a certain number of pounds (NJ)

**dibaabiishkoojiganezi** *vai* be a certain number of pounds (NJ)

**dibishkoojayi'ii** *pc* immediately above, directly above (NJ); *also* **dishkoojeyi'ii** (GJ)

**dinawigamig** *pc* type of lodge (RT, NJ, GJ)

**dipaabaawe** *vii* get damp (NJ, GJ)

**dipiiwan** *vii* be wet, moist (RT)

**dipiiwibagaa** *vii* be wet leaves (RT)

**dipiiwikamigaa** *vii* be moist soil (RT)

**dipiiwikamigaa** *vii* be wet soil (NJ, GJ)

**ditibaakowebiigise** *vai* roll, churn (log, or stick-like object) (NJ, GJ)

**ditibaakowebishkige** *vai* rolls logs (NJ, GJ)

**ditibaakowebishko'** /ditibaakowebishko'w-/ *vta* rolls s.o. (as in logs) (NJ, GJ)

**ditibiwebishkigani-madwewechigaans** *ni* bicycle bell; *pl* **ditibiwebishkigani-madwewechigaansan** (RT, NJ, GJ)

**ditibiwebin** *vta* roll s.o. across (RT, NJ, GJ)

**doodooshaaboowi-miijim** *ni* cheese (EO)

**dookinan** *vti* touch s.t., tap s.t. (RT, NJ, GJ)

**dootookigamide** *vii* be simmered (NJ, GJ)

**dootookigamizwi** /dootookigamizw-/ *vta* simmer s.o. (NJ); *also* **dootookigamizo** /dootookigamizw-/ (GJ)

**dootookigamizan** *vti* simmer s.t. (NJ, GJ)

**dootookigamizo** *vai* be simmered (as in a duck) (NJ, GJ)

**dootookikamigaa** *vii* be tundra (RT)

**dwaa'ibii** *vai* make a hole in the ice for water (NJ, GJ)

**dwaa'igan** *ni* hole in the ice; *pl* **dwaa'iganan** (NJ, GJ)
**dwaa'ige** *vai* make a hole in the ice (NJ, GJ)
**dwaashin** *vai* fall through the ice (RT, NJ, GJ)

# E

---

**edawayi'ii** *pc* on either side, one the sides (RT); *also* **eyiidawayi'ii** (NJ); *also* **edaweyi'ii** (GJ)
**edawaabide-waagaakwad** *ni* double bit ax; *pl* **edawaabide-waagaakwadoon** (NJ)
**edisod** *vai-prt* fruit; *pl* **edisojig** (RT)
**editeg** *vii-prt* berry, fruit; *pl* **editegin** (RT)
**enaabiigising** *vii-prt* line, crease; *pl* **enaabiigisingin** (NJ)
**enamanjichigaadeg** *vii-prt* feeling, sense (NJ)
**endaso-bezhig** *pc* every one, each one (RT)
**endazhi-boodaweng** *vai-prt* fire pit (RT, NJ, GJ)
**endazhi-diimiiyaamagak** *vii-prt* deep places (as in large bodies of water) (RT, NJ, GJ)
**endazhi-gipagaawanzhiiging** *vii-prt* thick stem; *pl* **endazhi-gipagaawanzhiigingin** (RT)
**endazhi-giziibiigiing** *vai-prt* bathtub (NJ)
**endazhi-obaashiiwang** *ni-prt* narrows (RT, NJ, GJ)
**eni-onji-bimaadak** *vii-prt* life cycle (RT)
**enigoonsigiwaam** *ni* ant hill; *pl* **enigoonsigiwaaman** (NJ, GJ)
**eniwekibidoon** *vti* steer s.t., control s.t. (TS)
**eshkan** *na* antler, horn; *pl* **eshkanag** (RT, NJ, GJ)
**eshkan** *ni* ice chisel; *pl* **eshkanan** (NJ, GJ)
**eshkan gwaaba'iskomaan** *ni* ice scooper; *pl* **eshkanan gwaaba'iskomaanan** (NJ, GJ)
**eshkandaming** *vii-prt* watermelon; **eshkandamingin** (RT, NJ, GJ)
**eshkani-bebezhigoganzhii** *na* unicorn; *pl* **eshkani-bebezhigoganzhiig** (RT, NJ, GJ)
**esibananjigesi** *na* raccoon; *pl* **esibananjigesiwag** [*lexicon note*: this is now considered an archaic form for most speakers if it is even known, but for some it is the original form, and esiban is an accepted short form, similar to the vocative, or an accepted short form like waashkesh for waawaashkeshi] (GJ)

---

**esikaanens** *na* conchigliette pasta, *pl* **esikaanensag** (RT, NJ, GJ)

**eyiidawayi'ii** *pc* on either side, one the sides (NJ); *also* **edawayi'ii** (RT); *also* **edaweyi'ii** (GJ)

**ezhegamoons** *na* crappie (GJ); *pl* **ezhegamoonsag**; *also* **gidagwadaashi** *na* crappie (KP); *pl* **gidagwadaashiwag**; also **odazhegamoons** *na* crappie (NJ); *pl* **odazhegamoonsag**

**ezhi-naanangin** *vii-prt* five of them (NJ)

# G

---

**gabaa'** *vta* disembark s.o., let s.o. off (RT, NJ, GJ)

**gabadoo** *vai* portage (NJ, GJ)

**gadaanaangwe** *vai* consume everything (NJ); *also* **gidaanawe** (RT)

**gagaanwaabajiishkaabid** *ni* long, pointed tooth; *pl* **gagaanwaabajiishkaabidan** (RT)

**gagaanwaabajiishkaabide** *vai* have long, pointed teeth (RT)

**gagaanwaabiigitawage** *vai* have long ears (NJ)

**gagaanwaajiibikeyaa** *vii* have long roots (NJ, GJ)

**gagaanwaajiibikezi** *vai* have long roots (NJ, GJ)

**gagiibiingwe** *vai* be blind (RT, NJ, GJ)

**gagiibiingwewasim** *na* guide dog; *pl* **gagiibiingwewasimoog** (NJ)

**gagiibishe** *vii* be deaf (RT, NJ, GJ)

**gagiikim** *vta* exhort s.o. (RT, NJ, GJ)

**gagiiniganzhii** *vai* have sharp claws (RT)

**gagiizhibaayaabiigibijigan** *ni* yoyo; *pl* **gagiizhibaayaabiigibijiganan** (NJ, GJ)

**gagwedwebii'igan** *ni* question mark (?) (JC)

**gakawadabi** *vai* sit dozing off (RT)

**ganawaabandamaazo** *vai* watch over, caretake things (NJ, GJ)

**ganwaapo** *vai+o* be unable to eat something because of spiritual prohibition, allergy, or overconsumption (NJ, GJ)

**ganwaapon** *vta* unable to eat s.o. because of spiritual prohibition, allergy, or overconsumption (NJ)

**gashka'oode** *vii* be knotted (NJ, GJ)

**gashka'oozo** *vai* be fastened, tied (NJ, GJ)

**gashkaabikada'an** *vti* squeeze s.t. shut with a tool (NJ, GJ)

**gashkaabikandan** *vti* bite s.t. shut (NJ, GJ)

---

**gashkaabikinan** *vti* squeeze s.t. shut with one's hand (NJ, GJ)

**gashkaagise** *vii* spring closed (NJ, GJ)

**gashkaagise-wanii'igan** *ni* conibear; *pl* **gashkaagise-wanii'iganan** (NJ, GJ)

**gashkigise** *vii* get pinched (as in a saw) (NJ, GJ)

**gawashkine** *vai* lay down from being full (as in a really full belly) (RT, NJ, GJ)

**gawaakizige** *vai* be falling-down drunk (NJ)

**Gaa-biitoogamaag** *place* Kabetogama (literally the place where there is one lake after another) (GJ)

**gaagaagiwaandag** *na* juniper; *pl* **gaagaagiwaandagoog** (RT, NJ, GJ)

**gaagaanjibizh** /gaagaanjibiN-/ *vta* push s.o., move s.o. (RT, NJ, GJ)

**gaagigebag** *ni* frog leaf, plantain; *pl* **gaagigebagoon** (NJ, GJ)

**gaagiimaa'** *vta* sneak up on s.o. (NJ, GJ)

**gaagiimaashimo** *vai* dance the sneak up (GJ)

**gaagiimaazi** *vai* sneak up in a crouched position (NJ, GJ)

**gaajida'ige** *vai* snag, commense an intimate relationship (RT); *also* **noojikaazo** (NJ, GJ, RT)

**gaajiji'** *vai* snag s.o., commense an intimate relationship with s.o. (RT)

**gaanjiba'ibaan** *ni* toilet plunger (NJ, GJ)

**gaanjiba'ibiise** *vii* water is pushed out, plunged down (NJ, GJ)

**gaanjwa'ibiise** *vii* water is pushed out, plunged down (NJ, GJ)

**gaashaa** *vii* sharp (as in a knife) (NJ, GJ)

**gaashaabide** *vai* have sharp teeth (NJ)

**gaashiboodoon** *vti* sharpen s.t. that is long and straight (NJ, GJ)

**gaashiingwe** *vai* has a bumpy face (as in not having shaved for a while), be partly shaved (NJ, GJ)

**gaashipoobizo** *vai* cross the line (as in driving out of lane), or miss a turnoff (as in driving) [*example*: Gigaashipoobizomin. = We missed the turn off.] (NJ, GJ)

**gaashkiboojige** *vai* sharpen things that are long and straight (NJ, GJ)

**gaasi-adisibii'igan** *ni* wipe off marker; *pl* **gaasi-adisibii'iganan** (RT, NJ, GJ)

**gaasiidoone'o** *vai* wipe one's mouth (RT, NJ, GJ)

**gaasiiyaabikishkan** *vti* wipe s.t. off of rocks with one's body (NJ, GJ)

**gaasiiyaamikishkige** *vai* wipe off rocks under water (NJ, GJ)

**gaaskaabasigewigamigoons** *ni* smokehouse; *pl* **gaaskaabasigewigamigoonsan** (NJ)

**gaaskanazomagad** *vii* whisper, sound softly (RT, NJ, GJ)

**gaaskiigino-odaminwaaganensikaan** *ni* plastic toy; *pl* **gaaskiigino-odaminwaaganensikaanan** (NJ, GJ)

**gaaskizwaan** *ni* smoke meat through to cured state (RT)

**gaawaa** *vii* be rough (RT, NJ, GJ)

**gaawaandag** *na* white spruce; *pl* **gaawaandagoog** (AM)

**gaawanzh** *ni* stem; *pl* **gaawanzhiin**; *loc* **gaawanzhiing** (RT)

**gaazhage** *vai* be gluttonous (NJ)

**gaazoomagad** *vii* be hidden (RT, NJ, GJ)

**gaazootaw** *vta* hide from s.o. (RT)

**gaazootaadiwag** /gaazootaadi-/ *vai* they play hide-and-seek with one another (NJ)

**gegwaanisagizid** *vai-prt* tyrannosaurus rex; *pl* **gegwaanisagiziwaad** (NJ)

**gete-awesiinh** *na* dinosaur; *pl* **gete-awesiinyag** (NJ, GJ)

**gete-ogiikadaanaangwe** *na* dinosour; *pl* **gete-ogiikadaanaangweg** (NJ)

**gete-ogiikadaanaangwe-waawan** *ni* dinosaur egg; *pl* **gete-ogiikadaanaangwe-waawanoon** (NJ)

**getemaagwad** *vii* smell ancient (GJ)

**giba'an** *vti* patch s.t., close s.t. (NJ, GJ)

**giba'igaade** *vii* be closed (as in a business or store) (NJ, GJ)

**giba'iganike** *vai* build a dam (NJ, GJ)

**gibaabikibidoon** *vti* squeeze s.t. shut (by using s.t.) (NJ, GJ)

**gibaabikinan** *vti* close s.t. with one's hand (as in damper on a stove) (NJ, GJ)

**gibaakiiginan** *vti* close s.t. (paper or sheet-like) (NJ, GJ)

**gibadoonh** *na* button; *pl* **gibadoonyag** (JC); *also* **zagaakwa'on** *na* button; *pl* **zagaakwa'onag** (NJ, GJ)

**gibichichige** *vai* block, prohibit, prevent (NJ, GJ)

**gibichii** *vai* stop (NJ, GJ)

**gibiigagoojigan** *ni* sheet-like material used for partition, window, or door of a lodge; **gibiigagoojiganan** (GJ)

**gibijaane** *vai* have a plugged or stuffy nose (RT, NJ, GJ)

**gibinde'amaw** *vta* close (s.t.) for s.o. (NJ, GJ)

**gibinde'an** *vta* close s.t. (as in cloth-like, e.g. wigwam door) (NJ, GJ)

**gibinde'igan** *ni* cloth door on wiigiwaam; *pl* **gibinde'iganan** (NJ)

**gibinde'ige** *vai* close the door (as in a cloth door) (NJ, GJ)

**gibinewen** *vta* choke s.o. (NJ, GJ)

**gibisidoon** *vti* block s.t. (as in using something to block light from a projector) (NJ, GJ)

**gibitagomo** *vai* stop floating, sink (NJ, GJ)

**gibitakwazhiwe** *vai* stop paddling (NJ, GJ)

**giboch** *expression* you don't know crap! dummy! (NJ, GJ)

**gibozige** *vai* bake (RT)

**gibwaabikada'an** *vti* pound s.t. shut with a tool (RT)

**gichi-babiikwajiwan** *vii* the water is really snarling (NJ, GJ)

**gichi-bikwaakwad** *ni* basketball; *pl* **gichi-bikwaakwadoon** (NJ)

**gichi-ogin** *na* tomato; *pl* **gichi-oginiig** (RT)

**gichi-oginii-waabigon** *ni* tomato flower; *pl* **gichi-oginii-waabigoniin** (NJ); *also* **gichi-oginii-waabigon** (RT)

**gichi-omakakii** *na* leopard frog; *pl* **gichi-omakakiig** (NJ, GJ)

**gichigamiiwashk** *ni* bulrush; *pl* **gichigamiiwashkoon** (NJ, GJ)

**gichigamiiwashkway** *na* bulrush; *pl* **gichigamiiwashkwayag** (NJ, GJ)

**gichiwakii'ige** *vai* stabilize a boat by bracing on bottom (NJ, GJ)

**gichiwaakwa'an** *vti* pin s.t. in place (as in clothes on clothesline) (NJ, GJ)

**gichiwashkishin** *vai* curls up (as into fetal position) (RT, NJ); *also* be stuck in the grass or mud (as when harvesting wild rice) (GJ)

**gichiwibiishkaa** *vii* glide slowly through water (NJ, GJ)

**gidaatabitaagozi** *vai* trill, fast sounding call (as in bird) (NJ, GJ)

**gidaatabose** *vai* walk fast (NJ)

**gidaatabowe** *vai* speaks fast (NJ, GJ)

**gidagwadaashi** *na* crappie (KP); *pl* **gidagwadaashiwag**; *also* **ezhegamoons** *na* crappie (GJ); *pl* **ezhegamoonsag**; *also* **odazhegamoons** *na* crappie (NJ); *pl* **odazhegamoonsag**

**gidinamegwe** *vai* pull fish from nets (RT)

**gidochige** *vai* learn music (NJ)

**gikendaagozi** *vai* be known, be around (NJ)

**gikendamaazo** *vai* sense things, know things by sense, discover (NJ, GJ)

**gikendamaazoon** *vti* sense s.t. (NJ)

**gikendamaazowin** *ni* sense; *pl* **gikendamaazowinan** (NJ, GJ)

**gikinoo'amaadii-zhinawa'oojiganens** *ni* school bell; *pl* **gikinoo'amaadii-zhinawa'oojiganensan** (NJ)

**gikinoo'amaadiiwidaabaan** *na* school bus; *pl* **gikinoo'amaadiiwidaabaanag** (NJ)

**gikinoo'amaagewidaaban** *na* school bus; *pl* **gikinoo'amaagewidaabanag** (NJ)

**gikinoonowagad** *vii* be a certain year (as in telling specific date) (NJ)

**gimiwanishi** *vai* make a structure to escape the rain, find shelter from rain (GJ); *also* get rained on (NJ)

**gimiwanoowaakwaa** *vii* be a rainforest (RT)

**gimiwanoowaakwaang** *pc* rainforest (RT)

**ginaabandamaa** *vai* don't want to go because of inclement weather (NJ, GJ)

**ginaanimanishi** *vai* be wind-bound, be stranded because of high wind (NJ, GJ)

**ginagazhe'wi** /**ginagazhe'w-**/ *vta* tickle s.o. (NJ); *also* **ginagazhe'o** /**ginagazhe'w-**/ (GJ)

**ginibiisaanishi** *vai* can't go because it is too rainy (NJ, GJ)

**ginigawaami** *vai* mingle (as in different species during fish spawn) (NJ, GJ)

**ginigawijigaazo** *vai* be mixed (RT)

**ginigawishkaw** *vta* mingle with s.o., mix in with s.o. (RT, NJ, GJ)

**ginigawisin** *vii* be mixed (RT)

**giniponishi** *vai* be snowed in (NJ, GJ)

**ginisinaa'ago** *vai* be wind-bound, be stranded because of high wind (NJ, GJ)

**ginoo-dibikad** *vii* be a long night (NJ, GJ)

**ginoo-giizhigad** *vii* be a long day (NJ, GJ)

**ginoogin** *vii* grow high, grow tall (RT)

**ginoozhe** *na* northern pike; *pl* **ginoozheg** (RT, NJ, GJ)

**ginwaabiigaanowe** *vai* have a long tail (NJ)

**ginwaabiigidenaniwe** *vai* have a long tongue (RT)

**ginwaabiigigwe** *vai* have a long neck (NJ)

**ginwaabiigijiichigom** *na* skin tag; **ginwaabiigijiichigomag** (NJ, GJ)

**ginwaabiko-jiimaan** *ni* metal boat; *pl* **ginwaabiko-jiimaanan** (RT, NJ, GJ)

**ginwaakwad** *vii* be long (tree-like) (NJ, GJ)

**ginwaashkanzhiiwi** *vai* have long claws or fingernails (NJ, GJ)

**ginwaasige** *vai* sun shines a long time, be a long day (as in a long summer day) (RT)

**ginwawe** *vai* have long fur or hair (RT)

**ginwiindimaa** *vii* be deep water (NJ, GJ)

**ginwiindimaasabii** *vai* set net in deep water (GJ, NJ)

**gipagawe** *vai* have thick fur (RT)

**gipagazhaan** *ni* callus, thick skin (NJ, GJ)

**gipagazhaga'e** *vai* have thick, callous, armor-like skin (NJ)

**gipagazhe** *vai* have thick, callous skin (RT)

**gipagadin** *vii* be frozen thick (as in a body of water) (NJ, GJ)

**gipagizigwazi** *vai* be frozen thick (as in ice) (NJ, GJ)

**gishewaabikad** *vii* hook is empty (NJ, GJ)

**gishkishenh** *na* female dog; *pl* **gishkishenyag** (RT, NJ, GJ)

**gitaakwa'iganaabik** *ni* sinker for drowning set (trap for animals); *pl*
     **gitaakwa'iganaabikoon** (NJ, GJ)

**gitaakwa'iganeyaab** *ni* anchor wire (for a trap); *pl*
     **gitaakwa'iganeyaabiin** (NJ, GJ)

**gitaakwapizon** *ni* dog leash, dog chain, seat belt; *pl* **gitaakwapizonan**
     (NJ, GJ)

**gitaamika'an** *vti* anchor s.t. (NJ, GJ)

**gitaamika'igan** *ni* anchor, weight for nets; *pl* **gitaamika'iganan** (NJ,
     GJ)

**gitaamika'iganeyaab** *ni* anchor line (NJ, GJ)

**gitaamikishkoodoon** *vti* sink s.t. to bottom of lake with heavy object
     (NJ, GJ)

**gitige** *vai* farm, garden, plant (RT)

**gizhaasige** *vai* shine hotly (as in the sun) (RT)

**gizhaawaso** *vai* be protective of one's young (NJ, GJ)

**gizhidaawangide** *vii* be warm sand (NJ, GJ)

**gizhibaabide** *vii* spin, rotate (as in the earth spinning on its axis) (RT)

**gizhibaajiwan** *vii* be swirling water (NJ, GJ)

**gizhibaapidoon** *vti* tie s.t. around (s.t.) (NJ, GJ)

**gizhibaashkaw** *vta* encircle s.o., go around s.o. (NJ, GJ)

**gizhigibizh** /**gizhigiN-**/ *vta* squeeze or tickle s.o. to urinate (NJ, GJ)

**gizhiikwazhiwe** *vai* paddle or swim fast (NJ, GJ)

**gizhiiwe** *vii* sound strong, have a loud, strong sound (NJ, GJ)

**gizhiiyaate** *vii* be bright, far-reaching, or penetrating light (NJ, GJ)

**giziibiiga'igan** *ni* soap; *pl* **giziibiiga'iganan** (RT, NJ, GJ)

**giziibiigitigwaane-giziibiiga'igan** *ni* shampoo (NJ)

**giziibishkam** *vai* have a joint illness (NJ, GJ); *also* **odoogiziibishkam**
     (GJ)

**gii'iwe** *vai* escape (from a predator) (RT, NJ, GJ)

**giige** *vai* heal up (RT, NJ, GJ)

**giigidoobii'igan** *ni* quotation mark; *pl* **giigidoobii'iganan** ("") (JC)

**giigoonsiwi** *vai* be a small fish (RT, NJ, GJ)

**giigoowaabid** *ni* fish teeth; *pl* **giigoowaabidan** (RT, NJ, GJ)

**giigoowensiwi** *vai* be a small fish (RT, NJ, GJ)

---

**giikiibiingwashi** *vai* fall asleep (LM)

**giikanaabasigaadeg wiiyaas** *vii-prt* smoked meat (GJ); *also* **nooka'iiwagwaan** (GJ)

**giikanaabasigaazod giigoonh** *vai-prt* smoked fish (GJ); *also* **nooka'iskawaan** (GJ)

**giikanaabate** *vii* be smoky (RT, NJ, GJ)

**giikawi-ezigaawe** *vai* succumb to ticks (NJ, GJ)

**giikawidikome** *vai* succumb to fleas (NJ, GJ)

**giinaa** *vii* sharp (knife) (RT, NJ, GJ)

**giiniboodoon** *vti* sharpen s.t. that has a jagged edge (NJ, GJ)

**giishkaabid** *ni* incisor; *pl* **giishkaabidan** (RT)

**giishkaabide** *vai* have incisors (RT)

**giishkaabideboojigan** *ni* swede saw; *pl* **giishkaabideboojiganan** (GJ)

**giishkandan** *vti* cut s.t. off with one's teeth (RT)

**giishkandizo** *vai* bite off a part of oneself (NJ, GJ)

**giishkanjige** *vai* cut with one's teeth (RT)

**giishkiganzhiizhiganaabikoons** *ni* fingernail clipper; *pl* **giishkiganzhiizhiganaabikoonsan** (NJ, GJ)

**giishkiganzhiizhige** *vai* cut fingernails or toenails (NJ, GJ)

**giishkitaa** *vai* breaks off a foot or paw (NJ, GJ)

**giishkadikwane'wi /giishkadikwane'w-/** *vta* limb s.o. (tree) using s.t. (ax, knife, or saw) (NJ)

**giishkashkosiwewidaabaan** *na* combine (mechanized harvesting machine); *pl* **giishkashkosiwewidaabaanag** (RT)

**giitaabikizh /giitaabikiN-/** *vta* let s.o. free (from a trap) (NJ, GJ)

**giitaabikinan** *vti* release s.t. (as in a trap) (NJ, GJ)

**giiwashkwebizh /giiwashkwebiN-/** vta get s.o. high or drunk (RT)

**giiwashkweyaabandam** *vai* be under the influence of narcotics, be "high" (NJ, GJ)

**giiwine** *vai* be in one's death throes (ES)

**giiwitaakamisab** *na* world wide web (NJ, GJ)

**giizhaami** *vai* stop spawning (RT, NJ, GJ)

**giizhibagaa** *vii* leaves are fully grown (NJ, GJ)

**giizhibagizi** *vai* has leaves fully grown (as in a tree) (NJ, GJ)

**giizhigin** *vii* mature, ripen, finish growing (RT, NJ, GJ)

**giizhikanagek** *na* cedar bark; *pl* **giizhikanagekwag** (RT, NJ, GJ)

**giizhizo** *vai* be cooked, be done cooking (RT)

**giizhoogami** *vii* be warm water (NJ)

**giizhookonaye** *vai* dress warmly, dress in warm clothes (RT, NJ, GJ)

**giiziz** /giizizw-/ *vta* fry s.o. (RT)

**goda'aakwaazh** /goda'aakwaaN-/ *vta* take a pot shot at s.o. (ES, RT, NJ, GJ)

**goji-giigido** *vai* try to speak (RT, NJ, GJ)

**gokokwaa** *vii* be tippy [*example*: Gokokwaa jiimaan. = The canoe is tippy.]

**gomaa go apii** *expression* before long (RT)

**gomaa go minik** *expression* not too much but enough (NJ)

**gonzaabiishkoojigan** *ni* net weight or sinker for drowning set (on trap for animals); *pl* **gonzaabiishkoojiganan** (RT, NJ, GJ)

**gonzaabiishkoojiganaabik** *na* rock weight; *pl* **gonzaabiishkoojiganaabikoog** (NJ, GJ)

**gonzaabiishkoozo** *vai* be submerged (as in ice weighed down by water) (NJ, GJ)

**gopimine** *vai* unload harvest from canoe and bring inland (NJ, GJ)

**gopiwidaaso** *vai* unload and bring inland (NJ, GJ)

**gopiwidoon** *vti* carry s.t. inland (NJ, GJ)

**goshkobizh** /goshkobiN-/ *vta* startle s.o by grabbing them (RT, NJ, GJ)

**goshkwaawaajishin** *vai* laying down relaxing, still (NJ, GJ)

**gotaagonezi** *vai* be scared (NJ)

**gozigon** *vii* feel heavy (NJ, GJ)

**goonzaabiishkomaan** *ni* net sinker, *pl* **goonzaabiishkomaanan** (RT)

**goopaataagozi** *vai* sound pathetic (NJ, GJ)

**gwanabaabago** *vai* capsize in rapids (NJ, GJ)

**gwanabaashi** *vai* capsize from wind (NJ, GJ)

**gwanabise** *vii* capsize (RT, NJ, GJ)

**gwayakobide** *vii* fly straight (NJ, GJ)

**gwayakobidoon** *vti* do s.t. right (NJ)

**gwayakobijige** *vai* tie or pull things straight (RT, NJ, GJ)

**gwayakopide** *vii* be tied straight (RT, NJ, GJ)

**gwazigwani** *vai* be heavy (NJ)

**gwaaba'adaawangwaan** *ni* sand scooper; *pl* **gwaaba'adaawangwaanan** (NJ, GJ)

**gwaabaajigan** *ni* shovel; *pl* **gwaabaajiganan** (NJ, GJ)

**gwaakwaashkwebiise** *vii* splash (NJ)

**gwaashkwesidoon** *vti* dribble s.t (as in a ball) (NJ); *also* **gweshkwesidoon** (GJ)

**gwekabowe** *vai* switch sides paddling (RT, NJ, GJ)

**gweki-zaswebiiga'anjigaawan** *vii* sprinkle water while turning (as in a lawn sprinkler) (GJ)

# I

---

**ikidowinensi-mazina'iganens** *ni* alphabet activity card; *pl* **ikidowinensi-mazina'iganensan** (RT)

**ikidowini-ataasowin** *ni* glossary; *pl* **ikidowini-ataasowinan** (RT)

**ikowaaginigaa** *vii* be a certain width (RT, NJ, GJ)

**ikoweba'wi** /ikoweba'w-/ *vta* push s.o. aside (NJ); *also* **akoweba'o** /akoweba'w-/ (GJ); *also* **ikoweba'** /ikoweba'w-/ (RT)

**ikwa'ibaan** *ni* water pump (RT, NJ, GJ)

**ikwa'ibii** *vii* water is pumped (RT, NJ, GJ)

**ikwa'ige** *vai* pump water (RT, NJ, GJ)

**ikwanaanjige** *vai* sniff, huff (NJ, GJ)

**ikwewaatig** *na* female tree; *pl* **ikwewaatigoog** (RT, NJ, GJ)

**inakwazhiwe** *vai* paddle to a certain place (RT, NJ, GJ)

**inamanjichigaade** *vii* be a feeling, be a sense (NJ)

**inawendangibii'igan** *ni* fact family number, *pl* **inawendangibii'iganan** (RT, NJ, GJ); *also* **asigiginjigemaagan**; *pl* **asigiginjigemaaganag** (GJ); *also* **inawendibii'igan**; *pl* **inawendibii'iganan** (RT, NJ, GJ)

**inaabadad** *vii* be used in a certain way (RT, NJ, GJ)

**inaabide-ayaa** *vii* be toothed (RT, NJ, GJ)

**inaabiigisin** *vii* be a line or crease in a certain way (NJ)

**inaadagaa** *vai* swim in a certain way (RT, NJ); *also* **inaadage** (GJ)

**inaadizokaw** *vta* teach s.o. by use of traditional legends (NJ, GJ)

**inaagamin** *vii* be a certain way (as in a liquid) (RT)

**inaajimotaw** *vta* tell s.o. s.t. (RT, NJ, GJ)

**inaakogomo** *vai* paddle to certain place (NJ, GJ)

**inaakogoojin** *vai* lie across (as in log) (NJ, GJ)

**inaakwad** *vii* be in a certain way (s.t. stick-like) (RT, NJ, GJ)

**inaandag** *na* balsam; *pl* **inaandagoog** (WI)

**inaasamii** *vai* facing (ES)

**inaatewin** *ni* light, illumination (RT)

**indanaaminingwiigan** *nid* my armpit; *loc* **indanaaminingwiiganaang** (NJ)

---

**indenaniw** *nid* my tongue (RT, NJ, GJ)

**inigokwaa** *vii* be such a size, be in a certain location, be everywhere [example: enigokwaag giiyaw = some parts of your body, all over your body] (NJ)

**ininamaw** *vta* hand s.t. to s.o. (RT, NJ, GJ)

**ininaandag** *na* balsam (WI), any evergreen (NJ); *pl* **ininaandagoog**

**ininiiwaatig** *na* male tree; *pl* **ininiiwaatigoog** (RT, NJ, GJ)

**ininishib** *na* drake mallard; *pl* **ininishibag** (RT, NJ, GJ)

**initaagwad** *vii* sound a certain way (RT, NJ, GJ)

**inwaazo** *vai* make one's best effort (ES)

**inweweyaashi** *vai* have a certain sound in the wind (RT, NJ, GJ)

**ipide** *vii* go a certain speed [*example:* Aaniin epidenig makwa ode' na'iid? = How fast does the bear's heart beat when in hibernation?] (RT)

**ipizo'** *vta* give s.o. a ride in a certain way (NJ)

**ipogwad** *vii* taste a certain way (RT, NJ, GJ)

**ishakonaa** *pc* usually (RT, NJ, GJ)

**ishaakozi** *vai* have an erection (LM)

**ishkaatig** *na* green wood (standing green trees); *pl* **ishkaatigoog** (GJ)

**ishkaatig** *ni* green wood (chopped); *pl* **ishkaatigoon** (GJ)

**ishko'** *vta* startle s.o. in a certain way (NJ, GJ)

**ishkodawe** *vai* make fire (NJ, GJ)

**ishkodekaan** *ni* fire maker (flint, stick kit); *pl* **ishkodekaanan** (NJ, GJ)

**ishkon** *vta*  set s.o. aside, save s.o. for later (RT)

**ishkondamaw** *vta* save, reserve s.t. for s.o. (of food) (RT, NJ, GJ)

**ishkonigaazo** *vai* be set aside, be reserved (RT)

**ishkwaakobijigan** *ni* tree or pole that is shaken; *pl* **ishkwaakobijiganan** (NJ, GJ)

**ishkwaakobijige** *vai* shake a tree (person or bear) (NJ, GJ)

**ishkwaakobizh /ishkwaakobiN-/** *vta* shake s.o. (tree-like) (NJ, GJ)

**ishkwebii'igan** *ni* period (.) (JC)

**ishkweyaabid** *ni* back tooth, molar; *pl* **ishkweyaabidan** (RT)

**ishpaakwa'igan** *ni* crutch, support; *pl* **ishpaakwa'iganan** (NJ, GJ)

**ishpaatigong** *pc* high in the trees (RT)

**ishpendaagwad** *vii* be important (RT, NJ, GJ)

**ishpidoondanekizin** *ni* high-heeled shoe; *pl* **ishpidoondanekizinan** (NJ, GJ)

**iska'ibaan** *ni* water bailer, sponge; *pl* **iska'ibaanan** (NJ, GJ)

**iska'ibii** *vai* bail (NJ, GJ)

**iska'ibiise** *vii* water forced up and out (NJ, GJ)

**iskaabiigiwebinan** *vti* flush s.t. (as in toilet) (NJ, GJ)

**iskaabiise** *vii* water level drops (NJ, GJ)

**iskatese** *vii* water level drops (NJ, GJ)

**ispwaabikada'an** *vti* bend s.t. (metal-like) down with a tool (as in bending over a protruding nail) (GJ); *also* **zipwaabikada'an** (JC)

**ispwaabikibidoon** *vti* bend s.t. (metal-like) down with hand (as in bending over a protruding nail) (GJ); *also* **zipwaabikibidoon** (JC)

**izhi-onde** *vii* it comes up in a certain way (as in lava) (GJ)

**izhigin** *vii* grow in a certain way (RT)

**izhijiwan** *vii* flow in a certain way (RT)

**izhiwanakowi** *vai* have a certain top (as in a tree) (NJ)

**izhiwijigaazo** *vai* be brought somewhere (RT)

# J

---

**jaagise** *vii* burn out, run out (in reference to community stick pile in moccasin game) (GJ)

**jaagizo** *vai* burn (RT, NJ, GJ)

**jiibwaabikad** *vii* have a point, come to a point (NJ, GJ)

**jiichiibizideni** *vai* tap one's foot (NJ)

**jiichiiga'amegwe** *vai* descale fish (NJ, GJ)

**jiichiigom** *na* wart; *pl* **jiichiigomag** (RT, NJ, GJ)

**jiiga'amegwe** *vai* descale fish, clean fish (RT, NJ, GJ)

**jiiga'oweshiinh** *na* cricket; *pl* **jiiga'oweshiinyag** (RT, NJ, GJ)

**jiigewe'am** *vai* swim or paddle along shore (RT, NJ, GJ)

**jiigizhwi** /jiigizhw-/ *vta* scale fish (NJ); *also* **jiigizho** /jiigizhw-/ (GJ); *also* **jiigizh** /jiigizhw-/ (RT)

**jiigwegizhige** *vai* fillet fish (GJ)

**jiingwe** *vai* voice carries long ways (NJ, GJ)

**jiingwewewag** /jiingwewe/ *vai* they rattle (as in thunderbirds) [*conjugation note*: requires plural to make sense, though this is not a reflexive verb] (NJ, GJ)

**jiishaakwa'ige** *vai* cut limbs off a tree (GJ); *also* scrape a hide (NJ)

---

**jiishaandawe'ige** *vai* limb small trees (as in cleaning saplings for use as lodge poles) (NJ)

**jiishaanda'wi** /**jiishaanda'w-**/ *vta* limb small tree (as in cleaning saplings for use as lodge poles) (NJ)

**jiishi'** *vta* offer food to s.o. and take back (as in coming out of a fast, when fed new foods in mourning, or for a first kill) (RT, NJ, GJ)

# M

**madaabiiga'igaazo** *vai* be exposed (from having trees are cut) (NJ, GJ)

**madaabiiga'ige** *vai* cut it right down to an open spot (NJ, GJ)

**madaabiijiwan** *vii* flows to shore (from inland) (RT, NJ, GJ)

**madwe-zaagaabate** *vii* smoke seen from a distance (NJ, GJ)

**madwenagwiiyaashi** *vai* make sound with one's wing in flight (GJ)

**madwenjige** *vai* be heard chewing (RT, NJ, GJ)

**madwese** *vai* be heard flying (NJ, GJ)

**madwewe** *vai* make a sound (RT, NJ, GJ)

**madwewe** *vii* make a sound (RT, NJ, GJ)

**madweyaashkaa** *vii* waves make a sound (RT, NJ, GJ)

**makadewiingwebinige** *vai* the dark side shows (as in bagese game) (GJ)

**makizineyaabiikaade** *vii* have laces (NJ, GJ)

**makoonsiwi** *vai* be sequestered for mensus (NJ)

**makoowizi** *vai* be sequestered for mensus (JC)

**makopinagaawanzh** *na* water lily plant; *pl* **makopinagaawanzhiig** (RT)

**mamaadaanimad** *vii* wind starts intermittently (RT)

**mamaajiwebishkan** *vti* make s.t. shake (NJ)

**mamaandido** *vai* be amazingly large (NJ)

**mamaangaabide** *vai* have wide teeth (RT)

**mamaangi-giinaabid** *ni* large, sharp teeth; *pl* **mamaangi-giinaabidan** (RT)

**mamaangi-giishkaabide** *vai* have large incisors (RT)

**mamaangibagaa** *vii* have large leaves (RT)

**mamaangibagizi** *vai* have large leaves (RT, NJ, GJ)

**mamaanginingwiigwane** *vai* have broad wings (RT)

**mamaanginowe** *vai* have big cheeks (RT)

**mamaangishkiinzhigwe** *vai* have large eyes (RT, NJ, GJ)

**mamaangizhigwane** *vai* have broad fins (as in a fish) (RT)

**mamaangizide** *vai* have big feet (RT)

**mamaazhiike** *pc* any old way, done hurriedly, not in a good way (NJ); *also* **mamaanzhii** (GJ)

**mamangideyaagoneshkige** *vai* make trail wider (in the snow) (GJ)

**mami'igaazo** *vai* be harvested, be taken (RT)

**mami'igewidaabaan** *na* combine (mechanized harvesting machine); *pl* **mami'igewidaabaanag** (RT)

**mamigobizh** /mamigobiN-/ *vta* give s.o. a backrub (RT, NJ, GJ)

**mamigowebizh** /mamigowebiN-/ *vta* shake s.o. (NJ, GJ)

**mamizhiganaabik** *ni* cookie cutters; *pl* **mamizhiganaabikoon** (RT, NJ, GJ)

**mamizhim** *vta* tattle on s.o. (RT, NJ, GJ)

**mamizhitam** *vai* tattle (RT, NJ, GJ)

**mamizhitaagozi** *vai* tattle (RT, NJ, GJ)

**mangade-bakwezhiganaabiins** *ni* lasagna noodle; *pl* **mangade-bakwezhiganaabiinsan** (RT, NJ, GJ)

**mangadebidoon** *vti* strip s.t. into wide (as in bark) strips (RT, NJ, GJ)

**mangadeyaagoneshkige** *vai* make a trail wider in the snow (NJ, GJ)

**mangadezhigaade** *vii* cut in wide strips (RT, NJ, GJ)

**mangademochige** *vai* make trail wider (in the snow) (NJ, GJ)

**mangadeyaakwa'ige** *vai* make trail wider (brush out) (NJ, GJ)

**mangibii'igan** *ni* capital letter; *pl* **mangibii'iganan** (JC)

**mangibii'ige** *vai* write in all capital letters (JC)

**mangigin** *vii* grow big (RT)

**mangitaagozi** *vai* have a deep voice (NJ)

**manidoomin** *na* bead; *pl* **manidoominag** (RT, NJ, GJ)

**manoominagaawanzh** *ni* rice stalk; *pl* **manoominagaawanzhiin** (RT, NJ, GJ)

**manoomini-manidoosh** *na* ladybug; *pl* **manoomini-manidoosh** (NJ, GJ)

**mashkawa'wi** /mashkawa'w-/ *vta* make s.o. strong, grow s.o. strong (NJ)

**mashkawaakamigaa** *vii* be strong (tree-like) (RT, NJ, GJ)

**mashkawaakogadin** *vii* be frozen and brittle (as in a fresh sapling cut in winter when first brought inside) (NJ)

**mashkawaanimad** *vii* wind blows hard, be a strong breeze (as from fan) (RT, NJ, GJ)

**mashkawaanimizi** *vai* be scared stiff (RT, NJ, GJ)

mashkawapidoon *vti* tie s.t. tight (RT, NJ, GJ)
mashkawigaade *vai* have strong legs (RT)
mashkawigin *vii* grow strong (RT)
mashkawikamigaa *vii* be tundra, be strong ground (RT)
mashkawikamigaaganoojiinh *na* lemming; *pl*
      mashkawikamigaaganoojiinyag (RT)
mashkawishkanzh *na* strong claw; *pl* mashkawishkanzhiig (RT)
mashkawishkanzii *vai* have strong claws (RT)
mashkinoozhe *na* muskellunge; *pl* mashkinoozheg; also ozhaawashko-
      ginoozhe (NJ)
mashkode-akakojiish *na* prairie dog; *pl* mashkode-akakojiishag (RT)
mashkodekamigaa *vii* be a prairieland (RT)
mashkodiisiminens *na* bean seed; *pl* mashkodiisiminensag (RT)
mashkosiinsigaawanzh *ni* grass stem; *pl* mashkosiinsigaawanzhiin
      (RT)
mashkosiinsikaa *vii* be a grassland, be lots of grass (RT)
mashkosiinsikaan *ni* lawn (RT)
mawine'ige *vai* be aggressive, retaliatory (RT, NJ, GJ)
mayaajiiging *vii-prt* plant; *pl* mayaajiigingin (RT)
mayagi-waawaabiganoojiinh *na* lemming; *pl* mayagi-
      waawaabiganoojiinyag (RT)
mayagitaagozi *vai* sound strange (RT, NJ); *also* mayegitaagozi (GJ)
mazina'igani-makak *ni* mailbox; *pl* mazina'igani-makakoon (RT, NJ,
      GJ)
mazinaakide *vii* be a picture, be illustrated (RT)
mazinaatebiigishin *vai* reflect in the water [*example*: Mazinaatebiigishin
      mitig. = The tree is reflecting in the water. *example*:
      Mazinaatebiigishin gaa-pimised bineshiinh. = The bird casts a
      reflection in the water flying.] (NJ, GJ)
mazinaateshin *vai* cast a shadow (NJ)
mazinadoobii'igan *ni* alphabet stamp; *pl* mazinadoobii'iganan (RT)
mazinadizh /mazinadiN-/ *vta* sculpt s.o. (with clay or dough) (GJ)
mazinibii'iganaatig *ni* drawing tool; *pl* mazinibii'iganaatigoon (GJ)
maziniganeshin *vai* be a fossil (NJ)
maziniiginige *vai* fold images, make images or pictures (using paper or
      cloth-like material) (GJ)
mazininjiishkiwagi *vai* sculpt (with clay or dough) (GJ)
mazinijiishkiwagin *vta* sculpt s.o. (with clay or dough) (NJ, GJ)
maadaadode *vii* story begins (RT)

**maadaami** *vai* start to spawn (RT, NJ, GJ)

**maagizhaa baamaa ingoding** *expression* perhaps at some later time (RT, NJ, GJ)

**maagoshkan** *vti* press s.t. down, pack s.t. down (RT, NJ, GJ)

**maagoshkaw** *vta* press s.o. down, pack s.o. down (as in snow) (NJ, GJ)

**maagwaagoneshkige** *vai* press foot in the snow, pack snow down with one's foot (GJ)

**maajiibide** *vii* start running, start operating (as in an engine), take off (RT, NJ, GJ)

**maajiibizo** *vai* start running, start operating, start driving, take off (RT, NJ, GJ)

**maajiigi** *vai* start to grow (RT)

**maajiigin** *vii* start to grow (RT)

**maajiiyaabagonde** *vii* take off on top of the water in a current (NJ, GJ)

**maajiiyaabogo** *vai* go off into the water (as in fish eggs) (NJ, GJ)

**maajiiyaaboode** *vii* take off in a current (NJ, GJ)

**maajiiyaadagaa** *vai* dart while swimming, quickly take off swimming (RT)

**maajiizh /maajiiN-/** *vta* send s.o. somewhere (RT)

**maamashkawadin** *vii* freeze strong (RT, NJ, GJ)

**maamawinigan** *ni* mixture; *pl* **maamawiniganan** (RT)

**maanadikoshens** *na* billy goat; *pl* **maanadikoshensag** (RT, NJ, GJ)

**maanzhi-ozaawizi** *vai* be the color of deer in the fall and winter (NJ)

**maawandoojiwan** *vii* pool (water); *also* waves come together (NJ, GJ)

**maawandoonan** *vti* sort s.t., group s.t. (RT, NJ, GJ)

**maawiin** *pc* must be (NJ)

**maazhaa ge baamaa ingoding** *expression* perhaps at some later time (RT, NJ, GJ)

**maazhi-miskozi** *vai* be pink (NJ, GJ)

**maazhipogwad** *vii* taste bad, taste bitter (RT, NJ, GJ)

**megwayaami** *vai* be in mid-spawn (NJ, GJ)

**memengwaa** *na* butterfly, swallowtail; *pl* **memengwaag** (RT, NJ, GJ)

**metasin** *vta* miss s.o. (one who is absent or dead) (RT, NJ); *also* **metisin** (GJ)

**michige'wi /michige'w-/** *vta* stick up fins to kill s.o. (NJ)

**michigwe'o /michigwe'w-/** *vta* stick up fins to kill s.o. (GJ)

**michinininjiitaw** *vta* communicate with s.o. using sign language (NJ)

**migisiwizh** *na* fishing sinker (RT, NJ, GJ)

**migiskan** *ni* fish hook; *pl* **migiskanan** (RT, NJ, GJ); *dim* **migiskanens**

**migiskanaatig** *ni* fishing pole; *pl* **migiskanaatigoon** (RT, NJ, GJ)

**mikawaam** *vta* remind s.o. (RT, NJ, GJ)

**mikigaade** *vii* be found (RT)

**mikigaazo** *vai* be found, be discovered (RT, NJ, GJ)

**mikond** *ni* reinforcing stick on end of birch bark roll or basket, a binding stick; *pl* **mikondiin**; *dim* **mikondiins** (GJ)

**mikwamii-waaginogaan** *ni* igloo; *pl* **mikwamii-waaginogaanan** (RT, NJ, GJ)

**mimigoshkamwaagan** *ni* threshing pit for wild rice; *pl* **mimigoshkamwaaganan** (RT)

**mina'igwaandag** *na* white spruce; *pl* **mina'igwaandagoog** (RT, NJ, GJ)

**minawaashkaa** *vii* be the pleasant motion of the waves (NJ)

**minaam** *vta* sniff s.o. [*example*: Niminaamig animosh. = The dog sniffs me.] (RT)

**mininaawa'o** *vai* take off from shore (as in a boat, or swimming) (GJ); *also* **niminaawa'o** (NJ, RT)

**mininaawaandawaagan** *ni* dock; *pl* **mininaawaandawaaganan** (GJ); *also* **niminaawaandawaagan** (NJ)

**mininaawebishkan** *vti* push s.t. off with one's body (as in a boat) (GJ); *also* **niminaawebishkan** (NJ)

**mininaawekii'o** *vai* push off while touching the ground (GJ); *also* **niminaawekii'o** (NJ)

**mininaawesabii** *vai* set close to shore (set goes perpendicular from shore) (GJ); *also* **niminaawesabii** (NJ)

**mininaawesaa** *vai* set nets out from shore (GJ); *also* **niminaawesaa** (NJ)

**mininaawesin** *vii* stand out from others in a row (GJ); *also* **niminaawesin** (NJ)

**Minisinaanakwad** *name* Lone Cloud (GJ)

**minisinaanakwad** *vii* be a solitary cloud (RT, NJ, GJ)

**minisinaanakwagoode** *vii* be a lone cloud (RT, NJ, GJ)

**minjikaawanikaw** *vta* make mittens for s.o. (RT)

**minjimaagoneshkaw** *vta* hold s.o. in snow (GJ)

**minjimaakwa'an** *vti* hold s.t. up with stick to stabilize it (GJ)

**minjimaakwa'iganens** *ni* spring safety clasp (as on a conibear trap); *pl* **minjimaakwa'iganensan** (NJ)

**minjimaakwa'o** /**minjimaakwa'w-**/ *vta* hold s.o. up with stick to stabilize it (GJ)

**minjimindaawangishkaw** *vta* hold s.o. in place in the sand (GJ)

**minjimin** *vta* cling to s.o., hold onto s.o. (RT)

**minjiminigaade** *vii* adhere, attach, clasp (RT)

**minjimishkaw** *vta* hold s.o. place with foot (GJ)

**minjimishkoode** *vii* be held in place (GJ)

**minjimishkoodoon** *vti* hold s.t. in place (GJ)

**minjimishkoojigan** *ni* place holder; *pl* **minjimishkoojiganan** (GJ)

**mino-ayi'iins** *ni* nutrient; *pl* **mino-ayi'iinsan** (RT)

**mino-giizhiganoke** *vai* have a fun-filled day (NJ)

**mino-zhooshkozideshimo** *vai* have nice sounding feet (as in a tap dancer) (NJ, GJ)

**minobii'ige** *vai* write well (RT, NJ, GJ)

**minobizo** *vai* have a happy ride (NJ)

**minogi** *vai* grow well (RT)

**minogin** *vii* grow well (RT, NJ, GJ)

**minokonaye** *vai* dress nicely

**minokone** *vai* burn well (NJ)

**minokosiwaagaasin** *vii* the grass is blowing nicely in the wind (NJ); *also* **minoshkosiiwagaasin** (GJ)

**minonaagozi'idizo** *vai* look one's best (NJ)

**minopogwad** *vii* taste good (RT, NJ, GJ)

**minotan** *vti* like the sound of s.t. (RT, NJ, GJ)

**minwaabide'igan** *ni* saw tooth straightener; *pl* **minwaabide'iganan** (GJ)

**minwaada'e** *vai* skate good (RT, NJ, GJ)

**minwaakizige** *vai* be good and drunk (NJ)

**minwaasigetamaw** *vta* shine pleasant light on s.o. (RT)

**minwaasin** *vii* be good wind (as from a fan) (NJ, GJ)

**minwewe'akokwe** *vai* make a nice sound drumming (RT, NJ, GJ)

**minwewebagaashi** *vai* tree makes a pleasant sound of leaves in the wind (NJ)

**minwewebagaasin** *vii* be a pleasant sound of wind in the tree leaves (NJ)

**minwewejiwan** *vii* good sound of water flowing (NJ)

**Minwewejiwanook** *name* Sweet Sound of Flowing Water Woman (NJ)

**minwewekosiwaagosin** *vii* be a pleasant sound of the grass blowing in the wind (NJ); ialso **minweweshkosiwagaasin** (NJ)

**minwewenaazhaabii'ige** *vai* make a pleasant sound playing fiddle (RT, NJ, GJ)

**minweweshkosiwagaasin** *vii* good sound of grass blowing in the wind (NJ); *also* **minwewekosiwaagosin** (NJ)

**minweweyaabiigibijige** *vai* make a pleasant sound playing guitar (RT, NJ, GJ)

**minweweyaabikaasin** *vii* good sound of metal (as in wind chimes) [*example*: Minweweyaabikaasinoon. = The (wind chimes) sound good.] (NJ)

**minweweyaandagaashi** *vai* pleasant sound of an evergreen tree in the wind (NJ)

**minweweyaandagaasin** *vii* pleasant sound of evergreen boughs in the wind (NJ)

**minweweyaashkaa** *vii* good sound of waves (NJ)

**misaakig** *na* whale; *pl* **misaakigoog** (GJ)

**misawaa** *vai* be so big (NJ); *also* **misawaa** *pc* although (JC)

**mishi-bizhii** *na* cougar; *pl* **mishi-bizhiig** (NJ); *also* **mishi-bizhiw** (RT)

**mishiimin** *na* apple; *pl* **mishiiminag** (RT, NJ, GJ)

**mishiiwaatigowi** *vai* be a dry (dead) tree (RT, NJ, GJ)

**miskodiye** *vai* have a red butt (RT, NJ, GJ)

**miskodiyeshiinh** *na* baboon; *pl* **miskodiyeshiinyag** (RT, NJ, GJ)

**miskojiidiye** *vai* have a bleeding anus, hemorrhoids  (RT, NJ, GJ)

**miskozhaanidizo** *vai* have a diaper rash (NJ, GJ)

**mitaamik** *pc* at the bottom of the lake (RT, NJ, GJ)

**mitaawangaa** *vii* be sandy (RT, NJ, GJ)

**mitaawangaang** *pc* on the sand (NJ)

**mitaawango-makakoons** *ni* sandbox; *pl* **mitaawango-makakoonsan**; *loc* **mitaawango-makakoonsing** (NJ)

**mitaawango-miikanens** *ni* dirt road, dirt trail; *pl* **mitaawango-miikanensan** (RT, NJ, GJ)

**mitigomin** *na* acorn; *pl* **mitigominag** (RT)

**mitigomizhiiwi** *vai* become an oak, turn into an oak tree (RT)

**mitigwaazh** *ni* burrow or nest inside a tree (RT)

**mizhakiikozhiwe** *vai* make it from below to land in the water (NJ, GJ)

**mizhakiinam** *vai* go from the sky all the way to ground like a thunderbird, or tornado touching down (NJ, GJ)

**mizhakiise** *vai* fly from the sky down to the earth, make land fall (then back up) (NJ, GJ)

**mizhodamowin** *ni* goal; *pl* **mizhodamowinan**; *also* **bakinaagewin** *ni* goal; *pl* **bakinaagewinan** (RT, NJ, GJ)

**mizise** *na* turkey; *pl* **miziseg** (NJ, GJ); *also* **misise** (RT)

**miziweginingwiigwane** *vai* have webbed wings, as in a bat (NJ)

**miziweyaashkaa** *vii* waves move all over (RT, NJ, GJ)

**miziweyiigizide** *vai* have webbed feet, as in a beaver or duck (NJ)

**miidaajise** *vai+o* run out of s.t. to eat (RT)

**miidanjige** *vai* eat feces (RT, NJ, GJ)

**miijibii** *vai* crap one's self from drinking too much (RT, NJ, GJ)

**miijidaajise** *vai+o* run out of s.t. (RT)

**miijishin** *vai* fall down and crap (RT, NJ, GJ)

**miijishkine** *vai* crap from eating too much (RT, NJ, GJ)

**miikinjii'** *vta* tease s.o. (RT, NJ, GJ)

**miinikaanagek** *na* seed shell; *pl* **miinikaanagekwag** (RT)

**miinikaanashk** *ni* seed pod; *pl* **miinikaanashkoon**; *loc* **miinikaanashkong** (RT)

**miinikaanens** *ni* seed; *pl* **miinikaanensan** (RT)

**miinikaanensike** *vai* make seeds (RT)

**miishaa** *vii* be fuzzy (NJ, GJ)

**miishaakigan** *ni* hairy chest *pl* **miishaakiganan** (RT, NJ, GJ)

**miishaakiganaan** *ni* chest hair; *pl* **miishaakiganaanan** (RT, NJ, GJ)

**miishaakigane** *vai* have a hairy chest (RT, NJ, GJ)

**miishaakiganesi** *na* s.o. with a hairy chest; *pl* **miishaakiganesiwag** (RT, NJ, GJ)

**miishanowaan** *ni* animal whisker; *pl* **miishanowaanan** (RT)

**miishaawiganaan** *ni* back or chest hair; *pl* **miishaawiganaanan** (RT, NJ, GJ)

**miishaawigane** *vai* have a hairy back (RT, NJ, GJ)

**miishidoonaan** *ni* animal whisker, feeler on fish; *pl* **miishidoonaanan** (NJ)

**miishidoone** *vai* have whiskers (RT, NJ, GJ)

**miishigaadaan** *ni* leg hair; *pl* **miishigaadaanan** (RT, NJ, GJ)

**miishigaade** *vai* have hairy legs (RT, NJ, GJ)

**miishinikaan** *ni* arm hair; *pl* **miishinikaanan** (RT, NJ, GJ)

**miishizi** *vai* hairy (RT, NJ, GJ)

**miiwishkodaadigin** *vii* grow crowded, grow close together (RT)

**miiwishkodaadimagad** *vii* be crowded (RT)

**miizii-aanimi'** *vta* make s.o. defecate from fear (RT, NJ, GJ)

**miiziibizh /miiziibiN-/** *vta* squeeze s.o. to the point of defecation (RT, NJ, GJ)

**mookibiigin** *vii* grow to the surface (as in lily pads to the surface of the water) (RT)

**mookibiise** *vii* emerge from water, suddenly pop out of water (NJ, GJ)

**mookii** *vai* surface (RT, NJ, GJ)

**mooshka'ogo** *vai* s.o. is flooding out (as in ice) (RT, NJ, GJ)

**mooshkamo** *vai* emerge from water (NJ, GJ)

**mooshkinebiise** *vii* fills with water (as in a canoe) (RT, NJ, GJ)

**mooshkinemaagod** *vii* have one's sense of smell filled or inhibited (as in by a cold) (NJ); *also* **mooshkinemaagwad** (RT)

# N

**na'aabi** *vai* see clearly, have sharp vision (RT)

**na'aakozi** *vai* be straight (treelike) (RT, NJ, GJ)

**na'emine** *vai* store grain (RT)

**na'enimo** *vai* cache, store food (RT, NJ, GJ)

**na'inibii** *vai* store water (NJ, GJ)

**na'inibiigin** *vii* store water (NJ)

**nabagaabide** *vai* have flat teeth (RT)

**nabagaanowe** *vai* have a flat tail (NJ)

**nabagashk** *ni* cattail; *pl* **nabagashkoon** (NJ)

**nabagi-ayaamagad** *vii* be flat (RT, NJ, GJ)

**nabagizidegaabawi** *vai* stand flat-footed (GJ)

**nabagizowe** *vai* have a flat tail (NJ)

**nabanemakadeyaaso** *vai* be dark on one side from sun (as in suntanned) (NJ, GJ)

**nabaneyaagad** *vii* there is a solo spring (as on a #6 conibear trap) (NJ)

**nabashkweyaasin** *vii* grass flattens in the wind (LM)

**nachiishkise** *vii* split or tear off (NJ); *also* **nichiishkise** (GJ)

**nagaakininjaan** *ni* palm of hand; *loc* **nagaakininjaaning** (NJ, GJ)

**nagaakizid** *ni* sole of the foot; *loc* **nagaakizidaang** (body part) (NJ, GJ)

**nagaakizidaaning** *pc* on the sole of the foot (referencing s.t. there) (NJ, GJ)

**nagadenim** *vta* befriend s.o. (NJ)

**nagajigaade** *vii* be left somewhere (RT)

**nagwaazo** *vai* get caught (in snare) (LW)

**nakwedenaniwem** *vta* catch s.o. with long, sticky tongue (as in a frog) (RT)

**nakwepwaa'** /nakwepwaa'w-/ *vta* catch s.o. with one's mouth (RT)

**namanjiin** *ni* unknown lodge pole [*lexicon note*: archaic word] (GJ)

**name** *na* sturgeon; *pl* **namewag** (RT, NJ, GJ)

**namebin** *na* sucker; *pl* **namebinag** (RT, NJ, GJ)

**namegos** *na* trout; *pl* **namegosag** (RT, NJ, GJ)

**namekwaan** *ni* sturgeon glue (NJ, GJ)

**nametegoke** *vai* take bones out in preparation for smoking (NJ, GJ)

**namewashkoons** *ni* field mint; *pl* **namewashkoonsan** (AM)

**namewashkoons** *ni* sweet fern; *pl* **namewashkoonsan** (NJ)

**nanaa'isabii** *vai* fix nets (RT, NJ, GJ)

**nanaa'itoon** *vti* resolve s.t., fix s.t. (RT, NJ, GJ)

**nanaandawishkaw** *vta* heal s.o. (RT, NJ, GJ)

**nanaaniizaanizi** *vai* have a dangerous disposition (NJ, GJ)

**nandawenjigan** *ni* objective; *pl* **nandawenjiganan** (LM); *also* **andawenjigan** (RT, NJ, GJ)

**nanepaadad** *vii* be odd, unmatched, opposite (NJ, GJ)

**nanepaadakizine** *vai* put one's shoes on the wrong foot (NJ, GJ)

**nanepaadendaagwad** *vii* be considered opposite (NJ, GJ)

**nanepaaj** *pc* opposite, inverse (NJ, GJ)

**naniizaanad** *vii* be unsafe, dangerous (NJ, GJ)

**naniizaanendaagwad** *vii* be considered dangerous (NJ, GJ)

**naniizaanizi** *vai* be dangerous (NJ, GJ)

**napaadaakwese** *vai* fall in the wrong direction (GJ)

**napaadakizine** *vai* wear shoes on wrong feet (GJ)

**napaadendaagwad** *vii* be considered opposite (NJ, GJ)

**napaaj** *pc* backwards, inverse (NJ, GJ)

**napaajibakwe** *vii* be roofed inside out (GJ)

**napaajiiginan** *vti* fold backwards, wrong way (GJ)

**napaajiigisin** *vii* be inside out (NJ, GJ)

**nawadide** *vii* catch on fire (RT, NJ, GJ)

**nawekide** *vii* be at a slant (GJ)

**naweyaashi** *vii* be bent by the wind (RT, NJ, GJ)

**naaba'oojigan** *ni* lace; *pl* **naaba'oojiganan** (NJ, GJ)

**naabaabiigigwebizh** /**naabaabiigigwebiN-**/ *vta* rope s.o. around the feet (NJ, GJ)

**naabaabiigizide** *vai* be roped around the feet (NJ, GJ)

**naabaabiigizidebizh** *vta* rope s.o. around the feet (GJ)

**naabaabiigose** *vai* be roped (NJ); *also* **naabaabiigise** (GJ)

**naabaabiigwebizh** /**naabaabiigwebiN-**/ *vta* lasso s.o. around the neck (NJ, GJ)

**naabaakose** *vii* be roped or caught on something (NJ, GJ)

**naabaaniigizide'on** *ni* stirrup, *pl* **naabaaniigizide'onan** (NJ, GJ)

**naabemeg** *na* male fish; *pl* **naabemegwag** (RT, NJ, GJ)

**naabemin** *ni* male fruit; *pl* **naabeminan** (RT, NJ, GJ)

**naabese** *na* male bird, rooster; *pl* **naabeseg** (RT, NJ, GJ)

**naabesim** *na* male dog, male horse, male wolf; *pl* **naabesimag** (RT, NJ, GJ)

**naadamaawaso** *vai* stick up for one's children (with negative consequences) (RT, NJ, GJ)

**naamiwana'o** *vai* paddle with the wind (NJ)

**naamiwana'ogo** *vai* be propelled faster by wind and waves (in watercaft) (NJ)

**naanaagadagagwegikenjigewin** *ni* science (JC)

**naanaagadawendam** *vai* ponder, reflect (RT, NJ, GJ)

**naanaagajitoon** *vti* notice s.t. (NJ)

**naanaanigaakobidoon** *vti* peel s.t. into strips, strip s.t. (as in basswood) (NJ, GJ)

**naanaanigaakobijige** *vai* peel into strips (as in basswood) (NJ, GJ)

**naanigaakobidoon** *vti* peel s.t. in a strip, strip s.t. (as in basswood) (NJ, GJ)

**naanigaakozhigan** *vti* cut s.t. into strips (NJ, GJ)

**naanigibidoon** *vti* tear s.t. (sheet-like) (NJ, GJ)

**naazhinan** *vti* roll s.t. down (NJ, GJ)

**naazhise** *vai* fly down, swoop down (RT)

**negwaabam** *vta* look at s.o. out of the corner of one's eye (RT, NJ, GJ)

**negwaabi** *vai* steal glances (RT, NJ, GJ)

**nemin** *na* lemon; *pl* **neminag** (RT)

**nenibaawizh iidog** *expression* it's about time [*example*: Nenibaawizh iidog gigoshkoz! = It's about time you woke up!] (NJ, GJ)

**neningodwaasinoon** *vii-pl* they number six, there are six of them (RT)

**nenoogibii'igan** *ni* comma (,); *pl* **nenoogibii'iganan** (JC)

**neso-eshkaned** *vai-prt* triceratops; *pl* **neso-eshkanewaad** (NJ)

**nesweshkaned** *vai-prt* triceratops; *pl* **nesweshkanewaad** (NJ)

**neweyaak** *na* tree that is bent by the wind; *pl* **neweyaakoog** (GJ)

**nibazagodenaniw** *ni* my sticky tongue (as in a frog) (RT)

**nibegaaziigaasing** *vii-prt* sprinkler; *pl* **nibegaaziigaasingin** (NJ)

**nibewemo** *vai* cry one's self to sleep (AG)

**nibeyaakizo** *vai* fall asleep because of the heat [*example*: Ginibeyaakizomin. = We're falling asleep because of the heat.] (RT, NJ, GJ)

**nibiiwaagamin** *vii* be runny (NJ)

**nibiiwadaawangaa** *vii* be wet sand (NJ)

**niboomagad** *vii* die (RT)

**nichiishkise** *vii* split or tear off (GJ); *also* **nachiishkise** (NJ)

**nidatagaagwan** /-datagaagwan-/ *nid* my spine; *pl* **nidatagaagwanan** (RT, NJ, GJ)

**nidatagaagwaneyaab** /-datagaagwaneyaab-/ *nid* my spinal cord; *pl* **nidatagaagwaneyaabiin** (RT, NJ, GJ)

**nikon** /-kon-/ *nid* my liver; *pl* **nikonan** (RT, NJ, GJ)

**nima'wi** /nima'w-/ *vta* feign at s.o. (as in a strike) [*example*: Ningii-nima'waa. = I acted like I was going to hit him.] (NJ); *also* **nima'o** /nima'w-/ (GJ)

**nimaamaa** *na* eyebrow; *pl* **nimaamaayag** (RT, NJ, GJ)

**nimashkiingwaan** /mashkiingwaan-/ *nid* my gill; *pl* **nimashkiingwaanan** (NJ)

**nimbikoninjaan** *nid* my knuckle [*example*: Nashke giga-bakite'win nimbikoninjaanan! = Hey I'm going to rap you with my knuckles!] (NJ, GJ)

**nimiishaabiwinaan** *nid* my eyelash; *pl* **nimiishaabiwinaanan** (NJ, GJ)

**niminaawa'o** *vai* take off from shore (as in a boat, or swimming) (RT, NJ); *also* **mininaawa'o** (GJ)

**niminaawaandawaagan** *ni* dock; *pl* **niminaawaandawaaganan** (NJ); *also* **mininaawaandawaagan** (GJ)

**niminaawebishkan** *vti* push s.t. off with one's body (as in a boat) (NJ); *also* **mininaawebishkan** (GJ)

**niminaawekii'o** *vai* push off while touching the ground (NJ); *also* **mininaawekii'o** (GJ)

**niminaawesabii** *vai* set close to shore (set goes perpendicular from shore) (NJ); *also* **mininaawesabii** (GJ)

**niminaawesaa** *vai* set nets out from shore (NJ); *also* **mininaawesaa** (GJ)

**niminaawesin** *vii* stand out from others in a row (NJ); *also* **mininaawesin** (GJ)

**nimiskam** *vta* throw the open hand at s.o. (all 5 fingers open and extended) [*cultural note*: considered extremely offensive, likely to be perceived as an intent to do spiritual harm or use bad medicine on s.o.] (NJ, GJ)

**nimiskandiwag** /nimiskandi-/ *vai* throw the open hand at one another (all 5 fingers open and extended) [*cultural note*: considered extremely offensive, likely to be perceived as an intent to do spiritual harm or use bad medicine on s.o.] (NJ, GJ)

**ninaga'ay** /**-naga'ay-**/ *nad* my scale (as of a fish or snake); *pl* **ninaga'ayag** (RT)

**ninashkid** /**-nashkidy-**/ *nid* my tail (of a bird); *pl* **ninashkidiin** (RT, NJ, GJ)

**ningaapoono** *vai* eat off the bush (RT)

**ningaasimoono** *vai* sail (NJ, GJ)

**ningigisin** *vii* be thawed (as in fresh cut sapling in winter being bent as a beaver hide stretching frame) (NJ)

**ningodwaasimidana ashi naanan dasing wekwaagindaasowin** *number* 65 million (NJ)

**ningodwaasokaan** *pc* the six spot (in moccasin game) (GJ)

**ningwa'** /**ningwa'w-**/ *vta* bury s.o. (RT)

**ningwiigad** *vii* be frost (RT)

**ningwiigane** *vai* have wings [*example*: Mii gaa-izhi-ningwiigwaned bapakwaanaajiinh. = A bat has wings like this. (NJ)

**niniisiigininjaan** *nid* my finger pad; *pl* **niniisiigininjaanan** (NJ)

**niniisiigizidaanens** *nid* between my toes; *loc* **niniisiigizidaanensing** (NJ, GJ)

**ninzhaga'ay** /**-zhaga'ay-**/ *nid* my skin; *also* **nishkatay** /**-shkatay-**/ (RT, NJ, GJ)

**ninzhigwan** /**-zhigwan-**/ *nid* my tail (of a fish, snake, or serpent); *pl* **ninzhigwanan** (RT, NJ, GJ)

**ninzow** /**-zow-**/ *nid* my tail (of an animal); *pl* **ninzowan** (NJ, GJ)

**nisawa'ogaan** *ni* long peaked lodge; *pl* **nisawa'ogaanan** (RT, NJ, GJ)

**nishangwan** *nid* my nasal cavity (NJ)

**nishkatay** /**-shkatay-**/ *nid* my skin; *also* **ninzhaga'ay** /**-zhaga'ay-**/ (RT, NJ, GJ)

**nishwaasokaan** *pc* the eight spot (in moccasin game) (GJ)

**nisidawendam** *vti* sense things (RT, NJ, GJ)

**nisidawendan** *vti* sense s.t. (RT, NJ, GJ)

**nisidawininjiinan** *vti* recognize s.t. by touch (NJ, GJ)

**nisidawishkaa** *vai* recognize things by touch (NJ, GJ)

**nisidawishkaawin** *ni* sense; *pl* **nisidawishkaawinan** (NJ, GJ)

**nisidawishkan** *vti* sense s.t., understand s.t with one's senses (NJ, GJ)

**nitaawan** *vii* be finely granulated, be fine sand (NJ, GJ)

**niibidegaabawi** *vai* stand in a row (RT, NJ, GJ)

**niibinibiisaa** *vii* be a summer rain (RT)

**niigaanaabid** *ni* front tooth; *pl* **niigaanaabidan** (RT)

**niigaanadenaniw** *ni* tip of the tongue (RT, NJ, GJ)

**niikimo** *vai* growl (RT, NJ, GJ)

**niingidodenaniwe** *vai* have a forked tongue (GJ)

**niingidowaakogi** *vai* grow in a forked shape (GJ)

**niingidowaakoninjiini** *vai* make the peace sign (GJ)

**niingidowaakoninjiitaw** *vai* give s.o. the peace sign (GJ)

**niingidowaakozi** *vai* forked, crotched (as in a tree) (GJ)

**niingidowaakwad** *vii* forked, crotched (as in a tree) (GJ)

**niisaajiwane'aadage** *vai* go downstream (GJ); *also* **niisaajiwanwe'aadage** (NJ)

**niisaajiwane'o** *vai* go downstream (GJ); *also* **niisaajiwanwe'o** (NJ)

**niisaajiwaneweyaaboono** *vai* go downstream on top of the water (GJ); *also* **niisaajiwanweweyaabono** (NJ)

**niisaajiwaneyaaboono** *vai* float downstream (as in an otter) (GJ); *also* **niisaajiwanweyaaboono** (NJ)

**niishiboono** *vai* shoot rapids (NJ, GJ)

**niisibizo** *vai* fly down, swoop down (RT)

**niisijiwan** *vii* flow down, roll down (as in water) (RT)

**niisinigan** *ni* trigger clasp (as on a conibear trap); *pl* **niisiniganan** (NJ)

**niisiniweba'igan** *ni* trap trigger (on conibear trap); *pl* **niisiniweba'iganan** (NJ)

**niiisise** *vai* fly down, swoop down (RT)

**niiskaweyaandibe** *vai* have snarly hair (NJ, GJ)

**niiyokaan** *pc* the four spot (as in moccasin game) (GJ)

**niizho-bimodan** *vti* double shoot (as in moccasin game) (GJ)

**niizho-gabenaage** *vai* score double (as in moccasin game) (GJ)

**niizhoobii'igewin** *ni* double vowel writing system (JC)

**niizhoopizh** /niizhoopiN-/ *vta* tie two together (NJ, GJ)

**noogaanimad** *vii* wind stops (RT, NJ, GJ)

**noogibizo** *vai* come to a stop while driving (RT, NJ, GJ)

**noogigin** *vii* stop growing (RT)

**noojiikaazo** *vai* try to commence an intimate relationship, snag (NJ, GJ, RT); *also* **gaajida'ige** (RT)

**noojiiwakiwenzii** *vai* try to commence an intimate relationship with an old man, snag (for old men) (NJ)

**nooka'iiwagwaan** *ni* pemmican (meat); *pl* **nooka'iiwagwaanan** (NJ, GJ)

**nooka'iskawaan** *na* pemmican (fish); *pl* **nooka'iskawaanag** (NJ, GJ)

**nookadawe** *vai* have soft fur (NJ)

**nookagwanjidoon** *vti* soften s.t. by soaking (RT, NJ, GJ)

**nookwewe** *vii* make a soft sound (RT, NJ, GJ)

**noondaagamo'** *vta* make s.o. sound a certain way (NJ, GJ)

**noondakiikozhiwe** *vai* try to reach the bottom unsuccessfully (NJ, GJ)

**noondakiise** *vai* throw s.t. in the water that cannot touch bottom (NJ, GJ)

**noondakiishkige** *vai* try in vain to feel for bottom with foot (NJ, GJ)

**noondamowin** *ni* sense of hearing (RT, NJ, GJ)

**noondegidaazo** *vai* be disinterested (TS)

**noondegwashi** *vai* be sleepy (RT, NJ, GJ); *also* **noondengwashi** (ES)

**noondendam** *vai* be envious, want what others have (NJ); want things from people (implies sexual arousal) (LM)

**noondenikaazh / noondenikaaN-/** *vta* desire s.o. to call s.o. by one's whole name [*cultural note*: some spirits long to be called by their full names rather than simply referred to as a thunderbird or water spirit] (NJ, GJ)

**noondenikaazo** *vai* long to be called by one's full name [*cultural note*: some spirits long to be called by their full names rather than simply referred to as a thunderbird or water spirit] (NJ, GJ)

**noosa'owesi** *na* smallmouth bass; *pl* **noosa'owesiwag**; also **odazhegomoo** *na* smallmouth bass; *pl* **odazhegomoog** (NJ, GJ)

**nooyoondam** *vai* feel with hearing (NJ)

**nooyoondan** *vti* feel s.t. with hearing (NJ)

**noozhemeg** *na* female fish; *pl* **noozhemegwag** (RT, NJ, GJ)

**noozhemin** *ni* female fruit; *pl* **noozheminan** (RT, NJ, GJ)

# O, OO, P, T

**obaashiiwan** *vii* be a narrows (RT, NJ, GJ)

**obikwaaj** *nid* air sack of a fish, swim bladder (NJ, GJ); *dim* **obikwaajiins**

**obikwaajiins** *nid* little air sack, swim bladder; *also ni* light bulb (NJ, GJ)

**obiibaagimakakii** *na* gray tree frog; *pl* **obiibaagimakakiig** (NJ)

**obiigomakakii** *na* toad; *pl* **obiigomakakiig** (NJ, GJ)

**odaminoowigamig** *ni* gym; *pl* **odaminoowigamigoon**; *loc* **odaminoowigamigong** (NJ)

**odatagwaagani-wesepikwaned** *vai-prt* spinosaurus; *pl* **odatagwaagani-wesepikwanewaad** (NJ)

**odazhegamoons** *na* crappie (NJ); *pl* **odazhegamoonsag**; *also*
    **gidagwadaashi** *na* crappie (KP); *pl* **gidagwadaashiwag**; *also*
    **ezhegamoons** *na* crappie (GJ); *pl* **ezhegamoonsag**
**odazhegomoo** *na* smallmouth bass; *pl* **odazhegomoog**; *also*
    **noosa'owesi** *na* smallmouth bass; *pl* **noosa'owesiwag** (NJ, GJ)
**odaabaan noondaagamo'ind** *vta-prt* car horn (NJ, GJ)
**odaabii'** *vta* drive s.o. (RT)
**odaanaam** *ni* background, personal history; *loc* **odaanaaming** (NJ)
    [*example*: Gii-wanii'ige mewinzha odoodaanaaming, gaawiin
    geyaabi noongom. = He used to trap long ago in his background,
    but not any more.]
**odaanaang endaayaan** *place* my backyard (NJ)
**odaanaang** *pc* the base of something, the back of something [*example*:
    odaanaang gidenaniw = the back of your tongue] (NJ, GJ)
**odaanzhenan** *vti* dim the lamp (NJ)
**odaanziyaani'** *vta* use s.t. for s.o.'s diaper [*example*: Giziingwe'onan
    odaanziyaani'. = Use towels for his diaper.] (NJ)
**ode'imini-waabigon** *ni* strawberry flower; *pl* **ode'imini-waabigoniin**
    (NJ); *also* **ode'imini-waabigwan** (RT)
**ode'iminoowan** *vii* become a strawberry [*example*: Ode'imini-
    waabigwaniin aanjiginoon ani-ode'iminoowangin. = Strawberry
    flowers grow into fruit.] (RT)
**odeshkani** *vai* have horns (as in an animal) (NJ)
**odikon** *ni* branch; *pl* odikonan (GJ)
**odoonibiins** *na* tulabee; *pl* **odoonibiinsag** (RT, NJ, GJ)
**ogaa** *na* walleye; *pl* **ogaawag** (RT, NJ, GJ)
**ogidaashkaabizo** *vai* surf (NJ, GJ)
**ogidaashkaabizwaanaak** *ni* surfboard (NJ, GJ)
**ogidaawangibatoo** *vai* run on sand (RT)
**ogidaawangwebizo** *vai* drive on sand (NJ, GJ)
**ogidikwam** *pc* on top of ice (GJ)
**ogijibiibizo** *vai* water ski (NJ, GJ)
**ogijikwam** *pc* on top of the ice (GJ); *also* **ogidikwam** (NJ)
**ogijizigwaang** *pc* on top of the ice (NJ, GJ)
**oginii-waabigoni-miskozi** *vai* be pink (NJ, GJ); *also* **oginii-
    waabigwani-miskozi** (RT)
**ogitebag** *ni* lily pad; *pl* **ogitebagoon** (RT)
**ogiziibishkami** *vai* have a joint strain (mild, not long-lasting) (NJ, GJ)
**ogiidaajiwane'o** *vai* swim upstream (GJ); *also* **ogiidaajiwanwe'o** (NJ)

**ogiidaajiwaneyaadagwe** *vai* swim upstream (GJ); *also* **ogiidaajiwanweyaadagwe** (NJ)

**ogokeyaw** *ni* bait made from fish (as in underside near gills or belly) (NJ); *pl* **ogokeyawan**; *also* **ogokeyawag** (GJ)

**ogokeyawi** *vai* use bait (NJ)

**ojaanimijiwan** *vii* be a fast current (NJ, GJ)

**ojichaagosin** *vii* reflect (RT, NJ)

**ojiibik** *ni* root; *pl* **ojiibikan**; *loc* **ojiibikaang** (RT, NJ, GJ)

**okaadiginebig** *na* lizard; *pl* **okaadiginebigoog** (RT)

**okeyaw** *na* decoy; *pl* **okeyawag** (KP)

**okijiinsikaanens** *ni* penne pasta, *pl* **okijiinsikaanensan** (RT, NJ, GJ)

**okikaandag** *na* jack pine; *pl* **okikaandagoog** (NJ)

**okoba'idaweshiinh** *na* lemming; *pl* **okoba'idaweshiinyag** (RT)

**okoba'idiganoojiinh** *na* lemming; *pl* **okoba'idiganoojiinyag** (RT)

**okonaw** *vta* crack shoot s.o., shoot more than one (line 'em up) (NJ, GJ)

**okonim** *ni* beaver dam; *pl* **okoniman**; *loc* **okoniming** (NJ)

**okoweba'** /**okoweba'w-**/ *vta* push s.o. into a mound (as in snow) (RT)

**okwaami** *vai* spawn in a school (as in fish) (NJ, GJ)

**omakakiibag** *ni* frog leaf, plantain; *pl* **omakakiibagoon** (NJ, GJ)

**omashkoziisimin** *na* lima bean; *pl* **omashkoziisiminag** (NJ)

**omba'an** *vti* set s.t. (as in a trap) (NJ, GJ)

**omba'ige** *vai* set traps (NJ, GJ)

**ombaakwa'igan** *ni* something used to lift things, crutch, jack (GJ)

**ombaashi** *vai* take off in flight (RT, NJ, GJ)

**ombaasijigan** *ni* kite; *pl* **ombaasigijiganan**; *dim* **ombaasijiganens** (NJ, GJ)

**ombimiigwanetaa** *vai* puff up one's feathers (NJ, GJ)

**ombin** *vta* raise s.o. up (RT, NJ, GJ)

**ombishidaakogibinewen** *vta* pin s.o. against the wall off the ground (GJ)

**omichigan** *ni* dorsal fin; *pl* **omichiganan** (RT, NJ, GJ)

**omichigegani** *vai* have spikes (as in a dinosaur) (NJ)

**omiimii** *na* dove, pigeon; *pl* **omiimiig** (RT, NJ, GJ)

**onaagamin** *vii* clear water (NJ, GJ)

**onadinigan** *na* dough (NJ, GJ)

**onadin** *vta* knead s.o. (NJ, GJ)

**onagizhiikaanens** *ni* macaroni, *pl* **onagizhiikaanensan** (RT, NJ, GJ)

**onawaangigan** *nid* fish cheek, operculum; *pl* **onawaangiganan** (NJ, GJ)

**onda'ibii** *vai* get water from a certain place (RT, NJ, GJ)

**ondamaabi** *vai* be busy looking around (NJ, GJ)

**ondami'** *vta* be responsible for s.o., take responsibility for s.o., be the reason for s.o.'s action or condition [*example*: Ningii-ondami'aa wenji-bezikaayaang. = I'm the reason we are late.] (NJ, GJ)

**ondandan** *vti* eat from s.t., obtain food from s.t. (RT)

**ondanjige** *vai+o* use s.t. for food, get food from somewhere (RT, NJ, GJ)

**ondaabate** *vii* smoke comes from somewhere (RT, NJ, GJ)

**ondaabateshin** *vii* dust billows when it hits the ground (NJ, GJ)

**ondaadigo'o** *vai* makes waves from a certain place (as in ripple from surfacing fish or muskrat) (NJ, GJ)

**ondaadigoshin** *vai* make waves from a certain place (as in ripple from diving fish or muskrat) (NJ, GJ)

**ondaadigotoo** *vai* s.o. is there making the waves (NJ, GJ)

**ondaadigwe** *vai* make waves (as an animal or person in a boat) [*example*: Nashke iwidi ondaadigwe! = Look over there something is making waves.] (NJ, GJ)

**ondaanike** *vai* dig from somewhere (RT, NJ, GJ)

**ondiziwin** *ni* nutrient; *pl* **ondiziwinan** (RT)

**oninamaa** *vai* be ready to go to bed (RT)

**oninasabii** *vai* prepare nets for setting (RT, NJ, GJ)

**oningwiiganaabik** *ni* side springs, tensioner springs (as on the sides of a conibear or leg-hold trap) (NJ)

**onji-gikendamaazon** *ni* sense; *pl* **onji-gikendamaazonan** (NJ, GJ)

**onji'idiwag** /**onji'idi-**/ *vai* they prohibit one another (ES); [*example:* Onji'idim. = There is a prohibition. (NJ)]

**onjigaa** *vii* flow, drip, run (as in water) (RT, NJ, GJ)

**onjigin** *vii* grow from a certain place, originate (RT)

**onjijiwan** *vii* water comes from somewhere, be a water source (NJ, RT)

**onjishkawa'o** *vai* paddle straight into waves (NJ, GJ)

**onzaam** *pc* overly, too much [*example*: Gaawiin nindizhaasiin onzaam nindaakoz. = I'm not going because I'm sick. *example*: Onzaam gizhide gaa-wii-onji-wi-nibaayang. It's too warm it makes us feel sleepy.] (NJ, GJ)

**onzaami'** *vta* eat too much of s.o. (NJ, GJ)

**onzaami'o** *vai* eat too much (NJ, GJ)

**onzaamiino** *vai* overpopulate (RT)

**onzaamipon** *vta* eat too much of s.o. (NJ, GJ)

**onzibii'** vta make s.o. water, get water from s.o. (NJ)

**onzonge** *vai* verbally attack people based on what your child told you [*example*: Gego onzongeken! = Don't (verbally) attack people based on what your child has come and told you! *cultural note*: It is considered inadvisable to do this because of possible spiritual consequences. Children need to fend for themselves and take responsibility for their actions.] (NJ, GJ)

**opimeshin** *vai* lie on one's side (NJ, GJ)

**oshkadin** *vii* new ice forms (NJ, GJ)

**oshkaabaanedin** *vii* ice over, ice forms for the first time (with no snow cover), new ice forms (NJ, GJ)

**oshkaatigoons** *ni* young stick; *pl* **oshkaatigoonsan** (GJ)

**oshki-nitaage** *vai* make a first kill (RT, NJ, GJ)

**oshkigin** *vii* s.t. new grows (RT)

**oshkiinzhigokaajiganan** *ni-pl* eye glasses (RT, NJ); *also* **oshkiinzhigokaanan** (GJ)

**oshkiinzhigoke** *vai* have glasses (RT, NJ, GJ)

**oshkiinzhigwaabid** *ni* canine tooth; *pl* **oshkiinzhigwaabidan** (RT)

**oshkiinzhigwaabide** *vai* have canine teeth (RT)

**owaako** *vai* release eggs, spawn (as in fish) (RT, NJ, GJ)

**owaziswani** *vai* have a nest (RT)

**ozaanaman** *na* soil (RT)

**ozaawaashkosiwe** *vii* grass turns golden (RT)

**ozaawi-memengwaa** *na* butterfly, tiger swallowtail; *pl* **ozaawi-memengwaag** (NJ, GJ)

**ozaawi-okosimaan** *ni* pumpkin; *pl* **ozaawi-okosimaanan** (NJ, GJ)

**ozaawi-zhooniyaawi-giigoozens** *na* goldfish; *pl* **ozaawi-zhooniyaawi-giigoozensag** (GJ)

**ozha'ige** *vai* accidentally chase things off (NJ); *also* **asho'ige** *vai* accidentally chase things off (GJ); *also* **ashwaa'ige** (GJ); *also* **ashwa'ige** (NJ)

**ozha'wi** /ozha'w-/ *vta* chase s.o. away (NJ)

**ozhaawashko-ginoozhe** *na* muskellunge; *pl* **ozhaawashko-ginoozheg** (NJ); *also* **mashkinoozhe** *na* muskellunge (AM); *pl* **mashkinoozheg**

**ozhaawashkwaagamin** *vii* be blue (water) (NJ, GJ)

**ozhibii'igaage** *vai+o* use s.t. as a pencil [*example:* Ashkikomaan ozhibii'igaagen. = Use the lead (metal, as in a bullet) as a pencil.] (NJ)

**ozhichigaazo** *vai+o* be made, be formed (RT)

**oziban** *ni* tree candy, the consumable part of inner tree bark (NJ) [*cultural note*: sweet, sticky substance in the inner bark (typically of poplar) was highly prized and consumed as a kind of candy]

**ozibanike** *vai* harvest tree candy, peel the outer bark to eat the inner bark (typically of a poplar) (NJ) [*cultural note*: sweet, sticky substance in the inner bark (typically of poplar) was highly prized and consumed as a kind of candy]

**oojiigaweshiinh** *na* cricket; **oojiigaweshiinyag** (NJ)

**ookomisi** *vai* menstruate (be visited by one's grandma) (NJ)

**ookweminaatig** *na* cherry tree; *pl* **ookweminaatigoog** (RT)

**piisaa** *ni* pizza; *pl* **piisaag** (NJ)

**tawagikaajigan** *ni* hearing aid; *pl* **tawagikaajiganan** (NJ, GJ)

# W

**wadikwan** *ni* tree branch, wood knot; *pl* **wadikwanan**; *loc* **wadikwaning** [*example*: Wadikwaning izhi-boonii. = He lands on a limb.] (NJ, GJ); *also* **odikon**; *pl* **odikonan** (GJ)

**wadiswan** *ni* nest (of a bird); *pl* **wadiswanan**; *dim* **wadiswanens** (RT, NJ, GJ)

**wadiswanike** *vai* make a nest (RT); *also* **waziswanike** (RT)

**wagidaawangibatoo** *vai* run on top of the sand (NJ, GJ)

**wake-ginagajii** *vii, vai* be ticklish (NJ)

**wake-nisidawishkaa** *vai* be physically sensitive (NJ, GJ)

**wakewaji** *vai* be sensitive to cold, can't take the cold (RT, NJ, GJ)

**wanaakizige** *vai* pass out from drinking (NJ)

**wanendam** *vai* pass out (NJ), forget (AM)

**wanenjigaazo** *vai* be forgotten (RT)

**wanimikoons** *ni* birch tree seed strings; *pl* **wanimikoonsan** (NJ, GJ)

**wanwewese** *vai* hiccough (NJ)

**washkwadab** *na* cattail root; *pl* **washkwadabiig** (NJ, GJ)

**wawaanendam** *vai* confused, undecided, unsure (RT, NJ, GJ)

**wawaawashkakozhiwe** *vai* be unable to keep a canoe straight (NJ, GJ)

**wawiyazh** *pc* cute, fun, just for fun [*example*: Wawiyazh ikido. = He is just saying it for fun.] (NJ, GJ)

**wayaabikweyaawiganed** *vai-prt* silver-back gorilla; *pl*
    **wayaabikweyaawiganejig** (RT, NJ, GJ)
**wayaawaasepikwaned** *vai-prt* kentrosaurus; *pl*
    **wayaawaasepikwanewaad** (NJ)
**wazhashkwedowens** *na* pinecone; *pl* **wazhashkwedowensag** (RT, NJ,
    GJ); *also* pink mushroom (NJ, GJ)
**waziswanike** *vai* make a nest (RT); *also* **wadiswanike** (RT)
**waabaabigan** *na* white or gray clay (NJ)
**waabigan** *na* clay (RT, NJ, GJ)
**waabigani-akik** *na* clay pot; *pl* **waabigani-akikoog**; *loc* **waabigani-**
    **akikong** (RT)
**waabigoni-akik** *na* flower pot; *pl* **waabigoni-akikoog** (NJ, GJ); *also*
    **waabigoni-akik** (RT)
**waabigoniikaa** *vii* be many flowers (NJ); *also* **waabigwaniikaa** (RT)
**waabijii-ozaawizi** *vai* be the color of deer in the fall and winter (NJ)
**waabikweyaawigane** *vai* have a silver-colored hairy back (RT, NJ, GJ)
**waabishkaagamin** *vii* be white (water) (NJ, GJ)
**waagigaadegaabawi** *vai* stand bow-legged (GJ)
**waagi-wiinizisens** *ni* hook (as in the burr of a plant); *pl* **waagi-**
    **wiinizisensan** (RT)
**waagigoode** *vii* hang in a bent position (NJ, GJ)
**waaginan** *vti* curve s.t., bend s.t. (RT, NJ, GJ)
**waaginogaan** *ni* domed lodge; *pl* **waaginogaanan** (RT, NJ, GJ)
**waagizidegaabawi** *vai* stand pigeon-toed (GJ)
**waak** *ni* egg (of a fish, frog, or turtle); *pl* **waakwan** (RT, NJ, GJ)
**waakaagamin** *vii* be clear water, be a clear lake (NJ, GJ)
**waanashkobaa** *vii* be a puddle (RT, NJ); *also* **waanishkobaa** (GJ); *also*
    **waanashkobiiyaa** (RT, NJ)
**waanashkobiiyaa** *vii* be a puddle (RT, NJ); *also* **waanashkobaa** *vii* be a
    puddle (RT, NJ); *also* **waanishkobaa** (GJ)
**waanichigaadeg** *vii-prt* pollution (RT, NJ, GJ)
**waanizhwi** /waanizhw-/ *vta* cut s.o. in a circular fashion (as in making
    snowshoe lacing) (NJ)
**waanizhaabii** *vai* cut hide or leather in a circular fashion (as in making
    snowshoe lacing) (NJ, GJ)
**waasaashkaa** *vii* there are white caps (RT, NJ, GJ)
**waasakonejiisag** *ni* glowing rotten wood (NJ, GJ)
**waasamoo-dakwaabiigizhoochigan** *ni* lawn mower; *pl* **waasamoo-**
    **dakwaabiigizhoochiganan** (RT, NJ, GJ)

---

**waasamoo-mangaanibaajigan** *ni* jack hammer; *pl* **waasamoo-mangaanibaajigan** (RT, NJ, GJ)

**waaseyaawin** *ni* sunlight (RT)

**waashaanzhe'an** *vti* dim, turn s.t. down (as in a kerosene lantern) (RT)

**waashaanzhenan** *vti* dim, turn s.t. down (as in a kerosene lantern) (NJ)

**waashaazheyaa** *vii* be dim light (RT)

**waasiingwewebinige** *vai* the white side shows (NJ, GJ)

**waasooskode'an** *vii* be a detached opening in the ice along the shore (GJ)

**waasooskodewan** *vii* be an opening in the ice along the shore (NJ)

**waawan** *ni* egg (of a bird); *pl* **waawanoon** (RT, NJ, GJ)

**waawanogek** *na* egg shell; *pl* **waawanogekwag** (NJ)

**waawiikobizh** /waawiikobiN-/ *vta* pull s.o. intermittently (RT, NJ, GJ)

**waawiyaagishin** *vai* curl up (as does a snake) (NJ, GJ)

**waawiyaagishin** *vai* grow in rings (NJ, GJ)

**waawiyeyaabijigan** *ni* encircling pole of a shake-tent; *pl* **waawiyeyaabijiganan** (GJ)

**webaabasigan** *ni* mosquito chaser smoke (NJ, GJ)

**wegaskendaagozi** *vai* be stubborn, fussy, hard to please (NJ, GJ); *redup* **weyagaskendaagozi** (GJ, NJ); *also* **wiiyagaskendaagozi** (NJ, GJ)

**Wekonimindaawangaans** *place* Maple Plain, Wisconsin (sandy beaver dam) (AM)

**wenji-zaagidaabateg** *vii-prt* smoke hole (NJ, GJ)

**wenjijiwang** *vii-prt* shower; *pl* **wenjijiwangin** (NJ)

**wewebaakowebinan** *vti* wave, swing s.t. (as in s.t. stick-like) (NJ)

**wewebaanoweni** *vai* wag one's tail (NJ, GJ)

**wewenabi** *vai* sit properly (RT, NJ, GJ); *also* **wawenabi** (LM)

**wewenose** *vai* walk properly, walk cautiously (RT, NJ, GJ)

**wewese'an** *vti* fan s.t. (RT, NJ, GJ)

**wewese'igan** *ni* fan; *pl* **wewese'iganan** (RT, NJ, GJ)

**wewese'wi** /wewese'w-/ *vta* fan s.o. (as in a drum) (NJ); *also* **wewese'o** /wewese'w-/ (GJ)

**wewiibizo** *vai* drive fast (RT, NJ, GJ)

**weyagaskendaagozi** *vai* picky, fussy, hard to please, finicky (NJ, GJ); *redup of* **wegaskendaagozi** *vai* be stubborn, fussy, hard to please (NJ, GJ); *also* **wiiyagaskendaagozi** (NJ, GJ)

**wiidookodaadiwin** *ni* cooperation (RT, NJ, GJ)

**wiigiwaam** *ni* wigwam lodge; *pl* **wiigiwaaman** (RT, NJ, GJ)

**wiigiwaaming dibendaasowin** *ni* furniture; *pl* **wiigiwaaming dibendaasowinan** (RT)

**wiigobiike** *vai* make string from basswood fiber (RT, NJ, GJ)

**wiigwaasabakwayike** *vai* make birch bark lodge coverings (RT, NJ, GJ)

**wiigwaasabakwaan** *ni* bark lodge covering; *pl* **wiigwaasabakwaanan** (RT, NJ, GJ)

**wiiji'** *vta* help s.o. (NJ, GJ)

**wiiji'idiwin** *ni* behavior (RT, NJ, GJ)

**wiiji'igoowizi** *vai* rely upon things, get help from things (NJ)

**wiijinaagozi** *vai* be camoflauged (RT, NJ, GJ)

**wiikonge'** *vta* feast s.o. (RT, NJ, GJ)

**wiikwa'ibiise** *vii* suck, vacuum water out (NJ, GJ)

**wiikwaji'o** *vai* try to get away (as in from a trap) (NJ, GJ)

**wiimbaagishkoode** *vii* hang low inverted (concave) (GJ)

**wiimbinaagan** *ni* bowl; *pl* **wiimbinaaganan** (GJ)

**wiinaabate** *vii* be dirty (as in something smoke-like) (RT, NJ, GJ)

**wiinaagamin** *vii* be dirty (as in a liquid) (RT, NJ, GJ)

**wiinichigaade** *vii* be polluted (NJ, GJ)

**wiininaamowin** *ni* dirty air (i.e. air pollution, polluted air) (RT, NJ, GJ)

**wiipe** *vai* sleep with people (RT)

**wiisagazheyaakizo** *vai* be painfully sunburned [*example*: Wiinge wiisagazheyaakizodog. = He must be really sunburned.] (NJ, GJ)

**wiisagi-ma'iingan** *na* coyote; *pl* **wiisagi-ma'iinganag** (RT); *also* **ma'iingaans** (TS)

**wiisigamaasin** *vii* wind causes small ripples on calm water (NJ, GJ)

**wiiwakwaan** *ni* hat; *pl* **wiiwakwaanan** (RT, NJ, GJ)

**wiiweginigaazo** *vai* be packaged (RT)

**wiiyaasanjige** *vai* be a carnivore (RT, NJ, GJ)

**wiiyagaskendaagozi** *vai* be pesty, fussy (NJ, GJ); *also* **wegaskendaagozi** *vai* be stubborn, fussy, hard to please (NJ, GJ); *redup* **weyagaskendaagozi** (GJ, NJ)


# Z

**zagaakwa'** /zagaakwa'w-/ *vta* button s.o. up (JC)

**zagaakwa'odizo** *vai* button one's self up (RT, NJ, GJ)

**zagaakwa'on** *na* button; *pl* **zagaakwa'onag** (NJ, GJ); *also* **gibadoonh** *na* button; *pl* **gibadoonyag** (JC)

**zagaakwa'oni-gizhibaayabiigibijigan** *ni* button spinner; *pl* **zagaakwa'oni-gizhibaayabiigibijiganan** (NJ, GJ)

**zagaakwaa** *vii* be dense, brushy woods, thick brush, thicket (ES, NJ) [*cultural note*: this term can be used as a metaphor for hard times; *example*: Da-zagaakwaa obimaadiziwin giishpin bizindawaasig ookomisan. = Her life will get hard if she doesn't listen to her grandmother.]

**zagigaadebizo** *vai* be flung up, caught by the leg (as a rabbit in a tree spring-noose trap) (NJ)

**zagigaadepizh** /zagigaadepiN-/ *vta* tie s.o. legs (NJ, GJ)

**zagigi-omichigegani** *vai* have an elongated spike (as in a dinosaur) (NJ)

**zagimewayaan** *ni* mosquito barrier (screen or sheet); *pl* **zagimewayaanan** (NJ, GJ)

**zakide** *vii* be a fire (RT)

**zanagendaagwad** *vii* be challenging (NJ)

**zasagigaadepizh** /zasagigaadepiN-/ *vta* tie s.o. legs repeatedly (NJ, GJ)

**zaswebiiga'anjigan** *ni* water sprinkler; *pl* **zaswebiiga'anjiganan** (RT, NJ, GJ)

**zaagaabate** *vii* smoke comes from somewhere (RT, NJ, GJ)

**zaagakii** *vii* sprout (RT)

**zaagisin** *vii* it protrudes (NJ, GJ)

**zaagidenaninjiitaw** *vta* give s.o. the dirty Ojibwe finger sign [*cultural note*: performed by sticking the thumb between the first two fingers,symbolically representing a phallus protruding between the legs, done teasingly, in jest, but only between male friends] (GJ)

**zaagidenaniweni** *vai* stick out one's tongue (NJ)

**zaagidenaniwetaw** *vta* stick one's tongue out at s.o. (NJ, GJ)

**zaagidiyeshin** *vai* have one's butt sticking out (RT, NJ, GJ)

**zaagiji-gwaashkwani** *vai* jump out (RT, NJ, GJ)

**zaagikwegomo** *vai* head is sticking out of water while floating (NJ, GJ)

**zaagizideni** *vai* stick one's foot out (RT, NJ, GJ)

**zaasaagidenaniwe** *vai* repeatedly stick out one's tongue (RT, NJ, GJ)

**zaasaagidiyezo** *vii* hind end repeatedly pops up from boiling (RT, NJ, GJ)

**zaasaagigamide** *vii* repeatedly pop up from boiling (RT, NJ, GJ)

**zaasaagiji-gwaashkwani** *vai* jump out repeatedly (RT, NJ, GJ)

**zaasaagikwezo** *vii* head repeatedly pops up from boiling (RT, NJ, GJ)

**zaasakokwe** *vai* fry things (RT, NJ, GJ)

**zaasibiibizo** *vai* heard coming through water (as in a motorboat) (GJ)

**zesab** *na* nettle; *pl* **zesabiig** (RT, NJ, GJ)

**zesegaandag** *na* black spruce; *pl* **zesegaandagoog** (NJ)

**zhagashkaanaamikwesi** *na* bottom dwelling fish; *pl*
       **zhagashkaanaamikwesiwag** (NJ, GJ)

**zhagashkaashi** *vai* be bent by the wind (GJ)

**zhagashkaasin** *vii* be bent from wind (GJ)

**zhagashkii** *vai* crouch down to ground (NJ, GJ)

**zhagashkosiweyaasin** *vii* grass bends down to ground from the wind, the
       grass is dancing (NJ, GJ)

**zhakamaw** *vta* put s.o. in one's mouth (RT, NJ, GJ)

**zhakamo** *vai* put things in one's mouth (RT, NJ, GJ)

**zhakamon** *vai+o* put (s.t.) in one's mouth (RT, NJ, GJ)

**zhakamoozh** /zhakamooN-/ *vta* put s.t. in s.o.'s mouth (NJ, GJ)

**zhamashkii** *vai* crouch down to ground (NJ, GJ)

**zhamashkishimo** *vai* do the grass dance (crouch while dancing) (GJ)

**zhamashkosiweyaasin** *vii* grass bends down to ground from the wind
       (NJ)

**zhamashkosiweyaasin** *vii* grass bends part-way down to ground from
       the wind (GJ)

**zhawabaaginan** *vti* bend s.t. (NJ)

**zhawoobaaginan** *vti* bend s.t. (GJ)

**zhazhiwaasin** *vii* get dull (GJ)

**zhazhwegigin** *vii* spread out (RT)

**zhaabobiiginigan** *ni* strainer; *pl* **zhaabobiiginiganan** (NJ, GJ)

**zhaabondawaan** *ni* teaching lodge, long-style wiigiwaam with doors
       and both ends; *pl* **zhaabondawaanan** (NJ)

**zhaaboshkaw** *vta* pass through s.o. (RT)

**zhaabwaate** *vii* shine through (as in light through glass or water) (NJ,
       GJ)

**zhaabwaate-omooday** *ni* vase; *pl* **zhaabwaate-omoodayan** (NJ, GJ)

**zhaangweshiwaabikoons** *na* quarter (coin) (NJ, GJ)

**zhaashaabobiiginigan** *ni* strainer (GJ)

**zhaashaabwaabiiginigaade** *vii* be woven (NJ, GJ)

**zhaashaabwaabiiginigan** *ni* woven item; *pl* **zhaashaabwaabiiginigan**
       (NJ, GJ)

**zhaashaaginizide** *vai* be barefoot (RT, NJ, GJ)

**zhaashaaginizidegaabawi** *vai* stand bare legged (RT, NJ, GJ)

**zhaashaagwanjige** *vai* chew, eat by chewing (RT)

**zhegwaabikin** *vta* bake s.o. (RT)

**zhegwaabikinige** *vai* put things in the oven (NJ, GJ)

**zhegwaakonan** *vti* slide s.t. into a tight area (of s.t. stick-like) (NJ)

**zhegwaakonan** *vti* stretch s.t. out (in moccasin game) (GJ)

**zhegwaakozh / zhegwaakoN-/** *vta* stick s.o. in a tight place (NJ)

**zhegwaakozh / zhegwaakoN-/** *vta* stretch s.o. out (in moccasin game, encouraging teammate to tease, do something to one's opponent) (GJ)

**zhinawa'oojiganens** *na* small bell; *pl* **zhinawa'oojiganensag** (NJ, GJ)

**zhinawese** *vii* rattle (as in sticks in a drum) (NJ, GJ)

**zhinawesin** *vai* make a metallic rattling sound (ball in a bell) (NJ, GJ)

**zhingibijiganaak** *ni* hoop for stretching beaver hide; *pl* **zhingibijiganaakoon** (NJ, GJ)

**zhingibijiganeyaab** *ni* wrapping string for beaver hide stretching hoop; *pl* **zhingibijiganeyaabiin** (NJ, GJ)

**zhingob** *na* balsam, evergreen; *pl* **zhingobiig** (RT, NJ, GJ); *also* black spruce (AM)

**zhingwaakwaandag** *na* pine needle; *pl* **zhingwaakwaandag** (RT, NJ)

**zhinoodaagan** *ni* net cord; *pl* **zhinoodaaganan** (NJ, GJ)

**zhiibaa-waanike** *vai* dig a tunnel (RT)

**zhiibaa-waazh** *ni* tunnel; *pl* **zhiibaa-waazhiin** (RT)

**zhiibaa'aabanjigan** *ni* telescope or binoculars; *pl* **zhiibaa'aabanjiganan** (GJ)

**zhiibaa'aabanjige** *vai* focus (GJ)

**zhiibine** *vai* doesn't die easily, dies hard (GJ, NJ)

**zhiigooganeshin** vai skeleton lies on the ground picked clean (NJ, GJ)

**zhiigwaami** *vai* be spawned out (NJ, GJ)

**zhiingendaagozi** *vai* be hated (NJ, GJ)

**zhiingenim** *vta* hate s.o. (RT, NJ, GJ)

**zhiiwan** *vii* be sweet (NJ, GJ); *also* be bitter (RT)

**zhiiwipogwad** *vii* taste sweet (NJ, GJ); *also* taste bitter (RT)

**zhiiwitaaganibiisin** *vii* be salty water (RT, NJ, GJ)

**zhiiwitaaganipogwad** *vii* taste salty (RT, NJ, GJ)

**zhooniyaa-giigoozens** *na* smelt; *pl* **zhooniyaa-giigoozensag** (NJ, GJ)

**zhooshkobiise** *vii* slides through the water easily (NJ, GJ)

**zhooshkojiwe** *vai* slide (NJ)

**zhooshkwazhe** *vai* have smooth skin (RT)

**zhooshkwaa** *vii* slide (RT, NJ, GJ)

**zhooshkwaakozhwi /zhooshkwaakozhw-/** *vta* cut s.o. smooth using s.t. (knife), as in trimming the knots off a sapling, making it smooth (NJ)

**zhooshkwaakozi** *vai* be smooth (s.t. treelike) (RT, NJ, GJ)

**zhwaaganib** *pc* spring melt water (NJ, GJ)

**zisiboojigan** *ni* flat file; *pl* **zisiboojiganan** (GJ)

**zisiboojiganens** *ni* chainsaw sharpening file; *pl* **zisiboojiganensan** (GJ)

**ziswebiiga'anjigan** *ni* lawn sprinkler; *pl* **ziswebiiga'anjiganan** (NJ)

**ziibiskaabi** *vai* squint, wink (NJ, GJ)

**ziigaakwa'igaade** *vii* be supported with a stick (GJ)

**ziigaakwa'igan** *ni* crutch pole (GJ)

**ziikoobiiginan** *vti* drain the water out of s.t. (NJ, GJ)

**ziikoobiiginigan** *ni* filter, strainer (RT, NJ, GJ)

**ziinaakwa'igan** *ni* wringer (RT)

**ziinibidoon** *vti* squeeze s.t. out (like toothpaste) (RT)

**ziinijaanese** *vai* cleanse one's nostrils (NJ, GJ)

**ziinikobiigaakwa'an** *vti* wring out twisting with stick (NJ, GJ)

**ziiniskiigome** *vai* blow one's nose (RT, NJ, GJ)

**ziiniskobiiga'an** *vti* wring out cloth or hide (NJ, GJ)

**ziiwiskipogwad** *vii* taste sour (NJ); *also* **ziiwaskipogod** (GJ)

**zoongibii'igan** *ni* exclamation point (!) (JC)

**zoongide'e** *vai* be brave (RT, NJ, GJ)

# ENGLISH-OJIBWE

ABANDON: **nagajigaade** *vii* be left somewhere (RT)

ABOUT TIME: **nenibaawizh iidog** *expression* it's about time [*example*: Nenibaawizh iidog gigoshkoz! = It's about time you woke up!] (NJ, GJ)

ABOVE: **dibishkoojayi'ii** *pc* immediately above, directly above (NJ); *also* **dishkoojeyi'ii** (GJ)

ACCIDENT: DROP ACCIDENTALLY: bishigonige *vai* miss and drop things (NJ)

ACORN: **mitigomin** *na* acorn; *pl* **mitigominag** (RT)

ACROSS:

> HELD ACROSS BY STICK: **bimaakobide** *vii* be held out across by a stick (as in lodge runners parallel to the ground) (GJ)
>
> LIE ACROSS: **inaakogoojin** *vai* lie across (as in log) (RT, NJ, GJ)
>
> ROLL SOMEONE ACROSS: **ditibiwebin** *vta* roll s.o. across (RT, NJ, GJ)
>
> STICK FOR HOLDING ACROSS: **bimaakobijigan** *ni* stick for holding s.t. across; *pl* **bimaakobijiganan** (GJ)

ACTIVITY: ALPHABET ACTIVITY CARD: **ikidowinensi-mazina'iganens** *ni* alphabet activity card; *pl* **ikidowinensi-mazina'iganensan** (RT)

ADD:

> ADD: **dagosijige** *vai* contribute, add to things (RT, NJ, GJ)
>
> ADD TO SOMETHING: **dagosidoon** *vti* contribute to s.t., add s.t. in (RT, NJ, GJ)

ADHERE: **minjiminigaade** *vii* adhere, attach, clasp (RT)

AGGRESSIVE: **mawine'ige** *vai* be aggressive, retaliatory (RT, NJ, GJ)

AIMING STICK: **bimoojiganaak** *ni* aiming stick (for moccasin game); *pl* **bimoojiganaakoon** (GJ)

AIR:

> HOLE IN ICE (AIR): **bagwaawanib** *ni* hole in the ice caused by air (as in from a beaver disturbing the lake bottom); *pl* **bagwaawanibiin** (NJ, GJ)
>
> DIRTY AIR: **wiininaamowin** *ni* dirty air (i.e. air pollution, polluted air) (RT, NJ, GJ)

AIRPLANE: **bemisemagak** *vii-prt* airplane; *pl* **bemisemagakin** (RT, NJ, GJ)

ALGAE: **ataagib** *ni* algae (RT, NJ, GJ)

ALPHABET:

ALPHABET ACTIVITY CARD: **ikidowinensi-mazina'iganens** *ni* alphabet activity card; *pl* **ikidowinensi-mazina'iganensan** (RT)

ALPHABET STAMP: **mazinadoobii'igan** *ni* alphabet stamp; *pl* **mazinadoobii'iganan** (RT)

AMBUSH:

AMBUSH FISH: **ashawaamiwe** *vai* lie in wait for fish (spearing) in open water or ice (RT, NJ, GJ)

AMBUSH SOMEONE: **akandamaw** *vta* lie in wait for s.o. (RT, NJ, GJ)

AMBUSH: **ashwabi** *vai* sit in wait (RT, NJ, GJ)

BLIND: **akandoowin** *ni* blind (RT, NJ, GJ)

LOOKOUT FOR SOMEONE: **ashawaabam** *vai* wait for s.o. to appear, be on lookout for s.o. (RT, NJ, GJ)

ANCHOR:

ANCHOR: ANCHOR: **boonakajigan** *ni* boat anchor; *pl* **boonakajiganan** (NJ, GJ, RT); *also* ANCHOR: **gitaamika'igan** *ni* anchor, weight for nets; *pl* **gitaamika'iganan** (RT, NJ, GJ)

ANCHOR IN: **badakakiiwebinigaade** *vii* anchor is thrown in (RT, NJ, GJ)

ANCHOR LINE: **gitaamika'iganeyaab** *ni* anchor line (RT, NJ, GJ)

ANCHOR ROCK: **agonjiwasin** *na* anchor rock (weight); *pl* **agonjiwasiniig** (RT, NJ, GJ)

ANCHOR SOMETHING: **gitaamika'an** *vti* anchor s.t. (RT, NJ, GJ)

ANCHOR WIRE: **gitaakwa'iganeyaab** *ni* anchor wire (for a trap); *pl* **gitaakwa'iganeyaabiin** (RT, NJ, GJ)

ANCHORED: **badakakiisin** *vii* stuck in, anchored in (RT, NJ, GJ)

ANCIENT: SMELL ANCIENT: **getemaagwad** *vii* smell ancient (GJ)

ANIMAL:

ANIMAL TAIL: **ninzow** /**-zow-**/ *nid* my tail (of an animal); *pl* **ninzowan** (RT, NJ, GJ)

HAVE HORNS: **odeshkani** *vai* have horns (as in an animal) (NJ)

ANNOUNCE STURGEON SPAWN: **biibaaginamewe** *vai* announce the coming of sturgeon spawn (as in gray tree frog) [*cultural note*: this particular tree frog sound is only heard at the start of the sturgeon spawn and is different from the characteristic call of other tree frogs] (NJ)

ANT HILL: **bikwadaawangisin** *vii* be a sand hill, be an ant hill (RT, NJ, GJ); *also* **enigoonsigiwaam** *ni* ant hill; *pl* **enigoonsigiwaaman** (RT, NJ, GJ)

ANTLER: **eshkan** *na* antler, horn; *pl* **eshkanag** (RT, NJ, GJ)

ANUS:

> ANAL PENETRATION: **boojidiyeshin** *vai* fall or sit on s.t. causing anal penetration (GJ)
>
> BLEEDING ANUS: **miskojiidiye** *vai* have a bleeding anus, hemorrhoids  (RT, NJ, GJ)

ANY OLD WAY: **debinaak** *pc* any old way, just barely sufficient (RT, NJ, GJ)

APPEAR: LOOK ONE'S BEST: **minonaagozi'idizo** *vai* look one's best (NJ)

APPLE: **mishiimin** *na* apple; *pl* **mishiiminag** (RT, NJ, GJ)

ARM HAIR: **miishinikaan** *ni* arm hair; *pl* **miishinikaanan** (RT, NJ, GJ)

ARMPIT: MY ARMPIT: **indanaaminingwiigan** *nid* my armpit; *loc* **indanaaminingwiiganaang**  (NJ)

AROUND: ENCIRCLE SOMEONE: **gizhibaashkaw** *vta* encircle s.o., go around s.o. (RT, NJ, GJ)

ARRIVE:

> LIGHT ARRIVES: **bagamaate** *vii*  light arrives in a certain place, light is captured in a certain place (RT)
>
> WATER ARRIVES: **bagamijiwan** *vii* water arrives in a certain place (RT)
>
> WIND ARRIVES: **bagamaanimad** *vii* wind comes up, gets windy (RT, NJ, GJ)

ARROWHEAD: **biiwaanagoons** *na* arrowhead; *pl* **biiwaanagoonsag** (NJ, GJ)

ATTACH:

> ATTACH: **agoke** *vii* attach, adhere, be stuck onto s.t. (RT, NJ, GJ)
>
> ATTACH TO SOMETHING: **dagobidoon** *vti* attach s.t. to an object (GJ)
>
> CLASP: **minjiminigaade** *vii* adhere, attach, clasp (RT)

ATTACK: VERBALLY ATTACK IN DEFENSE OF CHILD: **onzonge** *vai* verbally attack people based on what your child told you [*example*: Gego onzongeken! = Don't (verbally) attack people based on what your child has come and told you! *cultural note*: It is considered inadvisable to do this because of possible spiritual consequences. Children need to fend for themselves and take responsibility for their actions.] (RT, NJ, GJ)

AWARE OF WEATHER: **dadiibaabandamaazo** *vai* make sure one is aware of weather  (NJ, GJ)

AX:

DOUBLE BIT AX: **edawaabide-waagaakwad** *ni* double bit ax; *pl*
**edawaabide-waagaakwadoon** (NJ)

LIMB WITH AX: **bashkwatigwanezhwi** /**bashkwatigwanezhw-**/
*vta* limb s.o. (tree) using s.t. (like an ax, knife) (NJ)

BABOON: **miskodiyeshiinh** *na* baboon; *pl* **miskodiyeshiinyag** (RT, NJ,
GJ)

BACK:

BACK OR CHEST HAIR: **miishaawiganaan** *ni* back or chest hair;
*pl* **miishaawiganaanan** (RT, NJ, GJ)

BASE OF SOMETHING: **odaanaang** *pc* the base of something, the
back of something [*example*: odaanaang gidenaniw = the back of
your tongue] (NJ, GJ)

HAVE HAIRY BACK: **miishaawigane** *vai* have a hairy back (RT,
NJ, GJ)

HAVE SILVER-HAIRED BACK: **waabikweyaawigane** *vai* have a
silver-colored hairy back (RT, NJ, GJ)

SILVER-BACK GORILLA: **wayaabikweyaawiganed** *vai-prt* silver-
back gorilla; *pl* **wayaabikweyaawiganejig** (RT, NJ, GJ)

BACK FACING:

LIE BACK FACING: **animikoshin** *vai* lie with back facing up (RT,
NJ, GJ)

STAND BACK FACING OUT: **animikogaabawi** *vai* stand with back
facing (RT, NJ, GJ)

STAND BACK FACING SOMEONE: **animikogaabawitaw** *vai* stand
with back facing s.o. (RT, NJ, GJ)

BACK-AND-FORTH:

HIT BACK-AND-FORTH: **aayaazhawi-bakite'amaadiwag**
/**aayaazhawi-bakite'amaadi-**/ *vai+o* they hit s.t. back-and-forth
to one another [*example*: Aayaazhawi-bakite'amaadiwag
bikwaakwad. = They are hitting the ball to one another.] (NJ, GJ)

KICK BACK-AND-FORTH: **aayaazhawi-basikamaadiwag**
/**aayaazhawi-basikamaadi-**/ *vai+o* they kick s.t. back-and-forth
to one another [*example:* Aayaazhawi-basikamaadiwag
bikwaakwad. = They are kicking the ball to one another.] (NJ,
GJ)

THROW BACK-AND-FORTH: **aayaazhawi-webinamaadiwag**
/**aayaazhawi-webinamaadi-**/ *vai+o* they throw s.t. back-and-
forth to one another [*example*: Aayaazhawi-webinamaadiwag

bikwaakwad. = They are throwing the ball to one another.] (NJ, GJ)

BACK-TO-BACK:

STAND BACK-TO-BACK: **animikogaabawitaadiwag /animikogaabawitaadi-/** *vai* they stand back-to-back (RT, NJ, GJ); *also* **awasigaabawitaadiwag /awasigaabawitaadi-/** (NJ, GJ)

BACKBONE: **nidatagaagwan /-datagaagwan-/** *nid* my spine; *pl* **nidatagaagwanan** (RT, NJ, GJ)

BACKGROUND: **odaanaam** *ni* background, personal history (NJ) [*example*: Gii-wanii'ige mewinzha odoodaanaaming, gaawiin geyaabi noongom. = He used to trap long ago in his background, but not any more.]

BACKRUB: **mamigobizh /mamigobiN-/** *vta* give s.o. a backrub (RT, NJ, GJ)

BACKWARDS:

FOLD BACKWARDS: **napaajiiginan** *vti* fold backwards, wrong way (GJ)

INVERSE: **napaaj** *pc* backwards, inverse (NJ, GJ)

BACKYARD: **odaanaang endaayaan** *place* my backyard (NJ)

BAD WEATHER: CAUGHT IN BAD WEATHER: **bangisinamaa** *vai* caught in inclement weather (RT, NJ, GJ)

BAD: TASTE BITTER: **maazhipogwad** *vii* taste bad, taste bitter (RT, NJ, GJ)

BAGESE GAME:

DARK SIDE SHOWS: **makadewiingwebinige** *vai* the dark side shows (as in bagese game) (GJ)

GAME: **bagese** *na* bagese game (GJ)

GAME BOWL: **bagesewinaagan** *ni* bagese game bowl (GJ)

GAME PIECE: **bagesaan** *na* bagese game piece; *pl* **bagesaanag** (NJ)

PLAY: **bagese** *vai* play bagese game (GJ)

BAIL:

BAIL WATER: **iska'ibii** *vai* bail (RT, NJ, GJ)

WATER BAILER: **iska'ibaan** *ni* water bailer, sponge; *pl* **iska'ibaanan** (NJ, GJ)

BAIT:

BAIT MADE FROM FISH: **ogokeyaw** *ni* bait made from fish (as in underside near gills or belly) (NJ); *pl* **ogokeyawan**; *also* **ogokeyawag** (GJ)

USE BAIT: **ogokeyawi** *vai* use bait (NJ)

BAKE:

BAKE: **gibozige** *vai* bake (RT)

BAKE SOMEONE: **zhegwaabikin** *vta* bake s.o. (RT)

BAKERY: **bakwezhiganikewigamig** *ni* bakery; *pl* **bakwezhiganikewigamigooon**; *loc* **bakwezhiganikewigamigong** (RT)

BALL: BASKETBALL: **gichi-bikwaakwad** *ni* basketball; *pl* **gichi-bikwaakwadoon** (NJ)

BALLED UP: **bikwaakwadotaawag** /**bikwaakwadotaa**/ *vai* they are balled up (ducks, geese, bugs) [*conjugation note*: requires multiple actors to make sense even though this is not a reflexive verb] (NJ, GJ)

BALSAM: **inaandag** *na* balsam; *pl* **inaandagoog** (AM); *also* **ininaandag** (KP); *pl* **ininaandagoog**; *also* **zhingob**; *pl* **zhingobiig** (RT, NJ, GJ) [*translation note*: also means "any everygreen" to NJ, RT]

BARE:

BAREFOOT: **zhaashaaginizide** *vai* be barefoot (RT, NJ, GJ)

STAND BARELEGGED: **zhaashaaginizidegaabawi** *vai* stand barelegged (RT, NJ, GJ)

BARK:

BARK REINFORCEMENT TAB: **apigwaason** *ni* reinforcing tab on end of birch bark roll or basket (as a wide strip placed inside out on the end creating a double layer); *pl* **apigwaasonan** (GJ)

BIRCH BARK LODGE COVERING: **wiigwaasabakwaan** *ni* bark lodge covering; *pl* **wiigwaasabakwaanan** (RT, NJ, GJ)

CEDAR BARK: **giizhikanagek** *na* cedar bark; *pl* **giizhikanagekwag** (RT, NJ, GJ)

CUT WIDE STRIPS: **mangadezhigaade** *vii* cut in wide strips (RT, NJ, GJ)

MAKE BASSWOOD STRING: **wiigobiike** *vai* make string from basswood fiber (RT, NJ, GJ)

MAKE BIRCH BARK LODGE COVERING: **wiigwaasabakwayike** *vai* make birch bark lodge coverings (RT, NJ, GJ)

PEEL BARK (SHEET): **baabagonagekwe** *vai* peel bark (as in birch bark) (RT, NJ, GJ)

PEEL BARK (STRING): **bishagaakobijige** *vai* peeling bark (string of fiber) by hand (as in peeling basswood) (RT, NJ, GJ)

PEEL SOMEONE: **bishagaakobizh /bishagaakobiN-/** *vta* peel s.o. by hand (as in a tree) (RT, NJ, GJ)

PEEL SOMETHING: **bishagaakobidoon** *vti* peel s.t. (as in bark) by hand (RT, NJ, GJ)

SEARCH FOR BARK: **andawanagekwe** *vai* look for, search for bark (RT, NJ, GJ)

SHAPE BARK: **biitawinagekobijige** *vai* thin out layers of bark (as in basswood), shape basswood fiber to size (RT, NJ, GJ)

STRIP WIDE: **mangadebidoon** *vti* strip s.t. into wide (as in bark) strips (RT, NJ, GJ)

BARRIER: MOSQUITO BARRIER: **zagimewayaan** *ni* mosquito barrier (screen or sheet); *pl* **zagimewayaanan** (RT, NJ, GJ)

BASE OF SOMETHING: **odaanaang** *pc* the base of something, the back of something [*example*: odaanaang gidenaniw = the back of your tongue] (NJ, GJ)

BASKETBALL: **gichi-bikwaakwad** *ni* basketball; *pl* **gichi-bikwaakwadoon** (NJ)

BASS: SOUND LOW: **bedowe** *vii* have a soft voice (low and slow) (NJ, GJ)

BASSWOOD:

BASSWOOD FIBER: **asigobaan** *ni* processed basswood fiber (RT, NJ, GJ)

MAKE BASSWOOD STRING: **wiigobiike** *vai* make string from basswood fiber (RT, NJ, GJ)

PEEL IN STRIP: **naanigaakobidoon** *vti* peel s.t. in a strip, strip s.t. (as in basswood) (RT, NJ, GJ)

PEEL INTO STRIPS: **naanaanigaakobijige** *vai* peel into strips (as in basswood) (RT, NJ, GJ)

PEEL SOMETHING INTO STRIPS: **naanaanigaakobidoon** *vti* peel s.t. into strips, strip s.t. (as in basswood) (RT, NJ, GJ)

SEARCH FOR BASSWOOD: **andowiigobii** *vai* searching for basswood (NJ, GJ)

SHAPE BARK: **biitawinagekobijige** *vai* thin out layers of bark (as in basswood), shape basswood fiber to size (RT, NJ, GJ)

BATHTUB: **endazhi-giziibiigiing** *vai-prt* bathtub (NJ)

BEAD: **manidoomin** *na* bead; *pl* **manidoominag** (RT, NJ, GJ)

BEAN:

BEAN SEED: **mashkodiisiminens** *na* bean seed; *pl*
**mashkodiisiminensag** (RT)

LIMA BEAN: **omashkoziisimin** *na* lima bean; *pl*
**omashkoziisiminag** (NJ)

BEAR: **aniibiishanjige-makwa** *na* koala bear *pl* **aniibiishanjige-
makwag** (RT, NJ, GJ)

BEAT: SYNCOPATED BEAT: **biisiwebinige** vai make syncopated beat for
moccasin game song (GJ)

BEAVER HOUSE LAKE: **Asamikowiishiwi-zaaga'igan** *place* Beaver
House Lake (in Quetico Park) (GJ)

BEAVER:

BEAVER DAM: **okonim** *ni* beaver dam; *pl* **okoniman**; *loc*
**okoniming** (NJ)

BEAVER POND: **amikob** *ni* beaver pond; *pl* **amikobiin**; *loc*
**amikobiing** (RT, NJ, GJ)

BEAVER POND FORMS: **amikobiigaa** *vii* forming of a beaver lake
or pond (NJ); *also* **amikobiikaa** (GJ)

BEAVER STRETCHING HOOP: **zhingibijiganaak** *ni* hoop for
stretching beaver hide; *pl* **zhingibijiganaakoon** (NJ, GJ)

BEAVER TOOTH: **amikwaabid** *ni* beaver tooth; *pl* **amikwaabidan**
(RT, NJ, GJ)

STRING FOR BEAVER STRETCHING HOOP: **zhingibijiganeyaab** *ni*
wrapping string for beaver hide stretching hoop; *pl*
**zhingibijiganeyaabiin** (RT, NJ, GJ)

BED: *see* SLEEP

BEFORE LONG: **gomaa go apii** *expression* before long (RT)

BEGIN: *see* START

BEHAVIOR: **wiiji'idiwin** *ni* behavior (RT, NJ, GJ)

BELL:

BICYCLE BELL: **ditibiwebishkigani-madwewechigaans** *ni*
bicycle bell; *pl* **ditibiwebishkigani-madwewechigaansan** (RT,
NJ, GJ)

SCHOOL BELL: **gikinoo'amaadii-zhinawa'oojiganens** *ni* school
bell; *pl* **gikinoo'amaadii-zhinawa'oojiganensan** (NJ)

SMALL BELL: **zhinawa'oojiganens** *na* small bell; *pl*
**zhinawa'oojiganensag** (NJ, GJ)

BELT: SEAT BELT: **gitaakwapizon** *ni* dog leash, dog chain, seat belt; *pl*
**gitaakwapizonan** (RT, NJ, GJ)

BEND:

BEND AND JOIN: **aanikoowaaginan** *vti* bend together joining (as in lodge poles) (RT, NJ, GJ)

BEND DOWN WITH HAND: **ispwaabikibidoon** *vti* bend s.t. (metal-like) down with hand (as in bending over a protruding nail) (GJ)

BEND DOWN WITH TOOL: **ispwaabikada'an** *vti* bend s.t. (metal-like) down with a tool (as in bending over a protruding nail) (GJ)

BEND SOMETHING: **zhawabaaginan** *vti* bend s.t. (NJ); *also* **zhawoobaaginan** (GJ)

BEND SOMETHING DOWN: **biskada'an** *vti* bend s.t. down (NJ)

BEND SOMETHING METAL: **biskaabikada'an** *vti* bend s.t. (metal-like) down with a tool (as in bending over a protruding nail) (NJ)

BEND TOGETHER: **aanikwaaginan** *vti* bend together (as in lodge poles) (NJ)

BENT BY WIND: **naweyaashi** *vii* be bent by the wind (RT, NJ, GJ); *also* **zhagashkaasin** *vii* be bent from wind (GJ)

BENT BY WIND: **zhagashkaashi** *vai* be bent by the wind (GJ)

CURVE SOMETHING: **waaginan** *vti* curve s.t., bend s.t. (RT, NJ, GJ)

GRASS BENDS PART-WAY TO GROUND: **zhamashkosiweyaasin** *vii* grass bends part-way down to ground from the wind (GJ)

GRASS BENDS TO GROUND: **zhagashkosiweyaasin** *vii* grass bends down to ground from the wind, the grass is dancing (NJ, GJ); *also* **zhamashkosiweyaasin** (NJ)

HANG BENT: **waagigoode** *vii* hang in a bent position (RT, NJ, GJ)

TREE BENT BY THE WIND: **neweyaak** *na* tree that is bent by the wind; *pl* **neweyaakoog** (GJ)

BERRY: **editeg** *vii-prt* berry, fruit; *pl* **editegin** (RT)

BETWEEN TOES: **niniisiigizidaanens** *nid* between my toes; *loc* **niniisiigizidaanensing** (NJ, GJ)

BICYCLE BELL: **ditibiwebishkigani-madwewechigaans** *ni* bicycle bell; *pl* **ditibiwebishkigani-madwewechigaansan** (RT, NJ, GJ)

BIG: *see* LARGE

BINOCULARS: **zhiibaa'aabanjigan** *ni* telescope or binoculars; *pl* **zhiibaa'aabanjiganan** (GJ)

BIRCH:

BIRCH BARK LODGE COVERING: **wiigwaasabakwaan** *ni* bark lodge covering; *pl* **wiigwaasabakwaanan** (RT, NJ, GJ)

BIRCH TREE SEED STRINGS: **wanimikoons** *ni* birch tree seed strings; *pl* **wanimikoonsan** (RT, NJ, GJ)

MAKE BIRCH BARK LODGE COVERING: **wiigwaasabakwayike** *vai* make birch bark lodge coverings (RT, NJ, GJ)

BIRD:

BIRD EGG: **waawan** *ni* egg (of a bird); *pl* **waawanoon** (RT, NJ, GJ)

BIRD NEST: **wadiswan** *ni* nest (of a bird); *pl* **wadiswanan**; *dim* **wadiswanens** (RT, NJ, GJ)

BIRD TAIL: **ninashkid /-nashkidy-/** *nid* my tail (of a bird); *pl* **ninashkidiin** (RT, NJ, GJ)

DOVE, PIGEON: **omiimii** *na* dove, pigeon; *pl* **omiimiig** (RT, NJ, GJ)

MAKE BIRD NEST: **waziswanike** *vai* make a nest (RT); *also* **wadiswanike** (RT)

MALE BIRD: **naabese** *na* male bird, rooster; *pl* **naabeseg** (RT, NJ, GJ)

BITE:

BITE: **dakwanjige** *vai* bite and put in one's mouth (RT); *also* perform oral sex (TS)

BITE OFF PART OF SELF: **giishkandizo** *vai* bite off a part of oneself (RT, NJ, GJ)

BITE SHUT: **gashkaabikandan** *vti* bite s.t. shut (RT, NJ, GJ)

BITTER: **maazhipogwad** *vii* taste bad, taste bitter (RT, NJ, GJ)

BLACK SPRUCE: **zesegaandag** *na* black spruce; *pl* **zesegaandagoog** (NJ); *also* **zhingob**; *pl* **zhingobiig** (WI)

BLADDER: SWIM BLADDER: **obikwaajiins** *nid* little air sack, swim bladder; *also ni* light bulb (NJ, GJ); *also* **obikwaaj** *nid* air sack of a fish, swim bladder (NJ, GJ)

BLIND:

BLIND: **gagiibiigiingwe** *vai* be blind (RT, NJ, GJ); *also* **gagiibiingwe** *vai* be blind (RT, NJ, GJ)

HUNTING BLIND: **akandoowin** *ni* blind (RT, NJ, GJ)

BLINK:

BLINK: **basangwaabi** *vai* close one's eyes, blink (RT, NJ, GJ)

BLINK REPEATEDLY: **bapasangwaabi** *vai* blink one's eyes repeatedly (NJ, GJ)

BLINK REPEATEDLY AT SOMEONE: **bapasangwaabam** *vta* blink eyes at s.o. repeatedly [*example*: Gego bapasangwaabamaaken awiiya. = Don't keep blinking your eyes at anyone. *cultural note*: Considered extremely rude and offensive to repeatedly blink at someone.] (NJ, GJ)

BLISTER:

    BLISTER BREAKS: **baaskobiigishkaa** *vii* be a broken blister (RT, NJ, GJ)

    BLISTER ON FINGER: **apashkwebiigininjiishin** *vai* get a blister on one's hand, finger (RT, NJ, GJ)

    BLISTER ON FOOT: **apashkwebiigizideshin** *vai* get a blister on one's foot (RT, NJ, GJ)

BLOCK:

    BLOCK SOMETHING: **gibisidoon** *vti* block s.t. (as in using something to block light from a projector) (RT, NJ, GJ)

    PREVENT: **gibichichige** *vai* block, prohibit, prevent (NJ, GJ)

    STOP: **gibichii** *vai* stop (RT, NJ, GJ)

BLOOD: BLEEDING ANUS: **miskojiidiye** *vai* have a bleeding anus, hemorrhoids  (RT, NJ, GJ)

BLOW:

    BLOW ACROSS: **aazhawaasin** *vii* blows across (RT)

    BLOW IN SOMETHING: **biinji-boodaadan** *vti* blow in s.t. (RT, NJ, GJ)

    BLOW IN THINGS: **biinji-boodaajige** *vai* blow in things (RT, NJ, GJ)

    BLOW NOSE: **ziinijaanese** *vai* cleanse one's nostrils (RT, NJ, GJ); *also* **ziiniskiigome** *vai* blow one's nose (RT, NJ, GJ)

BLOW: *see also* WIND

BLUE WATER: **ozhaawashkwaagamin** *vii* be blue (water) (NJ, GJ)

BOAT: METAL BOAT: **ginwaabiko-jiimaan** *ni* metal boat; *pl* **ginwaabiko-jiimaanan** (RT, NJ, GJ)

BOAT: *see also* CANOE

BOBBER: **agonjiwinaaganens** *ni* bobber; *pl* **agonjiwinaaganensan** (GJ)

BODY:

    ARM HAIR: **miishinikaan** *ni* arm hair; *pl* **miishinikaanan** (RT, NJ, GJ)

    BACK OR CHEST HAIR: **miishaawiganaan** *ni* back or chest hair; *pl* **miishaawiganaanan** (RT, NJ, GJ)

    BETWEEN TOES: **niniisiigizidaanens** *nid* between my toes; *loc* **niniisiigizidaanensing** (NJ, GJ)

    BIG CHEEKS: **mamaanginowe** *vai* have big cheeks (RT)

BIG FEET: **mamaangizide** *vai* have big feet (RT)

BUTT STICKS OUT: **zaagidiyeshin** *vai* have one's butt sticking out (RT, NJ, GJ)

CHEST HAIR: **miishaakiganaan** *ni* chest hair; *pl* **miishaakiganaanan** (RT, NJ, GJ)

EYEBROW: **nimaamaa** *na* eyebrow; *pl* **nimaamaayag** (RT, NJ, GJ)

EYELASH: **nimiishaabiwinaan** *nid* my eyelash; *pl* **nimiishaabiwinaanan** (NJ, GJ)

FINGER PAD: **niniisiigininjaan** *nid* my finger pad; *pl* **niniisiigininjaanan** (NJ)

HAIRY CHEST: **miishaakigan** *ni* hairy chest *pl* **miishaakiganan** (RT, NJ, GJ)

HAVE HAIRY BACK: **miishaawigane** *vai* have a hairy back (RT, NJ, GJ)

HAVE HAIRY CHEST: **miishaakigane** *vai* have a hairy chest (RT, NJ, GJ)

HAVE HAIRY LEGS: **miishigaade** *vai* have hairy legs (RT, NJ, GJ)

HEAD POPS UP REPEATEDLY FROM BOILING: **zaasaagikwezo** *vii* head repeatedly pops up from boiling (RT, NJ, GJ)

HEAD STICKS OUT OF WATER FLOATING: **zaagikwegomo** *vai* head is sticking out of water while floating (NJ, GJ)

HIND END POPS UP FROM BOILING: **zaasaagidiyezo** *vii* hind end repeatedly pops up from boiling (RT, NJ, GJ)

KNUCKLE: **nimbikoninjaan** *nid* my knuckle [*example*: Nashke giga-bakite'win nimbikoninjaanan! = Hey I'm going to rap you with my knuckles!] (NJ, GJ)

LARGE EYES: **mamaangishkiinzhigwe** *vai* have large eyes (RT, NJ, GJ)

LEG HAIR: **miishigaadaan** *ni* leg hair; *pl* **miishigaadaanan** (RT, NJ, GJ)

LIVER: **nikon** /-kon-/ *nid* my liver; *pl* **nikonan** (RT, NJ, GJ)

MY ARMPIT: **indanaaminingwiigan** *nid* my armpit; *loc* **indanaaminingwiiganaang** (NJ)

MY TONGUE: **indenaniw** *nid* my tongue (RT, NJ, GJ)

NASAL CAVITY: **nishangwan** *nid* my nasal cavity (NJ)

ON SOLE OF FOOT: **nagaakizidaaning** *pc* on the sole of the foot (referencing s.t. there) (RT, NJ, GJ)

PALM OF HAND: **nagaakininjaan** *ni* palm of hand; *loc* **nagaakininjaaning** (RT, NJ, GJ)

PALM: **anaamininj** *pc* under the palm (NJ)

PUSH OFF: **mininaawebishkan** *vti* push s.t. off with one's body (as in a boat) (GJ); *also* **niminaawebishkan** (NJ)

SKIN: **ninzhaga'ay /-zhaga'ay-/** *nid* my skin; *also* **nishkatay /-shkatay-/** (RT, NJ, GJ)

SOLE: **anaamizid** *pc* under the foot, underneath (RT, NJ, GJ)

SOLE OF FOOT: **nagaakizid** *ni* sole of the foot; *loc* **nagaakizidaang** (body part) (RT, NJ, GJ)

SPINAL CORD: **nidatagaagwaneyaab /-datagaagwaneyaab-/** *nid* my spinal cord; *pl* **nidatagaagwaneyaabiin** (RT, NJ, GJ)

SPINE: **nidatagaagwan /-datagaagwan-/** *nid* my spine; *pl* **nidatagaagwanan** (RT, NJ, GJ)

STICK OUT FOOT: **zaagizideni** *vai* stick one's foot out (RT, NJ, GJ)

STICK OUT TONGUE AT SOMEONE: **zaagidenaniwetaw** *vta* stick one's tongue out at s.o. (RT, NJ, GJ)

STICK OUT TONGUE REPEATEDLY: **zaasaagidenaniwe** *vai* repeatedly stick out one's tongue (RT, NJ, GJ)

STICKY TONGUE: **nibazagodenaniw** *ni* my sticky tongue (as in a frog) (RT)

STRONG LEGS: **mashkawigaade** *vai* have strong legs (RT)

TIP OF THE TONGUE: **niigaanadenaniw** *ni* tip of the tongue (RT, NJ, GJ)

WRIST: **aanikawiganinjaan** *ni* wrist; *pl* **aanikawiganinjaanan** (RT, NJ); *also* **aanikawiganeninjaan** (GJ)

BOIL:

BREAK BY BOILING: **bigishkigamizige** *vai* break things up by boiling (NJ, GJ)

BREAK SOMEONE UP BY BOILING: **bigishkigamizwi /bigishkigamizw-/** *vta* break s.o. up by boiling (NJ); *also* **bigishkigamizo /bigishkigamizw-/** (GJ)

BREAK SOMETHING UP BY BOILING: **bigishkigamizan** *vti* break s.t. up by boiling (NJ, GJ)

BREAK UP BY BOILING: **bigishkigamide** *vii* breaks up while boiling (NJ, GJ)

HEAD POPS UP REPEATEDLY FROM BOILING: **zaasaagikwezo** *vii* head repeatedly pops up from boiling (RT, NJ, GJ)

HIND END POPS UP FROM BOILING: **zaasaagidiyezo** *vii* hind end repeatedly pops up from boiling (RT, NJ, GJ)

REPEATEDLY POP UP FROM BOILING: **zaasaagigamide** *vii* pops out of boiling water (RT, NJ, GJ)

BONE: DEBONE: **nametegoke** *vai* take bones out in preparation for smoking (RT, NJ, GJ)

BOTTOM:

BOTTOM: **asamiko-** *pv* at the bottom of the lake (RT, NJ, GJ)

BOTTOM DWELLING FISH: **zhagashkaanaamikwesi** *na* bottom dwelling fish; *pl* **zhagashkaanaamikwesiwag** (RT, NJ, GJ)

BOTTOM OF LAKE: **mitaamik** *pc* at the bottom of the lake (RT, NJ, GJ)

BOTTOM SWIM: **asamikozhiwe** *vai* swims on the bottom of the lake (GJ)

FEEL FOR BOTTOM WITH FOOT: **noondakiishkige** *vai* try in vain to feel for bottom with foot (NJ, GJ)

JUMP IN TOUCHING BOTTOM: **debakiise** *vai* jump in and hands or feet touch the bottom (GJ)

MUDDY BOTTOM: **azhashkiiyaamikaa** *vii* be a muddy bottom (as in a lake or pond) (RT)

STABILIZE BOAT: **gichiwakii'ige** *vai* stabilize a boat by bracing on bottom (RT, NJ, GJ)

STAND TOUCHING BOTTOM: **debakiishkige** *vai* stand and touch the bottom (GJ)

SWIM TO BOTTOM: **debakiikozhiwe** *vai* swim down to the bottom (touching), make contact with the bottom (GJ)

THROW IN WATER AND TOUCH BOTTOM: **noondakiise** *vai* throw s.t. in the water that cannot touch bottom (NJ, GJ)

TRY TO REACH BOTTOM UNSUCCESSFULLY: **noondakiikozhiwe** *vai* try to reach the bottom unsuccessfully (NJ, GJ)

BOUNCE: SKIP LAND: **detesabi-booniimagad** *vii* skip landing, land by bouncing on the water (as in duck or float plane) (RT, NJ, GJ)

BOW-LEGGED: STAND BOW-LEGGED: **waagigaadegaabawi** *vai* stand bow-legged (GJ)

BOWL:

BOWL: **wiimbinaagan** *ni* bowl; *pl* **wiimbinaaganan** (GJ)

GHOST BOWL: **andidaagan** *ni* ghost bowl (ES)

BRAID:

BE BRAIDED: **apikaade** *vii* be braided (NJ, GJ)

BRAID: **apikan** *ni* braid, braided tump line, shoulder strap; *pl* **apikanan** (NJ, GJ)

BRAID HAIR: **apikaazh** /apikaaN-/ *vta* braid s.o.'s hair (NJ, GJ)

BRAID SOMETHING: **apikaadan** *vti* braid s.t. (NJ, GJ)

WEAR BRAIDS: **apikaazo** *vai* be braided, wears braids (NJ, GJ)

BRANCH:

LIMB: **bashkwadikwane'ige** *vai* knock branches or limbs off a tree (RT, NJ, GJ)

LIMB WITH AX: **bashkwatigwanezhwi** /bashkwatigwanezhw-/ *vta* limb s.o. (tree) using s.t. (like an ax, knife) (NJ)

TREE BRANCH: **wadikwan** *ni* tree branch, wood knot; *pl* **wadikwanan**; *loc* **wadikwaning** [*example*: Wadikwaning izhiboonii. = He lands on a limb.] (NJ, GJ); *also* **odikon**; *pl* **odikonan** (GJ)

BRAVE: **zoongide'e** *vai* be brave (RT, NJ, GJ)

BREAK:

BLISTER BREAKS: **baaskobiigishkaa** *vii* be a broken blister (RT, NJ, GJ)

BREAK: **bookose** *vii* break (as in a sapling stick being bent for a hide stretching frame) (NJ)

BREAK BY BOILING: **bigishkigamizige** *vai* break things up by boiling (NJ, GJ)

BREAK BY WIND: **bookwaashi** *vai* broken off half way up by the wind (NJ, GJ)

BREAK DAM: **baakibidoon** *vii* break s.t. open (as in a dam) (RT, NJ, GJ)

BREAK IN WIND: **bakweyaandagaasin** *vii* be broken off in the wind (as in a pine bough) (RT, NJ, GJ)

BREAK OFF FOOT OR PAW: **giishkitaa** *vai* breaks off a foot or paw (RT, NJ, GJ)

BREAK SOMEONE: **bakiwebishkaw** break s.o. (as a fish in a net) (RT, NJ, GJ)

BREAK SOMEONE UP BY BOILING: **bigishkigamizwi** /bigishkigamizw-/ *vta* break s.o. up by boiling (NJ); *also* **bigishkigamizo** /bigishkigamizw-/ (GJ)

BREAK SOMETHING UP BY BOILING: **bigishkigamizan** *vti* break s.t. up by boiling (NJ, GJ)

BREAK SURFACE: **bagaskibiigishin** *vai* break the surface of water (as a beaver hitting water with tail) (RT, NJ, GJ)

BREAK THROUGH SNOW: **bajiba'am** *vai* break through and sink down in the snow, as when walking on crusty snow (NJ)

BREAK THROUGH SNOW AND SINK: **bajibashkobii'am** *vai* break through and sink down in the snow, as when walking on slushy snow [*morphological note:* "bii" pertains to water in this snow term] (NJ)

BREAK THROUGH SNOW WHILE DRIVING: **bajibashkobiigibizo** *vai* break through and sink down in the snow, as when driving on slushy snow (NJ)

BREAK UP BY BOILING: **bigishkigamide** *vii* breaks up while boiling (NJ, GJ)

BROKEN SNOWSHOE: **biigwaagime** *vai* have broken snowshoes (lacing or wood) (RT, NJ, GJ)

DAM BREAKS: **baakibiise** *vii* dam breaks open by itself (NJ, GJ)

FREEZE BRITTLE: **mashkawaakogadin** *vii* be frozen and brittle (as in a fresh sapling cut in winter when first brought inside) (NJ)

GROUND CRACKS: **baasikamigishkaa** *vii* ground cracks, be a fault line (RT, NJ, GJ)

SNAP OFF: **bookoganaandan** *vti* break s.t. by applying pressure, snap s.t. off (RT, NJ, GJ)

BREATHE: **bagidanaamo** *vai* breathe, exhale (RT, NJ, GJ)

BREEZE: see WIND

BRIGHT: **bagakaate** *vii* be bright light (RT, NJ, GJ)

BRING: **izhiwijigaazo** *vai* be brought somewhere (RT)

BRITTLE: FREEZE BRITTLE: **mashkawaakogadin** *vii* be frozen and brittle (as in a fresh sapling cut in winter when first brought inside) (NJ)

BROAD:

    BROAD FINS: **mamaangizhigwane** *vai* have broad fins (as in a fish) (RT)

    BROAD WINGS: **mamaanginingwiigwane** *vai* have broad wings (RT)

    BROAD: *see also* WIDE *and* LARGE

BROWN:

    BROWN: **waabijii-ozaawizi** *vai* be the color of deer in the fall and winter (NJ)

    COLOR OF DEER IN FALL: **maanzhi-ozaawizi** *vai* be the color of deer in the fall and winter (NJ)

BRUSH OFF: **bawega'am** *vai* brush off (RT)

BRUSH:

> BE DENSE BRUSH: **zagaakwaa** *vii* be dense, brushy woods, thick brush, thicket (ES, NJ) [*cultural note*: this term can be used as a metaphor for hard times; *example*: Da-zagaakwaa obimaadiziwin giishpin bizindawaasig ookomisan. = Her life will get hard if she doesn't listen to her grandmother.]

> BRUSH TRAIL WIDER: **mangadeyaakwa'ige** *vai* make trail wider (brush out) (NJ, GJ)

BUG: LADY BUG: **manoomini-manidoosh** *na* ladybug; *pl* **manoomini-manidoosh** (NJ, GJ)

BUILD DAM: **giba'iganike** *vai* build a dam (RT, NJ, GJ)

BULLET: **anwi** *ni* bullet, moccasin game bullet, or marble; *pl* **anwiin** (RT, NJ, GJ)

BULRUSH: **gichigamiiwashk** *ni* bulrush; *pl* **gichigamiiwashkoon** (RT, NJ, GJ); *also* **gichigamiiwashkway** *na* bulrush; *pl* **gichigamiiwashkwayag** (RT, NJ, GJ)

BUMPY FACE: **gaashiingwe** *vai* has a bumpy face (as in not having shaved for a while), be partly shaved (RT, NJ, GJ)

BUOY: **akandiikan** *ni* buoy (for net or navigation); *pl* **akandiikanan** (RT, NJ, GJ)

BURN:

> BURN: **jaagizo** *vai* burn (RT, NJ, GJ)

> BURN IN CERTAIN PLACE: **danakone** *vii* burn in certain place (RT, NJ, GJ)

> BURN OUT: **jaagise** *vii* burn out, run out (in reference to community stick pile in moccasin game) (GJ)

> BURN TO CHARCOAL: **akakanzhewaakizo** *vai* burn to a state of charcoal (NJ)

> BURN WELL: **minokone** *vai* burn well (NJ)

BURR: PLANT HOOK: **waagi-wiinizisens** *ni* hook (as in the burr of a plant); *pl* **waagi-wiinizisensan** (RT)

BURROW: TREE BURROW: **mitigwaazh** *ni* burrow or nest inside a tree (RT)

BURY SOMEONE: **ningwa'** /ningwa'w-/ *vta* bury s.o. (RT)

BUS: **bimoomigoodaabaan** *na* bus; *pl* **bimoomigoodaabaanag** (RT, NJ, GJ)

BUSH: EAT OFF THE BUSH: **ningaapoono** *vai* eat off the bush (RT)

BUSHY: **biigwawe** *vai* bushy (RT, NJ, GJ)

BUSY LOOKING: **ondamaabi** *vai* be busy looking around (RT, NJ, GJ)

BUTT:

> BUTT FLAP: **badagwanidiyegoojigan** *ni* butt flap; *pl* **badagwanidiyegoojiganan** (RT, NJ, GJ)
>
> BUTT STICKS OUT: **zaagidiyeshin** *vai* have one's butt sticking out (RT, NJ, GJ)
>
> COVER ONE'S HIND END: **badagwanidiye'o** *vai* cover one's hind end (RT, NJ, GJ)
>
> RED BUTT: **miskodiye** *vai* have a red butt (RT, NJ, GJ)

BUTTERFLY:

> BUTTERFULY: **memengwaa** *na* butterfly, swallowtail; *pl* **memengwaag** (RT, NJ, GJ)
>
> GOLDEN BUTTERLY: **ozaawi-memengwaa** *na* butterfly, tiger swallowtail; *pl* **ozaawi-memengwaag** (RT, NJ, GJ)

BUTTON:

> BUTTON: **zagaakwa'on** *na* button; *pl* **zagaakwa'onag** (NJ, RT, GJ); *also* **gibadoonh**; *pl* **gibadoonyag** (JC)
>
> BUTTON SELF UP: **zagaakwa'odizo** *vai* button one's self up (RT, NJ, GJ)
>
> BUTTON SOMEONE UP: **zagaakwa'** /**zagaakwa'w-**/ *vta* button s.o. up (JC)
>
> BUTTON SPINNER: **zagaakwa'oni-gizhibaayabiigibijigan** *ni* button spinner; *pl* **zagaakwa'oni-gizhibaayabiigibijiganan** (RT, NJ, GJ)

CACHE: **na'enimo** *vai* cache, store food (RT, NJ, GJ)

CACTUS: **bajiishkibag** *ni* cactus; *pl* **bajiishkibagoon** (RT)

CALLUS: **gipagazhaan** *ni* callus, thick skin (RT, NJ, GJ)

CALM AFTER RAIN: **anwaabiisaa** *vii* be a calm after raining (NJ, GJ)

CAMOFLAUGE: **wiijinaagozi** *vai* be camoflauged (RT, NJ, GJ)

CANDY: TREE CANDY: **oziban** *ni* tree candy, the consumable part of inner tree bark (NJ) [*cultural note*: sweet, sticky substance in the inner bark (typically of poplar) was highly prized and consumed as a kind of candy]

CANINE:

> CANINE TOOTH: **oshkiinzhigwaabid** *ni* canine tooth; *pl* **oshkiinzhigwaabidan** (RT)
>
> HAVE CANINE TOOTH: **oshkiinzhigwaabide** *vai* have canine teeth (RT)

CANOE:

ANCHOR: **boonakajigan** *ni* boat anchor; *pl* **boonakajiganan** (NJ, GJ)

ANCHOR: **boonikanjigan** *ni* anchor; *pl* **boonikanjiganan** (RT)

CANOE MAT: **apishkaamon** *ni* mat for the bottom of a canoe; *pl* **apishkaamonan** (RT, NJ, GJ)

CAPSIZE: **gwanabise** *vii* capsize (RT, NJ, GJ)

CAPSIZE FROM WIND: **gwanabaashi** *vai* capsize from wind (NJ, GJ)

CAPSIZE IN RAPIDS: **gwanabaabago** *vai* capsize in rapids (NJ, GJ)

EMPTY CANOE: **agwaanaaso** *vai* empty the canoe (RT, NJ, GJ)

GO UPSTREAM: **ogidaajiwanwe'o** *vai* go upstream (NJ, GJ)

MAKE NOISE PADDLING: **debweweshka'am** *vai* make noise paddling or poling from reeds sliding on a canoe (RT, NJ, GJ)

MAKE NOISE PADDLING AWAY: **animweweshka'am** *vai2* paddle or pole away making noise from reeds brushing against canoe (RT, NJ, GJ)

MAKE NOISE PADDLING BY: **bimweweshka'am** *vai2* make noise while paddling or poling by from reeds brushing against canoe (NJ, GJ)

MAKE SOMEONE DISEMBARK: **agwaashim** *vta* take s.o. out of the canoe (RT, NJ, GJ)

METAL CANOE: **ginwaabiko-jiimaan** *ni* metal boat; *pl* **ginwaabiko-jiimaanan** (RT, NJ, GJ)

PADDLE DOWNSTREAM: **niisaajiwane'aadage** *vai* go downstream (GJ); *also* **niisaajiwanwe'aadage** (NJ)

PADDLE INTO WAVES: **onjishkawa'o** *vai* paddle straight into waves (NJ, GJ)

PADDLE TO CERTAIN PLACE: **inaakogomo** *vai* paddle to certain place (RT, NJ, GJ)

PADDLE TO CERTAIN PLACE: **inakwazhiwe** *vai* paddle to a certain place (RT, NJ, GJ)

PADDLE WITH WIND: **naamiwana'o** *vai* paddle with the wind (NJ)

PROPEL: **naamiwana'ogo** *vai* be propelled faster by wind and waves (in watercaft) (NJ)

PORTAGE: **biminige** *vai* portage a canoe (RT, NJ, GJ)

PUSH OFF: **mininaawebishkan** *vti* push s.t. off with one's body (as in a boat) (GJ); *also* **niminaawebishkan** (NJ)

PUSH OFF FROM GROUND: **mininaawekii'o** *vai* push off while touching the ground (GJ); *also* **niminaawekii'o** (NJ)

SHOOT RAPIDS: **niishiboono** *vai* shoot rapids (NJ, GJ)

SOUND OF PADDLING THROUGH REEDS: **bimweweshka'am** *vai2* make noise while paddling or poling from reeds brushing against canoe (NJ, GJ)

STABILIZE (BRACE): **gichiwakii'ige** *vai* stabilize a boat by bracing on bottom (RT, NJ, GJ)

STABILIZE (CONTROL): **aadikwe'ige** *vai* stabilize, control (as in a paddle or pole on the bottom) (GJ)

SWITCH SIDES PADDLING: **gwekabowe** *vai* switch sides paddling (RT, NJ, GJ)

TAKE OFF FROM SHORE: **mininaawa'o** *vai* take off from shore (as in a boat, or swimming) (GJ); *also* **niminaawa'o** (NJ, RT)

UNABLE TO KEEP CANOE STRAIGHT: **wawaawashkakozhiwe** *vai* be unable to keep a canoe straight (RT, NJ, GJ)

UNLOAD AND BRING INLAND: **gopimine** *vai* unload harvest from canoe and bring inland (NJ, GJ)

CAPITAL:

CAPITAL LETTER: **mangibii'igan** *ni* capital letter; *pl* **mangibii'iganan** (JC)

WRITE IN ALL CAPITAL LETTERS: **mangibii'ige** *vai* write in all capital letters (JC)

CAPSIZE:

CAPSIZE: **gwanabise** *vii* capsize (RT, NJ, GJ)

CAPSIZE FROM WIND: **gwanabaashi** *vai* capsize from wind (NJ, GJ)

CAPSIZE IN RAPIDS: **gwanabaabago** *vai* capsize in rapids (NJ, GJ)

CAR:

CAR HORN: **odaabaan noondaagamo'ind** *vta-prt* car horn (NJ, GJ)

CAR JACK: **ombaakwa'igan** *ni*  something used to lift things, crutch, jack (GJ)

CARD: ALPHABET ACTIVITY CARD: **ikidowinensi-mazina'iganens** *ni* alphabet activity card; *pl* **ikidowinensi-mazina'iganensan** (RT)

CARETAKE: WATCH OVER: **ganawaabandamaazo** *vai* watch over, caretake things (RT, NJ, GJ)

CARNIVORE: **wiiyaasanjige** *vai* be a carnivore (RT, NJ, GJ)

CARRY INLAND: **gopiwidoon** *vti* carry s.t. inland (NJ, GJ)

CATCH:

> CATCH SOMEONE: **babaa-debam** *vta* go around catching s.o. (as in a bird catching bugs) (RT)
>
> CATCH SOMEONE: **debam** *vta* catch s.o. in the mouth (RT)
>
> CATCH WITH MOUTH: **nakwepwaa' /nakwepwaa'w-/** *vta* catch s.o. with one's mouth (RT)
>
> CATCH WITH TONGUE: **nakwedenaniwem** *vta* catch s.o. with long, sticky tongue (as in a frog) (RT)
>
> CAUGHT: **nagwaazo** *vai* get caught (in snare) (LW)
>
> CAUGHT BY LEG: **zagigaadebizo** *vai* be flung up, caught by the leg (as a rabbit in a tree spring-noose trap) (NJ)
>
> CAUGHT IN A NET: **biinda'agoo** *vai* get caught in a net (RT, NJ, GJ); *also* **biinda'am** (RT); *also* **biinda'ozo** (LW); *also* **bida'am** (NJ)
>
> CAUGHT IN BAD WEATHER: **bangisinamaa** *vai* caught in inclement weather (RT, NJ, GJ)
>
> CAUGHT IN RAIN: **bangibiisaanishi** *vai* be caught in a light rain (RT, NJ, GJ)
>
> GRAB: **debibizh /debibiN-/** *vta* catch, grab, or grasp s.o. (RT, NJ, GJ)

CATTAIL:

> CATTAIL: **apakweshkway** *na* cattail mat; cattail; *pl* **apakweshkwayag**; *also* **nabagashk**; *pl* **nabagashkoon** (NJ)
>
> CATTAIL ROOT: **washkwadab** *na* cattail root; *pl* **washkwadabiig** (RT, NJ, GJ)

CAUGHT: *see* CATCH

CAVATAAPI: **biimisko-onagizhiikaanens** *ni* cavataapi pasta, *pl* **biimisko-onagizhiikaanensan** (RT, NJ, GJ)

CEDAR BARK: **giizhikanagek** *na* cedar bark; *pl* **giizhikanagekwag** (RT, NJ, GJ)

CHAINSAW FILE: **zisiboojiganens** *ni* chainsaw sharpening file; *pl* **zisiboojiganensan** (GJ)

CHALLENGE: **zanagendaagwad** *vii* be challenging (NJ)

CHANGE:

> CHANGE APPEARANCE: **aanjinaagwad** *vii* change appearance, look different (RT, NJ, GJ)
>
> DIET CHANGES: **aandanjige** *vai* change diet (RT, NJ, GJ)
>
> LIGHT CHANGES: **aandaate** *vii* light changes (RT, NJ, GJ)

SEASON CHANGES: **aandakiiwin** *ni* changing season; *pl* **aandakiiwinan** (RT, NJ)

CHASE:

CHASE OFF: **asho'ige** *vai* accidentally chase things off (GJ); *also* **ashwa'ige** (NJ); *also* **ozha'ige** (NJ); *also* **ashwaa'ige** (GJ)

CHASE SOMEONE AWAY: **ozha'wi** /ozha'w-/ *vta* chase s.o. away (NJ)

CHEEK:

BIG CHEEKS: **mamaanginowe** *vai* have big cheeks (RT)

OPERCULUM: **onawaangigan** *nid* fish cheek, operculum; *pl* **onawaangiganan** (RT, NJ, GJ)

CHEESE: **chi-doodooshaaboo** *ni* cheese (RT); *also* **doodooshaaboowi-miijim** *ni* cheese (EO)

CHERRY TREE: **ookweminaatig** *na* cherry tree; *pl* **ookweminaatigoog** (RT)

CHEST:

BACK OR CHEST HAIR: **miishaawiganaan** *ni* back or chest hair; *pl* **miishaawiganaanan** (RT, NJ, GJ)

CHEST HAIR: **miishaakiganaan** *ni* chest hair; *pl* **miishaakiganaanan** (RT, NJ, GJ)

HAIRY CHEST: **miishaakigan** *ni* hairy chest *pl* **miishaakiganan** (RT, NJ, GJ)

HAVE HAIRY CHEST: **miishaakigane** *vai* have a hairy chest (RT, NJ, GJ)

PERSON WITH HAIRY CHEST: **miishaakiganesi** *na* s.o. with a hairy chest; *pl* **miishaakiganesiwag** (RT, NJ, GJ)

CHEW:

CHEW: **zhaashaagwanjige** *vai* chew, eat by chewing (RT)

HEARD CHEWING: **madwenjige** *vai* be heard chewing (RT, NJ, GJ)

HEARD CHEWING FROM DISTANCE: **debwewenjige** *vai* be heard chewing from a distance (RT, NJ, GJ)

CHIEF LAKE: **Akwa'wewin** *place* Chief Lake, Wisconsin (JS)

CHILD: VERBALLY ATTACK IN DEFENSE OF CHILD: **onzonge** *vai* verbally attack people based on what your child told you [*example*: Gego onzongeken! = Don't (verbally) attack people based on what your child has come and told you! *cultural note*: It is considered inadvisable to do this because of possible spiritual consequences.

Children need to fend for themselves and take responsibility for their actions.] (RT, NJ, GJ)

CHIME: BE PLEASANT SOUND OF CHIMES: **minweweyaabikaasin** *vii* good sound of metal (as in wind chimes) [*example*: Minweweyaabikaasinoon. = The (wind chimes) sound good.] (NJ)

CHIN: DIMPLED CHIN: **basiindaamikane** *vai* have a dimpled chin (RT, NJ, GJ)

CHISEL: ICE CHISEL: **eshkan** *ni* ice chisel; *pl* **eshkanan** (RT, NJ, GJ)

CHOKE SOMEONE: **gibinewen** *vta* choke s.o. (RT, NJ, GJ)

CHOP:

CHOP: **biisiga'igaade** *vii* be chopped into small pieces (as in wood) (NJ, GJ)

CHOP A SLIT: **beshiga'an** *vti* chop a slit in s.t. (as in bark) (RT, NJ, GJ)

CHURN:

CHURN: **ditibaakowebiigise** *vai* roll, churn (log, or stick-like object) (RT, NJ, GJ)

SNARLING WATER: **gichi-babiikwajiwan** *vii* the water is really snarling (RT, NJ, GJ)

CIRCLE:

CUT IN CIRCLE: **waanizhaabii** *vai* cut hide or leather in a circular fashion (as in making snowshoe lacing) (NJ, GJ)

CUT SOMEONE IN CIRCLE: **waanizhwi /waanizhw-/** *vta* cut s.o. in a circular fashion (as in making snowshoe lacing) (NJ)

ENCIRCLING POLE: **waawiyeyaabijigan** *ni* encircling pole of a shake-tent; *pl* **waawiyeyaabijiganan** (GJ)

GROW IN RINGS: **waawiyaagishin** *vai* grow in rings (RT, NJ, GJ)

CLASP:

CLASP: **minjiminigaade** *vii* adhere, attach, clasp (RT)

SAFETY CLASP: **minjimaakwa'iganens** *ni* spring safety clasp (as on a conibear trap); *pl* **minjimaakwa'iganensan** (NJ)

TRIGGER CLASP: **niisinigan** *ni* trigger clasp (as on a conibear trap); *pl* **niisiniganan** (NJ)

CLAW:

HAVE STRONG CLAWS: **mashkawishkanzii** *vai* have strong claws (RT)

LONG CLAWS: **ginwaashkanzhiiwi** *vai* have long claws or fingernails (RT, NJ, GJ)

SHARP CLAWS: **gagiiniganzhii** *vai* have sharp claws (RT)
STRONG CLAW: **mashkawishkanzh** *na* strong claw; *pl*
**mashkawishkanzhiig** (RT)

CLAY:

CLAY: **waabigan** *na* clay (RT, NJ, GJ)
CLAY POT: **waabigani-akik** *na* clay pot; *pl* **waabigani-akikoog**;
*loc* **waabigani-akikong** (RT)
WHITE CLAY: **waabaabigan** *na* white or gray clay (NJ)

CLEAN:

CLEAN: **biinichigemagad** *vii* it cleans (RT, NJ, GJ)
CLEAN WATER: **biinaagamin** *vii* be clean water (RT, NJ, GJ)
SKELETON LIES PICKED CLEAN: **zhiigooganeshin** vai skeleton
lies on the ground picked clean (RT, NJ, GJ)

CLEAR:

BE CLEAR WATER: **onaagamin** *vii* clear water (NJ, GJ); *also*
**waakaagamin** *vii* be clear water, be a clear lake (RT, NJ, GJ)
CLEAR CUT: **bashkoga'ige** *vai* make a clear cut, log by cutting all
trees in an area (RT, NJ, GJ)
HEAR CLEARLY: **bagakitam** *vai* hear clearly (NJ)
SEE CLEARLY: **bagakaabi** *vai* see clearly (RT, NJ, GJ)
SHARP VISION: **na'aabi** *vai* see clearly, have sharp vision (RT)

CLIMB: **babaamaandawe** *vai* climb around (RT)
CLING TO SOMEONE: **minjimin** *vta* cling to s.o., hold onto s.o. (RT)
CLIP:

CUT FINGERNAIL: **giishkiganzhiizhige** *vai* cut fingernails or
toenails (RT, NJ, GJ)
FINGERNAIL CLIPPER: **giishkiganzhiizhiganaabikoons** *ni*
fingernail clipper; *pl* **giishkiganzhiizhiganaabikoonsan** (RT,
NJ, GJ)

CLOSE:

BE CLOSED: **giba'igaade** *vii* be closed (as in a business or store)
(RT, NJ, GJ)
BITE SHUT: **gashkaabikandan** *vti* bite s.t. shut (RT, NJ, GJ)
CLOSE BY HAND: **gibaabikinan** *vti* close s.t. with one's hand (as
in damper on a stove) (RT, NJ, GJ)
CLOSE DOOR: **gibinde'ige** *vai* close the door (as in a cloth door)
(RT, NJ, GJ)
CLOSE EYES: **basangwaabi** *vai* close one's eyes (RT, NJ, GJ)

CLOSE FOR SOMEONE: **gibinde'amaw** *vta* close (s.t.) for s.o. (RT, NJ, GJ)

CLOSE SOMETHING (SHEET-LIKE): **gibaakiiginan** *vti* close s.t. (paper or sheet-like) (RT, NJ, GJ)

CLOSE SOMETHING (CLOTH-LIKE): **gibinde'an** *vta* close s.t. (cloth-like, such as a wigwam door) (RT, NJ, GJ)

PATCH SOMETHING: **giba'an** *vti* patch s.t., close s.t. (RT, NJ, GJ)

SPRING SHUT: **gashkaagise** *vii* spring closed (RT, NJ, GJ)

SQUEEZE SHUT (HAND): **gashkaabikinan** *vti* squeeze s.t. shut with one's hand (RT, NJ, GJ)

SQUEEZE SHUT (OBJECT): **gibaabikibidoon** *vti* squeeze s.t. shut (by using s.t.) (RT, NJ, GJ)

SQUEEZE SHUT (TOOL): **gashkaabikada'an** *vti* squeeze s.t. shut with a tool (RT, NJ, GJ)

CLOTH:

CLOSE SOMETHING (CLOTH-LIKE): **gibinde'an** *vta* close s.t. (cloth-like, such as a lodge door) (RT, NJ, GJ)

CLOTH WIGWAM DOOR: **gibinde'igan** *ni* cloth lodge door; *pl* **gibinde'iganan** (NJ)

WRING OUT CLOTH OR HIDE: **ziiniskobiiga'an** *vti* wring out cloth or hide (RT, NJ, GJ)

CLOTHESLINE: **agoojiganeyaab** *ni* clothesline; *pl* **agoojiganeyaabiin** (RT, NJ, GJ)

CLOUD:

LONE CLOUD: **Minisinaanakwad** *name* Lone Cloud (GJ)

LONE CLOUD: **minisinaanakwad** *vii* be a solitary cloud (RT, NJ, GJ); *also* **minisinaanakwagoode** *vii* be a lone cloud (RT, NJ, GJ)

CLUB: **bikwaakwadwaanawe** *vai* have clubs (as in a dinosaur) (NJ)

COLD:

COLD: **agigokaawin** *ni* headcold (RT, NJ, GJ)

COLD WIND: **dakaanimad** *vii* be a cold wind (RT, NJ, GJ)

HAVE COLD: **agikokaa** *vai* have a headcold (RT, NJ, GJ)

SENSITIVE TO COLD: **wakewaji** *vai* be sensitive to cold, can't take the cold (RT, NJ, GJ)

WET AND COLD: **dakibiigaji** *vai* be cold from being wet (rained on, sweaty) (NJ, GJ)

COLOR:

BLUE WATER: **ozhaawashkwaagamin** *vii* be blue (water) (NJ, GJ)

BROWN: **waabijii-ozaawizi** *vai* be the color of deer in the fall and winter (NJ)

COLOR OF DEER IN FALL: **maanzhi-ozaawizi** *vai* be the color of deer in the fall and winter (NJ)

COLOR OF DEER IN SUMMER: **bagaki-ozaawizi** *vai* be the color of deer in the spring and summer (NJ)

GOLDEN BUTTERLY: **ozaawi-memengwaa** *na* butterfly, tiger swallowtail; *pl* **ozaawi-memengwaag** (RT, NJ, GJ)

GRASS TURNS GOLD: **ozaawaashkosiwe** *vii* grass turns golden (RT)

HAVE SILVER-HAIRED BACK: **waabikweyaawigane** *vai* have a silver-colored hairy back (RT, NJ, GJ)

PINK: **maazhi-miskozi** *vai* be pink (NJ); *also* **oginii-waabigoni-miskozi** *vai* be pink (NJ, GJ); *also* **oginii-waabigoni-miskozi** (RT)

SILVER-BACK GORILLA: **wayaabikweyaawiganed** *vai-prt* silver-back gorilla; *pl* **wayaabikweyaawiganejig** (RT, NJ, GJ)

WHITE SIDE SHOWS: **waasiingwewebinige** *vai* the white side shows (RT, NJ, GJ)

WHITE WATER: **waabishkaagamin** *vii* be white (water) (NJ, GJ)

COMBINE: **mami'igewidaabaan** *na* combine (mechanized harvesting machine); *pl* **mami'igewidaabaanag** (RT)

COME:

COME AND TELL: **biidaajimo** *vai* come tell about things (RT, NJ, GJ)

COME AND TELL SOMETHING: **biidaadodan** *vti* come and tell about s.t. (RT, NJ, GJ)

COME PADDLING: **biidakwazhiwe** *vai* come paddling (RT, NJ, GJ)

COMMA: **nenoogibii'igan** *ni* comma (,); *pl* **nenoogibii'iganan** (JC)

CONCAVE: HANG LOW INVERTED: **wiimbaagishkoode** *vii* hang low inverted (concave) (GJ)

CONCHIGLIETTE: **esikaanens** *na* conchigliette pasta, *pl* **esikaanensag** (RT, NJ, GJ)

CONIBEAR: **gashkaagise-wanii'igan** *ni* conibear; *pl* **gashkaagise-wanii'iganan** (NJ, GJ)

CONIFER:

CONIFER SOUNDS PLEASANT IN WIND: **minweweyaandagaashi** *vai* pleasant sound of an evergreen tree in the wind (NJ)

EVERGREEN: **zhingob** *na* balsam, evergreen; *pl* **zhingobiig** (RT, NJ, GJ)

LIMB SAPLING: **jiishaandawe'ige** *vai* limb small trees (as in cleaning saplings for use as lodge poles) (NJ)

PINE NEEDLE: **zhingwaakwaandag** *na* pine needle; *pl* **zhingwaakwaandag** (RT, **zhinoodaagan** *ni* net cord; *pl* **zhinoodaaganan** (NJ, GJ)

PLEASANT SOUND OF CONIFER IN WIND: **minweweyaandagaasin** *vii* pleasant sound of evergreen boughs in the wind (NJ)

CONSTELLATION: ORION'S BELT: **Aadwaa'amoog** *name* Orion's Belt (constellation) (GJ)

CONSUME: **gadaanaangwe** *vai* consume everything (NJ); *also* **gidaanawe** (RT)

CONTRIBUTE:

ADD TO SOMETHING: **dagosidoon** *vti* contribute to s.t., add s.t. in (RT, NJ, GJ)

ADD: **dagosijige** *vai* contribute, add to things (RT, NJ, GJ)

CONTRIBUTOR: **degosijiged** *na-prt* contributor; *pl* **degosijigejig** (RT, NJ, GJ)

COOK: **giizhizo** *vai* be cooked, be done cooking (RT)

COOKIE CUTTER: **mamizhiganaabik** *ni* cookie cutters; *pl* **mamizhiganaabikoon** (RT, NJ, GJ)

COOL: **dakaagamisin** *vii* it cools (as in a liquid) (RT); *also* **dakigamisin** *vii* it cools (as in a liquid) (NJ)

COOPERATION: **wiidookodaadiwin** *ni* cooperation (RT, NJ, GJ)

CORRECT: **gwayakobidoon** *vti* do s.t. right (NJ)

COUGAR: **mishi-bizhii** *na* cougar; *pl* **mishi-bizhiig** (NJ); *also* **mishi-bizhiw** (RT)

COUNTING STICK: **bima'igan** *ni* counting stick for moccasin game; *pl* **bima'iganan** (GJ)

COVER:

COVER: **apakwe** *vai* cover things, roof (RT, NJ, GJ)

COVER: **apiigisin** *vii* lay as a protective layer (as in a trivet or pot holder) (RT, NJ, GJ)

COVER ONE'S EARS: **badagwanitawage'o** *vai* cover one's ears (RT, NJ, GJ)

COVER ONE'S EYES: **badagwanishkiinzhigwe'o** *vai* cover one's eyes (RT, NJ, GJ)

COVER ONE'S HIND END: **badagwanidiye'o** *vai* cover one's hind end (RT, NJ, GJ)

COVER SOMETHING: **agwana'an** *vti* cover s.t. (RT, NJ, GJ)

COVERED: **debashkine** *vai* be covered; *also* fit inside (NJ)

COVERING: **apakwaan** *ni* covering; *pl* **apakwaanan** (GJ)

COYOTE: **wiisagi-ma'iingan** *na* coyote; *pl* **wiisagi-ma'iinganag** (RT); *also* **ma'iingaans** (TS)

CRAP: *see* DEFECATE; *see also* FECES

CRAPPIE: **gidagwadaashi** *na* crappie (KP); *pl* **gidagwadaashiwag**; *also* **ezhegamoons** (GJ); *pl* **ezhegamoonsag**; *also* **odazhegamoons** (NJ); *pl* **odazhegamoonsag**

CRAWL: **bimoode** *vai* slither, crawl (RT, NJ, GJ)

CREASE:

    CREASE: **inaabiigisin** *vii* be a line or crease in a certain way (NJ)

    CREASE: **enaabiigising** *vii-prt* line, crease; *pl* **enaabiigisingin** (NJ)

CRICKET: **jiiga'oweshiinh** *na* cricket; *pl* **jiiga'oweshiinyag** (RT, GJ); *also* **oojiigaweshiinh**; *pl* **oojiigaweshiinyag** (NJ)

CROSS:

    CROSS LINE: **gaashipoobizo** *vai* cross the line (as in driving out of lane), or miss a turnoff (as in driving) [*example*: Gigaashipoobizomin. = We missed the turn off.] (NJ, GJ)

    CROSS POLE: **bimidaakobijigan** *ni* cross pole; *pl* **bimidaakobijiganan** (NJ, GJ)

    CROSS ROAD: **aazhookana** *ni* cross road, intersection; *loc* **aazhookanaang** (RT, NJ, GJ)

CROUCH:

    CROUCH TO GROUND: **zhagashkii** *vai* crouch down to ground (RT, NJ, GJ); *also* **zhamashkii** *vai* crouch down to ground (RT, NJ, GJ)

    GRASS DANCE: **zhamashkishimo** *vai* do the grass dance (crouch while dancing) (crouch dance) (GJ)

    SNEAK CROUCHED: **gaagiimaazi** *vai* sneak up in a crouched position (NJ, GJ)

CROWD:

    BE CROWDED: **miiwishkodaadimagad** *vii* be crowded (RT)

GROW CROWDED: **miiwishkodaadigin** *vii* grow crowded, grow close together (RT)

CRUTCH:

CRUTCH: **ishpaakwa'igan** *ni* crutch, support, jack; *pl* **ishpaakwa'iganan** (NJ, GJ); *also* **ombaakwa'igan** (GJ)

CRUTCH POLE: **ziigaakwa'igan** *ni* crutch pole (GJ)

CRY TO SLEEP: **nibewemo** *vai* cry one's self to sleep (AG)

CURL:

CURL UP (COIL): **waawiyaagishin** *vai* curl up (as does a snake) (RT, NJ, GJ)

CURL UP (FETAL): **gichiwashkishin** *vai* curls up (as into fetal position) (RT, NJ); *also* be stuck in the grass or mud (as when harvesting wild rice) (GJ)

CURR: MALE DOG, HORSE, WOLF: **naabesim** *na* male dog, male horse, male wolf; *pl* **naabesimag** (RT, NJ, GJ)

CURRENT:

CURRENT CUTS ICE: **bagonezigwaa** *vii* current cuts a hole in ice (RT, NJ, GJ); *also* **bagonezigojiwan** (GJ); *also* **bookizigwajiwan** (GJ)

FAST CURRENT: **ojaanimijiwan** *vii* be a fast current (NJ, GJ)

GO DOWNSTREAM: **niisaajiwane'aadage** *vai* go downstream (GJ); *also* **niisaajiwanwe'aadage** (NJ); *also* **niisaajiwane'o** *vai* go downstream (GJ); *also* **niisaajiwanwe'o** (NJ)

GO DOWNSTREAM ON TOP OF WATER: **niisaajiwaneweyaaboono** *vai* go downstream on top of the water (GJ); *also* **niisaajiwanweweyaabono** (NJ)

GO UPSTREAM: **ogidaajiwanwe'o** *vai* go upstream (NJ, GJ)

SWIM UPSTREAM: **ogiidaajiwane'o** *vai* swim upstream (GJ); *also* **ogiidaajiwanwe'o** (NJ); *also* **ogiidaajiwaneyaadagwe** (GJ); *also* **ogiidaajiwanweyaadagwe** (NJ)

TAKE OFF IN CURRENT: **maajiiyaaboode** *vii* take off in a current (NJ, GJ)

TAKE OFF ON WATER IN CURRENT: **maajiiyaabagonde** *vii* take off on top of the water in a current (NJ, GJ)

CURRENT: *see also* DOWNSTREAM; *see also* FLOW

CURVE SOMETHING: **waaginan** *vti* curve s.t., bend s.t. (RT, NJ, GJ)

CUT:

BITE OFF PART OF SELF: **giishkandizo** *vai* bite off a part of oneself (RT, NJ, GJ)

CLEAR CUT: **bashkoga'ige** *vai* make a clear cut, log by cutting all trees in an area (RT, NJ, GJ)

COMBINE: **giishkashkosiwewidaabaan** *na* combine (mechanized harvesting machine); *pl* **giishkashkosiwewidaabaanag** (RT)

COOKIE CUTTER: **mamizhiganaabik** *ni* cookie cutters; *pl* **mamizhiganaabikoon** (RT, NJ, GJ)

CUT DOWN TO OPEN SPOT: **madaabiiga'ige** *vai* cut it right down to an open spot (RT, NJ, GJ)

CUT FINGERNAIL: **giishkiganzhiizhige** *vai* cut fingernails or toenails (RT, NJ, GJ)

CUT FISH: **baanizhaawe** *vai* cut fish into strips, fillet (RT, NJ, GJ)

CUT IN CIRCLE: **waanizhaabii** *vai* cut hide or leather in a circular fashion (as in making snowshoe lacing) (NJ, GJ)

CUT IN HALF: **bookozhigaazo** *vai* be cut in half (NJ)

CUT LENGTHWISE: **daashkizhigaazo** *vai* be cut in half lengthwise, be slit (GJ)

CUT OFF WITH TEETH: **giishkandan** *vti* cut s.t. off with one's teeth (RT)

CUT SOMEONE IN CIRCLE: **waanizhwi** /**waanizhw-**/ *vta* cut s.o. in a circular fashion (as in making snowshoe lacing) (NJ)

CUT SOMETHING INTO STRIPS: **naanigaakozhigan** *vti* cut s.t. into strips (RT, NJ, GJ)

CUT WIDE STRIPS: **mangadezhigaade** *vii* cut in wide strips (RT, NJ, GJ)

CUT WITH TEETH: **giishkanjige** *vai* cut with one's teeth (RT)

EXPOSED: **madaabiiga'igaazo** *vai* be exposed (from having trees are cut) (RT, NJ, GJ)

LIMB BY CUTTING: **jiishaakwa'ige** *vai* cut limbs off a tree (GJ); *also* scrape a hide (NJ)

LIMB SOMEONE: **giishkadikwane'wi** /**giishkadikwane'w-**/ *vta* limb s.o. (tree) using s.t. (ax, knife, or saw) (NJ)

LIMB SOMEONE (SAPLING): **jiishaanda'wi** /**jiishaanda'w-**/ *vta* limb small tree (as in cleaning saplings for use as lodge poles) (NJ)

MAKE SOMEONE SMOOTH BY CUTTING: **zhooshkwaakozhwi** /**zhooshkwaakozhw-**/ *vta* cut s.o. smooth using s.t. (knife), as in trimming the knots off a sapling, making it smooth (NJ)

CUTE: **wawiyazh** *pc* cute, fun, just for fun [*example*: Wawiyazh ikido. = He is just saying it for fun.] (NJ, GJ)

CYCLE: LIFE CYCLE: **eni-onji-bimaadak** *vii-prt* life cycle (RT)

DAM:

> BEAVER DAM: **okonim** *ni* beaver dam; *pl* **okoniman**; *loc* **okoniming** (NJ)
>
> BREAK DAM: **baakibidoon** *vii* break s.t. open (as in a dam) (RT, NJ, GJ)
>
> BUILD DAM: **giba'iganike** *vai* build a dam (RT, NJ, GJ)
>
> DAM BREAKS: **baakibiise** *vii* dam breaks open by itself (NJ, GJ)
>
> DAM OPENS: **baakibiishkaa** *vii* be an opening (as in a dam opening) (NJ, GJ)
>
> LOOSEN DAM: **baakibiigibidoon** *vti* loosen dam to make partial leak (not break entirely) [*cultural note*: this is a common technique for setting beaver traps] (NJ, GJ)
>
> REPAIR DAM: **bi-andogiba'ige** *vai* come to repair dam (as in a beaver) (NJ, GJ)

DAMP: **dipaabaawe** *vii* get damp (RT, NJ, GJ)

DANCE:

> DANCE: **ando-zhooshkozideshimo** *vai* go dancing (NJ, GJ)
>
> DANCE SIDEWAYS: **bimijizideshimo** *vai* dance sideways (NJ, GJ)
>
> DANCE SNEAK-UP: **gaagiimaashimo** *vai* dance the sneak-up (GJ)
>
> GRASS DANCE: **zhamashkishimo** *vai* do the grass dance (crouch while dancing) (GJ)
>
> NICE SOUNDING FEET: **mino-zhooshkozideshimo** *vai* have nice sounding feet (as in a tap dancer) (NJ, GJ)

DANGER:

> BE CONSIDERED DANGEROUS: **naniizaanendaagwad** *vii* be considered dangerous (RT, NJ, GJ)
>
> BE DANGEROUS: **naniizaanad** *vii* be unsafe, dangerous (RT, NJ, GJ)
>
> BE DANGEROUS: **naniizaanizi** *vai* be dangerous (RT, NJ, GJ)
>
> HAVE DANGEROUS DISPOSITION: **nanaaniizaanizi** *vai* have a dangerous disposition (RT, NJ, GJ)

DARK:

> DARK ON ONE SIDE: **nabanemakadeyaaso** *vai* be dark on one side from sun (as in suntanned) (NJ, GJ)
>
> DARK SIDE SHOWS: **makadewiingwebinige** *vai* the dark side shows (as in bagese game) (GJ)

DART WHILE SWIMMING: **maajiiyaadagaa** *vai* dart while swimming, quickly take off swimming (RT)

DATE: BE A CERTAIN YEAR: **gikinoonowagad** *vii* be a certain year (as in telling specific date) (NJ)

DAY:

> LONG DAY: **ginoo-giizhigad** *vii* be a long day (RT, NJ, GJ)
>
> LONG DAY: **ginwaasige** *vai* sun shines a long time, be a long day (as in a long summer day) (RT)
>
> SHORT DAY: **dako-giizhigad** *vii* be a short day (RT, NJ, GJ)
>
> SHORT DAY: **dakwaasige** *vai* be short day, sun shines for a short period of time (as in short winter days) (RT)

DEAD TREE: **mishiiwaatigowi** *vai* be a dry (dead) tree (RT, NJ, GJ)

DEAF: **gagiibishe** *vii* be deaf (RT, NJ, GJ)

DEATH THROES: **giiwine** *vai* be in one's death throes (ES)

DECAY: **babinezi** *vai* decay (as in a tree becoming rotten) (GJ)

DECOY: **okeyaw** *na* decoy; *pl* **okeyawag** (KP)

DEEP:

> DEEP: **akwiindimaa** *vii* be a certain depth (water) (RT, NJ, GJ)
>
> DEEP PLACE: **endazhi-diimiiyaamagak** *vii-prt* deep places (as in large bodies of water) (RT, NJ, GJ)
>
> DEEP WATER: **ginwiindimaa** *vii* be deep water (RT, NJ, GJ)
>
> SET NET IN DEEP WATER: **ginwiindimaasabii** *vai* set net in deep water (GJ, NJ)

DEER:

> COLOR OF DEER IN FALL: **maanzhi-ozaawizi** *vai* be the color of deer in the fall and winter (NJ); *also* **waabijii-ozaawizi** *vai* be the color of deer in the fall and winter (NJ)
>
> COLOR OF DEER IN SUMMER: **bagaki-ozaawizi** *vai* be the color of deer in the spring and summer (NJ)

DEFECATE:

> DEFECATE FROM DRINKING: **miijibii** *vai* crap one's self from drinking too much (RT, NJ, GJ)
>
> DEFECATE FROM FEAR: **miizii-aanimi'** *vta* make s.o. defecate from fear (RT, NJ, GJ)
>
> DEFECATE FROM OVEREATING: **miijishkine** *vai* crap from eating too much (RT, NJ, GJ)
>
> FALL DOWN AND DEFECATE: **miijishin** *vai* fall down and crap (RT, NJ, GJ)

SQUEEZE TO MAKE SOMEONE DEFECATE: **miiziibizh** /miiziibiN-/ *vta* squeeze s.o. to the point of defecation (RT, NJ, GJ)

DEFEND:

DEFEND OFFSPRING: **naadamaawaso** *vai* stick up for one's children (with negative consequences) (RT, NJ, GJ)

VERBALLY ATTACK IN DEFENSE OF CHILD: **onzonge** *vai* verbally attack people based on what your child told you [*example*: Gego onzongeken! = Don't (verbally) attack people based on what your child has come and told you! *cultural note*: It is considered inadvisable to do this because of possible spiritual consequences. Children need to fend for themselves and take responsibility for their actions.] (RT, NJ, GJ)

DEHUSK WITH TEETH: **bashagam** *vta* dehusk s.o. with one's teeth (as in a squirrel to an acorn) (RT); *also* **bishagam** (GJ)

DENSE: BE DENSE BRUSH: **zagaakwaa** *vii* be dense, brushy woods, thick brush, thicket (ES, NJ) [*cultural note*: this term can be used as a metaphor for hard times; *example*: Da-zagaakwaa obimaadiziwin giishpin bizindawaasig ookomisan. = Her life will get hard if she doesn't listen to her grandmother.]

DESERT: **baatekamigaa** *vii* be a desert (RT)

DIAPER:

DIAPER RASH: **miskozhaanidizo** *vai* have a diaper rash (RT, NJ, GJ)

USE FOR DIAPER: **odaanziyaani'** *vta* use s.t. for s.o.'s diaper [*example*: Giziingwe'onan odaanziyaani'. = Use towels for his diaper.] (NJ)

DIE:

DEATH THROES: **giiwine** *vai* be in one's death throes (ES)

DIE: **niboomagad** *vii* die (RT)

DIE HARD: **zhiibine** *vai* doesn't die easily, dies hard (GJ, NJ)

DIET:

CHANGE DIET: **aandanjige** *vai* change diet (RT, NJ, GJ)

SPECIAL DIET: **ayinanjige** *vai* have a special, certain diet (RT)

DIFFERENT: USE DIFFERENT DISHES: **bakaaninaagane** *vai* use different dishes (as in when a girl on first menses, or anytime on menses) (RT, NJ, GJ)

DIFFICULT: BE CHALLENGING: **zanagendaagwad** *vii* be challenging (NJ)

DIG:

DIG: **ondaanike** *vai* dig from somewhere (RT, NJ, GJ)

DIM:

    DIG TUNNEL: **zhiibaa-waanike** *vai* dig a tunnel (RT)

DIM:

    BE DIM LIGHT: **waashaazheyaa** *vii* be dim light (RT)

    DIM LAMP: **odaanzhenan** *vti* dim the lamp (NJ)

    TURN SOMETHING DOWN: **waashaanzhe'an** *vti* dim, turn s.t. down (as in a kerosene lantern) (RT); *also* **waashaanzhenan** (NJ)

DIMPLE:

    DIMPLED: **basiingwe** *vai* have a dimple (RT, NJ, GJ)

    DIMPLED CHIN: **basiindaamikane** *vai* have a dimpled chin (RT, NJ, GJ)

DINOSAUR:

    CLUB: **bikwaakwadwaanawe** *vai* have clubs (as in a dinosaur) (NJ)

    DINOSAUR: **gete-awesiinh** *na* dinosaur; *pl* **gete-awesiinyag** (RT, NJ, GJ); *also* **gete-ogiikadaanaangwe** *na* dinosour; *pl* **gete-ogiikadaanaangweg** (NJ)

    DINOSAUR EGG: **gete-ogiikadaanaangwe-waawan** *ni* dinosaur egg; *pl* **gete-ogiikadaanaangwe-waawanoon** (NJ)

    ELONGATED SPIKE: **zagigi-omichigegani** *vai* have an elongated spike (as in a dinosaur) (NJ)

    HAVE SPIKES: **omichigegani** *vai* have spikes (as in a dinosaur) (NJ)

    KENTROSAURUS: **wayaawaasepikwaned** *vai-prt* kentrosaurus; *pl* **wayaawaasepikwanewaad** (NJ)

    SPINOSAURUS: **odatagwaagani-wesepikwaned** *vai-prt* spinosaurus; *pl* **odatagwaagani-wesepikwanewaad** (NJ)

    TRICERATOPS: **neso-eshkaned** *vai-prt* triceratops; *pl* **neso-eshkanewaad** (NJ); *also* **nesweshkaned** *vai-prt* triceratops; *pl* **nesweshkanewaad** (NJ)

    TYRANNOSAURAUS REX: **gegwaanisagizid** *vai-prt* tyrannosaurus rex; *pl* **gegwaanisagiziwaad** (NJ)

DIRT:

    BE POLLUTED: **wiinichigaade** *vii* be polluted (RT, NJ, GJ)

    DIRT ROAD: **mitaawango-miikanens** *ni* dirt road, dirt trail; *pl* **mitaawango-miikanensan** (RT, NJ, GJ)

    DIRTY AIR: **wiininaamowin** *ni* dirty air (i.e. air pollution, polluted air) (RT, NJ, GJ)

DIRTY SMOKE: **wiinaabate** *vii* be dirty (as in something smoke-like) (RT, NJ, GJ)

DIRTY WATER: **wiinaagamin** *vii* be dirty (as in a liquid) (RT, NJ, GJ)

DUSTY: **bizini** *vai* be dusty, be dirty (NJ); *also* get something in one's eye (GJ)

SOIL: **ozaanaman** *na* soil (RT)

DIRT: *see also* POLLUTE

DISCOVER:

BE FOUND: **mikigaade** *vii* be found (RT)

BE FOUND: **mikigaazo** *vai* be found, be discovered (RT, NJ, GJ)

KNOWN BY SENSE: **gikendamaazo** *vai* sense things, know things by sense, discover (RT, NJ, GJ)

DISEMBARK: **gabaa'** *vta* disembark s.o., let s.o. off (RT, NJ, GJ)

DISH: USE DIFFERENT DISHES: **bakaaninaagane** *vai* use different dishes (as in when a girl on first menses, or anytime on menses) (RT, NJ, GJ)

DISPOSITION: HAVE DANGEROUS DISPOSITION: **nanaaniizaanizi** *vai* have a dangerous disposition (RT, NJ, GJ)

DISTANCE:

BE SEEN AT A DISTANCE: **debinaagozi** *vai* be seen at a distance (ES)

HEARD CHEWING FROM DISTANCE: **debwewenjige** *vai* be heard chewing from a distance (RT, NJ, GJ)

DIVE IN SNOW: **bookaagonebizo** *vai* dive into the snow (RT, NJ, GJ)

DOCK: **mininaawaandawaagan** *ni* dock; *pl* **mininaawaandawaaganan** (GJ); *also* **niminaawaandawaagan** (NJ)

DOG:

DOG LEASH: **gitaakwapizon** *ni* dog leash, dog chain, seat belt; *pl* **gitaakwapizonan** (RT, NJ, GJ)

FEMALE DOG: **gishkishenh** *na* female dog; *pl* **gishkishenyag** (RT, NJ, GJ)

GUIDE DOG: **gagiibiingwewasim** *na* guide dog; *pl* **gagiibiingwewasimoog** (NJ)

MALE DOG, HORSE, WOLF: **naabesim** *na* male dog, male horse, male wolf; *pl* **naabesimag** (RT, NJ, GJ)

DOMED LODGE: **waaginogaan** *ni* domed lodge; *pl* **waaginogaanan** (RT, NJ, GJ)

DOOR:

CLOSE DOOR: **gibinde'ige** *vai* close the door (as in a cloth door) (RT, NJ, GJ)

CLOTH WIGWAM DOOR: **gibinde'igan** *ni* cloth door on wiigiwaam; *pl* **gibinde'iganan** (NJ)

OPEN DOOR: **baakiiginan** *vti* open s.t. (sheet-like) (RT, NJ, GJ); *also* **baakindenan** (RT, NJ, GJ)

OPEN: **baakindenamaw** *vta* open (s.t.) for s.o. (RT, NJ, GJ)

DORSAL FIN: **omichigan** *ni* dorsal fin; *pl* **omichiganan** (RT, NJ, GJ)

DOUBLE:

DOUBLE BIT AX: **edawaabide-waagaakwad** *ni* double bit ax; *pl* **edawaabide-waagaakwadoon** (NJ)

DOUBLE SHOOT: **niizho-bimodan** *vti* double shoot (as in moccasin game) (GJ)

DOUBLE VOWEL SYSTEM: **niizhoobii'igewin** *ni* double vowel writing system (JC)

SCORE DOUBLE: **niizho-gabenaage** *vai* score double (as in moccasin game) (GJ)

DOUGH:

DOUGH: **onadinigan** *na* dough (NJ, GJ)

KNEAD SOMEONE: **onadin** *vta* knead s.o. (NJ, GJ)

DOVE, PIGEON: **omiimii** *na* dove, pigeon; *pl* **omiimiig** (RT, NJ, GJ)

DOWN:

FLOW DOWN: **niisijiwan** *vii* flow down, roll down (as in water) (RT)

FLY DOWN: **naazhise** *vai* fly down, swoop down (RT); *also* **niisibizo** (RT); *also* **niisise** (RT)

PRESS SNOW DOWN BY FOOT: **maagwaagoneshkige** *vai* press foot in the snow, pack snow down with one's foot (GJ)

PRESS SOMEONE DOWN: **maagoshkaw** *vta* press s.o. down, pack s.o. down (as in snow) (RT, NJ, GJ)

PRESS SOMETHING DOWN: **maagoshkan** *vti* press s.t. down, pack s.t. down (RT, NJ, GJ)

ROLL DOWN: **naazhinan** *vti* roll s.t. down (RT, NJ, GJ)

DOWNSTREAM:

FLOAT DOWNSTREAM: **niisaajiwaneyaaboono** *vai* float downstream (as in an otter) (GJ); *also* **niisaajiwanweyaaboono** (NJ)

GO DOWNSTREAM: **niisaajiwane'aadage** *vai* go downstream (GJ); *also* **niisaajiwanwe'aadage** (NJ); *also* **niisaajiwane'o** *vai* go downstream (GJ); *also* **niisaajiwanwe'o** (NJ)

GO DOWNSTREAM ON TOP OF WATER: **niisaajiwaneweyaaboono** *vai* go downstream on top of the water (GJ); *also* **niisaajiwanweweyaabono** (NJ)

DOWNSTREAM: *see also* CURRENT

DOZE: SIT DOZING: **akawadabi** *vai* sit dozing off, spacing out vacuously (NJ, GJ); *also* **gakawadabi** *vai* sit dozing off (RT)

DRAIN WATER OUT OF SOMETHING: **ziikoobiiginan** *vti* drain the water out of s.t. (NJ, GJ)

DRAW: DRAWING TOOL: **mazinibii'iganaatig** *ni* drawing tool; *pl* **mazinibii'iganaatigoon** (GJ)

DRESS:

DRESS WARMLY: **giizhookonaye** *vai* dress warmly, dress in warm clothes (RT, NJ, GJ)

DRESS WELL: **minokonaye** *vai* dress nicely

DRIBBLE BALL: **gwaashkwesidoon** *vti* dribble s.t (as in a ball) (NJ); *also* **gweshkwesidoon** (GJ)

DRINK:

DRINK: **andoobii** *vai* get a drink from somewhere (NJ, GJ)

DEFECATE FROM DRINKING: **miijibii** *vai* crap one's self from drinking too much (RT, NJ, GJ)

FALLING DOWN DRUNK: **gawaakizige** *vai* be falling-down drunk (NJ)

GOOD AND DRUNK: **minwaakizige** *vai* be good and drunk (NJ)

PASS OUT FROM DRINKING: **wanaakizige** *vai* pass out from drinking (NJ)

DRIVE:

CROSS LINE: **gaashipoobizo** *vai* cross the line (as in driving out of lane), or miss a turnoff (as in driving) [*example*: Gigaashipoobizomin. = We missed the turn off.] (NJ, GJ)

DRIVE ACROSS: **aazhawagaakobizo** *vai* drive across ice (RT, NJ, GJ)

DRIVE FAST: **wewiibizo** *vai* drive fast (RT, NJ, GJ)

DRIVE ON SAND: **ogidaawangwebizo** *vai* drive on sand (NJ, GJ)

DRIVE SOMEONE: **odaabii'** *vta* drive s.o. (RT)

STOP DRIVING: **noogibizo** *vai* come to a stop while driving (RT, NJ, GJ)

DROP:

    DROP ACCIDENTALLY: **bishigonige** *vai* miss and drop things (NJ)

    WATER LEVEL DROPS: **iskaabiise** *vii* water level drops (RT, NJ, GJ); *also* **iskatese** *vii* water level drops (RT, NJ, GJ)

DRUM:

    SOUND GOOD DRUMMING: **minwewe'akokwe** *vai* make a nice sound drumming (RT, NJ, GJ)

    SYNCOPATED BEAT: **biisiwebinige** vai make syncopated beat for moccasin game song (GJ)

DRUNK: GET SOMEONE DRUNK: **giiwashkwebizh** /giiwashkwebiN-/ *vta* get s.o. high or drunk (RT)

DRY:

    DRY: **baate** *vii* be dry (RT)

    DRY SAND: **bengwadaawangaa** *vii* be dry sand (NJ, GJ)

DUCK: DRAKE: **ininishib** *na* drake mallard; *pl* **ininishibag** (RT, NJ, GJ)

DULL: **azhiwaasin** *vii* get dull (NJ); *also* **zhazhiwaasin** *vii* get dull (GJ)

DUMMY: **giboch** *expression* you don't know crap! dummy! (NJ, GJ)

DUST:

    DUST BILLOWS: **ondaabateshin** *vii* dust billows when it hits the ground (RT, NJ, GJ)

    DUSTY: **bizini** *vai* be dusty, be dirty (NJ); *also* get something in one's eye (GJ)

DYE:

    DYE: **adisigan** *ni* dye; *pl* **adisiganan** (RT, NJ, GJ)

    DYE SOMEONE: **adiswi** /adisw-/ *vta* dye s.o. (NJ); *also* **adiso** /adisw-/ *vta* dye s.o. (GJ); *also* **adis** /adisw-/ *vta* dye s.o. (RT)

EACH ONE: **endaso-bezhig** *pc* every one, each one (RT)

EAR:

    COVER ONE'S EARS: **badagwanitawage'o** *vai* cover one's ears (RT, NJ, GJ)

    LONG EARS: **gagaanwaabiigitawage** *vai* have long ears (NJ)

EARTH: **ozaanaman** *na* soil (RT)

EAT:

    BE A CARNIVORE: **wiiyaasanjige** *vai* be a carnivore (RT, NJ, GJ)

    CHEW: **zhaashaagwanjige** *vai* chew, eat by chewing (RT)

    DEFECATE FROM OVEREATING: **miijishkine** *vai* crap from eating too much (RT, NJ, GJ)

    EAT EVERYTHING: **gadaanaangwe** *vai* consume everything (NJ); *also* **gidaanawe** (RT)

EAT FECES: **miidanjige** *vai* eat feces  (RT, NJ, GJ)

EAT FROM SOMETHING: **ondandan** *vti* eat from s.t., obtain food from s.t. (RT)

EAT OFF BUSH: **ando-ningaapoono** *vai* eat off the bush (NJ); *also* **anda-ningaapoono** (ES, RT); *also* **ningaapoono** (RT)

EAT TOO MUCH: **ganwaapo** *vai+o* be unable to eat something because of spiritual prohibition, allergy, or overconsumption (NJ, GJ); *also* **onzaami'o** *vai* eat too much (RT, NJ, GJ)

EAT TOO MUCH OF SOMEONE: **ganwaapon** *vta* unable to eat s.o. because of spiritual prohibition, allergy, or overconsumption (NJ); *also* **onzaami'** *vta* eat too much of s.o. (RT, NJ, GJ); *also* **onzaamipon** (RT, NJ, GJ)

RUN OUT OF FOOD: **miidaajise** *vai+o* run out of s.t. to eat (RT)

ECHO:

ECHO: **baswewe** *vai* echo (RT, NJ, GJ)

ECHO: **baswewe** *vii* echo (RT, NJ, GJ)

EFFORT: MAKE BEST EFFORT: **inwaazo** *vai* make one's best effort (ES)

EGG:

EGG (BIRD): **waawan** *ni* egg (of a bird); *pl* **waawanoon** (RT, NJ, GJ)

EGG (AQUATIC CREATURE): **waak** *ni* egg (of a fish, frog, or turtle); *pl* **waakwan** (RT, NJ, GJ)

EGG SHELL: **waawanogek** *na* egg shell; *pl* **waawanogekwag** (NJ)

LAY EGG: **boonam** *vai2* lay an egg (RT, NJ, GJ)

RELEASE EGGS: **owaako** *vai* release eggs, spawn (as in fish) (RT, NJ, GJ)

EIGHT SPOT: **nishwaasokaan** *pc* the eight spot (in moccasin game) (GJ)

EITHER SIDE: **edawayi'ii** *pc* on either side, one the sides (RT); *also* **eyiidawayi'ii** (NJ); *also* **edaweyi'ii** (GJ)

EMERGE FROM WATER: **mookibiise** *vii* emerge from water, suddenly pop out of water (NJ, GJ); *also* **mooshkamo** *vai* emerge from water (NJ, GJ)

EMOTIONAL: **ando-mazitam** *vai2* be emotionally oversensitive, easy to offend, looking for fault (RT, NJ, GJ)

EMPTY:

BE EMPTY: **bizishigwaa** *vii* be empty (NJ); *also* **bizhishigwaa** (RT)

EMPTY CANOE: **agwaanaaso** *vai* empty the canoe (RT, NJ, GJ)

EMPTY SOMETHING: **agwaanaadan** *vti* empty s.t. (RT, NJ, GJ)

HOOK IS EMPTY: **gishewaabikad** *vii* hook is empty (RT, NJ, GJ)

MAKE SOMEONE DISEMBARK: **agwaashim** *vta* take s.o. out of the canoe (RT, NJ, GJ)

ENCIRCLE SOMEONE: **gizhibaashkaw** *vta* encircle s.o., go around s.o. (RT, NJ, GJ)

ENJOIN: **aanikoowaaginan** *vti* bend s.t. together, enjoin things (RT, NJ, GJ)

ENOUGH: NOT TOO MUCH BUT ENOUGH: **gomaa go minik** *expression* not too much but enough (NJ)

ENOUGH: *see also* SUFFICIENT

ENVY: **noondendam** *vai* be envious, want what others have (NJ); want things from people (implies sexual arousal) (LM)

ERA: **dasosagoons** *pc* era, a certain extent of time (RT)

ERECTION: **ishaakozi** *vai* have an erection (LM)

ERODE: **biigojiwan** *vii* erodes (from water flowing), erosion (RT)

ESCAPE:

    ESCAPE: **gii'iwe** *vai* escape (from a predator) (RT, NJ, GJ)

    TRY TO ESCAPE: **wiikwaji'o** *vai* try to get away (as in from a trap) (RT, NJ, GJ)

EVERGREEN: *see* CONIFER

EVERY ONE: **endaso-bezhig** *pc* every one, each one (RT)

EVERYWHERE: **inigokwaa** *vii* be such a size, be in a certain location, be everywhere [example: enigokwaag giiyaw = some parts of your body, all over your body] (NJ)

EXCLAMATION POINT: **zoongibii'igan** *ni* exclamation point (!) (JC)

EXHALE: **bagidanaamo** *vai* breathe, exhale (RT, NJ, GJ)

EXHORT: **gagiikim** *vta* exhort s.o. (RT, NJ, GJ)

EXIT: SMOKE COMES OUT: **zaagaabate** *vii* smoke comes out somewhere (RT, NJ, GJ)

EXPOSED: **madaabiiga'igaazo** *vai* be exposed (from having trees are cut) (RT, NJ, GJ)

EXTINGUISH: **aatawe-boodaadan** *vti* blow s.t. out (lamp) (RT, NJ, GJ)

EYE:

    CLOSE EYES: **basangwaabi** *vai* close one's eyes (RT, NJ, GJ)

    COVER ONE'S EYES: **badagwanishkiinzhigwe'o** *vai* cover one's eyes (RT, NJ, GJ)

    EYE GLASSES: **oshkiinzhigokaajiganan** *ni-pl* eye glasses (RT, NJ); *also* **oshkiinzhigokaanan** (GJ)

HAVE EYE GLASSES: **oshkiinzhigoke** *vai* have glasses (RT, NJ, GJ)

KEEP EYES OPEN: **ayinaabi** *vai* keep one's eyes open (RT, NJ, GJ)

LARGE EYES: **mamaangishkiinzhigwe** *vai* have large eyes (RT, NJ, GJ)

LOOK AT SOMEONE FROM CORNER OF EYE: **negwaabam** *vta* look at s.o. out of the corner of one's eye (RT, NJ, GJ)

EYEBROW: **nimaamaa** *na* eyebrow; *pl* **nimaamaayag** (RT, NJ, GJ)

EYELASH: **nimiishaabiwinaan** *nid* my eyelash; *pl* **nimiishaabiwinaanan** (NJ, GJ)

FACE:

BUMPY FACE: **gaashiingwe** *vai* has a bumpy face (as in not having shaved for a while), be partly shaved (RT, NJ, GJ)

FACING: **inaasamii** *vai* facing (ES)

FALL:

FALL CAUSING ANAL PENETRATION: **boojidiyeshin** *vai* fall or sit on s.t. causing anal penetration (GJ)

FALL DOWN AND DEFECATE: **miijishin** *vai* fall down and crap (RT, NJ, GJ)

FALL THROUGH ICE: **dwaashin** *vai* fall through the ice (RT, NJ, GJ)

FALL WRONG WAY: **napaadaakwese** *vai* fall in the wrong direction (GJ)

FALLING-DOWN DRUNK: **gawaakizige** *vai* be falling-down drunk (NJ)

FALL ASLEEP: **giikiibiingwashi** *vai* fall asleep (LM)

FAN:

FAN: **wewese'igan** *ni* fan; *pl* **wewese'iganan** (RT, NJ, GJ)

FAN SOMEONE: **wewese'wi** /wewese'w-/ *vta* fan s.o. (as in a drum) (NJ); *also* **wewese'o** /wewese'w-/ (GJ)

FAN SOMETHING: **wewese'an** *vti* fan s.t. (RT, NJ, GJ)

FARM:

FARM: **chi-gitigaan** *ni* farm; *pl* **chi-gitigaanan** (RT)

GARDEN: **gitige** *vai* farm, garden, plant (RT)

FART:

FART ON SOMETHING: **boogijidan** *vti* fart on s.t. (RT, NJ, GJ)

SQUEEZE SOMEONE TO FLATULENCE: **boogijibizh** /boogijibiN-/ *vta* squeeze s.o. to point of flatulence (RT, NJ, GJ)

WHOOPEE CUSHION: **boogidi-apikweshimon** *ni* whoopee cushion; *pl* **boogidi-apikweshimonan** (NJ)

FAST:

> DRIVE FAST: **wewiibizo** *vai* drive fast (RT, NJ, GJ)
>
> FAST CURRENT: **ojaanimijiwan** *vii* be a fast current (NJ, GJ)
>
> PADDLE FAST: **gizhiikwazhiwe** *vai* paddle or swim fast (RT, NJ, GJ)
>
> PROPEL: **naamiwana'ogo** *vai* be propelled faster by wind and waves (in watercaft) (NJ)
>
> SPEAK FAST: **gidaatabowe** *vai* speak fast (RT, NJ, GJ)
>
> TRILL: **gidaatabitaagozi** *vai* trill, fast sounding call (as in bird) (RT, NJ, GJ)
>
> WALK FAST: **dadaatabose** *vai* walk fast (RT, GJ); *also* **gidaatabose** (NJ)

FAULT LINE: **baasikamigishkaa** *vii* ground cracks, be a fault line (RT, NJ, GJ)

FEAR: MAKE DEFECATE FROM FEAR: **miizii-aanimi'** *vta* make s.o. defecate from fear (RT, NJ, GJ)

FEAST SOMEONE: **wiikonge'** *vta* feast s.o. (RT, NJ, GJ)

FEATHER: PUFF UP ONE'S FEATHERS: **ombimiigwanetaa** *vai* puff up one's feathers (NJ, GJ)

FECES: EAT FECES: **miidanjige** *vai* eat feces (RT, NJ, GJ)

FECES: *see also* DEFECATE

FEEL:

> FEEL BY HEARING: **nooyoondam** *vai* feel with hearing (NJ)
>
> FEEL BY SMELL: **biiyiijimaandam** *vai* feel by smell (NJ)
>
> FEEL FOR BOTTOM WITH FOOT: **noondakiishkige** *vai* try in vain to feel for bottom with foot (NJ, GJ)
>
> FEEL HEAVY: **gozigon** *vii* feel heavy (RT, NJ, GJ)
>
> FEEL SOMETHING BY HEARING: **nooyoondan** *vti* feel s.t. with hearing (NJ)
>
> FEEL SOMETHING BY SMELL: **biiyiijimaandan** *vti* feel s.t. by smell (NJ)
>
> FEEL SOMETHING BY TASTE: **biiyiijipidan** *vti* feel s.t. by taste (NJ)
>
> FEEL SOMETHING BY TOUCH: **biiyiijimanjitoon** *vti* feel s.t. by touch (NJ)
>
> FEELING: **inamanjichigaade** *vii* be a feeling, be a sense (NJ)
>
> FEELING: **enamanjichigaadeg** *vii-prt* feeling, sense (NJ)

FEIGN AT SOMEONE: **nima'wi** /**nima'w-**/ *vta* feign at s.o. (as in a strike) [*example*: Ningii-nima'waa. = I acted like I was going to hit him.] (NJ); *also* **nima'o** /**nima'w-**/ (GJ)

FEMALE:

>FEMALE DOG: **gishkishenh** *na* female dog; *pl* **gishkishenyag** (RT, NJ, GJ)

>FEMALE FISH: **noozhemeg** *na* female fish; *pl* **noozhemegwag** (RT, NJ, GJ)

>FEMALE FRUIT: **noozhemin** *ni* female fruit; *pl* **noozheminan** (RT, NJ, GJ)

>FEMALE TREE: **ikwewaatig** *na* female tree; *pl* **ikwewaatigoog** (RT, NJ, GJ)

FERN:

>FIDDLE FERN: **anaaganibag** *ni* fiddle fern; *pl* **anaaganibagoon** (AM)

>SWEET FERN: **namewashkoons** *ni* sweet fern; *pl* **namewashkoonsan** (NJ)

FIDDLE: SOUND PLEASANT PLAYING FIDDLE: **minwewenaazhaabii'ige** *vai* make a pleasant sound playing fiddle (RT, NJ, GJ)

FILE:

>CHAINSAW FILE: **zisiboojiganens** *ni* chainsaw sharpening file; *pl* **zisiboojiganensan** (GJ)

>FLAT FILE: **zisiboojigan** *ni* flat file; *pl* **zisiboojiganan** (GJ)

FILL WITH WATER: **mooshkinebiise** *vii* fills with water (as in a canoe) (RT, NJ, GJ)

FILTER: **ziikoobiiginigan** *ni* filter, strainer (RT, NJ, GJ)

FIN:

>BROAD FINS: **mamaangizhigwane** *vai* have broad fins (as in a fish) (RT)

>DORSAL FIN: **omichigan** *ni* dorsal fin; *pl* **omichiganan** (RT, NJ, GJ)

>STICK UP FINS TO KILL: **michige'wi** /**michige'w-**/ *vta* stick up fins to kill s.o. (NJ); *also* **michigwe'o** /**michigwe'w-**/ (GJ)

FIND:

>BE FOUND: **mikigaade** *vii* be found (RT)

>BE FOUND: **mikigaazo** *vai* be found, be discovered (RT, NJ, GJ)

FINELY GRANULATED: **nitaawan** *vii* be finely granulated, be fine sand (RT, NJ, GJ)

FINGER:

FINGER BLISTER: **apashkwebiigininjiishin** *vai* get a blister on one's hand, finger (RT, NJ, GJ)

FINGER PAD: **niniisiigininjaan** *nid* my finger pad; *pl* **niniisiigininjaanan** (NJ)

GIVE SOMEONE DIRTY FINGER SIGN: **zaagidenaninjiitaw** *vta* give s.o. the dirty Ojibwe finger sign [*cultural note*: performed by sticking the thumb between the first two fingers, symbolically representing a phallus protruding between the legs, done teasingly, in jest, but only between male friends] (GJ)

FINGERNAIL:

CLIP FINGERNAIL: **giishkiganzhiizhige** *vai* cut fingernails or toenails (RT, NJ, GJ)

FINGERNAIL CLIPPER: **giishkiganzhiizhiganaabikoons** *ni* fingernail clipper; *pl* **giishkiganzhiizhiganaabikoonsan** (RT, NJ, GJ)

LONG FINGERNAILS: **ginwaashkanzhiiwi** *vai* have long claws or fingernails (RT, NJ, GJ)

FIRE:

BURN IN CERTAIN PLACE: **danakone** *vii* burn in certain place (RT, NJ, GJ)

BURN WELL: **minokone** *vai* burn well (NJ)

FIRE: **zakide** *vii* be a fire (RT)

FIRE KETTLE: **boodawaanakik** *na* fire kettle; *pl* **boodawaanakikoog** (RT, NJ, GJ)

FIRE MAKER: **ishkodekaan** *ni* fire maker (flint, stick kit); *pl* **ishkodekaanan** (NJ, GJ)

FIRE PIT: **endazhi-boodaweng** *vai-prt* fire pit (RT, NJ, GJ)

FIREPLACE: **boodawaan** *ni* fireplace; *pl* **boodawaanan** (RT, NJ, GJ)

IGNITE: **nawadide** *vii* catch on fire (RT, NJ, GJ)

MAKE FIRE: **ishkodawe** *vai* make fire (NJ, GJ)

MAKE FIRE FOR SOMEONE: **boodawaazh /boodawaaN-/** *vta* build a fire for s.o. (RT, NJ); *also* **boodawaazho /boodawaaN-/** GJ)

MAKE FIRE IN SOMETHING: **boodawaadan** *vti* make a fire in s.t. (RT, NJ, GJ)

MAKE FIRE TO WARM SELF: **boodawaanidizo** *vai* build fire to warm oneself (NJ, GJ)

MAKE FIRE WITH SOMETHING: **boodawaage** *vai+o* make a fire with s.t. (RT, NJ, GJ)

MAKE WARMING FIRE: **boodawaazo** *vai* build fire for warming (RT, GJ)

UNABLE TO MAKE FIRE: **bwaanawi-ishkodawe** *vai* be unable to make a fire (RT, NJ, GJ)

FIRETRUCK: **aate'ishkodawewidaabaan** *na* firetruck; *pl* **aate'ishkodawewidaabaanag** (RT, NJ); *also* **aatawe'ishkodawewidaabaan** (GJ)

FIRST TIME: **bijiinag** *pc* for the first time, just now [*example*: Mii bijiinag gii-izhichigeyaan. = This is the first time I did this. *example*: Mii bijiinag wii-wiisiniyaang. = We're going to eat just now, we're just eating now (apologetic way of saying, because we were late in getting up).] (NJ, GJ)

FIRST KILL: **oshki-nitaage** *vai* make a first kill (RT, NJ, GJ)

FISH:

BAIT MADE FROM FISH: **ogokeyaw** *ni* bait made from fish (as in underside near gills or belly) (NJ); *pl* **ogokeyawan**; *also* **ogokeyawag** (GJ)

BE A SMALL FISH: **giigoonsiwi** *vai* be a small fish (RT, NJ, GJ); *also* **giigoowensiwi** *vai* be a small fish (RT, NJ, GJ)

BE IN MID-SPAWN: **megwayaami** *vai* be in mid-spawn (RT, NJ, GJ)

BOTTOM DWELLING FISH: **zhagashkaanaamikwesi** *na* bottom dwelling fish; *pl* **zhagashkaanaamikwesiwag** (RT, NJ, GJ)

BROAD FINS: **mamaangizhigwane** *vai* have broad fins (as in a fish) (RT)

CRAPPIE: **ezhegamoons** *na* crappie (GJ); *pl* **ezhegamoonsag**; *also* **gidagwadaashi** (KP); *pl* **gidagwadaashiwag**; *also* **odazhegamoons** (NJ); *pl* **odazhegamoonsag**

CUT FISH: **baanizhaawe** *vai* cut fish into strips, fillet (RT, NJ, GJ)

DEBONE: **nametegoke** *vai* take bones out in preparation for smoking (RT, NJ, GJ)

DORSAL FIN: **omichigan** *ni* dorsal fin; *pl* **omichiganan** (RT, NJ, GJ)

EGG: **waak** *ni* egg (of a fish, frog, or turtle); *pl* **waakwan** (RT, NJ, GJ)

FEELER: **miishidoonaan** *ni* animal whisker, feeler on fish; *pl* **miishidoonaanan** (NJ)

FEMALE FISH: **noozhemeg** *na* female fish; *pl* **noozhemegwag** (RT, NJ, GJ)

FISH HOOK: **migiskan** *ni* fish hook; *pl* **migiskanan** (RT, NJ, GJ)

FISH PEMMICAN: **nooka'iskawaan** *na* pemmican (fish); *pl* **nooka'iskawaanag** (RT, NJ, GJ)

FISH TAIL: **ninzhigwan /-zhigwan-/** *nid* my tail (of a fish, snake, or serpent); *pl* **ninzhigwanan** (RT, NJ, GJ)

FISH TOOTH: **giigoowaabid** *ni* fish tooth; *pl* **giigoowaabidan** (RT, NJ, GJ)

FISH TRAP: **biinjiboonaagan** *ni* fish trap; *pl* **biinjiboonaaganan** (NJ, GJ)

FISHING POLE: **migiskanaatig** *ni* fishing pole; *pl* **migiskanaatigoon** (RT, NJ, GJ)

GAFF HOOK: **aajibijigan** *ni* gaff hook; *pl* **aajibijiganan** (GJ)

GILL: **nimashkiingwaan /mashkiingwaan-/** *nid* my gill; *pl* **nimashkiingwaanan** (NJ)

GOLDFISH: **ozaawi-zhooniyaawi-giigoozens** *na* goldfish; *pl* **ozaawi-zhooniyaawi-giigoozensag** (GJ)

HATCH: **baashkaawanwe'o** *vai* hatch (NJ)

HERRING: **adikamegoons** *na* herring; *pl* **adikamegoonsag** (GJ)

MALE FISH: **naabemeg** *na* male fish; *pl* **naabemegwag** (RT, NJ, GJ)

MUSKELLUNGE: **ozhaawashko-ginoozhe** *na* muskellunge; *pl* **ozhaawashko-ginoozheg** (NJ); *also* **mashkinoozhe** (AM); *pl* **mashkinoozheg**

NORTHERN PIKE: **ginoozhe** *na* northern pike; *pl* **ginoozheg** (RT, NJ, GJ)

OPERCULUM: **onawaangigan** *nid* fish cheek, operculum; *pl* **onawaangiganan** (RT, NJ, GJ)

PULL FISH FROM NETS: **gidinamegwe** *vai* pull fish from nets (RT)

RELEASE EGGS: **owaako** *vai* release eggs, spawn (as in fish) (RT, NJ, GJ)

SCALE: **ninaga'ay /-naga'ay-/** *nad* my scale (as of a fish or snake); *pl* **ninaga'ayag** (RT)

SCALE FISH: **jiichiiga'amegwe** *vai* scale fish (RT, NJ, GJ); *also* **jiiga'amegwe** *vai* scale fish, clean fish (RT, NJ, GJ)

SCALE SOMEONE: **jiigizhwi /jiigizhw-/** *vta* scale fish (NJ); *also* **jiigizho /jiigizhw-/** (GJ); *also* **jiigizh /jiigizhw-/** (RT)

SMALLMOUTH BASS: **odazhegomoo** *na* smallmouth bass; *pl* **odazhegomoog**; *also* **noosa'owesi** *na* smallmouth bass; *pl* **noosa'owesiwag** (RT, NJ, GJ)

SMELT: **zhooniyaa-giigoozens** *na* smelt; *pl* **zhooniyaa-giigoozensag** (NJ, GJ)

SMOKED FISH: **giikanaabasigaazod giigoonh** *vai-prt* smoked fish (GJ)

SPAWN IN SCHOOL: **okwaami** *vai* spawn in a school (as in fish) (RT, NJ, GJ)

SPAWN: **aami** *vai* spawn (RT, NJ, GJ)

SPAWN SMELL: **aamimaagwad** *vii* smells of spawn (NJ, GJ)

SPAWN WATER: **aamiiwaagamin** *vii* be spawn water (NJ, GJ)

SPAWNED OUT: **zhiigwaami** *vai* be spawned out (RT, NJ, GJ)

SPEAR THROUGH ICE: **akwa'waa** *vai* spear through the ice (dark house) (RT); *also* **akwa'we** *vai* spear through the ice (dark house) (NJ, GJ)

START TO SPAWN: **maadaami** *vai* start to spawn (RT, NJ, GJ)

STURGEON: **name** *na* sturgeon; *pl* **namewag** (RT, NJ, GJ)

STURGEON GLUE: **namekwaan** *ni* sturgeon glue (RT, NJ, GJ)

SUCKER: **namebin** *na* sucker; *pl* **namebinag** (RT, NJ, GJ)

SWIM BLADDER: **obikwaajiins** *nid* little air sack, swim bladder; *also* *ni* light bulb (NJ, GJ); *also* **obikwaaj** *nid* air sack of a fish, swim bladder (NJ, GJ)

TROUT: **namegos** *na* trout; *pl* **namegosag** (RT, NJ, GJ)

TULABEE: **odoonibiins** *na* tulabee; *pl* **odoonibiinsag** (RT, NJ, GJ)

USE BAIT: **ogokeyawi** *vai* use bait (NJ)

WALLEYE: **ogaa** *na* walleye; *pl* **ogaawag** (RT, NJ, GJ)

WHITEFISH: **adikameg** *na* whitefish; *pl* **adikamegwag** (RT, NJ, GJ)

WHITEFISH PIPES: **adikamebinidis** *ni* whitefish pipes; *ni* **adikamebinidisiin** (RT, NJ, GJ)

WORK ON FISH: **ashkamegoke** *vai* work on raw fish (NJ); *also* **ashkimegoke** (GJ)

FIT INSIDE: **debashkine** *vai* be covered; *also* fit inside (NJ)

FIVE: **ezhi-naanangin** *vii-prt* five of them (NJ)

FIX:

FIX NETS: **nanaa'isabii** *vai* fix nets (RT, NJ, GJ)

FIX SOMETHING: **nanaa'itoon** *vti* resolve s.t., fix s.t. (RT, NJ, GJ)

FLAT:

BE FLAT: **nabagi-ayaamagad** *vii* be flat (RT, NJ, GJ)

FLAT: **desaa** *vii* be flat as in a shelf, be level (RT, NJ, GJ)

FLAT FILE: **zisiboojigan** *ni* flat file; *pl* **zisiboojiganan** (GJ)

FLAT TAIL: **nabagaanowe** *vai* have a flat tail (NJ); *also* **nabagizowe** *vai* have a flat tail (NJ)

FLAT TEETH: **nabagaabide** *vai* have flat teeth (RT)

GRASS FLATTENS IN WIND: **nabashkweyaasin** *vii* grass flattens in the wind (LM)

STAND FLAT-FOOTED: **nabagizidegaabawi** *vai* stand flat-footed (GJ)

FLEA: SUCCUMB TO FLEAS: **giikawidikome** *vai* succumb to fleas (NJ, GJ)

FLINT: **babigwaanag** *na* flint stone; *pl* **babigwaanagoog** (RT, NJ); *also* **biiwaanag** (GJ)

FLOAT:

FLOAT: **detebaa'angose** *vii* float up (as in beaver dam) (NJ)

FLOAT: **detebaa'angose** *vai* float up (as in ice) (RT, NJ, GJ)

FLOAT DOWNSTREAM: **niisaajiwaneyaaboono** *vai* float downstream (as in an otter) (GJ); *also* **niisaajiwanweyaaboono** (NJ)

FLOAT IN AIR: **bimaasin** *vii* float, travel on the air or wind (RT)

FLOAT LOGS: **bimaaboojige** *vai* float logs (RT, NJ, GJ)

FLOATATION DEVICE: **detebaa'agonji-gibide'ebizon** *ni* personal floatation device, life jacket (RT, NJ, GJ)

HEAD STICKS OUT OF WATER FLOATING: **zaagikwegomo** *vai* head is sticking out of water while floating (NJ, GJ)

HEAD STICKS OUT WHILE FLOATING: **bimi-zaagikwegomo** *vai* head sticks out while floating by (NJ, GJ)

NET FLOAT: **angooji-onaagan** *ni* net float; *pl* **angooji-onaaganan** (RT); *also* **agonjiwinaagan**; *pl* **agonjiwinaaganan** (GJ); *also* **agwinjiwinaagan**; *pl* **agwinjiwinaaganan** (NJ); *also* **agoonjoonaagan**; *pl* **agoonjoonaaganan** (JC)

SINK: **gibitagomo** *vai* stop floating, sink (RT, NJ, GJ)

TAKE OFF IN CURRENT: **maajiiyaaboode** *vii* take off in a current (NJ, GJ)

TAKE OFF IN WATER: **maajiiyaabogo** *vai* go off into the water (as in fish eggs) (NJ, GJ)

TAKE OFF ON WATER IN CURRENT: **maajiiyaabagonde** *vii* take off on top of the water in a current (NJ, GJ)

FLOOD: **mooshka'ogo** *vai* s.o. is flooding out (as in ice) (RT, NJ, GJ)
FLOUR: **bebinezid bakwezhigan** *vai-prt* flour (RT, NJ, GJ)
FLOW:

BE PLEASANT SOUND OF WATER FLOWING: **minwewejiwan** *vii* good sound of water flowing (NJ)

FLOW: **onjigaa** *vii* flow, run (as in water) (RT, NJ, GJ)

FLOW CERTAIN WAY: **izhijiwan** *vii* flow in a certain way (RT)

FLOW DOWN: **niisijiwan** *vii* flow down, roll down (as in water) (RT)

FLOW TO SHORE: **madaabiijiwan** *vii* flows to shore (from inland) (RT, NJ, GJ)

SWEET SOUND OF FLOWING WATER WOMAN: **Minwewejiwanook** *name* Sweet Sound of Flowing Water Woman (NJ)

FLOWER:

BE MANY FLOWERS: **waabigoniikaa** *vii* be many flowers (NJ); *also* **waabigwaniikaa** (RT)

FLOWER POT: **waabigoni-akik** *na* flower pot; *pl* **waabigoni-akikoog** (NJ, GJ); *also* **waabigwani-akik** (RT)

STRAWBERRY FLOWER: **ode'imini-waabigon** *ni* strawberry flower; *pl* **ode'imini-waabigoniin** (NJ); *also* **ode'imini-waabigwan**

TOMATO FLOWER: **gichi-oginii-waabigon** *ni* tomato flower; *pl* **gichi-oginii-waabigoniin** (NJ); *also* **gichi-oginii-waabigwan** (RT)

FUZZY: **miishaa** *vii* be fuzzy (RT, NJ, GJ)
FLUSH: **iskaabiigiwebinan** *vti* flush s.t. (as in toilet) (RT, NJ, GJ)
FLY:

FLY DOWN: **niisibizo** *vai* fly down, swoop down (RT); *also* **niisise** (RT); *also* **naazhise** (RT)

FLY STRAIGHT: **gwayakobide** *vii* fly straight (RT, NJ, GJ)

HEARD FLYING: **madwese** *vai* be heard flying (RT, NJ, GJ)

TAKE OFF FLYING: **bazigwa'o** *vai* take off in flight (RT, NJ, GJ)

TAKE OFF: **ombaashi** *vai* take off in flight (RT, NJ, GJ)

TOUCH LAND FROM SKY: **mizhakiinam** *vai* go from the sky all the way to ground like a thunderbird, or tornado touching down (NJ, GJ)

TOUCH LAND FROM SKY AND RETURN: **mizhakiise** *vai* fly from the sky down to the earth, make land fall (then back up) (NJ, GJ)

FOAM LETTER: **biitewegani-ozhibii'igan** *ni* foam letter; *pl* **biitewegani-ozhibii'iganan** (RT)

FOCUS: **zhiibaa'aabanjige** *vai* focus (GJ)

FOLD:

>FOLD BACKWARDS: **napaajiiginan** *vti* fold backwards, wrong way (GJ)

>MAKE IMAGE BY FOLDING: **maziniiginige** *vai* fold images, make images or pictures (using paper or cloth-like material) (GJ)

FOOD:

>EAT FROM SOMETHING: **ondandan** *vti* eat from s.t., obtain food from s.t. (RT)

>GET FOOD SOMEWHERE: **ondanjige** *vai+o* use s.t. for food, get food from somewhere (RT, NJ, GJ)

>OFFER FOOD AND TAKE BACK: **jiishi'** *vta* offer food to s.o. and take back (as in coming out of a fast, when fed new foods in mourning, or for a first kill) (RT, NJ, GJ)

>RUN OUT OF FOOD: **miidaajise** *vai+o* run out of s.t. to eat (RT)

>STORE FOOD: **na'enimo** *vai* cache, store food (RT, NJ, GJ)

FOOT:

>BAREFOOT: **zhaashaaginizide** *vai* be barefoot (RT, NJ, GJ)

>BE ROPED BY FEET: **naabaabiigizide** *vai* be roped around the feet (NJ, GJ)

>BIG FEET: **mamaangizide** *vai* have big feet (RT)

>BREAK OFF FOOT OR PAW: **giishkitaa** *vai* breaks off a foot or paw (RT, NJ, GJ)

>FEEL FOR BOTTOM WITH FOOT: **noondakiishkige** *vai* try in vain to feel for bottom with foot (NJ, GJ)

>FOOT BLISTER: **apashkwebiigizideshin** *vai* get a blister on one's foot (RT, NJ, GJ)

>HOLD SOMEONE WITH FOOT: **minjimishkaw** *vta* hold s.o. place with foot (GJ)

>NICE SOUNDING FEET: **mino-zhooshkozideshimo** *vai* have nice sounding feet (as in a tap dancer) (NJ, GJ)

>ON SOLE OF FOOT: **nagaakizidaaning** *pc* on the sole of the foot (referencing s.t. there) (RT, NJ, GJ)

>PRESS SNOW DOWN BY FOOT: **maagwaagoneshkige** *vai* press foot in the snow, pack snow down with one's foot (GJ)

>PUT SHOES ON WRONG FEET: **nanepaadakizine** *vai* put one's shoes on the wrong foot (NJ, GJ)

ROPE AROUND FEET: **naabaabiigigwebizh** /**naabaabiigigwebiN-**/ *vta* rope s.o. around the feet (NJ, GJ)

SOLE OF FOOT: **nagaakizid** *ni* sole of the foot; *loc* **nagaakizidaang** (body part) (RT, NJ, GJ)

STICK OUT FOOT: **zaagizideni** *vai* stick one's foot out (RT, NJ, GJ)

TAP FOOT: **jiichiibizideni** *vai* tap one's foot (NJ)

WEAR SHOE ON WRONG FOOT: **aabitanakakeyaa** *vii* a shoe is worn on the wrong foot (NJ) [*example:* Aabitanakakeyaawan. = Two left-footed/right-footed shoes are worn.]; *also* **aapidanakakeyaa** (GJ)

WEAR SHOES ON WRONG FEET: **napaadakizine** *vai* wear shoes on wrong feet (GJ)

WEBBED FOOT: **miziweyiigizide** *vai* have webbed feet, as in a beaver or duck (NJ)

FORCE WATER: **iska'ibiise** *vii* water forced up and out (RT, NJ, GJ)

FOREST: *see* TREE

FORGET: **wanendam** *vai* pass out (NJ), forget (AM)

FORGOTTEN: **wanenjigaazo** *vai* be forgotten (RT)

FORKED:

BE FORKED: **niingidowaakwad** *vii* forked, crotched (as in a tree) (GJ)

BE FORKED: **niingidowaakozi** *vai* forked, crotched (as in a tree) (GJ)

FORKED TONGUE: **niingidodenaniwe** *vai* have a forked tongue (GJ)

GROW FORKED: **niingidowaakogi** *vai* grow in a forked shape (GJ)

FORTUNATE: **dedeb** *expression* it's a good thing, it's fortunate (RT, NJ, GJ) [*example*: Dedeb igo gaa-wiisiniyaan zhebaa. = It's a good thing I ate this morning. *example*: Dedeb igo gaa-agwana'aman daa-gii-tibaabaawan. = It's is a good thing you covered them, they would have gotten damp.]

FOSSIL: **maziniganeshin** *vai* be a fossil (NJ)

FOUR SPOT: **niiyokaan** *pc* the four spot (as in moccasin game) (GJ)

FREE:

FREE SOMEONE: **giitaabikizh** /**giitaabikiN-**/ *vta* let s.o. free (from a trap) (NJ, GJ)

FREE SOMETHING: **giitaabikinan** *vti* release s.t. (as in a trap) (NJ, GJ)

FREEZE:

FREEZE BRITTLE: **mashkawaakogadin** *vii* be frozen and brittle (as in a fresh sapling cut in winter when first brought inside) (NJ)

FREEZE STRONG: **maamashkawadin** *vii* freeze strong (RT, NJ, GJ)

FREEZE THICK: **gipagadin** *vii* be frozen thick (as in a body of water) (RT, NJ, GJ)

FREEZE THICK: **gipagizigwazi** *vai* be frozen thick (as in ice) (RT, NJ, GJ)

FREEZE TO ICE: **agwaskodin** *vii* freeze to the ice (as in a net) (RT, NJ, GJ); *also* **agoskodin** (RT, NJ, GJ)

ICE SHELF FREEZES: **biitooskibiigadin** *vii* ice shelf freezes (RT, NJ, GJ)

FRIEND: **nagadenim** *vta* befriend s.o. (NJ)

FROG:

ANNOUNCE STURGEON SPAWN: **biibaaginamewe** *vai* announce the coming of sturgeon spawn (as in gray tree frog) [*cultural note*: this particular tree frog sound is only heard at the start of the sturgeon spawn and is different from the characteristic call of other tree frogs] (NJ)

BOREAL CHORUS FROG: **agoozimakakii** *na* boreal chorus frog (type of tree frog); *pl* **agoozimakakiig** (NJ, GJ)

EGG: **waak** *ni* egg (of a fish, frog, or turtle); *pl* **waakwan** (RT, NJ, GJ)

GRAY TREE FROG: **obiibaagimakakii**; gray tree frog; *pl* **obiibaagimakakiig** (NJ)

LEOPARD FROG: **gichi-omakakii** *na* leopard frog; *pl* **gichi-omakakiig** (RT, NJ, GJ)

FROG LEAF: **omakakiibag** *ni* frog leaf, plantain; *pl* **omakakiibagoon** (NJ, GJ); *also* **gaagigebag**; *pl* **gaagigebagoon** (NJ, GJ)

FRONT TOOTH: **niigaanaabid** *ni* front tooth; *pl* **niigaanaabidan** (RT)

FROST: **ningwiigad** *vii* be frost (RT)

FRUIT:

FRUIT: **edisod** *vai-prt* fruit; *pl* **edisojig** (RT)

FRUIT: **editeg** *vii-prt* berry, fruit; *pl* **editegin** (RT)

FEMALE FRUIT: **noozhemin** *ni* female fruit; *pl* **noozheminan** (RT, NJ, GJ)

MALE FRUIT: **naabemin** *ni* male fruit; *pl* **naabeminan** (RT, NJ, GJ)

FRY:

FRY: **zaasakokwe** *vai* fry things (RT, NJ, GJ)

FRY SOMEONE: **giiziz /giizizw-/** *vta* fry s.o. (RT)

FUN:

CUTE: **wawiyazh** *pc* cute, fun, just for fun [*example*: Wawiyazh ikido. = He is just saying it for fun.] (NJ, GJ)

HAVE FUN DAY: **mino-giizhiganoke** *vai* have a fun-filled day (NJ)

FUR:

LONG FUR: **ginwawe** *vai* have long fur or hair (RT)

SOFT FUR: **nookadawe** *vai* have soft fur (NJ)

THICK FUR: **gipagawe** *vai* have thick fur (RT)

FURNITURE: **wiigiwaaming dibendaasowin** *ni* furniture; *pl* **wiigiwaaming dibendaasowinan** (RT)

FUSILLI: **biimiskozhiganens** *ni* fusilli (pasta), *pl* **biimiskozhiganensan** (RT, NJ, GJ)

FUSSY: **wegaskendaagozi** *vai* be stubborn, fussy, hard to please (NJ, GJ); *redup* **weyagaskendaagozi** (GJ, NJ); *also* **wiiyagaskendaagozi** (NJ, GJ)

GAME: *see also* BAGESE *and* MOCCASIN GAME

GARDEN: **gitige** *vai* farm, garden, plant (RT)

GATHER: **asanjigo** *vai+o* store things (RT)

GHOST BOWL: **andidaagan** *ni* ghost bowl (ES)

GILL: **nimashkiingwaan /mashkiingwaan-/** *nid* my gill; *pl* **nimashkiingwaanan** (NJ)

GLANCE: *see* LOOK

GLASSES:

EYE GLASSES: **oshkiinzhigokaajiganan** *ni-pl* eye glasses (RT, NJ); *also* **oshkiinzhigokaanan** (GJ)

HAVE EYE GLASSES: **oshkiinzhigoke** *vai* have glasses (RT, NJ, GJ)

GLIDE THROUGH WATER: **gichiwibiishkaa** *vii* glide slowly through water (RT, NJ, GJ)

GLOSSARY: **ikidowini-ataasowin** *ni* glossary; *pl* **ikidowini-ataasowinan** (RT)

GLOWING ROTTEN WOOD: **waasakonejiisag** *ni* glowing rotten wood (NJ, GJ)

GLUE: STURGEON GLUE: **namekwaan** *ni* sturgeon glue (RT, NJ, GJ)

GLUTTON: **gaazhage** *vai* be gluttanous (NJ)

GOAL:

> GOAL: **bakinaagewin** *ni* goal; *pl* **bakinaagewinan**; *also* **mizhodamowin**; *pl* **mizhodamowinan** (RT, NJ, GJ)
>
> OBJECTIVE: **andawenjigan** *ni* objective; *pl* **andawenjiganan** (RT, NJ, GJ)

GOAT: **maanadikoshens** *na* billy goat; *pl* **maanadikoshensag** (RT, NJ, GJ)

GOLD:

> GOLDEN BUTTERLY: **ozaawi-memengwaa** *na* butterfly, tiger swallowtail; *pl* **ozaawi-memengwaag** (RT, NJ, GJ)
>
> GOLDFISH: **ozaawi-zhooniyaawi-giigoozens** *na* goldfish; *pl* **ozaawi-zhooniyaawi-giigoozensag** (GJ)
>
> GRASS TURNS GOLD: **ozaawaashkosiwe** *vii* grass turns golden (RT)

GONE: **aweniban** *pc* gone! (RT, NJ, GJ)

GOOD:

> LOOK ONE'S BEST: **minonaagozi'idizo** *vai* look one's best (NJ)
>
> NOT IN A GOOD WAY: **mamaazhiike** *pc* any old way, done hurriedly, not in a good way (NJ); *also* **mamaanzhii** (GJ)
>
> TASTE GOOD: **minopogwad** *vii* taste good (RT, NJ, GJ)

GOOD THING: **dedeb** *expression* it's a good thing, it's fortunate (RT, NJ, GJ) [*example*: Dedeb igo gaa-wiisiniyaan zhebaa. = It's a good thing I ate this morning. *example*: Dedeb igo gaa-agwana'aman daa-gii-tibaabaawan. = It's is a good thing you covered them they would have gotten damp.]

GORILLA: SILVER-BACK GORILLA: **wayaabikweyaawiganed** *vai-prt* silver-back gorilla; *pl* **wayaabikweyaawiganejig** (RT, NJ, GJ)

GRAB:

> GRAB SOMEONE: **debibizh** /debibiN-/ *vta* catch, grab, or grasp s.o. (RT, NJ, GJ)
>
> STARTLE BY GRABBING: **goshkobizh** /goshkobiN-/ *vta* startle s.o by grabbing them (RT, NJ, GJ)

GRAIN:

> GRAIN: **bakwezhiganimin** *na* grain; *pl* **bakwezhiganiminag** (RT)

STORE GRAIN: **na'emine** *vai* store grain (RT)

GRANULATE:

FINELY GRANULATED: **nitaawan** *vii* be finely granulated, be fine sand (RT, NJ, GJ)

GRANULATED: **biisiboojigaazo** *vai* be ground up, be granulated (RT)

GRASP SOMEONE: **debibizh** /**debibiN-**/ *vta* catch, grab, or grasp s.o. (RT, NJ, GJ)

GRASS:

BE PLEASANT SOUND OF GRASS BLOWING: **minwewekosiwaagosin** *vii* be a pleasant sound of the grass blowing in the wind (NJ); *also* **minweweshkosiwagaasin** *vii* good sound of grass blowing in the wind (NJ)

GRASS BENDS PART-WAY TO GROUND: **zhamashkosiweyaasin** *vii* grass bends part-way down to ground from the wind (GJ)

GRASS BENDS TO GROUND: **zhagashkosiweyaasin** *vii* grass bends down to ground from the wind, the grass is dancing (NJ, GJ); *also* **zhamashkosiweyaasin** (NJ)

GRASS BLOWING NICELY IN WIND: **minokosiwaagaasin** *vii* the grass is blowing nicely in the wind (NJ); *also* **minoshkosiiwagaasin** (GJ)

GRASS DANCE: **zhamashkishimo** *vai* do the grass dance (crouch while dancing) (GJ)

GRASS FLATTENS IN WIND: **nabashkweyaasin** *vii* grass flattens in the wind (LM)

GRASS STEM: **mashkosiinsigaawanzh** *ni* grass stem; *pl* **mashkosiinsigaawanzhiin** (RT)

GRASS TURNS GOLD: **ozaawaashkosiwe** *vii* grass turns golden (RT)

GRASSLAND: **mashkosiinsikaa** *vii* be a grassland, be lots of grass (RT)

LAWN: **mashkosiinsikaan** *ni* lawn (RT)

GRAY CLAY: **waabaabigan** *na* white or gray clay (NJ)

GREEN:

GREEN LEAF: **ashkibag** *ni* green leaf; *pl* **ashkibagoon** (RT)

GREEN LEAVES: **ashkibagokaa** *vii* be many green leaves (RT)

GREEN WOOD (CHOPPED): **ishkaatig** *ni* green wood (chopped); *pl* **ishkaatigoon** (GJ)

GREEN WOOD (STANDING): **ishkaatig** *na* green wood (as in standing green trees); *pl* **ishkaatigoog** (GJ)

GRIND:

GRIND: **bigishkanjige** *vai* grind, eat by grinding (RT)

GRIND SOMETHING: **bigishkandan** *vti* grind s.t. in one's mouth (RT)

GRIST MILL: **biisiboojigewigamig** *ni* grist mill; *pl* **biisiboojigewigamigoon**; *loc* **biisiboojigewigamigong** (RT)

GROOVE IN ROCK: **bakweyaabika'o** *vai* put a groove in rock (as in to attach an anchor line) (RT, NJ, GJ)

GROUND:

AGAINST GROUND: **ashidakamig** *pc* against the ground (GJ); *also* **ashoodakamig** (RT, NJ, GJ)

CROUCH TO GROUND: **zhagashkii** *vai* crouch down to ground (RT, NJ, GJ); *also* **zhamashkii** *vai* crouch down to ground (RT, NJ, GJ)

GRANULATED: **biisiboojigaazo** *vai* be ground up, be granulated (RT)

GRASS BENDS PART-WAY TO GROUND: **zhamashkosiweyaasin** *vii* grass bends part-way down to ground from the wind (GJ)

GRASS BENDS TO GROUND: **zhagashkosiweyaasin** *vii* grass bends down to ground from the wind, the grass is dancing (NJ, GJ); *also* **zhamashkosiweyaasin** (NJ)

PLANT IN GROUND: **badakamigisidoon** *vti* plant it in the ground (RT, NJ, GJ)

PUSH OFF FROM GROUND: **mininaawekii'o** *vai* push off while touching the ground (GJ); *also* **niminaawekii'o** (NJ)

GROUP:

BALLED UP: **bikwaakwadotaawag /bikwaakwadotaa/** *vai* they are balled up (ducks, geese, bugs) [*conjugation note*: requires multiple actors to make sense even though this is not a reflexive verb] (NJ, GJ)

SORT SOMETHING: **maawandoonan** *vti* sort s.t., group s.t. (RT, NJ, GJ)

GROW:

GROW ALONG: **bimigin** *vii* grow along (RT)

GROW BIG: **mangigin** *vii* grow big (RT)

GROW CERTAIN WAY: **izhigin** *vii* grow in a certain way (RT)

GROW CROWDED: **miiwishkodaadigin** *vii* grow crowded, grow close together (RT)

GROW FORKED: **niingidowaakogi** *vai* grow in a forked shape (GJ)

GROW IN CERTAIN PLACE: **dazhigi** *vai* grow in a certain place (RT)

GROW IN CERTAIN PLACE: **dazhigin** *vii* grow in a certain place (RT, NJ, GJ)

GROW IN RINGS: **waawiyaagishin** *vai* grow in rings (RT, NJ, GJ)

GROW IN WEIGHT: **aanjibo** *vai* change weight, grow in weight (as a child) (RT, NJ, GJ)

GROW INTO SOMETHING ELSE: **aanjigin** *vii* change while growing, grow into s.t. else (RT)

GROW SOMEONE STRONG: **mashkawa'wi /mashkawa'w-/** *vta* make s.o. strong, grow s.o. strong (NJ)

GROW STRONG: **mashkawigin** *vii* grow strong (RT)

GROW TALL: **ginoogin** *vii* grow high, grow tall (RT)

GROW TO A SMALL STATURE: **dakogin** *vii* grow to a small stature (RT)

GROW TO SURFACE: **mookibiigin** *vii* grow to the surface (as in lily pads to the surface of the water) (RT)

GROW WELL: **minogi** *vai* grow well (RT)

GROW WELL: **minogin** *vii* grow well (RT, NJ, GJ)

HAVE FULLY GROWN LEAVES: **giizhibagizi** *vai* has leaves fully grown (as in a tree) (RT, NJ, GJ)

LEAVES ARE FULLY GROWN: **giizhibagaa** *vii* leaves are fully grown (RT, NJ, GJ)

MATURE: **giizhigin** *vii* mature, ripen, finish growing (RT, NJ, GJ)

NEW GROWTH: **oshkigin** *vii* s.t. new grows (RT)

ORIGINATE: **onjigin** *vii* grow from a certain place, originate (RT)

SPROUT: **zaagakii** *vii* sprout (RT)

START GROWING: **maajiigi** *vai* start to grow (RT)

START GROWING: **maajiigin** *vii* start to grow (RT)

STOP GROWING: **noogigin** *vii* stop growing (RT)

GROWL: **niikimo** *vai* growl (RT, NJ, GJ)

GUIDE DOG: **gagiibiingwewasim** *na* guide dog; *pl* **gagiibiingwewasimoog** (NJ)

GUITAR: SOUND PLEASANT PLAYING GUITAR: **minweweyaabiigibijige**
*vai* make a pleasant sound playing guitar (RT, NJ, GJ)

GYMNASIUM: **odaminoowigamig** *ni* gym; *pl* **odaminoowigamigoon**; *loc*
**odaminoowigamigong** (NJ)

HAIR:

ARM HAIR: **miishinikaan** *ni* arm hair; *pl* **miishinikaanan** (RT,
NJ, GJ)

BACK OR CHEST HAIR: **miishaawiganaan** *ni* back or chest hair;
*pl* **miishaawiganaanan** (RT, NJ, GJ)

BE HAIRY: **miishizi** *vai* hairy (RT, NJ, GJ)

CHEST HAIR: **miishaakiganaan** *ni* chest hair; *pl*
**miishaakiganaanan** (RT, NJ, GJ)

EYEBROW: **nimaamaa** *na* eyebrow; *pl* **nimaamaayag** (RT, NJ,
GJ)

HAIRY CHEST: **miishaakigan** *ni* hairy chest *pl* **miishaakiganan**
(RT, NJ, GJ)

HAVE HAIRY BACK: **miishaawigane** *vai* have a hairy back (RT,
NJ, GJ)

HAVE HAIRY CHEST: **miishaakigane** *vai* have a hairy chest (RT,
NJ, GJ)

HAVE HAIRY LEGS: **miishigaade** *vai* have hairy legs (RT, NJ, GJ)

HAVE SILVER-HAIRED BACK: **waabikweyaawigane** *vai* have a
silver-colored hairy back (RT, NJ, GJ)

LEG HAIR: **miishigaadaan** *ni* leg hair; *pl* **miishigaadaanan** (RT,
NJ, GJ)

LONG HAIR: **ginwawe** *vai* have long fur or hair (RT)

PERSON WITH HAIRY CHEST: **miishaakiganesi** *na* s.o. with a
hairy chest; *pl* **miishaakiganesiwag** (RT, NJ, GJ)

SNARLY HAIR: **niiskaweyaandibe** *vai* have snarly hair (RT, NJ,
GJ)

HALF: CUT IN HALF: **bookozhigaazo** *vai* be cut in half (NJ)

HAMMER:

HAMMER SOUND: **bakitewe** *vii* make a hammering sound (RT,
NJ, GJ)

JACK HAMMER: **waasamoo-mangaanibaajigan** *ni* jack hammer;
*pl* **waasamoo-mangaanibaajigan** (RT, NJ, GJ)

USE AS HAMMER: **bakite'igaage** *vai+o* use s.t. for a hammer, use
s.t. to hit [*example*: Waagaakwadoon bakite'igaagen. = Use the
hatchet as a hammer.] (NJ)

HAND:

BEND DOWN WITH HAND: **ispwaabikibidoon** *vti* bend s.t. (metal-like) down with hand (as in bending over a protruding nail) (GJ)

GIVE SOMEONE THE PEACE SIGN: **niingidowaakoninjiitaw** *vai* give s.o. the peace sign (GJ)

HAND TO SOMEONE: **ininamaw** *vta* hand s.t. to s.o. (RT, NJ, GJ)

MAKE PEACE SIGN: **niingidowaakoninjiini** *vai* make the peace sign (GJ)

PALM OF HAND: **nagaakininjaan** *ni* palm of hand; *loc* **nagaakininjaaning** (RT, NJ, GJ)

THROW OPEN HAND AT ONE ANOTHER: **nimiskandiwag** /**nimiskandi-**/ *vai* throw the open hand at one another (all 5 fingers open and extended) [*cultural note*: considered extremely offensive, likely to be perceived as an intent to do spiritual harm or use bad medicine on s.o.] (RT, NJ, GJ)

THROW OPEN HAND AT SOMEONE: **nimiskam** *vta* throw the open hand at s.o. (all 5 fingers open and extended) [*cultural note*: considered extremely offensive, likely to be perceived as an intent to do spiritual harm or use bad medicine on s.o.] (RT, NJ, GJ)

WEAR MITTEN ON WRONG HAND: **aabitanakakezi** *vai* a mitten or glove is worn on the wrong hand (NJ) [*example*: Aabitanakakeziwag. = Two left-handed or right-handed gloves or mittens are worn.]; *also* **aapidanakakezi** (GJ)

WRING BY HAND: **ziikoobiiginan** *vti* wring s.t. by hand, drain the water out of s.t. (NJ)

HANG:

HANG BENT: **waagigoode** *vii* hang in a bent position (RT, NJ, GJ)

HANG LOW INVERTED: **wiimbaagishkoode** *vii* hang low inverted (concave) (GJ)

HANGER:

FIRE HANGER: **agoojiganaak** *ni* hanger for fire; *pl* **agoojiganaakoon** (RT, NJ, GJ)

KETTLE HANGER: **agoodakikwaanaak** *ni* kettle hanger (as in planted kettle hanger); *pl* **agoodakikwaanaakoon** (RT, NJ, GJ)

HAPPY: HAVE HAPPY RIDE: **minobizo** *vai* have a happy ride (NJ)

HARD: DIE HARD: **zhiibine** *vai* doesn't die easily, dies hard (GJ, NJ)

HARD: *see also* STRONG

---

HARVEST:

    COMBINE: **giishkashkosiwewidaabaan** *na* combine (mechanized harvesting machine); *pl* **giishkashkosiwewidaabaanag** (RT); *also* **mami'igewidaabaan** *na* combine (mechanized harvesting machine); *pl* **mami'igewidaabaanag** (RT)

    HARVEST: **mami'igaazo** *vai* be harvested, be taken (RT)

    HARVEST TREE CANDY: **ozibanike** *vai* harvest tree candy, peel the outer bark to eat the inner bark (typically of a poplar) (NJ) [*cultural note*: sweet, sticky substance in the inner bark (typically of poplar) was highly prized and consumed as a kind of candy]

    UNLOAD AND BRING INLAND: **gopimine** *vai* unload harvest from canoe and bring inland (NJ, GJ)

HAT: **wiiwakwaan** *ni* hat; *pl* **wiiwakwaanan** (RT, NJ, GJ)

HATCH: **baashkaawanwe'o** *vai* hatch (NJ)

HATE:

    BE HATED: **zhiingendaagozi** *vai* be hated (RT, NJ, GJ)

    HATE SOMEONE: **zhiingenim** *vta* hate s.o. (RT, NJ, GJ)

HEAD:

    HEAD POPS UP REPEATEDLY FROM BOILING: **zaasaagikwezo** *vii* head repeatedly pops up from boiling (RT, NJ, GJ)

    HEAD STICKS OUT WHILE FLOATING: **zaagikwegomo** *vai* head is sticking out of water while floating (NJ, GJ)

    HEAD STICKS OUT WHILE FLOATING BY: **bimi-zaagikwegomo** *vai* head sticks out while floating by (NJ, GJ)

    STRIKE HEAD: **bagaskindibe** *vai* strike (in moccasin game), smack on the head (RT, NJ, GJ)

    STRIKE SOMEONE ON HEAD: **bagaskindibe'wi /bagaskindibe'w-/** *vta* strike s.o. on the head (NJ); *also* **bagaskindibe'o /bagaskindibe'w-/** (GJ); *also* **bagaskindibe' /bagaskindibe'w-/** (RT)

HEAL:

    HEAL: **giige** *vai* heal up (RT, NJ, GJ)

    HEAL SOMEONE: **nanaandawishkaw** *vta* heal s.o. (RT, NJ, GJ)

HEAR:

    BE HEARD COMING THROUGH WATER: **zaasibiibizo** *vai* heard coming through water (as in a motorboat) (GJ)

    FEEL BY HEARING: **nooyoondam** *vai* feel with hearing (NJ)

FEEL SOMETHING BY HEARING: **nooyoondan** *vti* feel s.t. with hearing (NJ)

HEAR CLEARLY: **bagakitam** *vai* hear clearly (NJ)

HEAR SOMETHING CLEARLY: **debitan** *vti* hear s.t. clearly, identify the type or direction of a sound of s.t. (NJ, GJ)

HEARD CHEWING: **debwewenjige** *vai* be heard chewing from a distance (RT, NJ, GJ)

HEARING: **noondamowin** *ni* sense of hearing (RT, NJ, GJ)

HEARING AID: **tawagikaajigan** *ni* hearing aid; *pl* **tawagikaajiganan** (RT, NJ, GJ)

HEARD: *see* SOUND

HEAT: FALL ASLEEP FROM HEAT: **nibeyaakizo** *vai* fall asleep because of the heat [*example*: Ginibeyaakizomin. = We're falling asleep because of the heat.] (RT, NJ, GJ)

HEAVY:

BE HEAVY: **gwazigwani** *vai* be heavy (NJ)

FEEL HEAVY: **gozigon** *vii* feel heavy (RT, NJ, GJ)

HEEL: HIGH-HEELED SHOE: **ishpidoondanekizin** *ni* high-heeled shoe; *pl* **ishpidoondanekizinan** (RT, NJ, GJ)

HELP:

COOPERATION: **wiidookodaadiwin** *ni* cooperation (RT, NJ, GJ)

HELP SOMEONE: **wiiji'** *vta* help s.o. (NJ, GJ)

RELY: **wiiji'igoowizi** *vai* rely upon things, get help from things (NJ)

HEMORROID: **miskojiidiye** *vai* have a bleeding anus, hemorrhoids (RT, NJ, GJ)

HICCOUGH: **wanwewese** *vai* hiccough (NJ)

HICCUP: *see* HICCOUGH

HIDE:

HIDDEN: **gaazoomagad** *vii* be hidden (RT, NJ, GJ)

HIDE: **aapijigaazo** *vai* gone in hiding (RT, NJ, GJ)

HIDE FROM SOMEONE: **gaazootaw** *vta* hide from s.o. (RT)

PLAY HIDE-AND-SEEK: **gaazootaadiwag** /gaazootaadi-/ *vai* they play hide-and-seek with one another (NJ)

SCRAPE HIDE: **jiishaakwa'ige** *vai* scrape a hide (NJ); *also* cut limbs off a tree (GJ)

WRING OUT CLOTH OR HIDE: **ziiniskobiiga'an** *vti* wring out cloth or hide (RT, NJ, GJ)

HIGH:

BE HIGH: **giiwashkweyaabandam** *vai* be under the influence of narcotics, be "high" (RT, NJ, GJ)

GET SOMEONE HIGH: **giiwashkwebizh** /**giiwashkwebiN-**/ *vta* get s.o. high or drunk (RT)

HIGH IN TREES: **ishpaatigong** *pc* high in the trees (RT)

HIGH-HEELED SHOE: **ishpidoondanekizin** *ni* high-heeled shoe; *pl* **ishpidoondanekizinan** (RT, NJ, GJ)

HILL:

ANT HILL: **enigoonsigiwaam** *ni* ant hill; *pl* **enigoonsigiwaaman** (RT, NJ, GJ)

SAND OR ANT HILL: **bikwadaawangisin** *vii* be a sand hill, be an ant hill (RT, NJ, GJ)

HIND END POPS UP FROM BOILING: **zaasaagidiyezo** *vii* hind end repeatedly pops up from boiling (RT, NJ, GJ)

HISTORY: **odaanaam** *ni* background, personal history (NJ) [*example*: Gii-wanii'ige mewinzha odoodaanaaming, gaawiin geyaabi noongom. = He used to trap long ago in his background, but not any more.]

HIT:

FEIGN AT SOMEONE: **nima'wi** /**nima'w-**/ *vta* feign at s.o. (as in a strike) [*example*: Ningii-nima'waa. = I acted like I was going to hit him.] (NJ); *also* **nima'o** /**nima'w-**/ (GJ)

HIT BACK-AND-FORTH: **aayaazhawi-bakite'amaadiwag** /**aayaazhawi-bakite'amaadi-**/ *vai+o* they hit s.t. back-and-forth to one another [*example*: Aayaazhawi-bakite'amaadiwag bikwaakwad. = They are hitting the ball to one another.] (NJ, GJ)

HIT HEAD: **bagaskindibe** *vai* strike (in moccasin game), smack on the head (RT, NJ, GJ)

HIT REPEATEDLY: **bapakiteshka'igaade** *vii* be hit repeatedly (as in wheat being struck repeatedly by a combine) (RT)

STRIKE SOMEONE ON HEAD: **bagaskindibe'wi** /**bagaskindibe'w-**/ *vta* strike s.o. on the head (NJ); *also* **bagaskindibe'o** /**bagaskindibe'w-**/ (GJ); *also* **bagaskindibe'** /**bagaskindibe'w-**/ (RT)

HOLD:

BE HELD: **minjimishkoode** *vii* be held in place (GJ)

CLING TO SOMEONE: **minjimin** *vta* cling to s.o., hold onto s.o. (RT)

HELD ACROSS BY STICK: **bimaakobide** *vii* be held out across by a stick (as in lodge runners parallel to the ground) (GJ)

HOLD AGAINST EARTH: **ashoodakamigishkaw** *vta* hold s.o. in place against the earth (GJ)

HOLD SOMEONE IN SAND: **minjimindaawangishkaw** *vta* hold s.o. in place in the sand (GJ)

HOLD SOMEONE IN SNOW: **minjimaagoneshkaw** *vta* hold s.o. in snow (GJ)

HOLD SOMEONE WITH FOOT: **minjimishkaw** *vta* hold s.o. place with foot (GJ)

HOLD SOMETHING: **minjimishkoodoon** *vti* hold s.t. in place (GJ)

PLACE HOLDER: **minjimishkoojigan** *ni* place holder; *pl* **minjimishkoojiganan** (GJ)

STABILIZE SOMEONE WITH STICK: **minjimaakwa'o /minjimaakwa'w-/** *vta* hold s.o. up with stick to stabilize it (GJ)

STABILIZE WITH STICK: **minjimaakwa'an** *vti* hold s.t. up with stick to stabilize it (GJ)

STICK FOR HOLDING ACROSS: **bimaakobijigan** *ni* stick for holding s.t. across; *pl* **bimaakobijiganan** (GJ)

HOLD: *see also* PIN

HOLE:

BE A HOLE IN ICE: **bagwaawanibii** *vii* be a hole in the ice (NJ, GJ); *also* **bookizigwaa** (GJ)

CURRENT CUTS ICE: **bagonezigwaa** *vii* current cuts a hole in ice (RT, NJ, GJ); *also* **bagonezigojiwan** (GJ); *also* **bookizigwajiwan** (GJ)

HOLE IN ICE: **dwaa'igan** *ni* hole in the ice; *pl* **dwaa'iganan** (RT, NJ, GJ)

HOLE IN ICE (AIR): **bagwaawanib** *ni* hole in the ice caused by air (as in from a beaver disturbing the lake bottom); *pl* **bagwaawanibiin** (NJ, GJ)

HOLE IN ICE (CURRENT): **bagonib** *pc* hole through the ice caused by current, spring, or vortex (NJ, GJ)

MAKE HOLE IN ICE: **dwaa'ige** *vai* make a hole in the ice (RT, NJ, GJ)

MAKE HOLE IN ICE FOR WATER: **dwaa'ibii** *vai* make a hole in the ice for water (RT, NJ, GJ)

SMOKE HOLE: **wenji-zaagidaabateg** *vii-prt* smoke hole (RT, NJ, GJ)

WATER POOLS: **bagonebiiwan** *vii* there is a pool of water on the ice from a hole (NJ, GJ)

HOOK:

FISH HOOK: **migiskan** *ni* fish hook; *pl* **migiskanan** (RT, NJ, GJ); *dim* **migiskanens**; *pl* **migiskanensan** (RT)

GAFF HOOK: **aajibijigan** *ni* gaff hook; *pl* **aajibijiganan** (GJ)

HOOK IS EMPTY: **gishewaabikad** *vii* hook is empty (RT, NJ, GJ)

PLANT HOOK: **waagi-wiinizisens** *ni* hook (as in the burr of a plant); *pl* **waagi-wiinizisensan** (RT)

HOOP:

BEAVER STRETCHING HOOP: **zhingibijiganaak** *ni* hoop for stretching beaver hide; *pl* **zhingibijiganaakoon** (NJ, GJ)

STRING FOR BEAVER STRETCHING HOOP: **zhingibijiganeyaab** *ni* wrapping string for beaver hide stretching hoop; *pl* **zhingibijiganeyaabiin** (RT, NJ, GJ)

HOP: **aayaazhawi-boonii** *vai* hop from one branch to another (NJ, GJ)

HORN:

CAR HORN: **odaabaan noondaagamo'ind** *vta-prt* car horn (NJ, GJ)

HAVE HORNS: **odeshkani** *vai* have horns (as in an animal) (NJ)

HORSE: MALE DOG, HORSE, WOLF: **naabesim** *na* male dog, male horse, male wolf; *pl* **naabesimag** (RT, NJ, GJ)

HOT: SHINE HOTLY: **gizhaasige** *vai* shine hotly (as in the sun) (RT)

HUFF: **ikwanaanjige** *vai* sniff, huff (RT, NJ, GJ)

HURRIED: **mamaazhiike** *pc* any old way, done hurriedly, not in a good way (NJ); *also* **mamaanzhii** (GJ)

HUSK: SEED SHELL: **miinikaanagek** *na* seed shell; *pl* **miinikaanagekwag** (RT)

HYPHEN:

HYPHEN: **aanikebii'igan** *ni* hyphen (–) (JC)

HYPHENATE: **aanikebii'ige** *vai* hyphenate (JC)

ICE:

ANCHOR POLE FOR NETTING UNDER ICE: **anaamizigoneyaatig** *ni* anchor pole for ice netting; *pl* **anaamizigoneyaatigoon** (RT, NJ, GJ)

BE A HOLE IN ICE: **bagonezigwaa** *vii* be a hole in the ice (NJ, GJ); *also* **bagwaawanibii** (NJ, GJ); *also* **bookizigwaa** (GJ)

CURRENT CUTS ICE: **bagonezigwaa** *vii* current cuts a hole in ice (RT, NJ, GJ); *also* **bagonezigojiwan** (GJ); *also* **bookizigwajiwan** (GJ)

DETACHED OPENING IN ICE ALONG SHORE: **waasooskode'an** *vii* be a detached opening in the ice along the shore (GJ)

FALL THROUGH ICE: **dwaashin** *vai* fall through the ice (RT, NJ, GJ)

HOLE IN ICE: **dwaa'igan** *ni* hole in the ice; *pl* **dwaa'iganan** (RT, NJ, GJ)

HOLE IN ICE (AIR): **bagwaawanib** *ni* hole in the ice caused by air (as in from a beaver disturbing the lake bottom); *pl* **bagwaawanibiin** (NJ, GJ)

HOLE IN ICE (CURRENT): **bagonib** *pc* hole through the ice caused by current, spring, or vortex (NJ, GJ)

ICE CHISEL: **eshkan** *ni* ice chisel; *pl* **eshkanan** (RT, NJ, GJ)

ICE OVER: **oshkaabaanedin** *vii* ice over, ice forms for the first time (with no snow cover), new ice forms (NJ, GJ); *also* **oshkadin** *vii* (RT, NJ, GJ)

ICE SCOOPER: **eshkan gwaaba'iskomaan** *ni* ice scooper; *pl* **eshkanan gwaaba'iskomaanan** (NJ, GJ)

ICE SHELF FREEZES: **biitooskibiigadin** *vii* ice shelf freezes (RT, NJ, GJ)

ICE SHELF: **biitooskibiiyaa** *vii* be an ice shelf (RT, NJ, GJ)

MAKE HOLE IN ICE: **dwaa'ige** *vai* make a hole in the ice (RT, NJ, GJ)

MAKE HOLE IN ICE FOR WATER: **dwaa'ibii** *vai* make a hole in the ice for water (RT, NJ, GJ)

ON TOP OF ICE: **ogidikwam** *pc* on top of ice (GJ); *also* **ogijikwam** (RT, NJ, GJ); *also* **ogijizigwaang** (RT, NJ, GJ)

OPENING IN ICE ALONG SHORE: **waasooskodewan** *vii* be an opening in the ice along the shore (NJ)

POLE TO SET NET UNDER ICE: **anaamizigwaneyaatig** *ni* slider push-pole for setting net under ice; *pl* **anaamizigwaneyaatigoon** (RT, NJ, GJ)

PUT NET STRING UNDER ICE: **anaamizigoneyaabii** *vai* put net string under ice (RT, NJ, GJ)

SET NET UNDER ICE: **anaamizigosabii** *vai* set net under the ice (RT, NJ, GJ)

STRING FOR NETTING UNDER ICE: **anaamizigoneyaab** *ni* ice netting string (with pole); *pl* **anaamizigoneyaabiin** (RT, NJ, GJ)
UNDER ICE: **anaamizigwam** *pc* under the ice (RT, NJ, GJ); **anaamikwam** *pc* under the ice (RT, NJ, GJ)
WATER POOLS: **bagonebiiwan** *vii* there is a pool of water on the ice from a hole (NJ, GJ)
IGLOO: **mikwamii-waaginogaan** *ni* igloo; *pl* **mikwamii-waaginogaanan** (RT, NJ, GJ)
IGNITE: **biskaakonese** *vii* ignite, spark (RT, NJ, GJ); *also* **nawadide** *vii* catch on fire (RT, NJ, GJ)
ILL: JOINT ILLNESS: **giziibishkam** *vai* have a joint illness (RT, NJ, GJ)
ILLUMINATION: **inaatewin** *ni* light, illumination (RT)
ILLUSTRATE: **mazinaakide** *vii* be a picture, be illustrated (RT)
IMAGE: MAKE IMAGE BY FOLDING: **maziniiginige** *vai* fold images, make images or pictures (using paper or cloth-like material) (GJ)
IMPORTANT: **ishpendaagwad** *vii* be important (RT, NJ, GJ)
INCISOR:
    HAVE INCISORS: **giishkaabide** *vai* have incisors (RT)
    INCISOR: **giishkaabid** *ni* incisor; *pl* **giishkaabidan** (RT)
    LARGE INCISOR: **mamaangi-giishkaabide** *vai* have large incisors (RT)
INHIBIT: SMELL INHIBITED: **mooshkinemaagod** *vii* have one's sense of smell filled or inhibited (as in by a cold) (NJ); *also* **mooshkinemaagwad** (RT)
INK: **biitewegani-ozhibii'iganaaboo** *ni* ink (RT, NJ, GJ)
INLAND:
    CARRY SOMETHING INLAND: **gopiwidoon** *vti* carry s.t. inland (NJ, GJ)
    UNLOAD AND BRING INLAND: **gopiwidaaso** *vai* unload and bring inland (NJ, GJ)
    UNLOAD HARVEST AND BRING INLAND: **gopimine** *vai* unload harvest from canoe and bring inland (NJ, GJ)
INSERT:
    SLIDE SOMEONE IN TIGHT AREA: **zhegwaakozh / zhegwaakoN-/** *vta* stick s.o. in a tight place (NJ)
    SLIDE SOMETHING IN TIGHT AREA: **zhegwaakonan** *vti* slide s.t. into a tight area (of s.t. stick-like) (NJ)
INSIDE OUT:
    BE INSIDE OUT: **napaajiigisin** *vii* be inside out (NJ, GJ)

INSIDE OUT: **aaboojiigisin** *vii* be turned inside out (cloth-like) (RT, NJ, GJ)

ROOF INSIDE OUT: **napaajibakwe** *vii* be roofed inside out (GJ)

INSIDE: FIT INSIDE: **debashkine** *vai* be covered; *also* fit inside (NJ)

INSUFFICIENT: **ayiite** *pc* insufficient (NJ); *also* **aayiide** (GJ)

INTEREST: DISINTERESTED: **noondegidaazo** *vai* be disinterested (TS)

INTERMITTENT WIND: **mamaadaanimad** *vii* wind starts intermittently (RT)

INTERNET: WORLD WIDE WEB: **giiwitaakamisab** *na* world wide web (RT, NJ, GJ)

INVERSE:

INVERSE: **napaaj** *pc* backwards, inverse (NJ, GJ)

OPPOSITE: **nanepaaj** *pc* opposite, inverse (NJ, GJ)

INVERT: HANG LOW INVERTED: **wiimbaagishkoode** *vii* hang low inverted (concave) (GJ)

ITALICS: **ashawebii'igaade** *vii* be italicized (GJ)

JACK: CAR JACK: **ombaakwa'igan** *ni* something used to lift things, crutch, jack (GJ)

JACK HAMMER: **waasamoo-mangaanibaajigan** *ni* jack hammer; *pl* **waasamoo-mangaanibaajigan** (RT, NJ, GJ)

JACK PINE: **okikaandag** *na* jack pine; *pl* **okikaandagoog** (NJ); *also* **akikaandag**; *pl* **akikaandagoog** (RT, GJ)

JELLY: **baashkiminasigan** *ni* marmalade, jam, jelly (NJ); *pl* **baashkiminasiganan**; *also* **baashkominisigan** (RT)

JOINT:

JOINT ILLNESS: **giziibishkam** *vai* have a joint illness (RT, NJ, GJ)

JOINT STRAIN: **ogiziibishkami** *vai* have a joint strain (mild, not long-lasting) (RT, NJ, GJ)

JUMP:

JUMP IN TOUCHING BOTTOM: **debakiise** *vai* jump in and hands or feet touch the bottom (GJ)

JUMP INTO WATER: **bakobiigwaashkwani** *vai* leap into the water (RT)

JUMP OUT: **zaagiji-gwaashkwani** *vai* jump out (RT, NJ, GJ)

JUMP OUT REPEATEDLY: **zaasaagiji-gwaashkwani** *vai* jump out repeatedly (RT, NJ, GJ)

JUNIPER: **gaagaagiwaandag** *na* juniper; *pl* **gaagaagiwaandagoog** (RT, NJ, GJ)

KABETOGAMA: **Gaa-biitoogamaag** *place* Kabetogama (literally the place where there is one lake after another) (GJ)

KENTROSAURUS: **wayaawaasepikwaned** *vai-prt* kentrosaurus; *pl* **wayaawaasepikwanewaad** (NJ)

KETTLE: FIRE KETTLE: **boodawaanakik** *na* fire kettle; *pl* **boodawaanakikoog** (RT, NJ, GJ)

KICK:

    KICK: **basikawaadan** *vti* kick s.t. (NJ)

    KICK BACK-AND-FORTH: **aayaazhawi-basikamaadiwag /aayaazhawi-basikamaadi-/** *vai+o* they kick s.t. back-and-forth to one another [*example:* Aayaazhawi-basikamaadiwag bikwaakwad. = They are kicking the ball to one another.] (NJ, GJ)

KILL:

    FIRST KILL: **oshki-nitaage** *vai* make a first kill (RT, NJ, GJ)

    STICK UP FINS TO KILL: **michige'wi /michige'w-/** *vta* stick up fins to kill s.o. (NJ); *also* **michigwe'o /michigwe'w-/** (GJ)

KITE: **ombaasijigan** *ni* kite; *pl* **ombaasigijiganan**; *dim* **ombaasijiganens** (RT, NJ, GJ)

KNEAD SOMEONE: **onadin** *vta* knead s.o. (NJ, GJ)

KNOCK:

    KNOCK RICE: **bawa'am** *vai* knock rice (RT, NJ, GJ)

    KNOCK SOMETHING: **bawa'an** *vti* knock s.t. (as in rice) (RT, NJ, GJ)

    KNOCKED: **bawa'igaade** *vii* be knocked (as in rice) (RT, NJ, GJ)

KNOCK OFF LIMB: **bashkwadikwane'ige** *vai* knock branches or limbs off a tree (RT, NJ, GJ)

KNOT:

    BE KNOTTED: **aapidapide** *vii* be knotted to the point of being impossible to untie (RT, NJ, GJ)

    BE KNOTTED: **gashka'oode** *vii* be knotted (RT, NJ, GJ)

    BE TIED: **gashka'oozo** *vai* be fastened, tied (RT, NJ, GJ)

    KNOT: **aapidapidoon** *vti* knot s.t. to point of being unable to untie (RT, NJ, GJ)

    WOOD KNOT: **wadikwan** *ni* tree branch, wood knot; *pl* **wadikwanan**; *loc* **wadikwaning** [*example*: Wadikwaning izhi-boonii. = He lands on a limb.] (NJ, GJ); *also* **odikon**; *pl* **odikonan** (GJ)

KNOW:

BE KNOWN: **gikendaagozi** *vai* be known, be around (NJ)

KNOWN BY SENSE: **gikendamaazo** *vai* sense things, know things by sense, discover (RT, NJ, GJ)

KNUCKLE: **nimbikoninjaan** *nid* my knuckle [*example*: Nashke giga-bakite'win nimbikoninjaanan! = Hey I'm going to rap you with my knuckles!] (NJ, GJ)

KOALA: **aniibiishanjige-makwa** *na* koala bear *pl* **aniibiishanjige-makwag** (RT, NJ, GJ)

LACE:

HAVE LACES: **makizineyaabiikaade** *vii* have laces (RT, NJ, GJ)

LACE: **ashkimaazh /ashkimaaN-/** *vta* lace s.o. (as in a snowshoe) (NJ)

LACE: **naaba'oojigan** *ni* lace; *pl* **naaba'oojiganan** (RT, NJ, GJ)

SNOWSHOE LACE: **ashkimaneyaab** *ni* snowshoe lacing; *pl* **ashkimaneyaabiin** (NJ)

LADY BUG: **manoomini-manidoosh** *na* ladybug; *pl* **manoomini-manidoosh** (NJ, GJ)

LAKE:

BOTTOM OF LAKE: **mitaamik** *pc* at the bottom of the lake (RT, NJ, GJ)

LAKE BOTTOM: **asamiko-** *pv* at the bottom of the lake (RT, NJ, GJ)

LAKE BOTTOM SWIM: **asamikozhiwe** *vai* swims on the bottom of the lake (GJ)

LAKES LAYER: **biitoobiiyaa** *vii* the lakes are one after another (RT, NJ, GJ)

LAMP: DIM LAMP: **odaanzhenan** *vti* dim the lamp (NJ)

LAND:

LAND: **boonii** *vai, vii* land, perch (RT, NJ, GJ)

SKIP LAND: **detesabi-booniimagad** *vii* skip landing, land by bouncing on the water (as in duck or float plane) (RT, NJ, GJ)

TOUCH LAND FROM SKY: **mizhakiinam** *vai* go from the sky all the way to ground like a thunderbird, or tornado touching down (NJ, GJ)

TOUCH LAND FROM SKY AND RETURN: **mizhakiise** *vai* fly from the sky down to the earth, make land fall (then back up) (NJ, GJ)

TOUCH LAND IN WATER: **mizhakiikozhiwe** *vai* make it from below to land in the water (NJ, GJ)

LARGE:

BE LARGE: **misawaa** *vai* be so big (NJ)

BIG CHEEKS: **mamaanginowe** *vai* have big cheeks (RT)

BIG FEET: **mamaangizide** *vai* have big feet (RT)

BROAD FINS: **mamaangizhigwane** *vai* have broad fins (as in a fish) (RT)

GROW BIG: **mangigin** *vii* grow big (RT)

LARGE: **mamaandido** *vai* be amazingly large (NJ)

LARGE EYES: **mamaangishkiinzhigwe** *vai* have large eyes (RT, NJ, GJ)

LARGE LEAVES: **mamaangibagaa** *vii* have large leaves (RT)

LARGE LEAVES: **mamaangibagizi** *vai* have large leaves (RT, NJ, GJ)

LARGE, SHARP TEETH: **mamaangi-giinaabid** *ni* large, sharp teeth; *pl* **mamaangi-giinaabidan** (RT)

SUFFICIENTLY LARGE MOUTH: **debanendan** *vti* have a sufficiently large mouth to bite s.t. [*lexicon note*: from discussion of the size of a bagidaabaan, an item for ice fishing] (NJ)

LASAGNA NOODLE: **mangade-bakwezhiganaabiins** *ni* lasagna noodle; *pl* **mangade-bakwezhiganaabiinsan** (RT, NJ, GJ)

LASSO SOMEONE: **naabaabiigwebizh** /naabaabiigwebiN-/ *vta* lasso s.o. around the neck (NJ, GJ)

LASSO: *see also* ROPE

LATE: **bezikaa** *vai* go slow, be late [*example*: Ningii-ondami'aa wenji-bezikaayaang. = I'm the reason we are late. *example*: Hay' onzaam gibezikaamin, aazha gii-kiba'igaade. = Shoot, we're too late, it's already closed. *example*: Wiikaa ningii-koshkoz wenji-bezikaayaan. = I got up too late, which is why I'm late.] (NJ)

LATER: PERHAPS LATER: **maagizhaa baamaa ingoding** *expression* perhaps at some later time (RT, NJ, GJ); *also* **maazhaa ge baamaa ingoding** (RT, NJ, GJ)

LAUGH: **baapise** *vai* laugh suddenly (NJ)

LAWN:

    LAWN: **mashkosiinsikaan** *ni* lawn (RT)

    LAWN MOWER: **waasamoo-dakwaabiigizhoochigan** *ni* lawn mower; *pl* **waasamoo-dakwaabiigizhoochiganan** (RT, NJ, GJ)

    SPRINKLER: **ziswebiiga'anjigan** *ni* lawn sprinkler; *pl* **ziswebiiga'anjiganan** (NJ)

LAY EGG: **boonam** *vai2* lay an egg (RT, NJ, GJ)

LAY: *see* LIE

LAYER:

> LAYER: **apiigisijigan** *ni* layer or sheet; *pl* **apiigisijiganan** (RT, NJ, GJ)
>
> PEEL IN LAYERS: **biitoobiigibijige** *vai* peel in layers (RT, NJ, GJ); *also* **biitoobijigaade** *vii* be peeled in layers (RT, NJ, GJ)
>
> WEAR A LAYER: **apiigisijiganekonaye** *vai* wear a layer of clothing (RT, NJ, GJ)

LEAD: **ashkikomaan** *ni* lead (metal); *pl* **ashkikomaanan** (RT, NJ, GJ)

LEAF:

> BE PLEASANT SOUND OF LEAVES: **minwewebagaasin** *vii* be a pleasant sound of wind in the tree leaves (NJ)
>
> GREEN LEAF: **ashkibag** *ni* green leaf; *pl* **ashkibagoon** (RT)
>
> GREEN LEAVES: **ashkibagokaa** *vii* be many green leaves (RT)
>
> HAVE FULLY GROWN LEAVES: **giizhibagizi** *vai* has leaves fully grown (as in a tree) (RT, NJ, GJ)
>
> LARGE LEAVES: **mamaangibagaa** *vii* have large leaves (RT)
>
> LARGE LEAVES: **mamaangibagizi** *vai* have large leaves (RT, NJ, GJ)
>
> LEAVES ARE FULLY GROWN: **giizhibagaa** *vii* leaves are fully grown (RT, NJ, GJ)
>
> LOSE LEAVES: **binaakwii** *vai* lose leaves (as in a tree in autumn) (RT)
>
> TREE MAKES PLEASANT SOUND OF LEAVES: **minwewebagaashi** *vai* tree makes a pleasant sound of leaves in the wind (NJ)
>
> WET LEAVES: **dipiiwibagaa** *vii* be wet leaves (RT)

LEAP INTO WATER: **bakobiigwaashkwani** *vai* leap into the water (RT)

LEARN MUSIC: **gidochige** *vai* learn music (NJ)

LEASH: DOG LEASH: **gitaakwapizon** *ni* dog leash, dog chain, seat belt; *pl* **gitaakwapizonan** (RT, NJ, GJ)

LEFT: **nagajigaade** *vii* be left somewhere (RT)

LEG:

> CAUGHT BY LEG: **zagigaadebizo** *vai* be flung up, caught by the leg (as a rabbit in a tree spring-noose trap) (NJ)
>
> HAVE HAIRY LEGS: **miishigaade** *vai* have hairy legs (RT, NJ, GJ)
>
> LEG HAIR: **miishigaadaan** *ni* leg hair; *pl* **miishigaadaanan** (RT, NJ, GJ)
>
> STAND BARELEGGED: **zhaashaaginizidegaabawi** *vai* stand barelegged (RT, NJ, GJ)

STAND BOW-LEGGED: **waagigaadegaabawi** *vai* stand bow-legged (GJ)

STAND PIGEON-TOED: **waagizidegaabawi** *vai* stand pigeon-toed (GJ)

STRONG LEGS: **mashkawigaade** *vai* have strong legs (RT)

TIE SOMEONE'S LEGS: **zagigaadepizh** /**zagigaadepiN-**/ *vta* tie s.o. legs (RT, NJ, GJ)

TIE SOMEONE'S LEGS REPEATEDLY: **zasagigaadepizh** /**zasagigaadepiN-**/ *vta* tie s.o. legs repeatedly (RT, NJ, GJ)

LEGEND: TEACH WITH LEGENDS: **inaadizokaw** *vta* teach s.o. by use of traditional legends (NJ, GJ)

LEMMING: **mashkawikamigaaganoojiinh** *na* lemming; *pl* **mashkawikamigaaganoojiinyag** (RT); *also* **mayagi-waawaabiganoojiinh**; *pl* **mayagi-waawaabiganoojiinyag** (RT); *also* **okoba'idaweshiinh**; *pl* **okoba'idaweshiinyag** (RT); *also* **okoba'idiganoojiinh**; *pl* **okoba'idiganoojiinyag** (RT)

LEMON: **nemin** *na* lemon; *pl* **neminag** (RT)

LEOPARD FROG: **gichi-omakakii** *na* leopard frog; *pl* **gichi-omakakiig** (RT, NJ, GJ)

LETTER:

CAPITAL LETTER: **mangibii'igan** *ni* capital letter; *pl* **mangibii'iganan** (JC)

WRITE IN ALL CAPITAL LETTERS: **mangibii'ige** *vai* write in all capital letters (JC)

LEVEL:

LEVEL: **desaa** *vii* be flat as in a shelf, be level (RT, NJ, GJ)

WATER LEVEL DROPS: **iskaabiise** *vii* water level drops (RT, NJ, GJ); *also* **iskatese** *vii* water level drops (RT, NJ, GJ)

LIE:

LAYER: **apisin** *vii* lie as a protective layer (RT, NJ, GJ)

LIE ACROSS: **inaakogoojin** *vai* lie across (as in log) (RT, NJ, GJ)

LIE BACK FACING: **animikoshin** *vai* lie with back facing up (RT, NJ, GJ)

LIE DOWN FROM FULL BELLY: **gawashkine** *vai* lie down from being full (as in a really full belly) (RT, NJ, GJ)

LIE DOWN: **aazhigijishin** *vai* lie on one's back (RT, NJ, GJ)

LIE DOWN RELAXING: **goshkwaawaajishin** *vai* lie down relaxing, still (RT, NJ, GJ)

LIE ON: **apiigishin** *vai* lay as a protective layer (as in a trivet or pot holder) (RT, NJ, GJ)

LIE ON: **apiigisin** *vii* lay as a protective layer (as in a trivet or pot holder) (RT, NJ, GJ)

LIE ON SIDE: **opimeshin** *vai* lie on one's side (RT, NJ, GJ)

SKELETON LIES PICKED CLEAN: **zhiigooganeshin** vai skeleton lies on the ground picked clean (RT, NJ, GJ)

LIFE CYCLE: **eni-onji-bimaadak** *vii-prt* life cycle (RT)

LIFE JACKET: **detebaa'agonji-gibide'ebizon** *ni* personal floatation device, life jacket (RT, NJ, GJ)

LIFT SOMEONE: **ombin** *vta* lift s.o. up (RT, NJ, GJ)

LIGHT:

BE BRIGHT: **bagakaate** *vii* be bright light (RT, NJ, GJ)

BE DIM LIGHT: **waashaazheyaa** *vii* be dim light (RT)

LIGHT: **inaatewin** *ni* light, illumination (RT)

LIGHT ARRIVES: **bagamaate** *vii* light arrives in a certain place, light is captured in a certain place (RT)

LIGHT BULB: **obikwaajiins** *nid* little air sack, swim bladder; *also ni* light bulb (NJ, GJ)

LIGHT CHANGES: **aandaate** *vii* light changes (RT, NJ, GJ)

LIGHT GOES: **gizhiiyaate** *vii* be bright, far-reaching, or penetrating light (RT, NJ, GJ)

LIGHT SEPARATES: **babakeyaate** *vii* light separates (RT, NJ, GJ)

LIGHT SHINES: **akwaate** *vii* light shines a certain distance or length of time (RT, NJ, GJ)

SHINE ON SOMEONE: **minwaasigetamaw** *vta* shine pleasant light on s.o. (RT)

SUNLIGHT: **waaseyaawin** *ni* sunlight (RT)

TURN SOMETHING DOWN: **waashaanzhe'an** *vti* dim, turn s.t. down (as in a kerosene lantern) (RT); *also* **waashaanzhenan** (NJ)

LIKE SOUND: **minotan** *vti* like the sound of s.t. (RT, NJ, GJ)

LILY PAD:

LILY PAD: **ogitebag** *ni* lily pad; *pl* **ogitebagoon** (RT)

UNDER LILY PADS: **anaamibag** *pc* under the lily pads (RT)

LIMA BEAN: **omashkoziisimin** *na* lima bean; *pl* **omashkoziisiminag** (NJ)

LIMB:

LIMB (CUTTING): **jiishaakwa'ige** *vai* cut limbs off a tree (GJ); *also* scrape a hide (NJ)

LIMB (KNOCKING): **bashkwadikwane'ige** *vai* knock branches or limbs off a tree (RT, NJ, GJ)

LIMB SAPLING: **jiishaandawe'ige** *vai* limb small trees (as in cleaning saplings for use as lodge poles) (NJ)

LIMB SOMEONE: **giishkadikwane'wi** /**giishkadikwane'w-**/ *vta* limb s.o. (tree) using s.t. (ax, knife, or saw) (NJ)

LIMB SOMEONE (SAPLING): **jiishaanda'wi** /**jiishaanda'w-**/ *vta* limb small tree (as in cleaning saplings for use as lodge poles) (NJ)

LIMB WITH AX: **bashkwatigwanezhwi** /**bashkwatigwanezhw-**/ *vta* limb s.o. (tree) using s.t. (like an ax, knife) (NJ)

LINE:

CREASE: **inaabiigisin** *vii* be a line or crease in a certain way (NJ)

CROSS LINE: **gaashipoobizo** *vai* cross the line (as in driving out of lane), or miss a turnoff (as in driving) [*example*: Gigaashipoobizomin. = We missed the turn off.] (NJ, GJ)

LINE: **enaabiigising** *vii-prt* line, crease; *pl* **enaabiigisingin** (NJ)

LIQUID: *see* WATER

LIVE: **bimaadad** *vii* live (RT)

LIVER: **nikon** /**-kon-**/ *nid* my liver; *pl* **nikonan** (RT, NJ, GJ)

LIZARD: **okaadiginebig** *na* lizard; *pl* **okaadiginebigoog** (RT)

LOAD: **boozitaaso** *vai* load up (RT, NJ, GJ)

LOCATION: **inigokwaa** *vii* be such a size, be in a certain location, be everywhere [example: enigokwaag giiyaw = some parts of your body, all over your body] (NJ)

LODGE:

BIRCH BARK LODGE COVERING: **wiigwaasabakwaan** *ni* bark lodge covering; *pl* **wiigwaasabakwaanan** (RT, NJ, GJ)

CLOTH WIGWAM DOOR: **gibinde'igan** *ni* cloth door on wiigiwaam; *pl* **gibinde'iganan** (NJ)

DOMED LODGE: **waaginogaan** *ni* domed lodge; *pl* **waaginogaanan** (RT, NJ, GJ)

IGLOO: **mikwamii-waaginogaan** *ni* igloo; *pl* **mikwamii-waaginogaanan** (RT, NJ, GJ)

LODGE COVER TAB: **apigwaajigan** *ni* sewn covering reinforcement tab (as on birch bark lodge coverings) (RT, NJ, GJ)

LODGE POLE: **abanzh** *ni* lodge pole; *pl* **abanzhiin** (RT, NJ, GJ); *also* **abanzhiiwaatig** *ni* lodge pole; *pl* **abanzhiiwaatigoon** (GJ)

LODGE POLE: **namanjiin** *ni* unknown lodge pole [*lexicon note*: archaic word] (GJ)

LONG PEAKED LODGE: **nisawa'ogaan** *ni* long peaked lodge; *pl* **nisawa'ogaanan** (RT, NJ, GJ)

MAKE BIRCH BARK LODGE COVERING: **wiigwaasabakwayike** *vai* make birch bark lodge coverings (RT, NJ, GJ)

POINTED LODGE: **bajiishka'ogaan** *ni* pointed lodge (conical); *pl* **bajiishka'ogaanan** (NJ, GJ)

SEW ON: **agogwaade** *vii* sewn on, up against s.t. (as in ends of birch bark lodge coverings) (NJ, GJ)

TEACHING LODGE: **zhaabondawaan** *ni* teaching lodge, long-style wiigiwaam with doors and both ends; *pl* **zhaabondawaanan** (NJ)

TYPE OF LODGE: **dinawigamig** *pc* type of lodge (RT, NJ, GJ)

WIGWAM LODGE: **wiigiwaam** *ni* wigwam lodge; *pl* **wiigiwaaman** (RT, NJ, GJ)

LOG:

CLEAR CUT: **bashkoga'ige** *vai* make a clear cut, log by cutting all trees in an area (RT, NJ, GJ)

FLOAT LOGS: **bimaaboojige** *vai* float logs (RT, NJ, GJ)

ROLL LOGS: **ditibaakowebishkige** *vai* rolls logs (RT, NJ, GJ)

ROLL SOMEONE: **ditibaakowebishko'** /ditibaakowebishko'w-/ *vta* rolls s.o. (as in logs) (RT, NJ, GJ)

LONE:

LONE CLOUD: **Minisinaanakwad** *name* Lone Cloud (GJ)

LONE CLOUD: **minisinaanakwad** *vii* be a solitary cloud (RT, NJ, GJ); *also* **minisinaanakwagoode** *vii* be a lone cloud (RT, NJ, GJ)

LONG:

BE LONG: **ginwaakwad** *vii* be long (tree-like) (RT, NJ, GJ)

BEFORE LONG: **gomaa go apii** *expression* before long (RT)

ELONGATED SPIKE: **zagigi-omichigegani** *vai* have an elongated spike (as in a dinosaur) (NJ)

HAVE LONG ROOTS: **gagaanwaajiibikezi** *vai* have long roots (RT, NJ, GJ)

HAVE LONG TEETH: **gagaanwaabajiishkaabide** *vai* have long, pointed teeth (RT)

LONG CLAWS: **ginwaashkanzhiiwi** *vai* have long claws or fingernails (RT, NJ, GJ)

LONG DAY: **ginoo-giizhigad** *vii* be a long day (RT, NJ, GJ)
LONG EARS: **gagaanwaabiigitawage** *vai* have long ears (NJ)
LONG HAIR: **ginwawe** *vai* have long fur or hair (RT)
LONG NECK: **ginwaabiigigwe** *vai* have a long neck (NJ)
LONG NIGHT: **ginoo-dibikad** *vii* be a long night (RT, NJ, GJ)
LONG PEAKED LODGE: **nisawa'ogaan** *ni* long peaked lodge; *pl*
**nisawa'ogaanan** (RT, NJ, GJ)
LONG ROOTS: **gagaanwaajiibikeyaa** *vii* have long roots (RT, NJ,
GJ)
LONG TAIL: **ginwaabiigaanowe** *vai*  have a long tail (NJ)
LONG TONGUE: **ginwaabiigidenaniwe** *vai* have a long tongue
(RT)
LONG TOOTH: **gagaanwaabajiishkaabid** *ni* long, pointed tooth;
*pl* **gagaanwaabajiishkaabidan** (RT)
SUN SHINES LONG: **ginwaasige** *vai* sun shines a long time, be a
long day (as in a long summer day) (RT)

LOOK:
BUSY LOOKING: **ondamaabi** *vai* be busy looking around (RT,
NJ, GJ)
LOOK AT SOMEONE FROM CORNER OF EYE: **negwaabam** *vta* look
at s.o. out of the corner of one's eye (RT, NJ, GJ)
LOOK FOR BARK: **andawanagekwe** *vai* look for, search for bark
(RT, NJ, GJ)
LOOK FOR BASSWOOD: **andowiigobii** *vai* searching for basswood
(NJ, GJ)
LOOK FOR MINK: **andozhaangweshiwe** *vai* go after mink (NJ,
GJ)
LOOK FOR PITCH: **andobigiwe** *vai* go after pitch (NJ, GJ)
LOOK ONE'S BEST: **minonaagozi'idizo** *vai* look one's best (NJ)
STEAL GLANCES: **negwaabi** *vai* steal glances (RT, NJ, GJ)

LOOKOUT:
BE ON LOOKOUT: **andawaabi** *vai* be on lookout (RT)
BE ON LOOKOUT FOR SOMEONE: **ashawaabam** *vai* wait for s.o. to
appear, be on lookout for s.o. (RT, NJ, GJ)
LOOKOUT FOR FISH: **ashawaamiwe** *vai* lie in wait for fish
(spearing) in open water or ice (RT, NJ, GJ)
SIT WHILE ON LOOKOUT: **ashwabi** *vai* sit in wait (RT, NJ, GJ)

LOOSEN DAM: **baakibiigibidoon** *vti* loosen dam to make partial leak (not break entirely) [*cultural note*: this is a common technique for setting beaver traps] (NJ, GJ)

LOTION: **boozininjaan** *ni* lotion; *pl* **boozininjaanan** (NJ)

LOUD: VOICE CARRIES: **jiingwe** *vai* voice carries long ways (RT, NJ, GJ)

LOW:

> HANG LOW INVERTED: **wiimbaagishkoode** *vii* hang low inverted (concave) (GJ)
>
> LOW: **dabasi-ayaa** *vii* be low (as in on the ground or floor) (RT)
>
> SOUND LOW: **bedowe** *vii* have a soft voice (low and slow) (NJ, GJ)

MACARONI: **onagizhiikaanens** *ni* macaroni, *pl* **onagizhiikaanensan** (RT, NJ, GJ)

MADE FROM SOMETHING: **ozhichigaazo** *vai+o* be made, be formed (RT)

MAGNIFICENT: **bishigendaagwad** *vii* be magnificent (RT)

MAILBOX: **mazina'igani-makak** *ni* mailbox; *pl* **mazina'igani-makakoon** (RT, NJ, GJ)

MALE:

> DRAKE: **ininishib** *na* drake mallard; *pl* **ininishibag** (RT, NJ, GJ)
>
> MALE BIRD: **naabese** *na* male bird, rooster; *pl* **naabeseg** (RT, NJ, GJ)
>
> MALE DOG, HORSE, WOLF: **naabesim** *na* male dog, male horse, male wolf; *pl* **naabesimag** (RT, NJ, GJ)
>
> MALE FISH: **naabemeg** *na* male fish; *pl* **naabemegwag** (RT, NJ, GJ)
>
> MALE FRUIT: **naabemin** *ni* male fruit; *pl* **naabeminan** (RT, NJ, GJ)

MAPLE PLAIN: **Wekonimindaawangaans** *place* Maple Plain, Wisconsin (sandy beaver dam) (AM)

MARK: QUOTATION MARK: **giigidoobii'igan** *ni* quotation mark; *pl* **giigidoobii'iganan** ("") (JC)

MARKER: WIPE-OFF MARKER: **gaasi-adisibii'igan** *ni* wipe-off marker; *pl* **gaasi-adisibii'iganan** (RT, NJ, GJ)

MAT:

> CANOE MAT: **apishkaamon** *ni* mat for the bottom of a canoe; *pl* **apishkaamonan** (RT, NJ, GJ)
>
> CATTAIL MAT: **apakweshkway** *na* cattail mat; cattail; *pl* **apakweshkwayag**; *also* **nabagashk** (NJ)
>
> MAKE MATS: **anaakanike** *vai* make mats, rugs (RT, NJ, GJ)

PROTECTIVE MAT: **apisijigan** *ni* protective mat; *pl* **apisijiganan** (RT, NJ, GJ)

WOVEN MAT: **anaakan** *ni* woven mat; *pl* **anaakanan** (RT, NJ, GJ)

MATCH:

BE OPPOSITE: **nanepaadad** *vii* be odd, unmatched, opposite (NJ, GJ)

CONSIDERED OPPOSITE: **nanepaadendaagwad** *vii* be considered opposite (NJ, GJ)

OPPOSITE: **nanepaaj** *pc* opposite, inverse (NJ, GJ)

MATURE: **giizhigin** *vii* mature, ripen, finish growing (RT, NJ, GJ)

MEAT:

MEAT PEMMICAN: **nooka'iiwagwaan** *ni* pemmican (meat); *pl* **nooka'iiwagwaanan** (RT, NJ, GJ)

SMOKED MEAT: **giikanaabasigaadeg wiiyaas** *vii-prt* smoked meat (GJ)

MELT WATER: **zhwaaganib** *pc* spring melt water (NJ, GJ)

MENSTRUATE:

MENSTRUATE: **ookomisi** *vai* menstruate (be visited by one's grandma) (NJ)

SEQUESTER FOR MENSUS: **makoonsiwi** *vai* be sequestered for mensus (NJ); *also* **makoowizi** *vai* be sequestered for mensus (JC)

MESH:

MESH: **asabii-biiwabikoons** *ni* wire mesh, screen (RT, NJ, GJ)

MESH DIMENSION: **apiitadezi** *vai* be a certain width, be a certain dimension of mesh (as in a net) (RT, NJ, GJ)

MESH SIZE: **apiitashkizi** *vai* be a certain size mesh (as in a net) (RT, NJ, GJ)

METAL:

BE PLEASANT SOUND OF CHIMES: **minweweyaabikaasin** *vii* good sound of metal (as in wind chimes) [*example*: Minweweyaabikaasinoon. = The (wind chimes) sound good.] (NJ)

METAL CANOE: **ginwaabiko-jiimaan** *ni* metal boat; *pl* **ginwaabiko-jiimaanan** (RT, NJ, GJ)

MILL: GRIST MILL: **biisiboojigewigamig** *ni* grist mill; *pl* **biisiboojigewigamigoon**; *loc* **biisiboojigewigamigong** (RT)

MILLION: SIXTY-FIVE MILLION: **ningodwaasimidana ashi naanan dasing wekwaagindaasowin** *number* 65 million (NJ)

MINGLE:

>BE MIXED: **ginigawijigaazo** *vai* be mixed (RT)

>BE MIXED: **ginigawisin** *vii* be mixed (RT)

>MINGLE WITH SOMEONE: **ginigawishkaw** *vta* mingle with s.o., mix in with s.o. (RT, NJ, GJ)

>MINGLE: **ginigawaami** *vai* mingle (as in different species during fish spawn) (RT, NJ, GJ)

MINK: **andozhaangweshiwe** *vai* go after mink (NJ, GJ)

MINT: FIELD MINT: **namewashkoons** *ni* field mint; *pl* **namewashkoonsan** (AM)

MISS SOMEONE: **metasin** *vta* miss s.o. (one who is absent or dead) (RT, NJ); *also* **metisin** (GJ)

MIST: PRECIPITATE: **binawanise** *vii* precipitate (cross between snow and rain but misty-like, tiny particles of precipitation) (NJ)

MITTEN: **minjikaawanikaw** *vta* make mittens for s.o. (RT)

MIX:

>BE MIXED: **ginigawijigaazo** *vai* be mixed (RT)

>BE MIXED: **ginigawisin** *vii* be mixed (RT)

>MINGLE WITH SOMEONE: **ginigawishkaw** *vta* mingle with s.o., mix in with s.o. (RT, NJ, GJ)

>MINGLE: **ginigawaami** *vai* mingle (as in different species during fish spawn) (RT, NJ, GJ)

>MIXTURE: **maamawinigan** *ni* mixture; *pl* **maamawiniganan** (RT)

MOCCASIN GAME:

>AIMING STICK: **bimoojiganaak** *ni* aiming stick (for moccasin game); *pl* **bimoojiganaakoon** (GJ)

>BURN OUT: **jaagise** *vii* burn out, run out (in reference to community stick pile in moccasin game) (GJ)

>COUNTING STICK: **bima'igan** *ni* counting stick for moccasin game; *pl* **bima'iganan** (GJ)

>DOUBLE SHOOT: **niizho-bimodan** *vti* double shoot (as in moccasin game) (GJ)

>EIGHT SPOT: **nishwaasokaan** *pc* the eight spot (in moccasin game) (GJ)

>FOUR SPOT: **niiyokaan** *pc* the four spot (as in moccasin game) (GJ)

GOAL: **bakinaagewin** *ni* goal; *pl* **bakinaagewinan**; *also* **mizhodamowin** *ni* goal; *pl* **mizhodamowinan** (RT, NJ, GJ)

SCORE DOUBLE: **niizho-gabenaage** *vai* score double (as in moccasin game) (GJ)

SIX SPOT: **ningodwaasokaan** *pc* the six spot (in moccasin game) (GJ)

STRETCH SOMEONE OUT: **zhegwaakozh / zhegwaakoN-/** *vta* stretch s.o. out (in moccasin game, encouraging teammate to tease, do something to one's opponent) (GJ)

STRETCH SOMETHING OUT: **zhegwaakonan** *vti* stretch s.t. out (in moccasin game) (GJ)

STRIKE: **bagaskindibe** *vai* strike (in moccasin game), smack on the head (RT, NJ, GJ)

SYNCOPATED BEAT: **biisiwebinige** vai make syncopated beat for moccasin game song (GJ)

MOIST:

MOIST SOIL: **dipiiwikamigaa** *vii* be moist soil (RT)

WET: **dipiiwan** *vii* be wet, moist (RT)

MOLAR:

HAVE MOLARS: **bigishkaabide** *vai* have molars (RT)

MOLAR: **bigishkaabid** *ni* molar; *pl* **bigishkaabidan** (RT); *also* **ishkweyaabid** *ni* back tooth, molar; *pl* **ishkweyaabidan** (RT)

MONEY: QUARTER: **zhaangweshiwaabikoons** *na* quarter (coin) (NJ, GJ)

MOON:

WANE: **animaasige** *vai* wane (as in moon phase) (JC)

WAX: **biidaasige** *vai* wax (as in cycle of the moon) (JC)

MOSQUITO:

MAKE MOSQUITO SMUDGE: **ashawi-zagimeweke** *vai* make smudge to chase off mosquitoes (NJ, GJ)

MOSQUITO BARRIER: **zagimewayaan** *ni* mosquito barrier (screen or sheet); *pl* **zagimewayaanan** (RT, NJ, GJ)

MOSQUITO SMUDGE: **baashkijiinesijigan** *ni* smudge to ward off mosquitoes; *pl* **baashkijiinesijiganan** (NJ, GJ); *also* **webaabasigan** *ni* mosquito chaser smoke (NJ, GJ)

MOTION: WAVE MOTION: **minawaashkaa** *vii* be the pleasant motion of the waves (NJ)

MOUNTAIN LION: **mishi-bizhii** *na* cougar; *pl* **mishi-bizhiig** (NJ); *also* **mishi-bizhiw** (RT)

MOURN: STOP ACTIVITY: **boonikamigizi** *vai* stop doing certain activities, refrain from doing special activities (as when in mourning) (RT, NJ, GJ)

MOUTH:

CATCH WITH MOUTH: **nakwepwaa' /nakwepwaa'w-/** *vta* catch s.o. with one's mouth (RT)

GRIND: **bigishkanjige** *vai* grind, eat by grinding (RT)

GRIND SOMETHING: **bigishkandan** *vti* grind s.t. in one's mouth (RT)

OPEN MOUTH: **ashkidaawani** *vai* open one's mouth wide (RT, NJ, GJ)

PUT SOMEONE IN MOUTH: **zhakamaw** *vta* put s.o. in one's mouth (RT, NJ, GJ)

PUT SOMETHING IN MOUTH: **zhakamon** *vai+o* put (s.t.) in one's mouth (RT, NJ, GJ)

PUT SOMETHING IN SOMEONE'S MOUTH: **zhakamoozh /zhakamooN-/** *vta* put s.t. in s.o.'s mouth (NJ, GJ)

PUT THINGS IN MOUTH: **zhakamo** *vai* put things in one's mouth (RT, NJ, GJ)

SUFFICIENTLY LARGE MOUTH: **debanendan** *vti* have a sufficiently large mouth to bite s.t. [*lexicon note*: from discussion of the size of a bagidaabaan, an item for ice fishing] (NJ)

WIPE MOUTH: **gaasiidoone'o** *vai* wipe one's mouth (RT, NJ, GJ)

MOVE:

MOVE: **bimibide** *vii* be running, be moving, be in use (as in something motorized) (NJ)

PUSH SOMEONE: **gaagaanjibizh /gaagaanjibiN-/** *vta* push s.o., move s.o. (RT, NJ, GJ)

MOWER: **waasamoo-dakwaabiigizhoochigan** *ni* lawn mower; *pl* **waasamoo-dakwaabiigizhoochiganan** (RT, NJ, GJ)

MUCH: NOT TOO MUCH BUT ENOUGH: **gomaa go minik** *expression* not too much but enough (NJ)

MUD:

MUDDY BOTTOM: **azhashkiiyaamikaa** *vii* be a muddy bottom (as in a lake or pond) (RT)

MUDDY WATER: **azhashkiiwaagamin** *vii* be murky water, be muddy water (RT, NJ, GJ)

STUCK IN MUD: **aadakiise** *vii* get stuck in the mud in the water (NJ, GJ)

MUSHROOM: PINK MUSHROOM: **wazhashkwedowens** *na* pink mushroom; *pl* **wazhashkwedowensag** (RT, NJ, GJ)

MUSIC: LEARN MUSIC: **gidochige** *vai* learn music (NJ)

MUSKELLUNGE: **ozhaawashko-ginoozhe** *na* muskellunge; *pl* **ozhaawashko-ginoozheg** (NJ); *also* **mashkinoozhe** (AM); *pl* **mashkinoozheg**

MUST BE: **maawiin** *pc* must be (NJ)

NAME:

> CALL BY WHOLE NAME: **noondenikaazh / noondenikaaN-/** *vta* desire s.o. to call s.o. by one's whole name [*cultural note*: some spirits long to be called by their full names rather than simply referred to as a thunderbird or water spirit] (NJ, GJ)
>
> CALLED BY WHOLE NAME: **noondenikaazo** *vai* long to be called by one's full name [*cultural note*: some spirits long to be called by their full names rather than simply referred to as a thunderbird or water spirit] (NJ, GJ)

NARROWS: **endazhi-obaashiiwang** *ni-prt* narrows (RT, NJ, GJ)

NASAL CAVITY: **nishangwan** *nid* my nasal cavity (NJ)

NECK: LONG NECK: **ginwaabiigigwe** *vai* have a long neck (NJ)

NEEDLE:

> NEEDLE: **ashishawe-zhaabonigan** *ni* glovers needle, three-sided needle; *pl* **ashishawe-zhaaboniganan** (NJ, GJ)
>
> PINE NEEDLE: **zhingwaakwaandag** *na* pine needle; *pl* **zhingwaakwaandag** (RT, NJ)

NEST:

> BIRD NEST: **wadiswan** *ni* nest (of a bird); *pl* **wadiswanan**; *dim* **wadiswanens** (RT, NJ, GJ)
>
> HAVE NEST: **owaziswani** *vai* have a nest (RT)
>
> MAKE BIRD NEST: **wadiswanike** *vai* make a nest (RT); *also* **waziswanike** (RT)
>
> MAKE NEST IN CERTAIN PLACE: **dazhe** *vai* build a nest in a certain place (RT)
>
> TREE NEST: **mitigwaazh** *ni* burrow or nest inside a tree (RT)

NET:

> ANCHOR POLE FOR NETTING UNDER ICE: **anaamizigoneyaatig** *ni* anchor pole for ice netting; *pl* **anaamizigoneyaatigoon** (RT, NJ, GJ)
>
> ANCHOR ROCK: **agonjiwasin** *na* anchor rock (weight); *pl* **agonjiwasiniig** (RT, NJ, GJ)

CAUGHT IN A NET: **biinda'agoo** *vai* get caught in a net (RT, NJ, GJ); *also* **biinda'am** (RT); *also* **biinda'ozo** (LW); *also* **bida'am** (NJ)

FIX NETS: **nanaa'isabii** *vai* fix nets (RT, NJ, GJ)

FLOAT: **angooji-onaagan** *ni* net float; *pl* **angooji-onaaganan** (RT); *also* **agonjiwinaagan**; *pl* **agonjiwinaaganan** (GJ); *also* **agwinjiwinaagan**; *pl* **agwinjiwinaaganan** (NJ); *also* **agoonjoonaagan**; *pl* **agoonjoonaaganan** (JC)

HANG NETS: **agoodasabii** *vai* hang nets (NJ); *also* **agoodisabii** (GJ)

MAKE NETS: **asabike** *vai* make nets (RT, NJ, GJ)

NET DRYING RACK: **adoodasabaanaak** *ni* net drying rack; *pl* **adoodasabaanaakoon** (RT, NJ, GJ)

NET MESH: **apiitashkizi** *vai* be a certain size mesh (as in a net) (RT, NJ, GJ)

NET SINKER (ANCHOR LINE): **gitaamika'igan** *ni* anchor, weight for nets; *pl* **gitaamika'iganan** (RT, NJ, GJ)

NET SINKER (BELOW FLOAT): **asinaab** *na* net sinker (below each net float) made from rocks; *pl* **asinaabiig** (NJ, GJ); *also* **goonzaabiishkomaan**; *pl* **goonzaabiishkomaanan** (RT)

NET SINKER (GENERAL): **gonzaabiishkoojigan** *ni* net weight or sinker for drowning set (on trap for animals); *pl* **gonzaabiishkoojiganan** (RT, NJ, GJ)

NET STICK: **asabikewaatig** *ni* net making stick; *pl* **asabikewaatigoon** (RT, NJ, GJ)

NET STRING: **asabikeyaab** *ni* net string; *pl* **asabikeyaabiin** (NJ)

POLE TO SET NET UNDER ICE: **anaamizigwaneyaatig** *ni* slider push-pole for setting net under ice; *pl* **anaamizigwaneyaatigoon** (RT, NJ, GJ)

PREPARE NETS: **oninasabii** *vai* prepare nets for setting (RT, NJ, GJ)

PULL FISH FROM NETS: **gidinamegwe** *vai* pull fish from nets (RT)

PUT NET STRING UNDER ICE: **anaamizigoneyaabii** *vai* put net string under ice (RT, NJ, GJ)

ROCK WEIGHT: **gonzaabiishkoojiganaabik** *na* rock weight; *pl* **gonzaabiishkoojiganaabikoog** (RT, NJ, GJ)

SET NET IN DEEP WATER: **ginwiindimaasabii** *vai* set net in deep water (GJ, NJ)

SET NET OUT FROM SHORE: **niminaawesaa** *vai* set nets out from shore (NJ); *also* **mininaawesaa** (GJ)

SET NET PERPENDICULAR TO SHORE: **mininaawesabii** *vai* set net close to shore (set goes perpendicular from shore) (GJ); *also* **niminaawesabii** (NJ)

SET NET UNDER ICE: **anaamizigosabii** *vai* set net under the ice (RT, NJ, GJ)

SOFTEN NETS: **biniskosabii** *vai* soften nets (RT)

STRING FOR NETTING UNDER ICE: **anaamizigoneyaab** *ni* ice netting string (with pole); *pl* **anaamizigoneyaabiin** (RT, NJ, GJ)

NETTLE: **zesab** *na* nettle; *pl* **zesabiig** (RT, NJ, GJ)

NEW POST: **Bakwewaang** *place* where the thunder beings touched down, New Post, WI (on Lac Courte Oreilles Reservation) (JS); *also* **Bakweweyaang** (GJ)

NEW GROWTH: **oshkigin** *vii* s.t. new grows (RT)

NEWS: **babaamaajimo** *vai, vii* tell news (RT, NJ, GJ)

NEXT ROOM: **awasigamig** *pc* the next room (RT, NJ, GJ); *also* **awasisag** (GJ)

NIGHT:

LONG NIGHT: **ginoo-dibikad** *vii* be a long night (RT, NJ, GJ)

SHORT NIGHT: **dako-dibikad** *vii* be a short night (RT, NJ, GJ)

NOISE OF REEDS:

MAKE NOISE PADDLING: **debweweshka'am** *vai* make noise paddling or poling from reeds sliding on a canoe (RT, NJ, GJ)

MAKE NOISE PADDLING AWAY: **animweweshka'am** *vai2* paddle or pole away making noise from reeds brushing against canoe (RT, NJ, GJ)

MAKE NOISE PADDLING BY: **bimweweshka'am** *vai2* make noise while paddling or poling by from reeds brushing against canoe (NJ, GJ)

NOODLE: *see* PASTA

NORTHERN PIKE: **ginoozhe** *na* northern pike; *pl* **ginoozheg** (RT, NJ, GJ)

NOSE:

BLOW NOSE: **ziinijaanese** *vai* cleanse one's nostrils (RT, NJ, GJ); *also* **ziiniskiigome** *vai* blow one's nose (RT, NJ, GJ)

STUFFY NOSE: **gibijaane** *vai* have a plugged or stuffy nose (RT, NJ, GJ)

NOTCH: **bakwekode** *vii* be notched (as in nettle strings) (RT, NJ, GJ)

NOTICE SOMETHING: **naanaagajitoon** *vti* notice s.t. (NJ)

NUMBER:

    BE CERTAIN NUMBER: **dasin** *vii* be a certain number (RT, NJ, GJ)

FACT FAMILY: **inawendangibii'igan** *ni* fact family number, *pl* **inawendangibii'iganan** (RT, NJ, GJ); *also* **asigiginjigemaagan**; *pl* **asigiginjigemaaganag** (GJ); *also* **inawendibii'igan**; *pl* **inawendibii'iganan** (RT, NJ, GJ)

    FOUR SPOT: **niiyokaan** *pc* the four spot (as in moccasin game) (GJ)

    NUMBER: **asigibii'iganens** *ni* number; *pl* **asigibii'iganensan** (NJ)

    NUMBER OF POUNDS: **dibaabiishkoojiganeyaa** *vii* be a certain number of pounds (NJ)

    NUMBER OF POUNDS: **dibaabiishkoojiganezi** *vai* be a certain number of pounds (NJ)

    NUMBER SIX: **neningodwaasinoon** *vii-pl* they number six, there are six of them (RT)

    SIXTY-FIVE MILLION: **ningodwaasimidana ashi naanan dasing wekwaagindaasowin** *number* 65 million (NJ)

    MILLION: **aabiding wekwaagindaasowin** *ni* one million (RT, NJ, GJ)

NUTRIENT: **mino-ayi'iins** *ni* nutrient; *pl* **mino-ayi'iinsan** (RT); *also* **ondiziwin** *ni* nutrient; *pl* **ondiziwinan** (RT)

OAK: BECOME OAK: **mitigomizhiiwi** *vai* become an oak, turn into an oak tree (RT)

OBJECTIVE: **andawenjigan** *ni* objective; *pl* **andawenjiganan** (RT, NJ, GJ)

OCTOPUS: **baataniinoonikesi** *na* octopus; *pl* **baataniinoonikesiwag** (RT, NJ, GJ)

ODD:

    CONSIDERED OPPOSITE: **nanepaadendaagwad** *vii* be considered opposite (NJ, GJ)

    OPPOSITE: **nanepaadad** *vii* be odd, unmatched, opposite (NJ, GJ)

    OPPOSITE: **nanepaaj** *pc* opposite, inverse (NJ, GJ)

OFFEND: **ando-mazitam** *vai2* be emotionally oversensitive, easy to offend, looking for fault (RT, NJ, GJ)

OFFER:

    OFFER FOOD AND TAKE BACK: **jiishi'** *vta* offer food to s.o. and take back (as in coming out of a fast, when fed new foods in mourning, or for a first kill) (RT, NJ, GJ)

    OFFER TOBACCO: **asemaakandan** *vti* offer tobacco to s.t. (NJ)

OFFER TOBACCO: **asemaakande** *vii* tobacco is offered to it (NJ)

OFFSPRING: DEFEND OFFSPRING: **naadamaawaso** *vai* stick up for one's children (with negative consequences) (RT, NJ, GJ)

OLD MAN: SNAG AN OLD MAN: **noojiiwakiwenzii** *vai* try to commence an intimate relationship with an old man, snag (for old men) (NJ)

ONE: EVERY ONE: **endaso-bezhig** *pc* every one, each one (RT)

OPEN:

DAM OPENS: **baakibiishkaa** *vii* be an opening (as in a dam opening) (NJ, GJ)

OPEN: **baakindenamaw** *vta* open (s.t.) for s.o. (RT, NJ, GJ)

OPEN DOOR: **baakiiginan** *vti* open s.t. (sheet-like) (RT, NJ, GJ); *also* **baakindenan** (RT, NJ, GJ)

OPERCULUM: **onawaangigan** *nid* fish cheek, operculum; *pl* **onawaangiganan** (RT, NJ, GJ)

OPPOSITE:

CONSIDERED OPPOSITE: **nanepaadendaagwad** *vii* be considered opposite (NJ, GJ); *also* **napaadendaagwad** (NJ, GJ)

INVERSE: **napaaj** *pc* backwards, inverse (NJ, GJ)

OPPOSITE: **nanepaadad** *vii* be odd, unmatched, opposite (NJ, GJ)

OPPOSITE: **nanepaaj** *pc* opposite, inverse (NJ, GJ)

ORAL: **dakwanjige** *vai* bite and put in one's mouth (RT); *also* perform oral sex (TS)

ORIGINATE: **onjigin** *vii* grow from a certain place, originate (RT)

ORION'S BELT: **Aadwaa'amoog** *name* Orion's Belt (constellation) (GJ)

OUT:

JUMP OUT: **zaagiji-gwaashkwani** *vai* jump out (RT, NJ, GJ)

JUMP OUT REPEATEDLY: **zaasaagiji-gwaashkwani** *vai* jump out repeatedly (RT, NJ, GJ)

OUT: *see also* STICK OUT

OVEN: PUT THINGS IN OVEN: **zhegwaabikinige** *vai* put things in the oven (RT, NJ, GJ)

OVERLY: **onzaam** *pc* overly, too much [*example*: Gaawiin nindizhaasiin onzaam nindaakoz. = I'm not going because I'm sick. *example*: Onzaam gizhide gaa-wii-onji-wi-nibaayang. It's too warm it makes us feel sleepy.] (NJ, GJ)

OVERPOPULATE: **onzaamiino** *vai* overpopulate (RT)

PACK:

PACK TRAIL WITH SNOWSHOE: **daataagwaagoneshkige** *vai* pack trail with snowshoes or shoes (NJ, GJ)

PRESS SOMEONE DOWN: **maagoshkaw** *vta* press s.o. down, pack s.o. down (as in snow) (RT, NJ, GJ)

PRESS SOMETHING DOWN: **maagoshkan** *vti* press s.t. down, pack s.t. down (RT, NJ, GJ)

PACKAGE: **wiiweginigaazo** *vai* be packaged (RT)

PAD: FINGER PAD: **niniisiigininjaan** *nid* my finger pad; *pl* **niniisiigininjaanan** (NJ)

PADDLE:

COME PADDLING: **biidakwazhiwe** *vai* come paddling (RT, NJ, GJ)

MAKE NOISE PADDLING: **debweweshka'am** *vai* make noise paddling or poling from reeds sliding on a canoe (RT, NJ, GJ)

MAKE NOISE PADDLING AWAY: **animweweshka'am** *vai2* paddle or pole away making noise from reeds brushing against canoe (RT, NJ, GJ)

MAKE NOISE PADDLING BY: **bimweweshka'am** *vai2* make noise while paddling or poling by from reeds brushing against canoe (NJ, GJ)

PADDLE: **bimakwazhiwe** *vai* paddle, swim underwater (RT, NJ, GJ)

PADDLE DOWNSTREAM: **niisaajiwane'aadage** *vai* go downstream (GJ); *also* **niisaajiwanwe'aadage** (NJ)

PADDLE FAST: **gizhiikwazhiwe** *vai* paddle or swim fast (RT, NJ, GJ)

PADDLE INTO WAVES: **onjishkawa'o** *vai* paddle straight into waves (NJ, GJ)

PADDLE SLOWLY (FLOAT): **bedaakogomo** *vai* paddle slowly (implies floating) (RT, NJ, GJ)

PADDLE SLOWLY (FORCED MOVEMENT): **bedakwazhiwe** *vai* paddle slowly (implies forced movement) (RT, NJ, GJ)

PADDLE TO CERTAIN PLACE (FLOAT): **inaakogomo** *vai* paddle to certain place (RT, NJ, GJ)

PADDLE TO CERTAIN PLACE (FORCED MOVEMENT): **inakwazhiwe** *vai* paddle to a certain place (RT, NJ, GJ)

PADDLE WITH WIND: **naamiwana'o** *vai* paddle with the wind (NJ)

PROPEL: **naamiwana'ogo** *vai* be propelled faster by wind and waves (in watercaft) (NJ)

SHOOT RAPIDS: **niishiboono** *vai* shoot rapids (NJ, GJ)

STOP PADDLING: **gibitakwazhiwe** *vai* stop paddling (RT, NJ, GJ)

SWITCH SIDES PADDLING: **gwekabowe** *vai* switch sides paddling (RT, NJ, GJ)

PAGE: **agaamiigin** *pc* the next page (NJ, GJ)

PAINFUL SUNBURN: **wiisagazheyaakizo** *vai* be painfully sunburned [*example*: Wiinge wiisagazheyaakizodog. = He must be really sunburned.] (NJ, GJ)

PALM:

    PALM OF HAND: **anaamininj** *pc* under the palm (NJ)

    PALM OF HAND: **nagaakininjaan** *ni* palm of hand; *loc* **nagaakininjaaning** (RT, NJ, GJ)

PARTITION: **gibiigagoojigan** *ni* sheet-like material used for partition, window, or door of a lodge; **gibiigagoojiganan** (GJ)

PASS OUT: **wanendam** *vai* pass out (NJ), forget (AM)

PASS THROUGH SOMEONE: **zhaaboshkaw** *vta* pass through s.o. (RT)

PASTA:

    CAVATAAPI: **biimisko-onagizhiikaanens** *ni* cavataapi pasta, *pl* **biimisko-onagizhiikaanensan** (RT, NJ, GJ)

    CONCHIGLIETTE: **esikaanens** *na* conchigliette pasta, *pl* **esikaanensag** (RT, NJ, GJ)

    FUSILLI: **biimiskozhiganens** *ni* fusilli (pasta), *pl* **biimiskozhiganensan** (RT, NJ, GJ)

    LASAGNA NOODLE: **mangade-bakwezhiganaabiins** *ni* lasagna noodle, *pl* **mangade-bakwezhiganaabiinsan** (RT, NJ, GJ)

    MACARONI: **onagizhiikaanens** *ni* macaroni, *pl* **onagizhiikaanensan** (RT, NJ, GJ)

    PENNE: **okijiinsikaanens** *ni* penne pasta, *pl* **okijiinsikaanensan** (RT, NJ, GJ)

    SPAGHETTI: **bakwezhiganaabiins** *na* pasta, spaghetti; *pl* **bakwezhiganaabiinsag** (RT)

PATCH:

    CLOSE SOMETHING WITH PATCH: **giba'an** *vti* patch s.t., close s.t. (RT, NJ, GJ)

    PATCH: **bagwa'ige** *vai* patch things (RT, NJ, GJ)

    PATCH SOMETHING: **bagwa'an** *vti* patch s.t. (RT, NJ, GJ)

PATHETIC: SOUND PATHETIC: **goopaataagozi** *vai* sound pathetic (RT, NJ, GJ)

PAW: BREAK OFF FOOT OR PAW: **giishkitaa** *vai* breaks off a foot or paw (RT, NJ, GJ)

PAY:

PAY SELF: **diba'amaazo** *vai* pay one's self (RT, NJ, GJ)

TAX: **diba'amaazowin** *ni* tax; *pl* **diba'amaazowinan** (RT, NJ, GJ)

PEACE:

GIVE SOMEONE THE PEACE SIGN: **niingidowaakoninjiitaw** *vai* give s.o. the peace sign (GJ)

MAKE PEACE SIGN: **niingidowaakoninjiini** *vai* make the peace sign (GJ)

PEAKED LODGE: **nisawa'ogaan** *ni* long peaked lodge; *pl* **nisawa'ogaanan** (RT, NJ, GJ)

PEEL:

DIFFICULT TO PEEL: **asanii** *vii* difficult to peel (as in dry birch bark, basswood fiber) (GJ)

EASY TO PEEL (POPS OFF): **baabagose** *vii* peels easily (as in when bark pops off tree on its own) (RT, NJ, GJ)

EASY TO PEEL (SEPARATE): **bakwanii** *vii* peels easy (as in birch bark, basswood fiber) (RT, NJ, GJ)

PEEL: **baabagonige** *vai* peel bark (RT, NJ, GJ)

PEEL BARK (SHEET): **baabagonagekwe** *vai* peel bark (as in birch bark) (RT, NJ, GJ)

PEEL BARK (STRING): **bishagaakobijige** *vai* peeling bark (string of fiber) by hand (as in peeling basswood) (RT, NJ, GJ)

PEEL IN LAYERS: **biitoobiigibijige** *vai* peel in layers (RT, NJ, GJ)

PEEL IN LAYERS: **biitoobijigaade** *vii* be peeled in layers (RT, NJ, GJ)

PEEL IN LONG STRIPS: **daashkibiigibijige** *vai* peel into long strips (GJ); *also* **daashkibiigobijige** *vai* peel into long strips (NJ)

PEEL IN SINGLE STRIP: **naanigaakobidoon** *vti* peel s.t. in a strip, strip s.t. (as in basswood) (RT, NJ, GJ)

PEEL INTO STRIPS: **naanaanigaakobijige** *vai* peel into strips (as in basswood) (RT, NJ, GJ)

PEEL SOMEONE: **bishagaakobizh /bishagaakobiN-/** *vta* peel s.o. by hand (as in a tree) (RT, NJ, GJ)

PEEL SOMETHING: **bishagaakobidoon** *vti* peel s.t. (as in bark) by hand (RT, NJ, GJ)

PEEL SOMETHING INTO STRIPS: **naanaanigaakobidoon** *vti* peel s.t. into strips, strip s.t. (as in basswood) (RT, NJ, GJ)

PEMMICAN:

FISH PEMMICAN: **nooka'iskawaan** *na* pemmican (fish); *pl*
**nooka'iskawaanag** (RT, NJ, GJ)

MEAT PEMMICAN: **nooka'iiwagwaan** *ni* pemmican (meat); *pl*
**nooka'iiwagwaanan** (RT, NJ, GJ)

PENCIL: USE AS PENCIL: **ozhibii'igaage** *vai+o* use s.t. as a pencil
[*example:* Ashkikomaan ozhibii'igaagen. = Use the lead (metal,
as in a bullet) as a pencil.] (NJ)

PENNE PASTA: **okijiinsikaanens** *ni* penne pasta, *pl* **okijiinsikaanensan**
(RT, NJ, GJ)

PERCH:

    HOP TO NEW PERCH: **aanji-boonii** *vai* hop to a new perch (RT,
NJ, GJ)

    PERCH: **asaawens** *na* perch (fish); *pl* **asaawensag** (RT, NJ, GJ)

    PERCH: **boonii** *vai, vii* land, perch (RT, NJ, GJ)

PERHAPS LATER: **maagizhaa baamaa ingoding** *expression* perhaps at
some later time (RT, NJ, GJ); *also* **maazhaa ge baamaa
ingoding** (RT, NJ, GJ)

PERIOD: **ishkwebii'igan** *ni* period (.) (JC)

PERPENDICULAR: SET NET PERPENDICULAR TO SHORE: **mininaawesabii**
*vai* set net close to shore (set goes perpendicular from shore)
(GJ); *also* **niminaawesabii** (NJ)

PESTY: **wiiyagaskendaagozi** *vai* be pesty, fussy (RT, NJ, GJ)

PHYSICALLY SENSITIVE: **wake-nisidawishkaa** *vai* be physically sensitive
(RT, NJ, GJ)

PICKY: **wegaskendaagozi** *vai* be stubborn, fussy, hard to please (NJ, GJ);
*redup* **weyagaskendaagozi** (GJ, NJ); *also* **wiiyagaskendaagozi**
(NJ, GJ)

PICTURE: **mazinaakide** *vii* be a picture, be illustrated (RT)

PIE: **bakwezhiganikaan** *na* pie; *pl* **bakwezhiganikaanag** (NJ)

PIERCING SOUND: **bagakitaagod** *vii* sound sharp, have a piercing sound;
*also* **bagakitaagwad** (NJ, GJ)

PIGEON: **omiimii** *na* dove, pigeon; *pl* **omiimiig** (RT, NJ, GJ)

PIN:

    CHOKE PIN SOMEONE AGAINST WALL: **ashidaako-gibinewen** *vta*
pin s.o. against the wall by choke-hold (GJ)

    PIN BY REPEATED SPEECH: **ashidakamigwewem** *vta* hold s.o. in
place by repeated speech (GJ)

    PIN BY SPEECH: **ashidakamigwem** *vta* hold s.o. in place by
speech (GJ)

PIN DOWN: **ashidakamigishkaw** *vta* hold down, pin down s.o. by voice or with body (GJ, NJ)

PIN SOMEONE AGAINST WALL: **ashidaakobizh /ashidaakobiN-/** *vta* pin s.o. against something wooden (as in wall or floor) (GJ); *also* **ashidaakoshkaw** (GJ)

PIN SOMEONE AGAINST WALL OFF GROUND: **ombishidaakogibinewen** *vta* pin s.o. against the wall off the ground (GJ)

PIN SOMETHING: **gichiwaakwa'an** *vti* pin s.t. in place (as in clothes on clothesline) (RT, NJ, GJ)

PIN WITH FOOT OR BODY: **ashoodakamigishkaw** *vta* pin s.o. down with foot or body against ground, submit so. (GJ)

PINCH: **gashkigise** *vii* get pinched (as in a saw) (RT, NJ, GJ)

PINECONE: **wazhashkwedowens** *na* pinecone; *pl* **wazhashkwedowensag** (RT, NJ, GJ)

PINE: *see* CONIFER

PINK:

PINK: **maazhi-miskozi** *vai* be pink (NJ, GJ); *also* **oginii-waabigoni-miskozi** *vai* be pink (NJ, GJ); *also* **oginii-waabigwani-miskozi** (RT)

PINK MUSHROOM: **wazhashkwedowens** *na* pink mushroom; *pl* **wazhashkwedowensag** (RT, NJ, GJ)

PIT:

FIRE PIT: **endazhi-boodaweng** *vai-prt* fire pit (RT, NJ, GJ)

THRESHING PIT: **mimigoshkamwaagan** *ni* threshing pit for wild rice; *pl* **mimigoshkamwaaganan** (RT)

PITCH: **andobigiwe** *vai* go after pitch (NJ, GJ)

PIZZA: **piisaa** *ni* pizza; *pl* **piisaag** (NJ); *also* **niiyo-biitoosijigan** (AG)

PLACE:

GROW IN CERTAIN PLACE: **dazhigi** *vai* grow in a certain place (RT)

GROW IN CERTAIN PLACE: **dazhigin** *vii* grow in a certain place (RT)

MAKE NEST IN CERTAIN PLACE: **dazhe** *vai* build a nest in a certain place (RT)

PLANT:

BE STRONG: **mashkawaakamigaa** *vii* be strong (tree-like) (RT, NJ, GJ)

CATTAIL: **nabagashk** *ni* cattail; *pl* **nabagashkoon** (NJ)

FIELD MINT: **namewashkoons** *ni* field mint; *pl*
**namewashkoonsan** (AM)
FROG LEAF: **omakakiibag** *ni* frog leaf, plantain; *pl*
**omakakiibagoon** (NJ, GJ)
GARDEN: **gitige** *vai* farm, garden, plant (RT)
LILY PAD: **ogitebag** *ni* lily pad; *pl* **ogitebagoon** (RT)
NETTLE: **zesab** *na* nettle; *pl* **zesabiig** (RT, NJ, GJ)
PLANT: **mayaajiiging** *vii-prt* plant; *pl* **mayaajiigingin** (RT)
PLANT HOOK: **waagi-wiinizisens** *ni* hook (as in the burr of a
plant); *pl* **waagi-wiinizisensan** (RT)
PLANT IN GROUND: **badakamigisidoon** *vti* plant it in the ground
(RT, NJ, GJ)
RICE STALK: **manoominagaawanzh** *ni* rice stalk; *pl*
**manoominagaawanzhiin** (RT, NJ, GJ)
STEM: **gaawanzh** *ni* stem; *pl* **gaawanzhiin**; *loc* **gaawanzhiing**
(RT)
SWEET FERN: **namewashkoons** *ni* sweet fern; *pl*
**namewashkoonsan** (NJ)
VINE: **bemiging** *vii-prt* vine, plant (as in one that grows along the
ground); *pl* **bemigingin** (RT)
WATER LILY: **makopinagaawanzh** *na* water lily plant; *pl*
**makopinagaawanzhiig** (RT)
PLANTAIN: **omakakiibag** *ni* frog leaf, plantain; *pl* **omakakiibagoon** (NJ,
GJ); *also* **gaagigebag**; *pl* **gaagigebagoon** (NJ, GJ)
PLASTIC TOY: **gaaskiigino-odaminwaaganensikaan** *ni* plastic toy; *pl*
**gaaskiigino-odaminwaaganensikaanan** (NJ, GJ)
PLAY:
SOUND PLEASANT PLAYING FIDDLE: **minwewenaazhaabii'ige**
*vai* make a pleasant sound playing fiddle (RT, NJ, GJ)
SOUND PLEASANT PLAYING GUITAR: **minweweyaabiigibijige** *vai*
make a pleasant sound playing guitar (RT, NJ, GJ)
PLEASANT SOUND: *see* SOUND
PLIER: **dakonjigaans** *ni* pliers, vice grip; *pl* **dakonjigaansan** (NJ, GJ);
*also* **dakwanjigaans** (RT)
PLUGGED NOSE: **gibijaane** *vai* have a plugged or stuffy nose (RT, NJ,
GJ)
PLUM: **bagesaan** *na* plum; *pl* **bagesaanag** (RT, NJ, GJ)
PLUNGE:

PLUNGE DOWN: **gaanjiba'ibiise** *vii* water is pushed out, plunged down (NJ, GJ); *also* **gaanjwa'ibiise** (NJ, GJ)

TOILET PLUNGER: **gaanjiba'ibaan** *ni* toilet plunger (NJ, GJ)

POINT: HAVE POINT: **jiibwaabikad** *vii* have a point, come to a point (NJ, GJ)

POLE:

CROSS POLE: **bimidaakobijigan** *ni* cross pole; *pl* **bimidaakobijiganan** (NJ, GJ)

CRUTCH POLE: **ziigaakwa'igan** *ni* crutch pole (GJ)

ENCIRCLING POLE: **waawiyeyaabijigan** *ni* encircling pole of a shake-tent; *pl* **waawiyeyaabijiganan** (GJ)

FISHING POLE: **migiskanaatig** *ni* fishing pole; *pl* **migiskanaatigoon** (RT, NJ, GJ)

LODGE POLE: **namanjiin** *ni* unknown lodge pole [*lexicon note:* archaic word] (GJ)

MAKE NOISE POLING: **debweweshka'am** *vai* make noise paddling or poling from reeds sliding on a canoe (RT, NJ, GJ)

MAKE NOISE POLING AWAY: **animweweshka'am** *vai2* paddle or pole away making noise from reeds brushing against canoe (RT, NJ, GJ)

MAKE NOISE POLING BY: **bimweweshka'am** *vai2* make noise while paddling or poling by from reeds brushing against canoe (NJ, GJ)

POLLUTE:

AIR POLLUTION: **wiininaamowin** *ni* dirty air (i.e. air pollution, polluted air) (RT, NJ, GJ)

BE POLLUTED: **wiinichigaade** *vii* be polluted (RT, NJ, GJ)

POLLUTION: **waanichigaadeg** *vii-prt* pollution (RT, NJ, GJ)

WATER POLLUTION: **wiinaagamin** *vii* be dirty (as in a liquid) (RT, NJ, GJ)

POLLUTE: *see also* DIRT

PONDER: **naanaagadawendam** *vai* ponder, reflect (RT, NJ, GJ)

POOL: **maawandoojiwan** *vii* pool (water); *also* waves come together (RT, NJ, GJ)

POOP: *see* FECES *and* DEFECATE

PORTAGE:

PORTAGE: **biminige** *vai* portage a canoe (RT, NJ, GJ)

PORTAGE: **gabadoo** *vai* portage (RT, NJ, GJ)

POT:

CLAY POT: **waabigani-akik** *na* clay pot; *pl* **waabigani-akikoog**; *loc* **waabigani-akikong** (RT)

FLOWER POT: **waabigoni-akik** *na* flower pot; *pl* **waabigoni-akikoog** (NJ, GJ); *also* **waabigwani-akik** (RT)

POUND:

> NUMBER OF POUNDS: **dibaabiishkoojiganeyaa** *vii* be a certain number of pounds (NJ)
>
> NUMBER OF POUNDS: **dibaabiishkoojiganezi** *vai* be a certain number of pounds (NJ)
>
> POUND SHUT: **gibwaabikada'an** *vti* pound s.t. shut with a tool (RT)

POWDER:

> POWDER: **bebinewang** *vii-prt* powder; *pl* **bebinewangin** (RT, NJ, GJ)
>
> POWDERY: **bibinewan** *vii* fine, powdery (RT, NJ, GJ)
>
> POWDERY: **bibinezi** *vai* be fine, powdery (RT, NJ, GJ)

PRAIRIE: BE PRAIRIE: **mashkodekamigaa** *vii* be a prairieland (RT)

PRAIRIE DOG: **mashkode-akakojiish** *na* prairie dog; *pl* **mashkode-akakojiishag** (RT)

PRECIPITATE: **binawanise** *vii* precipitate (cross between snow and rain but misty-like, tiny particles of precipitation) (NJ)

PREDATOR: ESCAPE: **gii'iwe** *vai* escape (from a predator) (RT, NJ, GJ)

PREPARE NETS: **oninasabii** *vai* prepare nets for setting (RT, NJ, GJ)

PRESS:

> PRESS SOMEONE DOWN: **maagoshkaw** *vta* press s.o. down, pack s.o. down (as in snow) (RT, NJ, GJ)
>
> PRESS SOMETHING DOWN: **maagoshkan** *vti* press s.t. down, pack s.t. down (RT, NJ, GJ)

PREVENT:

> BLOCK SOMETHING: **gibisidoon** *vti* block s.t. (as in using something to block light from a projector) (RT, NJ, GJ)
>
> PREVENT: **gibichichige** *vai* block, prohibit, prevent (NJ, GJ)
>
> STOP: **gibichii** *vai* stop (RT, NJ, GJ)

PRISM: **ashishaweyaa** *vii* be a triangular prism (NJ, GJ)

PROHIBIT:

> BE PROHIBITED: **onji'idim** *vai* there is a prohibition (NJ)
>
> PREVENT: **gibichichige** *vai* block, prohibit, prevent (NJ, GJ)
>
> PROHIBIT ONE ANOTHER: **onji'idiwag /onji'idi-/** *vai* they prohibit one another (ES)

STOP: **gibichii** *vai* stop (RT, NJ, GJ)

PROPER:

>SIT PROPERLY: **wewenabi** *vai* sit properly (RT, NJ, GJ)

>WALK PROPERLY: **wewenose** *vai* walk properly, walk cautiously (RT, NJ, GJ)

PROTECTIVE: **gizhaawaso** *vai* be protective of one's young (RT, NJ, GJ)

PROTRUDE: **zaagisin** *vii* it protrudes (RT, NJ, GJ)

PROTRUDE: *see also* OUT *and* STICK OUT

PUDDLE: **waanashkobaa** *vii* be a puddle (RT, NJ); *also* **waanishkobaa** (GJ); *also* **waanashkobiiyaa** (RT, NJ)

PUFF UP ONE'S FEATHERS: **ombimiigwanetaa** *vai* puff up one's feathers (NJ, GJ)

PULL:

>PULL FISH FROM NETS: **gidinamegwe** *vai* pull fish from nets (RT)

>PULL OUT: **bashkobijigaade** *vii* be pulled out, be weeded, be removed from somewhere (RT)

>PULL PLANTS: **bashkobijige** *vai* pull out plants, weed (RT)

>PULL SOMEONE: **waawiikobizh** /**waawiikobiN-**/ *vta* pull s.o. intermittently (RT, NJ, GJ)

>PULL STRAIGHT: **gwayakobijige** *vai* tie or pull things straight (RT, NJ, GJ)

>PULLED BY WIND: **bakwadaasin** *vii* be pulled up by the wind (RT, NJ, GJ)

PUMP:

>BE PUMPED: **ikwa'ibii** *vii* be pumped (water) (RT, NJ, GJ)

>PUMP WATER: **ikwa'ige** *vai* pump water (RT, NJ, GJ)

>WATER PUMP: **ikwa'ibaan** *ni* water pump (RT, NJ, GJ)

PUMPKIN: **ozaawi-okosimaan** *ni* pumpkin; *pl* **ozaawi-okosimaanan** (RT, NJ, GJ)

PUSH:

>PLUNGE DOWN: **gaanjiba'ibiise** *vii* water is pushed out, plunged down (NJ, GJ); *also* **gaanjwa'ibiise** (NJ, GJ)

>PUSH OFF FROM GROUND: **mininaawekii'o** *vai* push off while touching the ground (GJ); *also* **niminaawekii'o** (NJ)

>PUSH OFF: **mininaawebishkan** *vti* push s.t. off with one's body (as in a boat) (GJ); *also* **niminaawebishkan** (NJ)

>PUSH SNOW ASIDE: **akoweba'o** /**akoweba'w-**/ *vta* push s.o. aside (as in snow) (GJ); *also* **ikoweba'wi** /**ikoweba'w-**/ (NJ); *also* **ikoweba'** /**ikoweba'w-**/ (RT)

PUSH SOMEONE: **gaagaanjibizh** /gaagaanjibiN-/ *vta* push s.o., move s.o. (RT, NJ, GJ)

PUT:

PUT: **achigaazo** *vai* be put somewhere (RT)

PUT ON SOMETHING: **apiigisidoon** *vti* put it on s.t. (as in hot plate) (RT, NJ, GJ)

PYRAMID: **ashishawe-bajiishkaa** *vii* be a three-sided pyramid (NJ, GJ)

QUARTER: **zhaangweshiwaabikoons** *na* quarter (coin) (NJ, GJ)

QUESTION: **gagwedwebii'igan** *ni* question mark (?) (JC)

QUOTATION MARK: **giigidoobii'igan** *ni* quotation mark; *pl* **giigidoobii'iganan** ("") (JC)

RACCOON: **esibananjigesi** *na* raccoon; *pl* **esibananjigesiwag** [*lexicon note*: this is now considered an archaic form for most speakers if it is even known, but for some it is the original form, and esiban is an accepted short form, similar to the vocative, or an accepted short form like waashkesh for waawaashkeshi] (GJ)

RAIN:

BE A RAINFOREST: **gimiwanoowaakwaa** *vii* be a rainforest (RT)

CALM AFTER RAIN: **anwaabiisaa** *vii* be a calm after raining (NJ, GJ)

CAUGHT IN RAIN: **bangibiisaanishi** *vai* be caught in a light rain (RT, NJ, GJ)

PRECIPITATE: **binawanise** *vii* precipitate (cross between snow and rain but misty-like, tiny particles of precipitation) (NJ)

RAINFOREST: **gimiwanoowaakwaang** *pc* rainforest (RT)

SEEK SHELTER FROM RAIN: **gimiwanishi** *vai* make a structure to escape the rain, find shelter from rain (GJ); *also* get rained on (NJ)

STRANDED BY RAIN: **ginibiisaanishi** *vai* can't go because it is too rainy (NJ, GJ)

SUMMER RAIN: **niibinibiisaa** *vii* be a summer rain (RT)

RAPIDS:

SHOOT RAPIDS: **niishiboono** *vai* shoot rapids (NJ, GJ)

CAPSIZE IN RAPIDS: **gwanabaabago** *vai* capsize in rapids (NJ, GJ)

RASH: DIAPER RASH: **miskozhaanidizo** *vai* have a diaper rash (RT, NJ, GJ)

RATTLE:

METALLIC RATTLE: **zhinawesin** *vai* make a metallic rattling sound (ball in a bell) (RT, NJ, GJ)

RATTLE: **zhinawese** *vii* rattle (as in sticks in a drum) (RT, NJ, GJ)

RUMBLE: **jiingwewewag** /jiingwewe/ *vai* they rattle (as in thunderbirds) [*conjugation note*: requires plural to make sense, though this is not a reflexive verb] (NJ, GJ)

READY FOR BED: **oninamaa** *vai* be ready to go to bed (RT)

RECOGNIZE:

SENSE SOMETHING BY TOUCH: **nisidawininjiinan** *vti* recognize s.t. by touch (RT, NJ, GJ)

SENSE THINGS BY TOUCH: **nisidawishkaa** *vai* recognize things by touch (RT, NJ, GJ)

RECTUM: SHOOT IN RECTUM: **biinjidiyeshkozo** *vai* shoot s.o. right in the rectum (NJ, GJ)

RED BUTT: **miskodiye** *vai* have a red butt (RT, NJ, GJ)

REED:

MAKE NOISE PADDLING IN REEDS: **debweweshka'am** *vai* make noise paddling or poling from reeds sliding on a canoe (RT, NJ, GJ)

MAKE NOISE PADDLING AWAY IN REEDS: **animweweshka'am** *vai2* paddle or pole away making noise from reeds brushing against canoe (RT, NJ, GJ)

MAKE NOISE PADDLING BY IN REEDS: **bimweweshka'am** *vai2* make noise while paddling or poling by from reeds brushing against canoe (NJ, GJ)

REFLECT:

PONDER: **naanaagadawendam** *vai* ponder, reflect (RT, NJ, GJ)

REFLECT: **ojichaagosin** *vii* reflect (RT, NJ)

REFLECT IN WATER: **mazinaatebiigishin** *vai* reflect in the water [*example*: Mazinaatebiigishin mitig. = The tree is reflecting in the water. *example*: Mazinaatebiigishin gaa-pimised bineshiinh. = The bird casts a reflection in the water flying.] (NJ, GJ)

REFRAIN: **boonikamigizi** *vai* stop doing certain activities, refrain from doing special activities (as when in mourning) (RT, NJ, GJ)

REINFORCE:

REINFORCEMENT TAB FOR BARK ROLL: **apigwaason** *ni* reinforcing tab on end of birch bark roll or basket (as a wide strip

placed inside out on the end creating a double layer); *pl*
**apigwaasonan** (GJ)

REINFORCEMENT TAB FOR LODGE BARK: **apigwaajigan** *ni* sewn
covering reinforcement tab (as on birch bark lodge coverings)
(RT, NJ, GJ)

REINFORCING STICK: **mikond** *ni* reinforcing stick on end of birch
bark roll or basket, a binding stick; *pl* **mikondiin**; *dim*
**mikondiins** (GJ)

REJECT: **aanawendan** *vti* reject s.t. (as in food offered to s.o., as in being
picky) (NJ, GJ)

RELATIONSHIP:

SNAG: **noojiikaazo** *vai* snag, commense an intimate relationship
(NJ, GJ, RT); *also* **gaajida'ige** (RT)

SNAG AN OLD MAN: **noojiiwakiwenzii** *vai* try to commence an
intimate relationship with an old man, snag (for old men) (NJ)

SNAG SOMEONE: **gaajiji'** *vai* snag s.o., commense an intimate
relationship with s.o. (RT)

RELAX (PRONE): **goshkwaawaajishin** *vai* lie down relaxing, still (RT,
NJ, GJ)

RELEASE:

FREE SOMEONE: **giitaabikizh** /**giitaabikiN-**/ *vta* let s.o. free
(from a trap) (NJ, GJ)

FREE SOMETHING: **giitaabikinan** *vti* release s.t. (as in a trap) (NJ,
GJ)

RELEASE EGGS: **owaako** *vai* release eggs, spawn (as in fish) (RT,
NJ, GJ)

RELUCTANT BECAUSE OF WEATHER: **ginaabandamaa** *vai* don't want to
go because of inclement weather (NJ, GJ)

RELY: **wiiji'igoowizi** *vai* rely upon things, get help from things (NJ)

REMIND SOMEONE: **mikawaam** *vta* remind s.o. (RT, NJ, GJ)

REPAIR DAM: **bi-andogiba'ige** *vai* come to repair dam (as in a beaver)
(NJ, GJ)

REPEAT:

BLINK REPEATEDLY: **bapasangwaabi** *vai* blink repeatedly (RT,
NJ, GJ)

BLINK REPEATEDLY AT SOMEONE: **bapasangwaabam** *vta* blink
eyes at s.o. repeatedly [*example*: Gego bapasangwaabamaaken
awiiya. = Don't keep blinking your eyes at anyone. *cultural note*:

Considered extremely rude and offensive to repeatedly blink at someone.] (NJ, GJ)

HEAD POPS UP REPEATEDLY FROM BOILING: **zaasaagikwezo** *vii* head repeatedly pops up from boiling (RT, NJ, GJ)

HIT REPEATEDLY: **bapakiteshka'igaade** *vii* be hit repeatedly (as in wheat being struck repeatedly by a combine) (RT)

JUMP OUT REPEATEDLY: **zaasaagiji-gwaashkwani** *vai* jump out repeatedly (RT, NJ, GJ)

REPEATEDLY POP UP FROM BOILING: **zaasaagigamide** *vii* repeatedly pop up from boiling (RT, NJ, GJ)

TIE SOMEONE'S LEGS REPEATEDLY: **zasagigaadepizh /zasagigaadepiN-/** *vta* tie s.o. legs repeatedly (RT, NJ, GJ)

REPRODUCE: **ani-aanjigin** *vii* reproduce (RT)

RESERVE:

BE RESERVED: **ishkonigaazo** *vai* be set aside, be reserved (RT)

SAVE SOMEONE FOR LATER: **ishkon** *vta* set s.o. aside, save s.o. for later (RT)

SAVE SOMETHING FOR SOMEONE: **ishkondamaw** *vta* save, reserve s.t. for s.o. (of food) (RT, NJ, GJ)

RESOLVE SOMETHING: **nanaa'itoon** *vti* resolve s.t., fix s.t. (RT, NJ, GJ)

RESPONSIBLE: BE RESPONSIBLE FOR SOMEONE: **ondami'** *vta* be responsible for s.o., take responsibility for s.o., be the reason for s.o.'s action or condition [*example*: Ningii-ondami'aa wenji-bezikaayaang. = I'm the reason we are late.] (NJ, GJ)

REST: **anweshim** *vta* make s.o. rest [*example*: Nindanweshimigoo. = I am being made to rest. *cultural note*: High wind or rain that forces one to rest on a journey may be taken as a sign that it's not wise to try to beat the weather.] (NJ, GJ)

RETALIATORY: **mawine'ige** *vai* be aggressive, retaliatory (RT, NJ, GJ)

RICE:

KNOCK RICE: **bawa'am** *vai* knock rice (RT, NJ, GJ)

KNOCK SOMETHING: **bawa'an** *vti* knock s.t. (as in rice) (RT, NJ, GJ)

KNOCKED: **bawa'igaade** *vii* be knocked (as in rice) (RT, NJ, GJ)

RICE STALK: **manoominagaawanzh** *ni* rice stalk; *pl* **manoominagaawanzhiin** (RT, NJ, GJ)

THRESHING PIT: **mimigoshkamwaagan** *ni* threshing pit for wild rice; *pl* **mimigoshkamwaaganan** (RT)

RIDE:

GIVE SOMEONE A RIDE: **ipizo'** *vta* give s.o. a ride in a certain way (NJ)

HAVE HAPPY RIDE: **minobizo** *vai* have a happy ride (NJ)

RIGHT: DO RIGHT: **gwayakobidoon** *vti* do s.t. right (NJ)

RING: GROW IN RINGS: **waawiyaagishin** *vai* grow in rings (RT, NJ, GJ)

RIPEN:

MATURE: **giizhigin** *vii* mature, ripen, finish growing (RT, NJ, GJ)

RIPEN: **adiso** *vai* ripen (RT)

RIPEN: **adite** *vii* ripen (RT)

RIPPLE: WIND CAUSES RIPPLE: **wiisigamaasin** *vii* wind causes small ripples on calm water (RT, NJ, GJ)

ROAD: DIRT ROAD: **mitaawango-miikanens** *ni* dirt road, dirt trail; *pl* **mitaawango-miikanensan** (RT, NJ, GJ)

ROAST WEINERS: **abwenagizhiinsi** *vai* roast wieners over a fire (NJ)

ROASTING STICK: **abwaanaak** *ni* roasting stick; *pl* **abwaanaakoon** (NJ, GJ)

ROCK:

ROCK WEIGHT: **gonzaabiishkoojiganaabik** *na* rock weight; *pl* **gonzaabiishkoojiganaabikoog** (RT, NJ, GJ)

WIPE OFF ON ROCK: **gaasiiyaabikishkan** *vti* wipe s.t. off of rocks with one's body (NJ, GJ)

WIPE OFF ROCK: **gaasiiyaamikishkige** *vai* wipe off rocks under water  (NJ, GJ)

ROLL:

ROLL: **ditibaakowebiigise** *vai* roll, churn (log, or stick-like object) (RT, NJ, GJ)

ROLL DOWN: **naazhinan** *vti* roll s.t. down (RT, NJ, GJ)

ROLL LOGS: **ditibaakowebishkige** *vai* rolls logs (RT, NJ, GJ)

ROLL SOMEONE: **ditibaakowebishko'** /ditibaakowebishko'w-/ *vta* rolls s.o. (as in logs) (RT, NJ, GJ)

ROLL SOMEONE ACROSS: **ditibiwebin** *vta* roll s.o. across (RT, NJ, GJ)

ROOF:

ROOF INSIDE OUT: **napaajibakwe** *vii* be roofed inside out (GJ)

ROOF RIPPED BY WIND: **bakwadanabakweyaasin** *vii* roof ripped off by the wind (of a house) (RT, NJ, GJ)

ROOF RIPPED BY WIND: **bakwadanabakweyaashi** *vai* have one's roof ripped off by the wind (RT, NJ, GJ)

ROOM:

>BE SUFFICIENT ROOM: **dawaa** *vii* be sufficient room, space (RT); *also* **dawaasin** *vii* be sufficient room, space (RT)
>NEXT ROOM: **awasigamig** *pc* the next room (RT, NJ, GJ); *also* **awasisag** (GJ)
>ROOM DIVIDER: **aajisaga'igan** *ni* room divider; *pl* **aajisaga'iganan** (RT); *also* **aajisaginigan** (GJ)

ROOSTER: **naabese** *na* male bird, rooster; *pl* **naabeseg** (RT, NJ, GJ)

ROOT:

>CATTAIL ROOT: **washkwadab** *na* cattail root; *pl* **washkwadabiig** (RT, NJ, GJ)
>HAVEST ROOTS: **andojiibike** *vai* harvest roots (NJ, GJ)
>HAVE LONG ROOTS: **gagaanwaajiibikezi** *vai* have long roots (RT, NJ, GJ)
>LONG ROOTS: **gagaanwaajiibikeyaa** *vii* have long roots (RT, NJ, GJ)
>ROOT: **ojiibik** *ni* root; *pl* **ojiibikan**; *loc* **ojiibikaang** (RT, NJ, GJ)
>SPLIT ROOTS: **daashkibiiwadabiigobijige** *vai* split roots [*cultural note*: typically done with jack pine or black spruce to prepare heavy sewing fiber] (NJ, GJ)

ROPE:

>BE ROPED: **naabaabiigose** *vai* be roped (NJ); *also* **naabaabiigise** (GJ)
>BE ROPED: **naabaakose** *vii* be roped or caught on something (NJ, GJ)
>BE ROPED BY FEET: **naabaabiigizide** *vai* be roped around the feet (NJ, GJ)
>LASSO SOMEONE: **naabaabiigwebizh** /naabaabiigwebiN-/ *vta* lasso s.o. around the neck (NJ, GJ)
>ROPE AROUND FEET: **naabaabiigigwebizh** /naabaabiigigwebiN-/ *vta* rope s.o. around the feet (NJ, GJ)

ROT:

>GLOWING ROTTEN WOOD: **waasakonejiisag** *ni* glowing rotten wood (NJ, GJ)
>ROT: **biigijiisagowan** *vii* be rotten (as in wood) (GJ)
>ROTTEN TREE: **biigijiisagowi** *vai* be a decayed tree (standing) (GJ)

ROTTEN WOOD (ANY KIND): **biigijiisagaatig** *ni* rotten wood; *pl*
**biigijiisagaatigoon** (GJ); *also* **biigijiisagwaatig**; *pl*
**biigijiisagwaatigoon** (NJ)

ROTTEN WOOD (DOWN): **biigijiisag** *ni* rotten wood (downed); *pl*
**biigijiisagoon** (GJ)

ROTTEN WOOD (STANDING): **biigijiisag** *na* rotten wood (still
standing); *pl* **biigijiisagoog** (GJ)

ROTATE: **gizhibaabide** *vii* spin, rotate (as in the earth spinning on its
axis) (RT)

ROUGH: **gaawaa** *vii* be rough (RT, NJ, GJ)

ROW:

STAND IN A ROW: **niibidegaabawi** *vai* stand in a row (RT, NJ,
GJ)

STAND OUT IN ROW: **mininaawesin** *vii* stand out from others in a
row (GJ); *also* **niminaawesin** (NJ)

RUB: BACKRUB: **mamigobizh** /mamigobiN-/ *vta* give s.o. a backrub (RT,
NJ, GJ)

RUMBLE:

COME RUMBLING: **bi-bakwewe** *vai* come rumbling (like
thunderbird) (GJ)

RATTLE: **jiingwewewag** /jiingwewe/ *vai* they rattle (as in
thunderbirds) [*conjugation note*: requires plural to make sense,
though this is not a reflexive verb] (NJ, GJ)

RUMBLE: **bakweweyaa** *vii* rumble (RT, NJ, GJ)

RUN:

RUN: **bimibide** *vii* be running, be moving, be in use (as in
something motorized) (NJ)

RUN ON SAND: **bimidaawangibatoo** *vai* run on sand (NJ, GJ)

RUN ON TOP OF SAND: **ogidaawangibatoo** *vai* run on sand (RT);
*also* **wagidaawangibatoo** *vai* run on top of the sand (NJ, GJ)

START RUNNING: **maajiibide** *vii* start running, start operating (as
in an engine), take off (RT, NJ, GJ)

START RUNNING: **maajiibizo** *vai* start running, start operating,
start driving, take off (RT, NJ, GJ)

RUN OUT:

BURN OUT: **jaagise** *vii* burn out, run out (in reference to
community stick pile in moccasin game) (GJ)

RUN OUT: **miijidaajise** *vai+o* run out of s.t. (RT)

RUN OUT OF FOOD: **miidaajise** *vai+o* run out of s.t. to eat (RT)

RUNNY: **nibiiwaagamin** *vii* be runny (NJ)

RUT: **aamanozo** *vai* be in rut (RT, NJ, GJ)

SAFE:

> BE CONSIDERED DANGEROUS: **naniizaanendaagwad** *vii* be considered dangerous (RT, NJ, GJ)
>
> BE DANGEROUS: **naniizaanad** *vii* be unsafe, dangerous (RT, NJ, GJ)
>
> BE DANGEROUS: **naniizaanizi** *vai* be dangerous (RT, NJ, GJ)
>
> SAFE: **boome** *vai* be safe (RT)
>
> SAFETY CLASP: **minjimaakwa'iganens** *ni* spring safety clasp (as on a conibear trap); *pl* **minjimaakwa'iganensan** (NJ)

SAIL:

> SAIL: **ningaasimoono** *vai* sail (NJ, GJ)
>
> SAIL BY: **bimaasimoono** *vai* sail along, sail by (NJ, GJ)

SALT:

> BE SALTY WATER: **zhiiwitaaganibiisin** *vii* be salty water (RT, NJ, GJ)
>
> TASTE SALTY: **zhiiwitaaganipogwad** *vii* taste salty (RT, NJ, GJ)

SAND:

> BE SANDY: **mitaawangaa** *vii* be sandy (RT, NJ, GJ)
>
> DIRT ROAD: **mitaawango-miikanens** *ni* dirt road, dirt trail; *pl* **mitaawango-miikanensan** (RT, NJ, GJ)
>
> DRIVE ON SAND: **ogidaawangwebizo** *vai* drive on sand (NJ, GJ)
>
> DRY SAND: **bengwadaawangaa** *vii* be dry sand (NJ, GJ)
>
> FINELY GRANULATED: **nitaawan** *vii* be finely granulated, be fine sand (RT, NJ, GJ)
>
> HOLD SOMEONE IN SAND: **minjimindaawangishkaw** *vta* hold s.o. in place in the sand (GJ)
>
> ON SAND: **mitaawangaang** *pc* on the sand (NJ)
>
> RUN BY ON SAND: **bimidaawangibatoo** *vai* run by on sand (NJ, GJ)
>
> RUN ON TOP OF SAND: **ogidaawangibatoo** *vai* run on top of sand (RT); *also* **wagidaawangibatoo** (NJ, GJ)
>
> SAND OR ANT HILL: **bikwadaawangisin** *vii* be a sand hill, be an ant hill (RT, NJ, GJ)
>
> SAND SCOOPER: **gwaaba'adaawangwaan** *ni* sand scooper; *pl* **gwaaba'adaawangwaanan** (NJ, GJ)

SANDBOX: **mitaawango-makakoons** *ni* sandbox; *pl*
**mitaawango-makakoonsan**; *loc* **mitaawango-makakoonsing**
(NJ)
TRUDGE THROUGH SAND: **bimidaawangii** *vai* trudge through
sand (NJ, GJ)
WARM SAND: **gizhidaawangide** *vii* be warm sand (NJ, GJ)
WET SAND: **nibiiwadaawangaa** *vii* be wet sand (NJ)
SAVE:
BE RESERVED: **ishkonigaazo** *vai* be set aside, be reserved (RT)
SAVE SOMEONE FOR LATER: **ishkon** *vta* set s.o. aside, save s.o.
for later (RT)
SAVE SOMETHING FOR SOMEONE: **ishkondamaw** *vta* save,
reserve s.t. for s.o. (of food) (RT, NJ, GJ)
SAW:
SAW TOOTH STRAIGHTENER: **minwaabide'igan** *ni* saw tooth
straightener; *pl* **minwaabide'iganan** (GJ)
SWEDE SAW: **giishkaabideboojigan** *ni* swede saw; *pl*
**giishkaabideboojiganan** (GJ)
SCALE:
SCALE: **ninaga'ay** /**-naga'ay-**/ *nad* my scale (as of a fish or
snake); *pl* **ninaga'ayag** (RT)
SCALE FISH: **jiichiiga'amegwe** *vai* scale fish (RT, NJ, GJ); *also*
**jiiga'amegwe** *vai* scale fish, clean fish (RT, NJ, GJ)
SCALE SOMEONE: **jiigizhwi** /**jiigizhw-**/ *vta* scale fish (NJ); *also*
**jiigizho** /**jiigizhw-**/ (GJ); *also* **jiigizh** /**jiigizhw-**/ (RT)
SCARE:
BE SCARED: **gotaagonezi** *vai* be scared (NJ)
BE SCARED OF UNSEEN: **amaniso** *vai* be frightened of the unseen
(LM)
SCARED STIFF: **mashkawaanimizi** *vai* be scared stiff (RT, NJ,
GJ)
STARTLE BY GRABBING: **goshkobizh** /**goshkobiN-**/ *vta* startle
s.o by grabbing them (RT, NJ, GJ)
SCHOOL:
GO TO SCHOOL: **ando-gikinoo'amaagozi** *vai* go to school (NJ)
SCHOOL BELL: **gikinoo'amaadii-zhinawa'oojiganens** *ni* school
bell; *pl* **gikinoo'amaadii-zhinawa'oojiganensan** (NJ)
SCHOOL BUS: **gikinoo'amaadiiwidaabaan** *na* school bus; *pl*
**gikinoo'amaadiiwidaabaanag** (NJ); *also*

**gikinoo'amaagewidaaban** *na* school bus; *pl*
**gikinoo'amaagewidaabanag** (NJ)

SCIENCE: **naanaagadagagwegikenjigewin** *ni* science (JC)

SCOOP:

> ICE SCOOPER: **eshkan gwaaba'iskomaan** *ni* ice scooper; *pl*
> **eshkanan gwaaba'iskomaanan** (NJ, GJ)
>
> SAND SCOOPER: **gwaaba'adaawangwaan** *ni* sand scooper; *pl*
> **gwaaba'adaawangwaanan** (NJ, GJ)

SCORE:

> SCORE: **bakinaagewin** *ni* goal; *pl* **bakinaagewinan**; *also*
> **mizhodamowin** *ni* goal; *pl* **mizhodamowinan** (RT, NJ, GJ)
>
> SCORE: **biinjiweba'ige** *vai* score, score a goal, score a point (as
> in soccer or lacrosse) [*example*: Ningii-biinjiweba'ige. = I scored
> a point.] (GJ)
>
> SCORE DOUBLE: **niizho-gabenaage** *vai* score double (as in
> moccasin game) (GJ)
>
> SCORE ON SOMEONE: **biinjiweba'amaw** *vta* score a point on s.o.
> [*example*: Gigii-biinjiweba'amawin. = I scored on you.] (GJ)

SCRAPE:

> SCRAPE HIDE: **jiishaakwa'ige** *vai* scrape a hide (NJ); *also* cut
> limbs off a tree (GJ)
>
> SCRAPE SOMETHING: **bashagaakwa'an** *vti* scrape s.t. (as in bark
> off a tree) (RT); *also* **bishagaakwa'an** (GJ)

SCREWDRIVER: **biima'igan** *ni* screwdriver; *pl* **biima'iganan** (RT, NJ);
> *also* **biimiskwa'igan** *ni* screwdriver; *pl* **biimiskwa'iganan** (GJ)

SCULPT:

> SCULPT: **mazininjiishkiwagi** *vai* sculpt (with clay or dough) (NJ,
> GJ)
>
> SCULPT SOMEONE: **mazinadizh /mazinadiN-/** *vta* sculpt s.o.
> (with clay or dough) (GJ); *also* **mazinijiishkiwagin** (GJ)

SEARCH:

> SEARCH FOR BARK: **andawanagekwe** *vai* look for, search for
> bark (RT, NJ, GJ)
>
> SEARCH FOR BASSWOOD: **andowiigobii** *vai* searching for
> basswood (NJ, GJ)
>
> SEARCH FOR MINK: **andozhaangweshiwe** *vai* go after mink (NJ,
> GJ)
>
> SEARCH FOR PITCH: **andobigiwe** *vai* go after pitch (NJ, GJ)

SEARCH: *see also* LOOK

---

SEASON CHANGES: **aandakiiwin** *ni* changing season; *pl* **aandakiiwinan** (RT, NJ)

SEAT BELT: **gitaakwapizon** *ni* dog leash, dog chain, seat belt; *pl* **gitaakwapizonan** (RT, NJ, GJ)

SEAWEED: **anzanz** *ni* seaweed; *pl* **anzanziin** (RT, NJ, GJ)

SEE:

> BE SEEN AT A DISTANCE: **debinaagozi** *vai* be seen at a distance (ES)
>
> DARK SIDE SHOWS: **makadewiingwebinige** *vai* the dark side shows (as in bagese game) (GJ)
>
> SEE CLEARLY (SHARP VISION): **na'aabi** *vai* see clearly, have sharp vision (RT)
>
> SEE CLEARLY (VISUALIZE): **bagakaabi** *vai* see clearly (RT, NJ, GJ)
>
> SEE SMOKE: **madwe-zaagaabate** *vii* see smoke from a distance (RT, NJ, GJ)

SEED:

> ACORN: **mitigomin** *na* acorn; *pl* **mitigominag** (RT)
>
> BEAN SEED: **mashkodiisiminens** *na* bean seed; *pl* **mashkodiisiminensag** (RT)
>
> BIRCH TREE SEED STRINGS: **wanimikoons** *ni* birch tree seed strings; *pl* **wanimikoonsan** (RT, NJ, GJ)
>
> MAKE SEEDS: **miinikaanensike** *vai* make seeds (RT)
>
> SEED: **miinikaanens** *ni* seed; *pl* **miinikaanensan** (RT)
>
> SEED POD: **miinikaanashk** *ni* seed pod; *pl* **miinikaanashkoon**; *loc* **miinikaanashkong** (RT)
>
> SEED SHELL: **miinikaanagek** *na* seed shell; *pl* **miinikaanagekwag** (RT)

SEEK SHELTER: **dabinoo'ige** *vai* seek shelter (RT)

SEND SOMEONE: **maajiizh** /**maajiiN-**/ *vta* send s.o. somewhere (RT)

SENSE:

> FEEL BY HEARING: **nooyoondam** *vai* feel with hearing (NJ)
>
> FEEL BY SMELL: **biiyiijimaandam** *vai* feel by smell (NJ)
>
> FEEL SOMETHING BY HEARING: **nooyoondan** *vti* feel s.t. with hearing (NJ)
>
> FEEL SOMETHING BY SMELL: **biiyiijimaandan** *vti* feel s.t. by smell (NJ)
>
> FEEL SOMETHING BY TASTE: **biiyiijipidan** *vti* feel s.t. by taste (NJ)

FEEL SOMETHING BY TOUCH: **biiyiijimanjitoon** *vti* feel s.t. by touch (NJ)

FEELING: **inamanjichigaade** *vii* be a feeling, be a sense (NJ)

HEARING: **noondamowin** *ni* sense of hearing (RT, NJ, GJ)

KNOWN BY SENSE: **gikendamaazo** *vai* sense things, know things by sense, discover (RT, NJ, GJ)

SENSE: **gikendamaazowin** *ni* sense; *pl* **gikendamaazowinan** (RT, NJ, GJ); *also* **nisidawishkaawin**; *pl* **nisidawishkaawinan** (RT, NJ, GJ); *also* **onji-gikendamaazon** *ni* sense; *pl* **onji-gikendamaazonan** (RT, NJ, GJ); *also* **enamanjichigaadeg** *vii-prt* feeling, sense (NJ)

SENSE OF SMELL: **biijimaanjige** *vai* smell, have a sense of smell, sense or identify things by smell (RT, NJ, GJ)

SENSE OF TASTE: **biijipijigaage** *vai* taste, sense things by taste (RT, NJ, GJ)

SENSE OF TOUCH: **biijimanjitoon** *vti* feel s.t. all around (by touch), sense by touch s.t. all around (as in a foot soaking in warm water) (RT, NJ, GJ)

SENSE SOMETHING BY TASTE: **biijipidan** *vti* taste s.t., sense s.t. by taste (RT, NJ, GJ)

SENSE SOMETHING BY TOUCH: **nisidawininjiinan** *vti* recognize s.t. by touch (RT, NJ, GJ)

SENSE SOMETHING: **gikendamaazoon** *vti* sense s.t. (NJ); *also* **nisidawendan** (RT, NJ, GJ); *also* **nisidawishkan** (RT, NJ, GJ)

SENSE THINGS: **nisidawendam** *vti* sense things (RT, NJ, GJ)

SENSE THINGS BY TOUCH: **nisidawishkaa** *vai* recognize things by touch (RT, NJ, GJ)

SMELL INHIBITED: **mooshkinemaagod** *vii* have one's sense of smell filled or inhibited (as in by a cold) (NJ); *also* **mooshkinemaagwad** (RT)

SENSITIVE:

OVERSENSITIVE: **ando-mazitam** *vai2* be emotionally oversensitive, easy to offend, looking for fault (RT, NJ, GJ)

PHYSICALLY SENSITIVE: **wake-nisidawishkaa** *vai* be physically sensitive (RT, NJ, GJ)

SENSITIVE TO COLD: **wakewaji** *vai* be sensitive to cold, can't take the cold (RT, NJ, GJ)

SEPARATE: LIGHT SEPARATES: **babakeyaate** *vii* light separates (RT, NJ, GJ)

---

SEQUESTER FOR MENSUS: **makoonsiwi** *vai* be sequestered for mensus (NJ); *also* **makoowizi** *vai* be sequestered for mensus (JC)

SET:

SET:
> PREPARE NETS: **oninasabii** *vai* prepare nets for setting (RT, NJ, GJ)
>
> SET SOMETHING: **omba'an** *vti* set s.t. (as in a trap) (NJ, GJ)
>
> SET TRAPS: **omba'ige** *vai* set traps (NJ, GJ)

SET: *see also* NET

SET ASIDE:
> BE RESERVED: **ishkonigaazo** *vai* be set aside, be reserved (RT)
>
> SAVE SOMEONE FOR LATER: **ishkon** *vta* set s.o. aside, save s.o. for later (RT)
>
> SAVE SOMETHING FOR SOMEONE: **ishkondamaw** *vta* save, reserve s.t. for s.o. (of food) (RT, NJ, GJ)

SEW:
> SEW EXTENSION: **aanikoogwaajigan** *ni* sewn on extension; *pl* **aanikoogwaajiganan** (RT, NJ, GJ)
>
> SEW IN SUCCESSION: **aanikoogwaade** *vii* be sewn on in succession, in a linear fashion (RT, NJ, GJ)
>
> SEW ON: **agogwaade** *vii* sewn on, up against s.t. (as in ends of birch bark lodge coverings) (NJ, GJ)

SEXUAL AROUSAL: **noondendam** *vai* be envious, want what others have (NJ); want things from people (implies sexual arousal) (LM)

SHADE: **agawaateshkaa** *vii* be shade, be a shadow (RT, NJ); *also* **aagawaateshkaa** (GJ)

SHADOW:
> BE A SHADOW: **agawaate** *vii* be a shadow (RT); *also* **aagawaate** (GJ)
>
> CAST A SHADOW: **mazinaateshin** *vai* cast a shadow (NJ)

SHAKE:
> MAKE SOMETHING SHAKE: **mamaajiwebishkan** *vti* make s.t. shake (NJ)
>
> SHAKE SOMEONE: **ishkwaakobizh** /**ishkwaakobiN-**/ *vta* shake s.o. (tree-like) (NJ, GJ); *also* **mamigowebizh** /**mamigowebiN-**/ (RT, NJ, GJ)
>
> SHAKE TENT ENCIRCLING POLE: **waawiyeyaabijigan** *ni* encircling pole of a shake-tent; *pl* **waawiyeyaabijiganan** (GJ)
>
> SHAKE TREE: **ishkwaakobijige** *vai* shake a tree (person or bear) (RT, NJ, GJ)

SHAKING TREE: **ishkwaakobijigan** *ni* tree or pole that is shaken; *pl* **ishkwaakobijiganan** (RT, NJ, GJ)

SHALLOW: **dakwiindimaa** *vii* be shallow (a short depth of water) (RT, NJ, GJ)

SHAMPOO: **giziibiigitigwaane-giiziibiiga'igan** *ni* shampoo (NJ)

SHARP:

BE SHARP: **gaashaa** *vii* sharp (as in a knife) (RT, NJ, GJ)

CHAINSAW FILE: **zisiboojiganens** *ni* chainsaw sharpening file; *pl* **zisiboojiganensan** (GJ)

HAVE POINT: **jiibwaabikad** *vii* have a point, come to a point (NJ, GJ)

LARGE, SHARP TEETH: **mamaangi-giinaabid** *ni* large, sharp teeth; *pl* **mamaangi-giinaabidan** (RT)

SHARP: **giinaa** *vii* sharp (knife) (RT, NJ, GJ)

SHARP CLAWS: **gagiiniganzhii** *vai* have sharp claws (RT)

SHARP TEETH: **gaashaabide** *vai* have sharp teeth (NJ)

SHARPEN: **gaashkiboojige** *vai* sharpen things that are long and straight (RT, NJ, GJ)

SHARPEN SOMETHING JAGGED: **giiniboodoon** *vti* sharpen s.t. that has a jagged edge (NJ, GJ)

SHARPEN SOMETHING STRAIGHT: **gaashiboodoon** *vti* sharpen s.t. that is long and straight (RT, NJ, GJ)

SHELF: **desaakwa'iganaak** *ni* smoking shelf, storage shelf; *pl* **desaakwa'iganaakoon** (RT, NJ, GJ)

SHELL: EGG SHELL: **waawanogek** *na* egg shell; *pl* **waawanogekwag** (NJ)

SHELTER:

SHELTER: **dabinoo'ige** *vai* seek shelter (RT)

SEEK SHELTER FROM RAIN: **gimiwanishi** *vai* make a structure to escape the rain, find shelter from rain (GJ); *also* get rained on (NJ)

SEEK SHELTER FROM WATER: **agwaaba'iwe** *vai* get off water to safety, seek shelter (NJ, GJ)

SHINE:

LIGHT GOES: **gizhiiyaate** *vii* be bright, far-reaching, or penetrating light (RT, NJ, GJ)

SHINE CERTAIN WAY: **ayinaate** *vii* shine in a certain way or color (RT, NJ, GJ)

SHINE HOTLY: **gizhaasige** *vai* shine hotly (as in the sun) (RT)

SHINE ON SOMEONE: **minwaasigetamaw** *vta* shine pleasant light on s.o. (RT)

SHINE SO LONG: **akwaate** *vii* light shines a certain length of time or distance (RT, NJ, GJ)

SHINE THROUGH: **zhaabwaate** *vii* shine through (as in light through glass or water) (RT, NJ, GJ)

SHOCK: **det** *expression* shocking (ES)

SHOE:

HIGH-HEELED SHOE: **ishpidoondanekizin** *ni* high-heeled shoe; *pl* **ishpidoondanekizinan** (RT, NJ, GJ)

PUT SHOES ON WRONG FEET: **nanepaadakizine** *vai* put one's shoes on the wrong foot (NJ, GJ)

SHOOT:

DOUBLE SHOOT: **niizho-bimodan** *vti* double shoot (as in moccasin game) (GJ)

SHOOT IN RECTUM: **biinjidiyeshkozo** *vai* shoot s.o. right in the rectum (NJ, GJ)

SHOOT MULTIPLE: **okonaw** *vta* crack shoot s.o., shoot more than one (line 'em up) (NJ, GJ)

TAKE POT SHOT AT SOMEONE: **goda'aakwaazh** /**goda'aakwaaN-**/ *vta* take a pot shot at s.o. (ES, RT, NJ, GJ)

SHORE:

DETACHED OPENING IN ICE ALONG SHORE: **waasooskode'an** *vii* be a detached opening in the ice along the shore (GJ)

OPENING IN ICE ALONG SHORE: **waasooskodewan** *vii* be an opening in the ice along the shore (NJ)

SET NET PERPENDICULAR TO SHORE: **mininaawesabii** *vai* set net close to shore (set goes perpendicular from shore) (GJ); *also* **niminaawesabii** (NJ)

SET NETS OUT FROM SHORE: **niminaawesaa** *vai* set nets out from shore (NJ); *also* **mininaawesaa** (GJ)

TAKE OFF FROM SHORE: **mininaawa'o** *vai* take off from shore (as in a boat, or swimming) (GJ); *also* **niminaawa'o** (NJ, RT)

SHORT:

GROW TO A SMALL STATURE: **dakogin** *vii* grow to a small stature (RT)

SHORT DAY: **dako-giizhigad** *vii* be a short day (RT, NJ, GJ)

SHORT DAY: **dakwaasige** *vai* be short day, sun shines for a short period of time (as in short winter days) (RT)

SHORT NIGHT: **dako-dibikad** *vii* be a short night (RT, NJ, GJ)

SHOVEL: **gwaabaajigan** *ni* shovel; *pl* **gwaabaajiganan** (RT, NJ, GJ)

SHOW: WHITE SIDE SHOWS: **waasiingwewebinige** *vai* the white side shows (RT, NJ, GJ)

SHOWER: **wenjijiwang** *vii-prt* shower; *pl* **wenjijiwangin** (NJ)

SHUT:

    BITE SHUT: **gashkaabikandan** *vti* bite s.t. shut (RT, NJ, GJ)

    POUND SHUT: **gibwaabikada'an** *vti* pound s.t. shut with a tool (RT)

    SPRING SHUT: **gashkaagise** *vii* spring closed (RT, NJ, GJ)

    SQUEEZE SHUT (HAND): **gashkaabikinan** *vti* squeeze s.t. shut with one's hand (RT, NJ, GJ)

    SQUEEZE SHUT (OBJECT): **gibaabikibidoon** *vti* squeeze s.t. shut (by using s.t.) (RT, NJ, GJ)

    SQUEEZE SHUT (TOOL): **gashkaabikada'an** *vti* squeeze s.t. shut with a tool (RT, NJ, GJ)

SIDE:

    DARK ON ONE SIDE: **nabanemakadeyaaso** *vai* be dark on one side from sun (as in suntanned) (NJ, GJ)

    EITHER SIDE: **edawayi'ii** *pc* on either side, one the sides (RT); *also* **eyiidawayi'ii** (NJ); *also* **edaweyi'ii** (GJ)

SIDEWAYS:

    DANCE SIDEWAYS: **bimijizideshimo** *vai* dance sideways (NJ, GJ)

    MAKE TRAIL SIDEWAYS: **bimijizide-miikanaake** *vai* make trail sideways (NJ, GJ)

SIGN:

    GIVE SOMEONE DIRTY FINGER SIGN: **zaagidenaninjiitaw** *vta* give s.o. the dirty Ojibwe finger sign [*cultural note*: performed by sticking the thumb between the first two fingers, symbolically representing a phallus protruding between the legs, done teasingly, in jest, but only between male friends] (GJ)

    GIVE SOMEONE THE PEACE SIGN: **niingidowaakoninjiitaw** *vai* give s.o. the peace sign (GJ)

    MAKE PEACE SIGN: **niingidowaakoninjiini** *vai* make the peace sign (GJ)

SIGN LANGUAGE: **michinininjiitaw** *vta* communicate with s.o. using sign language (NJ)

SILO: **atoominesigan** *ni* silo; *pl* **atoominesiganan**; *loc* **atoominesiganing** (RT)

SILVER:

> HAVE SILVER-HAIRED BACK: **waabikweyaawigane** *vai* have a silver-colored hairy back (RT, NJ, GJ)
>
> SILVER-BACK GORILLA: **wayaabikweyaawiganed** *vai-prt* silver-back gorilla; *pl* **wayaabikweyaawiganejig** (RT, NJ, GJ)

SIMMER:

> SIMMER: **dootookigamide** *vii* be simmered (NJ, GJ)
>
> SIMMER: **dootookigamizo** *vai* be simmered (as in a duck) (NJ, GJ)
>
> SIMMER SOMEONE: **dootookigamizwi** /**dootookigamizw-**/ *vta* simmer s.o. (NJ); *also* **dootookigamizo** /**dootookigamizw-**/ (GJ)
>
> SIMMER SOMETHING: **dootookigamizan** *vti* simmer s.t. (NJ, GJ)

SINK:

> SINK: **gibitagomo** *vai* stop floating, sink (RT, NJ, GJ)
>
> SINK SOMETHING: **asamishkoodoon** *vti* sink s.t. by weighting it down (GJ); *also* **gitaamikishkoodoon** *vti* sink s.t. to bottom of lake with heavy object (RT, NJ, GJ)
>
> SINKER (FISHING): **migisiwizh** *na* fishing sinker (RT, NJ, GJ)
>
> SINKER (NET): **goonzaabiishkomaan** *ni* net sinker, *pl* **goonzaabiishkomaanan** (RT)
>
> SINKER (NET OR TRAP): **gonzaabiishkoojigan** *ni* net weight or sinker for drowning set (on trap for animals); *pl* **gonzaabiishkoojiganan** (RT, NJ, GJ)
>
> SINKER (TRAP): **gitaakwa'iganaabik** *ni* sinker for drowning set (trap for animals); *pl* **gitaakwa'iganaabikoon** (RT, NJ, GJ)

SIT:

> SIT: **ayate** *vii* just sitting there (NJ, GJ)
>
> SIT CAUSING ANAL PENETRATION: **boojidiyeshin** *vai* fall or sit on s.t. causing anal penetration (GJ)
>
> SIT DOZING: **gakawadabi** *vai* sit dozing off (RT)
>
> SIT PROPERLY: **wewenabi** *vai* sit properly (RT, NJ, GJ)
>
> STRADDLE: **desabi** *vai* straddle, sit straddling (RT, NJ, GJ)

SIX:

> NUMBER SIX: **neningodwaasinoon** *vii-pl* they number six, there are six of them (RT)
>
> SIX SPOT: **ningodwaasokaan** *pc* the six spot (in moccasin game) (GJ)

SIXTY-FIVE MILLION: **ningodwaasimidana ashi naanan dasing wekwaagindaasowin** *number* 65 million (NJ)

SIZE:

> DIMENSION: **ayinigokwaa** *vii* be a certain size, be a certain dimension (RT)
>
> SIZE: **ayizhinaagwad** *vii* be a certain size (RT)

SKATE WELL: **minwaada'e** *vai* skate well (RT, NJ, GJ)

SKELETON LIES PICKED CLEAN: **zhiigooganeshin** vai skeleton lies on the ground picked clean (RT, NJ, GJ)

SKI: WATER SKI: **ogijibiibizo** *vai* water ski (RT, NJ, GJ)

SKIN:

> HAVE THICK SKIN: **gipagazhaga'e** *vai* have thick, callous, armor-like skin (NJ); *also* **gipagazhe** *vai* have thick, callous skin (RT)
>
> SKIN: **ninzhaga'ay** /-zhaga'ay-/ *nid* my skin; *also* **nishkatay** /-shkatay-/ (RT, NJ, GJ)
>
> SKIN TAG: **ginwaabiigijiichigom** *na* skin tag; **ginwaabiigijiichigomag** (RT, NJ, GJ)
>
> SMOOTH SKIN: **zhooshkwazhe** *vai* have smooth skin (RT)
>
> THICK SKIN: **gipagazhaan** *ni* callus, thick skin (RT, NJ, GJ)
>
> WART: **jiichiigom** *na* wart; *pl* **jiichiigomag** (RT, NJ, GJ)

SKY:

> TOUCH LAND FROM SKY: **mizhakiinam** *vai* go from the sky all the way to ground like a thunderbird, or tornado touching down (NJ, GJ)
>
> TOUCH LAND FROM SKY AND RETURN: **mizhakiise** *vai* fly from the sky down to the earth, make land fall (then back up) (NJ, GJ)

SLANT: **nawekide** *vii* be at a slant (GJ)

SLAP TAIL ON WATER: **damoo'am** *vai* slap one's tail on the water (as in a beaver) (NJ)

SLEEP:

> CRY TO SLEEP: **nibewemo** *vai* cry one's self to sleep (AG)
>
> DOZE: **akawadabi** *vai* sit dozing off, spacing out vacuously (RT, NJ, GJ)
>
> FALL SLEEP: **giikiibiingwashi** *vai* fall asleep (LM)
>
> FALL ASLEEP FROM HEAT: **nibeyaakizo** *vai* fall asleep because of the heat [*example*: Ginibeyaakizomin. = We're falling asleep because of the heat.] (RT, NJ, GJ)
>
> READY FOR BED: **oninamaa** *vai* be ready to go to bed (RT)
>
> SLEEP WITH PEOPLE: **wiipe** *vai* sleep with people (RT)
>
> SLEEPY: **akongoshi** *vai* be very sleepy (GJ, NJ)
>
> SLEEPY: **noondegwashi** *vai* be sleepy (RT, NJ, GJ)

SLIDE:

    SLIDE: **zhooshkojiwe** *vai* slide (NJ)

    SLIDE: **zhooshkwaa** *vii* slide (RT, NJ, GJ)

    SLIDE SOMEONE IN TIGHT AREA: **zhegwaakozh / zhegwaakoN-/** *vta* stick s.o. in a tight place (NJ)

    SLIDE SOMETHING IN TIGHT AREA: **zhegwaakonan** *vti* slide s.t. into a tight area (of s.t. stick-like) (NJ)

    SLIDE THROUGH WATER EASILY: **zhooshkobiise** *vii* slides through the water easily (RT, NJ, GJ)

SLINGSHOT: **basitebijigan** *ni* slingshot; *pl* **basitebijiganan** (RT, NJ, GJ)

SLIT:

    CHOP A SLIT: **beshiga'an** *vti* chop a slit in s.t. (as in bark) (RT, NJ, GJ)

    CUT LENGTHWISE: **daashkizhigaazo** *vai* be cut in half lengthwise, be slit (GJ)

SLITHER: **bimoode** *vai* slither, crawl (RT, NJ, GJ)

SLOTH: **bedakwaandaweshiinh** *na* sloth; *pl* **bedakwaandaweshiinyag** (RT)

SLOW:

    PADDLE SLOWLY (FLOATING): **bedaakogomo** *vai* paddle slowly (implies floating) (RT, NJ, GJ)

    PADDLE SLOWLY (FORCED MOVEMENT): **bedakwazhiwe** *vai* paddle slowly (implies forced movement) (RT, NJ, GJ)

    SOUND SLOW: **bejitaagod** *vii* sound slow (as in a fog horn) (NJ); *also* **bejitaagwad**

    SOUND SLOW: **bejitaagozi** *vai* slow sounding call (as in a bird call) (RT, NJ, GJ)

SLUSH:

    SLUSH WATER: **biitooskobiig** *pc* slush water (RT, NJ, GJ)

    SLUSH WATER: **biitooskobiigaaboo** *ni* slush water; *pl* **biitooshkobiigaaboon** (RT, NJ, GJ)

    SLUSH WATER UNDER SNOW: **biitooskobiigaa** *vii* be water under snow, be slush (RT, NJ, GJ)

SMALL:

    BE SMALL: **babiiwizhenhyi** *vai* be small in stature (NJ)

    GROW TO A SMALL STATURE: **dakogin** *vii* grow to a small stature (RT)

SMALLMOUTH BASS: **noosa'owesi** *na* smallmouth bass; *pl*
**noosa'owesiwag**; also **odazhegomoo** *na* smallmouth bass; *pl*
**odazhegomoog** (NJ, GJ)

SMELL:

FEEL BY SMELL: **biiyiijimaandam** *vai* feel by smell (NJ)

FEEL SOMETHING BY SMELL: **biiyiijimaandan** *vti* feel s.t. by
smell (NJ)

SENSE OF SMELL: **biijimaanjige** *vai* smell, have a sense of smell,
sense or identify things by smell (RT, NJ, GJ)

SMELL: **biijimaate** *vii* smell issues forth, aroma emanates (RT,
NJ, GJ)

SMELL ANCIENT: **getemaagwad** *vii* smell ancient (GJ)

SMELL INHIBITED: **mooshkinemaagod** *vii* have one's sense of
smell filled or inhibited (as in by a cold) (NJ); *also*
**mooshkinemaagwad** (RT)

SMELL SOMEONE: **biijimaam** *vta* smell s.o. (RT, NJ, GJ)

SMELL SOMETHING: **biijimaandan** *vti* smell s.t., sense s.t. by
smell (RT, NJ, GJ)

SNIFF SOMEONE: **minaam** *vta* sniff s.o. [*example*: Niminaamig
animosh. = The dog sniffs me.] (RT)

SMELT: **zhooniyaa-giigoozens** *na* smelt; *pl* **zhooniyaa-giigoozensag** (NJ,
GJ)

SMOKE:

CONTINUOUS SMOKE: **baashkijiinesin** *vii* continuous smoke (RT,
NJ, GJ)

DEBONE: **nametegoke** *vai* take bones out in preparation for
smoking (RT, NJ, GJ)

DIRTY SMOKE: **wiinaabate** *vii* be dirty (as in something smoke-
like) (RT, NJ, GJ)

MOSQUITO CHASER SMOKE: **webaabasigan** *ni* mosquito chaser
smoke (NJ, GJ)

SEE SMOKE: **madwe-zaagaabate** *vii* see smoke from a distance
(RT, NJ, GJ)

SMOKE COMES FROM SOMEWHERE: **ondaabate** *vii* smoke comes
from somewhere (RT, NJ, GJ)

SMOKE COMES OUT: **zaagaabate** *vii* smoke comes out
somewhere (RT, NJ, GJ)

SMOKE HOLE: **wenji-zaagidaabateg** *vii-prt* smoke hole (RT, NJ,
GJ)

SMOKE MEAT: **agwaawe** *vai* curing meat/fish by smoking (NJ)

SMOKE RACK: **agwaawaanaakoons** *ni* smoking rack stick; *pl* **agwaawaanaakoonsan** (RT, NJ, GJ)

SMOKE SOMEONE: **agwaawen** *vta* cure s.o. by smoking (NJ)

SMOKED FISH: **giikanaabasigaazod giigoonh** *vai-prt* smoked fish (GJ)

SMOKED MEAT: **gaaskizwaan** *ni* meat smoked through to cured state (RT); *also* **giikanaabasigaadeg wiiyaas** *vii-prt* smoked meat (GJ)

SMOKEHOUSE: **agwaawaanaak** *ni* A-frame pointed smokehouse; *pl* **agwaawaanaakoon** (RT, NJ, GJ); *also* **gaaskaabasigewigamigoons** *ni* smokehouse; *pl* **gaaskaabasigewigamigoonsan** (NJ)

SMOKY: **giikanaabate** *vii* be smoky (RT, NJ, GJ)

SMOOTH:

BE SMOOTH: **zhooshkwaakozi** *vai* be smooth (s.t. treelike) (RT, NJ, GJ)

MAKE SOMEONE SMOOTH BY CUTTING: **zhooshkwaakozhwi /zhooshkwaakozhw-/** *vta* cut s.o. smooth using s.t. (knife), as in trimming the knots off a sapling, making it smooth (NJ)

SMOOTH SKIN: **zhooshkwazhe** *vai* have smooth skin (RT)

SMUDGE:

SMUDGE: **ashawi-zagimeweke** *vai* make smudge to chase off mosquitoes (NJ, GJ)

SMUDGE: **baashkijiinesin** *vii* continuous smoke (RT, NJ, GJ)

MOSQUITO SMUDGE: **baashkijiinesijigan** *ni* smudge to ward off mosquitoes; *pl* **baashkijiinesijiganan** (NJ, GJ)

SNAG:

SNAG: **noojiikaazo** *vai* snag, commense an intimate relationship (NJ, GJ, RT); *also* **gaajida'ige** (RT)

SNAG AN OLD MAN: **noojiiwakiwenzii** *vai* try to commence an intimate relationship with an old man, snag (for old men) (NJ)

SNAG SOMEONE: **gaajiji'** *vai* snag s.o., commense an intimate relationship with s.o. (RT)

SNAKE:

SCALE: **ninaga'ay /-naga'ay-/** *nad* my scale (as of a fish or snake); *pl* **ninaga'ayag** (RT)

SNAKE TAIL: **ninzhigwan /-zhigwan-/** *nid* my tail (of a fish, snake, or serpent); *pl* **ninzhigwanan** (RT, NJ, GJ)

SNAP OFF: **bookoganaandan** *vti* break s.t. by applying pressure, snap s.t. off (RT, NJ, GJ)

SNARL:

SNARLING WATER: **gichi-babiikwajiwan** *vii* the water is really snarling (RT, NJ, GJ)

SNARLY HAIR: **niiskaweyaandibe** *vai* have snarly hair (RT, NJ, GJ)

SNEAK:

DANCE SNEAK-UP: **gaagiimaashimo** *vai* dance the sneak-up (GJ)

SNEAK CROUCHED: **gaagiimaazi** *vai* sneak up in a crouched position (NJ, GJ)

SNEAK UP ON SOMEONE: **gaagiimaa'** *vta* sneak up on s.o. (RT, NJ, GJ)

SNIFF:

SNIFF: **ikwanaanjige** *vai* sniff, huff (RT, NJ, GJ)

SNIFF SOMEONE: **minaam** *vta* sniff s.o. [*example*: Niminaamig animosh. = The dog sniffs me.] (RT)

SNOW:

BREAK THROUGH SNOW (CRUST): **bajiba'am** *vai* break through and sink down in the snow, as when walking on crusty snow (NJ)

BREAK THROUGH SNOW (DRIVING): **bajibashkobiigibizo** *vai* break through and sink down in the snow, as when driving on slushy snow (NJ)

BREAK THROUGH SNOW (SLUSH): **bajibashkobii'am** *vai* break through and sink down in the snow, as when walking on slushy snow [*morphological note:* "bii" pertains to water in this snow term] (NJ)

DIVE IN SNOW: **bookaagonebizo** *vai* dive into the snow (RT, NJ, GJ)

HAVE A HARD TIME GOING THROUGH SNOW: **aadaagoneshin** *vai* have a hard time going through snow [*cultural note*: indicates a deep snowy winter to come] (NJ, GJ)

HOLD SOMEONE IN SNOW: **minjimaagoneshkaw** *vta* hold s.o. in snow (GJ)

MAKE TRAIL WIDER: **mamangideyaagoneshkige** *vai* make trail wider (in the snow) (GJ); *also* **mangadeyaagoneshkige** (NJ, GJ); *also* **mangademochige** (NJ, GJ)

PACK TRAIL WITH SNOWSHOE: **daataagwaagoneshkige** *vai* pack trail with snowshoes or shoes (NJ, GJ)

PRECIPITATE: **binawanise** *vii* precipitate (cross between snow and rain but misty-like, tiny particles of precipitation) (NJ)

PRESS SNOW DOWN BY FOOT: **maagwaagoneshkige** *vai* press foot in the snow, pack snow down with one's foot (GJ)

PUSH SNOW: **akoweba'o** /akoweba'w-/ *vta* push s.o. aside (as in snow) (GJ); *also* **ikoweba'wi** /ikoweba'w-/ (NJ); *also* **ikoweba'** /ikoweba'w-/ (RT)

SLUSH WATER UNDER SNOW: **biitooskobiigaa** *vii* be water under snow, be slush (RT, NJ, GJ)

STRANDED BY SNOW: **giniponishi** *vai* be snowed in (NJ, GJ)

SNOWSHOE:

BROKEN SNOWSHOE: **biigwaagime** *vai* have broken snowshoes (lacing or wood) (RT, NJ, GJ)

CUT IN CIRCLE: **waanizhaabii** *vai* cut hide or leather in a circular fashion (as in making snowshoe lacing) (NJ, GJ)

CUT SOMEONE IN CIRCLE: **waanizhwi** /waanizhw-/ *vta* cut s.o. in a circular fashion (as in making snowshoe lacing) (NJ)

LACE: **ashkimaazh** /ashkimaaN-/ *vta* lace s.o. (as in a snowshoe) (NJ)

PACK TRAIL WITH SNOWSHOE: **daataagwaagoneshkige** *vai* pack trail with snowshoes or shoes (NJ, GJ)

SNOWSHOE BINDING: **adiman** *ni* snowshoe binding; *pl* **adimanan** (NJ)

SOAK:

SOAK: **agwanjidoon** *vti* soak s.t. (RT, NJ); *also* **agonjidoon** (GJ)

SOFTEN BY SOAKING: **nookagwanjidoon** *vti* soften s.t. by soaking (RT, NJ, GJ)

SOAP: **giziibiiga'igan** *ni* soap; *pl* **giziibiiga'iganan** (RT, NJ, GJ)

SOCCER: **basikawaadam** *vai* play soccer (NJ)

SOFT:

SOFT FUR: **nookadawe** *vai* have soft fur (NJ)

SOFTEN BY SOAKING: **nookagwanjidoon** *vti* soften s.t. by soaking (RT, NJ, GJ)

SOFTEN NETS: **biniskosabii** *vai* soften nets (RT)

SOUND SOFT: **nookwewe** *vii* make a soft sound (RT, NJ, GJ)

SOIL:

MOIST SOIL: **dipiiwikamigaa** *vii* be moist soil (RT)

SOIL: **ozaanaman** *na* soil; *pl* **ozaanamanag** (RT)

SOLE:

> ON SOLE OF FOOT: **nagaakizidaaning** *pc* on the sole of the foot (referencing s.t. there) (RT, NJ, GJ)
>
> SOLE: **anaamizid** *pc* under the foot, underneath (RT, NJ, GJ)
>
> SOLE OF FOOT: **nagaakizid** *ni* sole of the foot; *loc* **nagaakizidaang** (body part) (RT, NJ, GJ)

SOLITARY: *see* LONE

SOLO SPRING: **nabaneyaagad** *vii* there is a solo spring (as on a #6 conibear trap) (NJ)

SORT SOMETHING: **maawandoonan** *vti* sort s.t., group s.t. (RT, NJ, GJ)

SOUND:

> BE PLEASANT SOUND OF CHIMES: **minweweyaabikaasin** *vii* good sound of metal (as in wind chimes) [*example*: Minweweyaabikaasinoon. = The (wind chimes) sound good.] (NJ)
>
> BE PLEASANT SOUND OF GRASS BLOWING: **minwewekosiwaagosin** *vii* be a pleasant sound of the grass blowing in the wind (NJ); *also* **minweweshkosiwagaasin** *vii* good sound of grass blowing in the wind (NJ)
>
> BE PLEASANT SOUND OF LEAVES: **minwewebagaasin** *vii* be a pleasant sound of wind in the tree leaves (NJ)
>
> BE PLEASANT SOUND OF WATER FLOWING: **minwewejiwan** *vii* good sound of water flowing (NJ)
>
> CONIFER SOUNDS PLEASANT IN WIND: **minweweyaandagaashi** *vai* pleasant sound of an evergreen tree in the wind (NJ)
>
> DEEP VOICE: **mangitaagozi** *vai* have a deep voice (NJ)
>
> HEAR CLEARLY: **debitan** *vti* hear s.t. clearly, identify the type or direction of a sound of s.t. (NJ, GJ)
>
> HEARD CHEWING: **madwenjige** *vai* be heard chewing (RT, NJ, GJ)
>
> HEARD FLYING: **madwese** *vai* be heard flying (RT, NJ, GJ)
>
> LIKE SOUND: **minotan** *vti* like the sound of s.t. (RT, NJ, GJ)
>
> MAKE NOISE PADDLING: **debweweshka'am** *vai* make noise paddling or poling from reeds sliding on a canoe (RT, NJ, GJ)
>
> MAKE NOISE PADDLING AWAY: **animweweshka'am** *vai2* paddle or pole away making noise from reeds brushing against canoe (RT, NJ, GJ)

MAKE NOISE PADDLING BY: **bimweweshka'am** *vai2* make noise while paddling or poling by from reeds brushing against canoe (NJ, GJ)

MAKE SOMEONE SOUND: **noondaagamo'** *vta* make s.o. sound a certain way (NJ, GJ)

MAKE SOUND: **madwewe** *vai* make a sound (RT, NJ, GJ)

MAKE SOUND: **madwewe** *vii* make a sound (RT, NJ, GJ)

NICE SOUNDING FEET: **mino-zhooshkozideshimo** *vai* have nice sounding feet (as in a tap dancer) (NJ, GJ)

PIERCING SOUND: **bagakitaagod** *vii* sound sharp, have a piercing sound; *also* **bagakitaagwad** (NJ, GJ)

PLEASANT SOUND OF CONIFER IN WIND: **minweweyaandagaasin** *vii* pleasant sound of evergreen boughs in the wind (NJ)

PLEASANT SOUND OF WAVES: **minweweyaashkaa** *vii* good sound of waves (NJ)

RUMBLE: **jiingwewewag** /jiingwewe/ *vai* they rattle (as in thunderbirds) [*conjugation note*: requires plural to make sense, though this is not a reflexive verb] (NJ, GJ)

SOFT VOICE: **bedowe** *vii* have a soft voice (low and slow) (NJ, GJ)

SOUND CERTAIN WAY: **initaagwad** *vii* sound a certain way (RT, NJ, GJ)

SOUND GOOD DRUMMING: **minwewe'akokwe** *vai* make a nice sound drumming (RT, NJ, GJ)

SOUND IN WIND: **inweweyaashi** *vai* have a certain sound in the wind (RT, NJ, GJ)

SOUND OF PADDLING THROUGH REEDS: **bimweweshka'am** *vai2* make noise while paddling or poling from reeds brushing against canoe (NJ, GJ)

SOUND PATHETIC: **goopaataagozi** *vai* sound pathetic (RT, NJ, GJ)

SOUND PLEASANT PLAYING FIDDLE: **minwewenaazhaabii'ige** *vai* make a pleasant sound playing fiddle (RT, NJ, GJ)

SOUND PLEASANT PLAYING GUITAR: **minweweyaabiigibijige** *vai* make a pleasant sound playing guitar (RT, NJ, GJ)

SOUND SLOW: **bejitaagod** *vii* sound slow (as in a fog horn) (NJ); *also* **bejitaagwad**

SOUND SLOW: **bejitaagozi** *vai* slow sounding call (as in a bird call) (RT, NJ, GJ)

SOUND SOFT: **nookwewe** *vii* make a soft sound (RT, NJ, GJ)

SOUND STRANGE: **mayagitaagozi** *vai* sound strange (RT, NJ); *also* **mayegitaagozi** (GJ)

SOUND STRONG: **gizhiiwe** *vii* sound strong, have a loud, strong sound (NJ, GJ)

SWEET SOUND OF FLOWING WATER WOMAN: **Minwewejiwanook** *name* Sweet Sound of Flowing Water Woman (NJ)

TREE MAKES PLEASANT SOUND OF LEAVES: **minwewebagaashi** *vai* tree makes a pleasant sound of leaves in the wind (NJ)

TRILL: **gidaatabitaagozi** *vai* trill, fast sounding call (as in bird) (RT, NJ, GJ)

VOICE CARRIES: **jiingwe** *vai* voice carries long ways (RT, NJ, GJ)

WAVE SOUND: **madweyaashkaa** *vii* waves make a sound (RT, NJ, GJ)

SOUR TASTE: **ziiwiskipogwad** *vii* taste sour (NJ); *also* **ziiwaskipogod** (GJ)

SOURCE: WATER SOURCE: **onjijiwan** *vii* water comes from somewhere, be a water source (NJ, RT)

SPACE:

BE SUFFICIENT ROOM: **dawaa** *vii* be sufficient room, space (RT); *also* **dawaasin** *vii* be sufficient room, space (RT)

LEAVE SPACE: **dawisidoon** *vti* leave a space (RT, NJ, GJ)

SPAGHETTI: **bakwezhiganaabiins** *na* pasta, spaghetti; *pl* **bakwezhiganaabiinsag** (RT)

SPARK: **biskaakonese** *vii* ignite, spark (RT, NJ, GJ)

SPAWN:

ANNOUNCE STURGEON SPAWN: **biibaaginamewe** *vai* announce the coming of sturgeon spawn (as in gray tree frog) [*cultural note*: this particular tree frog sound is only heard at the start of the sturgeon spawn and is different from the characteristic call of other tree frogs] (NJ)

BE IN MID-SPAWN: **megwayaami** *vai* be in mid-spawn (RT, NJ, GJ)

MINGLE: **ginigawaami** *vai* mingle (as in different species during fish spawn) (RT, NJ, GJ)

RELEASE EGGS: **owaako** *vai* release eggs, spawn (as in fish) (RT, NJ, GJ)

SPAWN: **aami** *vai* spawn (RT, NJ, GJ)

SPAWN IN CERTAIN PLACE: **danaami** *vai* spawn in a certain place (RT, NJ, GJ)

SPAWN IN SCHOOL: **okwaami** *vai* spawn in a school (as in fish) (RT, NJ, GJ)

SPAWN SMELL: **aamimaagwad** *vii* smells of spawn (NJ, GJ)

SPAWN WATER: **aamiiwaagamin** *vii* be spawn water (NJ, GJ)

SPAWNED OUT: **zhiigwaami** *vai* be spawned out (RT, NJ, GJ)

START TO SPAWN: **maadaami** *vai* start to spawn (RT, NJ, GJ)

STOP SPAWNING: **giizhaami** *vai* stop spawning (RT, NJ, GJ)

SPEAK:

SPEAK FAST: **gidaatabowe** *vai* speak fast  (RT, NJ, GJ)

TRY TO SPEAK: **goji-giigido** *vai* try to speak (RT, NJ, GJ)

SPEAR: **anit** *ni* spear; *pl* **anitiin** (RT, NJ, GJ)

SPEAR THROUGH ICE: **akwa'waa** *vai* spear through the ice (dark house) (RT); *also* **akwa'we** *vai* spear through the ice (dark house) (NJ, GJ)

SPEED: **ipide** *vii* go a certain speed [*example:* Aaniin epidenig makwa ode' na'iid? = How fast does the bear's heart beat when in hibernation?] (RT)

SPIKE:

ELONGATED SPIKE: **zagigi-omichigegani** *vai* have an elongated spike (as in a dinosaur) (NJ)

HAVE SPIKES: **omichigegani** *vai* have spikes (as in a dinosaur) (NJ)

SPIN:

BUTTON SPINNER: **zagaakwa'oni-gizhibaayabiigibijigan** *ni* button spinner; *pl* **zagaakwa'oni-gizhibaayabiigibijiganan** (RT, NJ, GJ)

ROTATE: **gizhibaabide**  *vii* spin, rotate (as in the earth spinning on its axis) (RT)

SPINE:

SPINAL CORD: **nidatagaagwaneyaab** /-datagaagwaneyaab-/ *nid* my spinal cord; *pl* **nidatagaagwaneyaabiin** (RT, NJ, GJ)

SPINE: **nidatagaagwan** /-datagaagwan-/ *nid* my spine; *pl* **nidatagaagwanan** (RT, NJ, GJ)

SPLASH: **gwaakwaashkwebiise** *vii* splash (NJ)

SPLIT:

ELONGATED SPLIT: **baakishkaa** *vii* open up lengthwise (as in a metal sinker) (GJ)

SPLIT ALONG GRAIN: **danachiishkise** *vii* split along the grain (as in bark) (GJ)

SPLIT ROOTS: **daashkibiiwadabiigobijige** *vai* split roots [*cultural note*: typically done with jack pine or black spruce to prepare heavy sewing fiber] (NJ, GJ)

SPLIT WITH TOOL: **daashkiga'an** *vti* split s.t. into pieces lengthwise using a tool (GJ)

TEAR OFF: **nachiishkise** *vii* split or tear off (NJ); *also* **nichiishkise** (GJ)

SPONGE: **iska'ibaan** *ni* water bailer, sponge; *pl* **iska'ibaanan** (NJ, GJ)

SPREAD OUT: **zhazhwegigin** *vii* spread out (RT)

SPRING:

SOLO SPRING: **nabaneyaagad** *vii* there is a solo spring (as on a #6 conibear trap) (NJ)

SPRING MELT WATER: **zhwaaganib** *pc* spring melt water (NJ, GJ)

SPRING SHUT: **gashkaagise** *vii* spring closed (RT, NJ, GJ)

TENSIONER SPRING: **oningwiiganaabik** *ni* side springs, tensioner springs (as on the sides of a conibear or leg-hold trap) (NJ)

SPRINKLE:

SPRINKLE WATER TURNING: **gweki-zaswebiiga'anjigaawan** *vii* sprinkle water while turning (as in a lawn sprinkler) (RT, NJ, GJ)

WATER SPRINKLER: **zaswebiiga'anjigan** *ni* water sprinkler; *pl* **zaswebiiga'anjiganan** (RT, GJ); *also* **ziswebiiga'anjigan**; *pl* **ziswebiiga'anjiganan** (NJ)

SPRINKLER: **nibegaaziigaasing** *vii-prt* sprinkler; *pl* **nibegaaziigaasingin** (NJ)

SPROUT: **zaagakii** *vii* sprout (RT)

SPRUCE:

BLACK SPRUCE: **zesegaandag** *na* black spruce; *pl* **zesegaandagoog** (NJ); *also* **zhingob**; *pl* **zhingobiig** (WI)

WHITE SPRUCE: **mina'igwaandag** *na* white spruce; *pl* **mina'igwaandagoog** (RT, NJ, GJ); *also* **gaawaandag**; *pl* **gaawaandagoog** (RT, NJ, GJ)

SQUEEZE:

SQUEEZE SHUT (HAND): **gashkaabikinan** *vti* squeeze s.t. shut with one's hand (RT, NJ, GJ)

SQUEEZE SHUT (OBJECT): **gibaabikibidoon** *vti* squeeze s.t. shut (by using s.t.) (RT, NJ, GJ)

SQUEEZE SHUT (TOOL): **gashkaabikada'an** *vti* squeeze s.t. shut with a tool (RT, NJ, GJ)

SQUEEZE SOMEONE TO DEFECATION: **miiziibizh /miiziibiN-/** *vta* squeeze s.o. to the point of defecation (RT, NJ, GJ)

SQUEEZE SOMEONE TO FLATULENCE: **boogijibizh /boogijibiN-/** *vta* squeeze s.o. to point of flatulence (RT, NJ, GJ)

SQUEEZE SOMEONE TO URINATION: **gizhigibizh /gizhigiN-/** *vta* squeeze or tickle s.o. to urinate (RT, NJ, GJ)

SQUEEZE SOMETHING OUT: **ziinibidoon** *vti* squeeze s.t. out (like toothpaste) (RT)

SQUINT: **ziibiskaabi** *vai* squint, wink (RT, NJ, GJ)

STABILIZE:

BE HELD: **minjimishkoode** *vii* be held in place (GJ)

HOLD SOMETHING: **minjimishkoodoon** *vti* hold s.t. in place (GJ)

STABILIZE (BRACE): **gichiwakii'ige** *vai* stabilize a boat by bracing on bottom (RT, NJ, GJ)

STABILIZE (CONTROL): **aadikwe'ige** *vai* stabilize, control (as in a paddle or pole on the bottom) (GJ)

STABILIZE SOMEONE WITH STICK: **minjimaakwa'o /minjimaakwa'w-/** *vta* hold s.o. up with stick to stabilize it (GJ)

STABILIZE SOMETHING WITH STICK: **minjimaakwa'an** *vti* hold s.t. up with stick to stabilize it (GJ)

STALK: RICE STALK: **manoominagaawanzh** *ni* rice stalk; *pl* **manoominagaawanzhiin** (RT, NJ, GJ)

STAMP: ALPHABET STAMP: **mazinadoobii'igan** *ni* alphabet stamp; *pl* **mazinadoobii'iganan** (RT)

STAND:

STAND: **animikogaabawi** *vai* stand with back facing (RT, NJ, GJ)

STAND BACK FACING: **animikogaabawitaw** *vai* stand with back facing s.o. (RT, NJ, GJ)

STAND BACK-TO-BACK: **awasigaabawitaadiwag /awasigaabawitaadi-/** *vai* they stand back-to-back (NJ, GJ)

STAND BARELEGGED: **zhaashaaginizidegaabawi** *vai* stand barelegged (RT, NJ, GJ)

STAND BOW-LEGGED: **waagigaadegaabawi** *vai* stand bow-legged (GJ)

STAND FLAT-FOOTED: **nabagizidegaabawi** *vai* stand flat-footed (GJ)

STAND IN A ROW: **niibidegaabawi** *vai* stand in a row (RT, NJ, GJ)

STAND LEANING: **aaswaakogaabawi** *vai* stand leaning up against s.t. (RT, NJ, GJ)

STAND PIGEON-TOED: **waagizidegaabawi** *vai* stand pigeon-toed (GJ)

STAND TOUCHING BOTTOM: **debakiishkige** *vai* stand and touch the bottom (GJ)

STAND OUT IN ROW: **mininaawesin** *vii* stand out from others in a row (GJ); *also* **niminaawesin** (NJ)

STAR: ORION'S BELT: **Aadwaa'amoog** *name* Orion's Belt (constellation) (GJ)

START:

START GROWING: **maajiigi** *vai* start to grow (RT)

START GROWING: **maajiigin** *vii* start to grow (RT)

START RUNNING: **maajiibide** *vii* start running, start operating (as in an engine), take off (RT, NJ, GJ)

START RUNNING: **maajiibizo** *vai* start running, start operating, start driving, take off (RT, NJ, GJ)

START TO SPAWN: **maadaami** *vai* start to spawn (RT, NJ, GJ)

STORY BEGINS: **maadaadode** *vii* story begins (RT)

WIND STARTS INTERMITTENTLY: **mamaadaanimad** *vii* wind starts intermittently (RT)

STARTLE:

STARTLE SOMEONE: **ishko'** *vta* startle s.o. in a certain way (RT, NJ, GJ)

STARTLE SOMEONE BY GRABBING: **goshkobizh** /**goshkobiN-**/ *vta* startle s.o by grabbing them (RT, NJ, GJ)

STEER:

STEER: **eniwekibidoon** *vti* steer s.t., control s.t. (TS)

UNABLE TO KEEP CANOE STRAIGHT: **wawaawashkakozhiwe** *vai* be unable to keep a canoe straight (RT, NJ, GJ)

STEM:

GRASS STEM: **mashkosiinsigaawanzh** *ni* grass stem; *pl* **mashkosiinsigaawanzhiin** (RT)

STEM: **gaawanzh** *ni* stem; *pl* **gaawanzhiin**; *loc* **gaawanzhiing** (RT)

RICE STALK: **manoominagaawanzh** *ni* rice stalk; *pl* **manoominagaawanzhiin** (RT, NJ, GJ)

THICK STEM: **endazhi-gipagaawanzhiiging** *vii-prt* thick stem; *pl* **endazhi-gipagaawanzhiigingin** (RT)

STEP: **dakokii** *vai+o* step on things (RT, NJ, GJ)

STICK:

AIMING STICK: **bimoojiganaak** *ni* aiming stick (for moccasin game); *pl* **bimoojiganaakoon** (GJ)

BE A CERTAIN WAY: **inaakwad** *vii* be in a certain way (s.t. stick-like) (RT, NJ, GJ)

COUNTING STICK: **bima'igan** *ni* counting stick for moccasin game; *pl* **bima'iganan** (GJ)

CRUTCH POLE: **ziigaakwa'igan** *ni* crutch pole (GJ)

HELD ACROSS BY STICK: **bimaakobide** *vii* be held out across by a stick (as in lodge runners parallel to the ground) (GJ)

REINFORCING STICK: **mikond** *ni* reinforcing stick on end of birch bark roll or basket, a binding stick; *pl* **mikondiin**; *dim* **mikondiins** (GJ)

STABILIZE SOMEONE WITH STICK: **minjimaakwa'o** /**minjimaakwa'w-**/ *vta* hold s.o. up with stick to stabilize it (GJ)

STABILIZE WITH STICK: **minjimaakwa'an** *vti* hold s.t. up with stick to stabilize it (GJ)

STICK FOR HOLDING ACROSS: **bimaakobijigan** *ni* stick for holding s.t. across; *pl* **bimaakobijiganan** (GJ)

SUPPORT WITH STICK: **ziigaakwa'igaade** *vii* be supported with a stick (GJ)

WRING OUT TWISTING WITH STICK: **ziinikobiigaakwa'an** *vti* wring out twisting with stick (RT, NJ, GJ)

YOUNG STICK: **oshkaatigoons** *ni* young stick; *pl* **oshkaatigoonsan** (GJ)

STICK IN:

SLIDE SOMEONE IN TIGHT AREA: **zhegwaakozh** / **zhegwaakoN-**/ *vta* stick s.o. in a tight place (NJ)

SLIDE SOMETHING IN TIGHT AREA: **zhegwaakonan** *vti* slide s.t. into a tight area (of s.t. stick-like) (NJ)

STICK OUT:

BUTT STICKS OUT: **zaagidiyeshin** *vai* have one's butt sticking out (RT, NJ, GJ)

GIVE SOMEONE DIRTY FINGER SIGN: **zaagidenaninjiitaw** *vta* give s.o. the dirty Ojibwe finger sign [*cultural note*: performed by sticking the thumb between the first two fingers, symbolically representing a phallus protruding between the legs, done teasingly, in jest, but only between male friends] (GJ)

HEAD POPS UP REPEATEDLY FROM BOILING: **zaasaagikwezo** *vii* head repeatedly pops up from boiling (RT, NJ, GJ)

HEAD STICKS OUT OF WATER FLOATING: **zaagikwegomo** *vai* head is sticking out of water while floating (NJ, GJ)

HIND END POPS UP FROM BOILING: **zaasaagidiyezo** *vii* hind end repeatedly pops up from boiling (RT, NJ, GJ)

PROTRUDE: **zaagisin** *vii* protrude (RT, NJ, GJ)

REPEATEDLY POP UP FROM BOILING: **zaasaagigamide** *vii* repeatedly pop up from boiling (RT, NJ, GJ)

STICK OUT FOOT: **zaagizideni** *vai* stick one's foot out (RT, NJ, GJ)

STICK OUT TONGUE: **zaagidenaniweni** *vai* stick out one's tongue (NJ)

STICK OUT TONGUE AT SOMEONE: **zaagidenaniwetaw** *vta* stick one's tongue out at s.o. (RT, NJ, GJ)

STICK OUT TONGUE REPEATEDLY: **zaasaagidenaniwe** *vai* repeatedly stick out one's tongue (RT, NJ, GJ)

STICK OUT: *see also* OUT

STICK UP FOR OFFSPRING: **naadamaawaso** *vai* stick up for one's children (with negative consequences) (RT, NJ, GJ)

STICKY:

STICKY TONGUE: **bazagodenaniwe** *ni* have a sticky tongue (as in a frog) (RT)

STICKY TONGUE: **nibazagodenaniw** *ni* my sticky tongue (as in a frog) (RT)

STIFF: SCARED STIFF: **mashkawaanimizi** *vai* be scared stiff (RT, NJ, GJ)

STIRRUP: **naabaaniigizide'on** *ni* stirrup, *pl* **naabaaniigizide'onan** (NJ, GJ)

STOP:

PREVENT: **gibichichige** *vai* block, prohibit, prevent (NJ, GJ)

SINK: **gibitagomo** *vai* stop floating, sink (RT, NJ, GJ)

STOP: **gibichii** *vai* stop (RT, NJ, GJ)

STOP ACTIVITY: **boonikamigizi** *vai* stop doing certain activities, refrain from doing special activities (as when in mourning) (RT, NJ, GJ)

STOP DRIVING: **noogibizo** *vai* come to a stop while driving (RT, NJ, GJ)

STOP GROWING: **noogigin** *vii* stop growing (RT)

STOP PADDLING: **gibitakwazhiwe** *vai* stop paddling (RT, NJ, GJ)

STOP SPAWNING: **giizhaami** *vai* stop spawning (RT, NJ, GJ)

WIND STOPS: **noogaanimad** *vii* wind stops (RT, NJ, GJ)

STORE:

STORE: **asanjigo** *vai+o* store things (RT)

STORE FOOD: **na'enimo** *vai* cache, store food (RT, NJ, GJ)

STORE GRAIN: **na'emine** *vai* store grain (RT)

STORE WATER: **na'inibii** *vai* store water (NJ, GJ)

STORE WATER: **na'inibiigin** *vii* store water (NJ)

STORY BEGINS: **maadaadode** *vii* story begins (RT)

STRADDLE: **desabi** *vai* straddle, sit straddling (RT, NJ, GJ)

STRAIGHT:

BE STRAIGHT: **na'aakozi** *vai* be straight (treelike) (RT, NJ, GJ)

BE TIED STRAIGHT: **gwayakopide** *vii* be tied straight (RT, NJ, GJ)

FLY STRAIGHT: **gwayakobide** *vii* fly straight (RT, NJ, GJ)

SAW TOOTH STRAIGHTENER: **minwaabide'igan** *ni* saw tooth straightener; *pl* **minwaabide'iganan** (GJ)

TIE STRAIGHT: **gwayakobijige** *vai* tie or pull things straight (RT, NJ, GJ)

UNABLE TO KEEP CANOE STRAIGHT: **wawaawashkakozhiwe** *vai* be unable to keep a canoe straight (RT, NJ, GJ)

STRAIN:

JOINT STRAIN: **ogiziibishkami** *vai* have a joint strain (mild, not long-lasting) (RT, NJ, GJ)

STRAINER: **zhaabobiiginigan** *ni* strainer; *pl* **zhaabobiiginiganan** (RT, NJ, GJ); *also* **zhaashaabobiiginigan** *ni* strainer (GJ)

STRAINER: **ziikoobiiginigan** *ni* filter, strainer (RT, NJ, GJ)

STRANDED:

STRANDED BY RAIN: **ginibiisaanishi** *vai* can't go because it is too rainy (NJ, GJ)

STRANDED BY SNOW: **giniponishi** *vai* be snowed in (NJ, GJ)

STRANDED BY WIND: **ginaanimanishi** *vai* be wind-bound, be stranded because of high wind (NJ, GJ); *also* **ginisinaa'ago** *vai* be wind-bound, be stranded because of high wind (NJ, GJ)

STRANGE: SOUND STRANGE: **mayagitaagozi** *vai* sound strange (RT, NJ); *also* **mayegitaagozi** (GJ)

STRAWBERRY:

    BECOME A STRAWBERRY: **ode'iminoowan** *vii* become a strawberry [*example*: Ode'imini-waabigwaniin aanjiginoon ani-ode'iminoowangin. = Strawberry flowers grow into fruit.] (RT)

    STRAWBERRY FLOWER: **ode'imini-waabigon** *ni* strawberry flower; *pl* **ode'imini-waabigoniin** (NJ); *also* **ode'imini-waabigwan** (RT)

STRETCH:

    BEAVER STRETCHING HOOP: **zhingibijiganaak** *ni* hoop for stretching beaver hide; *pl* **zhingibijiganaakoon** (NJ, GJ)

    STRING FOR BEAVER STRETCHING HOOP: **zhingibijiganeyaab** *ni* wrapping string for beaver hide stretching hoop; *pl* **zhingibijiganeyaabiin** (RT, NJ, GJ)

STRIKE: *see* HIT

STRIKE HEAD:

    STRIKE HEAD: **bagaskindibe** *vai* strike (in moccasin game), smack on the head (RT, NJ, GJ)

    STRIKE SOMEONE'S HEAD: **bagaskindibe'wi** /bagaskindibe'w-/ *vta* strike s.o. on the head (NJ); *also* **bagaskindibe'o** /bagaskindibe'w-/ (GJ); *also* **bagaskindibe'** /bagaskindibe'w-/ (RT)

STRING:

    BIRCH TREE SEED STRINGS: **wanimikoons** *ni* birch tree seed strings; *pl* **wanimikoonsan** (RT, NJ, GJ)

    MAKE BASSWOOD STRING: **wiigobiike** *vai* make string from basswood fiber (RT, NJ, GJ)

    STRING FOR BEAVER STRETCHING HOOP: **zhingibijiganeyaab** *ni* wrapping string for beaver hide stretching hoop; *pl* **zhingibijiganeyaabiin** (RT, NJ, GJ)

STRIP:

    CUT SOMETHING INTO STRIPS: **naanigaakozhigan** *vti* cut s.t. into strips (RT, NJ, GJ)

    PEEL IN STRIP: **naanigaakobidoon** *vti* peel s.t. in a strip, strip s.t. (as in basswood) (RT, NJ, GJ)

PEEL INTO STRIPS: **naanaanigaakobijige** *vai* peel into strips (as in basswood) (RT, NJ, GJ)

PEEL SOMETHING INTO STRIPS: **naanaanigaakobidoon** *vti* peel s.t. into strips, strip s.t. (as in basswood) (RT, NJ, GJ)

STRIP WIDE: **mangadebidoon** *vti* strip s.t. into wide (as in bark) strips (RT, NJ, GJ)

STRONG:

BE STRONG: **mashkawaakamigaa** *vii* be strong (tree-like) (RT, NJ, GJ)

FREEZE STRONG: **maamashkawadin** *vii* freeze strong (RT, NJ, GJ)

GROW STRONG: **mashkawa'wi /mashkawa'w-/** *vta* make s.o. strong, grow s.o. strong (NJ)

GROW STRONG: **mashkawigin** *vii* grow strong (RT)

HAVE STRONG CLAWS: **mashkawishkanzii** *vai* have strong claws (RT)

SOUND STRONG: **gizhiiwe** *vii* sound strong, have a loud, strong sound (NJ, GJ)

STRONG BREEZE: **mashkawaanimad** *vii* wind blows hard, be a strong breeze (as from fan) (RT, NJ, GJ)

STRONG CLAW: **mashkawishkanzh** *na* strong claw; *pl* **mashkawishkanzhiig** (RT)

STRONG LEGS: **mashkawigaade** *vai* have strong legs (RT)

STUBBORN: **wegaskendaagozi** *vai* be stubborn, fussy, hard to please (NJ, GJ); *redup* **weyagaskendaagozi** (GJ, NJ); *also* **wiiyagaskendaagozi** (NJ, GJ)

STUCK:

STUCK IN GRASS OR MUD: **gichiwashkishin** *vai* curls up (as into fetal position) (RT, NJ); *also* be stuck in the grass or mud (as when harvesting wild rice) (GJ)

STUCK IN MUD: **aadakiise** *vii* get stuck in the mud in the water (NJ, GJ)

STUFFY NOSE: **gibijaane** *vai* have a plugged or stuffy nose (RT, NJ, GJ)

STURGEON:

ANNOUNCE STURGEON SPAWN: **biibaaginamewe** *vai* announce the coming of sturgeon spawn (as in gray tree frog) [*cultural note*: this particular tree frog sound is only heard at the start of the sturgeon spawn and is different from the characteristic call of other tree frogs] (NJ)

STURGEON: **name** *na* sturgeon; *pl* **namewag** (RT, NJ, GJ)

STURGEON GLUE: **namekwaan** *ni* sturgeon glue (RT, NJ, GJ)

SUBMERGE: **gonzaabiishkoozo** *vai* be submerged (as in ice weighed down by water) (RT, NJ, GJ)

SUCCUMB:

> SUCCUMB TO FLEAS: **giikawidikome** *vai* succumb to fleas (NJ, GJ)
>
> SUCCUMB TO TICKS: **giikawi-ezigaawe** *vai* succumb to ticks (NJ, GJ)

SUCK WATER: **wiikwa'ibiise** *vii* suck, vacuum water out (RT, NJ, GJ)

SUCKER: **namebin** *na* sucker; *pl* **namebinag** (RT, NJ, GJ)

SUFFICIENT:

> BARELY SUFFICIENT: **debinaak** *pc* any old way, just barely sufficient (RT, NJ, GJ)
>
> BE SUFFICIENT ROOM: **dawaa** *vii* be sufficient room, space (RT); *also* **dawaasin** *vii* be sufficient room, space (RT)
>
> BE SUFFICIENT TIME: **dawate** *vii* be sufficient time (RT)
>
> HAVE INSUFFICIENT TIME: **dajise** *vai* have insufficient time to do s.t. [*example*: Ningii-tajise ji-gii-andawaabandamaan. = I didn't have time to go pick it up.] (NJ, GJ)
>
> HAVE SUFFICIENT TIME: **dawise** *vai* have sufficient time to do s.t. (GJ, NJ)
>
> MAKE SOMEONE LATE: **daji'** *vai* make s.o. late, run s.o. out of time
>
> SUFFICIENT: **debise** *vii* be sufficient, be enough (RT)
>
> SUFFICIENT TIME: **dawi-ayaa** *vii* be sufficient time (GJ)
>
> SUFFICIENT WIND: **debaasin** *vii* be sufficient wind (as from a fan) (RT, NJ, GJ)
>
> SUFFICIENTLY LARGE MOUTH: **debanendan** *vti* have a sufficiently large mouth to bite s.t. [*lexicon note*: from discussion of the size of a bagidaabaan, an item for ice fishing] (NJ)
>
> SUFFICIENTLY THICK: **debizigwaa** *vii* be sufficiently thick (as in the ice) (RT, NJ, GJ)

SUMMER RAIN: **niibinibiisaa** *vii* be a summer rain (RT)

SUN:

> DARK ON ONE SIDE: **nabanemakadeyaaso** *vai* be dark on one side from sun (as in suntanned) (NJ, GJ)
>
> LIGHT CHANGES: **aandaate** *vii* light changes (RT, NJ, GJ)

LIGHT SHINES: **akwaate** *vii* light shines a certain distance or length of time (RT, NJ, GJ)

PAINFUL SUNBURN: **wiisagazheyaakizo** *vai* be painfully sunburned [*example*: Wiinge wiisagazheyaakizodog. = He must be really sunburned.] (NJ, GJ)

SHINE: **aabawaasige** *vai* shine warmly (RT, NJ, GJ)

SUN SHINES LONG: **ginwaasige** *vai* sun shines a long time, be a long day (as in a long summer day) (RT)

SUNLIGHT: **waaseyaawin** *ni* sunlight (RT)

SUNTAN LOTION: **abaasindekeboozazhaan** sun tan lotion, suntain oil (NJ)

SUPPORT:

CRUTCH: **ishpaakwa'igan** *ni* crutch, support; *pl* **ishpaakwa'iganan** (NJ, GJ)

SUPPORT WITH STICK: **ziigaakwa'igaade** *vii* be supported with a stick (GJ)

SURF:

SURF: **ogidaashkaabizo** *vai* surf (RT, NJ, GJ)

SURFBOARD: **ogidaashkaabizwaanaak** *ni* surfboard (RT, NJ, GJ)

SURFACE:

EMERGE FROM WATER: **mookibiise** *vii* emerge from water, suddenly pop out of water (NJ, GJ)

EMERGE FROM WATER: **mooshkamo** *vai* emerge from water (NJ, GJ)

GROW TO SURFACE: **mookibiigin** *vii* grow to the surface (as in lily pads to the surface of the water) (RT)

SURFACE: **mookii** *vai* surface (RT, NJ, GJ)

SWALLOWTAIL:

SWALLOWTAIL: **memengwaa** *na* butterfly, swallowtail; *pl* **memengwaag** (RT, NJ, GJ)

TIGER SWALLOWTAIL: **ozaawi-memengwaa** *na* butterfly, tiger swallowtail; *pl* **ozaawi-memengwaag** (RT, NJ, GJ)

SWEAT:

SWEATY FOREHEAD: **abwebiigaskatigwe** *vai* have a sweaty forehead (GJ)

SWEATY SKIN: **abwebiigazhe** *vai* have sweaty skin, have sweaty body (NJ, GJ)

SWEET:

BE SWEET: **zhiiwan** *vii* be sweet (NJ, GJ); *also* be bitter (RT)

TASTE SWEET: **zhiiwipogwad** *vii* taste sweet (NJ, GJ); *also* taste bitter (RT)

SWIM:

DART WHILE SWIMMING: **maajiiyaadagaa** *vai* dart while swimming, quickly take off swimming (RT)

SWIM: **inaadagaa** *vai* swim in a certain way (RT, NJ); *also* **inaadage** (GJ)

SWIM ALONG: **jiigewe'am** *vai* swim or paddle along shore (RT, NJ, GJ)

SWIM BLADDER: **obikwaajiins** *nid* little air sack, swim bladder; *also ni* light bulb (NJ, GJ); *also* **obikwaaj** *nid* air sack of a fish, swim bladder (NJ, GJ)

SWIM ON BOTTOM: **asamikozhiwe** *vai* swims on the bottom of the lake (GJ)

SWIM TO BOTTOM: **debakiikozhiwe** *vai* swim down to the bottom (touching), make contact with the bottom (GJ)

SWIM UNDERWATER: **bimakwazhiwe** *vai* paddling, swimming underwater (RT, NJ, GJ)

SWIM UPSTREAM: **ogiidaajiwane'o** *vai* swim upstream (GJ); *also* **ogiidaajiwanwe'o** (NJ); *also* **ogiidaajiwaneyaadagwe** (GJ); *also* **ogiidaajiwanweyaadagwe** (NJ)

TAKE OFF FROM SHORE: **mininaawa'o** *vai* take off from shore (as in a boat, or swimming) (GJ); *also* **niminaawa'o** (NJ, RT)

TRY TO REACH BOTTOM UNSUCCESSFULLY: **noondakiikozhiwe** *vai* try to reach the bottom unsuccessfully (NJ, GJ)

SWING SOMETHING: **wewebaakowebinan** *vti* wave, swing s.t. (as in s.t. stick-like) (NJ)

SWIRLING WATER: **gizhibaajiwan** *vii* be swirling water (RT, NJ, GJ)

SWITCH SIDES PADDLING: **gwekabowe** *vai* switch sides paddling (RT, NJ, GJ)

SWOOP: **naazhise** *vai* fly down, swoop down (RT); *also* **niisibizo** (RT); *also* **niisise** (RT)

SYNCOPATED BEAT: **biisiwebinige** vai make syncopated beat for moccasin game song (GJ)

TAB:

TAB FOR BARK: **apigwaason** *ni* reinforcing tab on end of birch bark roll or basket (as a wide strip placed inside out on the end creating a double layer); *pl* **apigwaasonan** (GJ)

TAB FOR LODGE BARK: **apigwaajigan** *ni* sewn covering reinforcement tab (as on birch bark lodge coverings) (RT, NJ, GJ)

TAIL:

ANIMAL TAIL: **ninzow /-zow-/** *nid* my tail (of an animal); *pl* **ninzowan** (RT, NJ, GJ)

BIRD TAIL: **ninashkid /-nashkidy-/** *nid* my tail (of a bird); *pl* **ninashkidiin** (RT, NJ, GJ)

FISH TAIL: **ninzhigwan /-zhigwan-/** *nid* my tail (of a fish, snake, or serpent); *pl* **ninzhigwanan** (RT, NJ, GJ)

FLAT TAIL: **nabagaanowe** *vai* have a flat tail (NJ); *also* **nabagizowe** *vai* have a flat tail (NJ)

LONG TAIL: **ginwaabiigaanowe** *vai* have a long tail (NJ)

SLAP TAIL ON WATER: **damoo'am** *vai* slap one's tail on the water (as in a beaver) (NJ)

WAG TAIL: **wewebaanoweni** *vai* wag one's tail (RT, NJ, GJ)

TAKE: **mami'igaazo** *vai* be harvested, be taken (RT)

TAKE OFF:

DART WHILE SWIMMING: **maajiiyaadagaa** *vai* dart while swimming, quickly take off swimming (RT)

START RUNNING: **maajiibide** *vii* start running, start operating (as in an engine), take off (RT, NJ, GJ)

START RUNNING: **maajiibizo** *vai* start running, start operating, start driving, take off (RT, NJ, GJ)

TAKE OFF AND LAND: **akwaandawe-boonii** *vai* take off to land at a higher location (RT, NJ, GJ)

TAKE OFF FLYING: **bazigwa'o** *vai* take off in flight (RT, NJ, GJ); *also* **ombaashi** *vai* take off in flight (RT, NJ, GJ)

TAKE OFF FROM SHORE: **mininaawa'o** *vai* take off from shore (as in a boat, or swimming) (GJ); *also* **niminaawa'o** (NJ, RT)

TAKE OFF IN WATER: **maajiiyaabogo** *vai* go off into the water (as in fish eggs) (NJ, GJ)

TAKE OFF ON WATER IN CURRENT: **maajiiyaabagonde** *vii* take off on top of the water in a current (NJ, GJ)

TALK ABOUT WOMEN: **dazhimikwewe** *vai* talk about women (RT, NJ, GJ)

TALL: GROW TALL: **ginoogin** *vii* grow high, grow tall (RT)

TANGLE: **bimiskwa'oozo** *vai* he is tangled (as a fish in the net) (RT, NJ, GJ)

TAP:

    TAP FOOT: **jiichiibizideni** *vai* tap one's foot (NJ)

    TAP SOMETHING: **dookinan** *vti* touch s.t., tap s.t. (RT, NJ, GJ)

TASTE:

    CERTAIN TASTE: **ipogwad** *vii* taste a certain way (RT, NJ, GJ)

    FEEL SOMETHING BY TASTE: **biiyiijipidan** *vti* feel s.t. by taste (NJ)

    SENSE OF TASTE: **biijipijigaage** *vai* taste, sense things by taste (RT, NJ, GJ)

    SENSE SOMETHING BY TASTE: **biijipidan** *vti* taste s.t., sense s.t. by taste (RT, NJ, GJ)

    TASTE BITTER: **maazhipogwad** *vii* taste bad, taste bitter (RT, NJ, GJ)

    TASTE CERTAIN WAY: **biijipogwad** *vii* have a certain taste, come to have a certain taste (RT, NJ, GJ)

    TASTE GOOD: **minopogwad** *vii* taste good (RT, NJ, GJ)

    TASTE SOUR: **ziiwiskipogwad** *vii* taste sour (NJ); *also* **ziiwaskipogod** (GJ)

    TASTE SWEET: **zhiiwipogwad** *vii* taste sweet (NJ, GJ); *also* taste bitter (RT)

TATTLE:

    TATTLE: **mamizhitam** *vai* tattle (RT, NJ, GJ); *also* **mamizhitaagozi** *vai* tattle (RT, NJ, GJ)

    TATTLE ON SOMEONE: **mamizhim** *vta* tattle on s.o. (RT, NJ, GJ)

TAX: **diba'amaazowin** *ni* tax; *pl* **diba'amaazowinan** (RT, NJ, GJ)

TEACH WITH LEGENDS: **inaadizokaw** *vta* teach s.o. by use of traditional legends (NJ, GJ)

TEACHING LODGE: **zhaabondawaan** *ni* teaching lodge, long-style wiigiwaam with doors and both ends; *pl* **zhaabondawaanan** (NJ)

TEAR:

    TEAR OFF: **nachiishkise** *vii* split or tear off (NJ); *also* **nichiishkise** (GJ)

    TEAR SOMETHING: **naanigibidoon** *vti* tear s.t. (sheet-like) (RT, NJ, GJ)

TEASE SOMEONE: **miikinjii'** *vta* tease s.o. (RT, NJ, GJ)

TEEPEE: **bajiishka'ogaan** *ni* pointed lodge (conical); *pl* **bajiishka'ogaanan** (NJ, GJ)

TEETH: *see* TOOTH

TELESCOPE: **zhiibaa'aabanjigan** *ni* telescope or binoculars; *pl* **zhiibaa'aabanjiganan** (GJ)

TELL:

COME AND TELL: **biidaajimo** *vai* come tell about things (RT, NJ, GJ)

COME AND TELL SOMETHING: **biidaadodan** *vti* come and tell about s.t. (RT, NJ, GJ)

TELL NEWS: **babaamaajimo** *vai, vii* tell news (RT, NJ, GJ)

TELL SOMEONE: **inaajimotaw** *vta* tell s.o. s.t. (RT, NJ, GJ)

TENSIONER SPRING: **oningwiiganaabik** *ni* side springs, tensioner springs (as on the sides of a conibear or leg-hold trap) (NJ)

THAW: **ningigisin** *vii* be thawed (as in fresh cut sapling in winter being bent as a beaver hide stretching frame) (NJ)

THICK:

FREEZE THICK: **gipagadin** *vii* be frozen thick (as in a body of water) (RT, NJ, GJ)

FREEZE THICK: **gipagizigwazi** *vai* be frozen thick (as in ice) (RT, NJ, GJ)

HAVE THICK SKIN: **gipagazhaga'e** *vai* have thick, callous, armor-like skin (NJ); *also* **gipagazhe** *vai* have thick, callous skin (RT)

SUFFICIENTLY THICK: **debizigwaa** *vii* be sufficiently thick (as in the ice) (RT, NJ, GJ)

THICK FUR: **gipagawe** *vai* have thick fur (RT)

THICK SKIN: **gipagazhaan** *ni* callus, thick skin (RT, NJ, GJ)

THICK STEM: **endazhi-gipagaawanzhiiging** *vii-prt* thick stem; *pl* **endazhi-gipagaawanzhiigingin** (RT)

THICKET: **zagaakwaa** *vii* be dense, brushy woods, thick brush, thicket (ES, NJ) [*cultural note*: this term can be used as a metaphor for hard times; *example*: Da-zagaakwaa obimaadiziwin giishpin bizindawaasig ookomisan. = Her life will get hard if she doesn't listen to her grandmother.]

THIN:

SHAPE BARK: **biitawinagekobijige** *vai* thin out layers of bark (as in basswood), shape basswood fiber to size (RT, NJ, GJ)

THIN: **bibagadin** *vii* be thin (as in ice) (RT, NJ, GJ)

THREE MILE: **Biinjiboonaaganing** *place* the shoot between Three Mile and Woseley Lake (in Quetico Park) (GJ)

THRESHING PIT: **mimigoshkamwaagan** *ni* threshing pit for wild rice; *pl* **mimigoshkamwaaganan** (RT)

THRIVE:

THRIVE: **baashkiinad** *vii* thrive (RT)

THRIVE: **baashkiino** *vai* thrive, be prolific (as in a baby boom) (RT, NJ, GJ)

THROUGH:

PASS THROUGH SOMEONE: **zhaaboshkaw** *vta* pass through s.o. (RT)

SHINE THROUGH: **zhaabwaate** *vii* shine through (as in light through glass or water) (RT, NJ, GJ)

THROW:

THROW BACK-AND-FORTH: **aayaazhawi-webinamaadiwag** **/aayaazhawi-webinamaadi-/** *vai+o* they throw s.t. back-and-forth to one another [*example*: Aayaazhawi-webinamaadiwag bikwaakwad. = They are throwing the ball to one another.] (NJ, GJ)

THROW IN WATER AND TOUCH BOTTOM: **noondakiise** *vai* throw s.t. in the water that cannot touch bottom (NJ, GJ)

THROW OPEN HAND AT ONE ANOTHER: **nimiskandiwag** **/nimiskandi-/** *vai* throw the open hand at one another (all 5 fingers open and extended) [*cultural note*: considered extremely offensive, likely to be perceived as an intent to do spiritual harm or use bad medicine on s.o.] (RT, NJ, GJ)

THROW OPEN HAND AT SOMEONE: **nimiskam** *vta* throw the open hand at s.o. (all 5 fingers open and extended) [*cultural note*: considered extremely offensive, likely to be perceived as an intent to do spiritual harm or use bad medicine on s.o.] (RT, NJ, GJ)

TICK: SUCCUMB TO TICKS: **giikawi-ezigaawe** *vai* succumb to ticks (NJ, GJ)

TICKLE:

BE TICKLISH: **wake-ginagajii** *vii, vai* be ticklish  (NJ)

TICKLE SOMEONE: **ginagazhe'wi** **/ginagazhe'w-/** *vta* tickle s.o. (NJ); *also* **ginagazhe'o** **/ginagazhe'w-/** (GJ)

TICKLE UNTIL URINATION: **gizhigibizh** **/gizhigiN-/** *vta* squeeze or tickle s.o. to urinate (RT, NJ, GJ)

TIDE:

TIDE COMES IN: **biidaashkaa** *vii* waves or tide roll in (RT, NJ, GJ); *also* **agwaayaashkaa** *vii* tide comes in (RT, NJ, GJ)

TIDE GOES OUT: **animaashkaa** *vii* tide goes out (RT, NJ, GJ)

TIE:

> BE KNOTTED: **gashka'oode** *vii* be knotted (RT, NJ, GJ)
>
> BE TIED: **gashka'oozo** *vai* be fastened, tied (RT, NJ, GJ)
>
> BE TIED STRAIGHT: **gwayakopide** *vii* be tied straight (RT, NJ, GJ)
>
> TIE AROUND: **gizhibaapidoon** *vti* tie s.t. around (s.t.) (RT, NJ, GJ)
>
> TIE SOMEONE'S LEGS REPEATEDLY: **zasagigaadepizh** /**zasagigaadepiN-**/ *vta* tie s.o. legs repeatedly (RT, NJ, GJ)
>
> TIE SOMEONE'S LEGS: **zagigaadepizh** /**zagigaadepiN-**/ *vta* tie s.o. legs (RT, NJ, GJ)
>
> TIE STRAIGHT: **gwayakobijige** *vai* tie or pull things straight (RT, NJ, GJ)
>
> TIE TIGHT: **mashkawapidoon** *vti* tie s.t. tight (RT, NJ, GJ)
>
> TIE TWO TOGETHER: **niizhoopizh** /**niizhoopiN-**/ *vta* tie two together (RT, NJ, GJ)

TIGER SWALLOWTAIL: **ozaawi-memengwaa** *na* butterfly, tiger swallowtail; *pl* **ozaawi-memengwaag** (RT, NJ, GJ)

TIGHT:

> RETIGHTEN: **aanji-baabisapidoon** *vti* retighten (RT, NJ, GJ)
>
> TIE TIGHT: **mashkawapidoon** *vti* tie s.t. tight (RT, NJ, GJ)
>
> TIGHTEN: **baabisapidoon** *vti* tighten s.t. down (RT, NJ, GJ)

TIME:

> ABOUT TIME: **nenibaawizh iidog** *expression* it's about time [*example*: Nenibaawizh iidog gigoshkoz! = It's about time you woke up!] (NJ, GJ)
>
> BE SUFFICIENT TIME: **dawate** *vii* be sufficient time (RT)
>
> ERA: **dasosagoons** *pc* era, a certain extent of time (RT)
>
> HAVE INSUFFICIENT TIME: **dajise** *vai* have insufficient time to do s.t. [*example*: Ningii-tajise ji-gii-andawaabandamaan. = I didn't have time to go pick it up.] (NJ, GJ)
>
> HAVE SUFFICIENT TIME: **dawise** *vai* have sufficient time to do s.t. (GJ, NJ)
>
> MAKE SOMEONE LATE: **daji'** *vai* make s.o. late, run s.o. out of time
>
> SUFFICIENT TIME: **dawi-ayaa** *vii* be sufficient time (GJ)

TIP:

> BE TIPPY: **gokokwaa** *vii* be tippy [*example*: Gokokwaa jiimaan. = The canoe is tippy.]

TIP OF THE TONGUE: **niigaanadenaniw** *ni* tip of the tongue (RT, NJ, GJ)

TIRE: **detibiseg** *vii-prt* tires, wheels; *pl* **detibisegin** (RT, NJ, GJ)

TIRED: **ayekomanji'o** *vai* be tired (NJ)

TOAD: **obiigomakakii** *na* toad; *pl* **obiigomakakiig** (NJ, GJ)

TOBACCO:

> OFFER TOBACCO TO SOMETHING: **asemaakandan** *vti* offer tobacco to s.t. (NJ)

> TOBACCO IS OFFERED TO SOMETHING: **asemaakande** *vii* tobacco is offered to it (NJ)

TOE: BETWEEN TOES: **niniisiigizidaanens** *nid* between my toes; *loc* **niniisiigizidaanensing** (NJ, GJ)

TOENAIL: CUT TOENAIL: **giishkiganzhiizhige** *vai* cut fingernails or toenails (RT, NJ, GJ)

TOILET PLUNGER: **gaanjiba'ibaan** *ni* toilet plunger (NJ, GJ)

TOMATO:

> TOMATO: **gichi-ogin** *na* tomato; *pl* **gichi-oginiig** (RT)

> TOMATO FLOWER: **gichi-oginii-waabigon** *ni* tomato flower; *pl* **gichi-oginii-waabigwaniin** (RT); *also* **gichi-oginii-waabigwan** (RT)

TONGUE:

> CATCH WITH TONGUE: **nakwedenaniwem** *vta* catch s.o. with long, sticky tongue (as in a frog) (RT)

> FORKED TONGUE: **niingidodenaniwe** *vai* have a forked tongue (GJ)

> LONG TONGUE: **ginwaabiigidenaniwe** *vai* have a long tongue (RT)

> MY TONGUE: **indenaniw** *nid* my tongue (RT, NJ, GJ)

> MY STICKY TONGUE: **nibazagodenaniw** *ni* my sticky tongue (as in a frog) (RT)

> STICK OUT TONGUE: **zaagidenaniweni** *vai* stick out one's tongue (NJ)

> STICK OUT TONGUE AT SOMEONE: **zaagidenaniwetaw** *vta* stick one's tongue out at s.o. (RT, NJ, GJ)

> STICK OUT TONGUE REPEATEDLY: **zaasaagidenaniwe** *vai* repeatedly stick out one's tongue (RT, NJ, GJ)

> STICKY TONGUE: **bazagodenaniwe** *ni* have a sticky tongue (as in a frog) (RT)

TIP OF THE TONGUE: **niigaanadenaniw** *ni* tip of the tongue (RT, NJ, GJ)

TOO MUCH:

EAT TOO MUCH OF SOMEONE: **onzaami'** *vta* eat too much of s.o. (RT, NJ, GJ); *also* **onzaamipon** *vta* eat too much of s.o. (RT, NJ, GJ)

EAT TOO MUCH: **onzaami'o** *vai* eat too much (RT, NJ, GJ)

OVERLY: **onzaam** *pc* overly, too much [*example*: Gaawiin nindizhaasiin onzaam nindaakoz. = I'm not going because I'm sick. *example*: Onzaam gizhide gaa-wii-onji-wi-nibaayang. It's too warm it makes us feel sleepy.] (NJ, GJ)

OVERPOPULATE: **onzaamiino** *vai* overpopulate (RT)

TOOL:

BEND DOWN WITH TOOL: **ispwaabikada'an** *vti* bend s.t. (metal-like) down with a tool (as in bending over a protruding nail) (GJ)

DRAWING TOOL: **mazinibii'iganaatig** *ni* drawing tool; *pl* **mazinibii'iganaatigoon** (GJ)

SPLIT WITH TOOL: **daashkiga'an** *vti* split s.t. into pieces lengthwise using a tool (GJ)

TOOTH:

CANINE TOOTH: **oshkiinzhigwaabid** *ni* canine tooth; *pl* **oshkiinzhigwaabidan** (RT)

CUT OFF WITH TEETH: **giishkandan** *vti* cut s.t. off with one's teeth (RT)

CUT WITH TEETH: **giishkanjige** *vai* cut with one's teeth (RT)

DEHUSK WITH TEETH: **bashagam** *vta* dehusk s.o. with one's teeth (as in a squirrel to an acorn) (RT); *also* **bishagam** (GJ)

FISH TOOTH: **giigoowaabid** *ni* fish tooth; *pl* **giigoowaabidan** (RT, NJ, GJ)

FLAT TEETH: **nabagaabide** *vai* have flat teeth (RT)

FRONT TOOTH: **niigaanaabid** *ni* front tooth; *pl* **niigaanaabidan** (RT)

HAVE CANINE TOOTH: **oshkiinzhigwaabide** *vai* have canine teeth (RT)

HAVE INCISORS: **giishkaabide** *vai* have incisors (RT)

HAVE MOLARS: **bigishkaabide** *vai* have molars (RT)

HAVE POINTED TEETH: **gagaanwaabajiishkaabide** *vai* have long, pointed teeth (RT)

HAVE TEETH: **inaabide-ayaa** *vii* be toothed (RT, NJ, GJ)

INCISOR: **giishkaabid** *ni* incisor; *pl* **giishkaabidan** (RT)

LARGE INCISOR: **mamaangi-giishkaabide** *vai* have large incisors (RT)

LARGE, SHARP TEETH: **mamaangi-giinaabid** *ni* large, sharp teeth; *pl* **mamaangi-giinaabidan** (RT)

MOLAR: **bigishkaabid** *ni* molar; *pl* **bigishkaabidan** (RT); *also* **ishkweyaabid**; *pl* **ishkweyaabidan** (RT)

POINTED TOOTH: **gagaanwaabajiishkaabid** *ni* long, pointed tooth; *pl* **gagaanwaabajiishkaabidan** (RT)

SAW TOOTH STRAIGHTENER: **minwaabide'igan** *ni* saw tooth straightener; *pl* **minwaabide'iganan** (GJ)

SHARP TEETH: **gaashaabide** *vai* have sharp teeth (NJ)

WIDE TEETH: **mamaangaabide** *vai* have wide teeth (RT)

TOP:

DRIVE ON SAND: **ogidaawangwebizo** *vai* drive on sand (NJ, GJ)

HAVE CERTAIN TOP: **izhiwanakowi** *vai* have a certain top (as in a tree) (NJ)

ON TOP OF ICE: **ogidikwam** *pc* on top of the ice (GJ); *also* **ogijikwam** (RT, NJ); *also* **ogijizigwaang** *pc* on top of the ice (NJ)

RUN ON SAND: **ogidaawangibatoo** *vai* run on sand (RT); *also* **wagidaawangibatoo** (NJ, GJ)

TORTILLA: **bibine-bakwezhiganiigin** *na* tortilla; *pl* **bibine-bakwezhiganiiginag** (RT)

TOUCH:

FEEL SOMETHING BY TASTE: **biiyiijipidan** *vti* feel s.t. by taste (NJ)

FEEL SOMETHING BY TOUCH: **biiyiijimanjitoon** *vti* feel s.t. by touch (NJ)

JUMP IN TOUCHING BOTTOM: **debakiise** *vai* jump in and hands or feet touch the bottom (GJ)

SENSE OF TOUCH: **biijimanjitoon** *vti* feel s.t. all around (by touch), sense by touch s.t. all around (as in a foot soaking in warm water) (RT, NJ, GJ)

SENSE SOMETHING BY TOUCH: **nisidawininjiinan** *vti* recognize s.t. by touch (RT, NJ, GJ)

SENSE THINGS BY TOUCH: **nisidawishkaa** *vai* recognize things by touch (RT, NJ, GJ)

STAND TOUCHING BOTTOM: **debakiishkige** *vai* stand and touch the bottom (GJ)

SWIM TO BOTTOM: **debakiikozhiwe** *vai* swim down to the bottom (touching), make contact with the bottom (GJ)

THROW IN WATER AND TOUCH BOTTOM: **noondakiise** *vai* throw s.t. in the water that cannot touch bottom (NJ, GJ)

TOUCH LAND FROM SKY AND RETURN: **mizhakiise** *vai* fly from the sky down to the earth, make land fall (then back up) (NJ, GJ)

TOUCH LAND FROM SKY: **mizhakiinam** *vai* go from the sky all the way to ground like a thunderbird, or tornado touching down (NJ, GJ)

TOUCH LAND IN WATER: **mizhakiikozhiwe** *vai* make it from below to land in the water (NJ, GJ)

TOUCH SOMETHING: **dookinan** *vti* touch s.t., tap s.t. (RT, NJ, GJ)

TOY: **gaaskiigino-odaminwaaganensikaan** *ni* plastic toy; *pl* **gaaskiigino-odaminwaaganensikaanan** (NJ, GJ)

TRAIL:

BRUSH TRAIL WIDER: **mangadeyaakwa'ige** *vai* make trail wider (brush out) (NJ, GJ)

DIRT ROAD: **mitaawango-miikanens** *ni* dirt road, dirt trail; *pl* **mitaawango-miikanensan** (RT, NJ, GJ)

MAKE TRAIL SIDEWAYS: **bimijizide-miikanaake** *vai* make trail sideways (NJ, GJ)

MAKE TRAIL WIDER: **mamangideyaagoneshkige** *vai* make trail wider (in the snow) (GJ); *also* **mangadeyaagoneshkige** (NJ, GJ); *also* **mangademochige** (NJ, GJ)

PACK TRAIL WITH SNOWSHOE: **daataagwaagoneshkige** *vai* pack trail with snowshoes or shoes (NJ, GJ)

TRAP:

ANCHOR WIRE: **gitaakwa'iganeyaab** *ni* anchor wire (for a trap); *pl* **gitaakwa'iganeyaabiin** (RT, NJ, GJ)

CONIBEAR: **gashkaagise-wanii'igan** *ni* conibear; *pl* **gashkaagise-wanii'iganan** (NJ, GJ)

FISH TRAP: **biinjiboonaagan** *ni* fish trap; *pl* **biinjiboonaaganan** (NJ, GJ)

FREE SOMEONE: **giitaabikizh** /giitaabikiN-/ *vta* let s.o. free (from a trap) (NJ, GJ)

FREE SOMETHING: **giitaabikinan** *vti* release s.t. (as in a trap) (NJ, GJ)

SAFETY CLASP: **minjimaakwa'iganens** *ni* spring safety clasp (as on a conibear trap); *pl* **minjimaakwa'iganensan** (NJ)

SET SOMETHING: **omba'an** *vti* set s.t. (as in a trap) (NJ, GJ)

SET TRAPS: **omba'ige** *vai* set traps (NJ, GJ)

SINKER: **gitaakwa'iganaabik** *ni* sinker for drowning set (trap for animals); *pl* **gitaakwa'iganaabikoon** (RT, NJ, GJ); *also* **gonzaabiishkoojigan** *ni* net weight or sinker for drowning set (on trap for animals); *pl* **gonzaabiishkoojiganan** (RT, NJ, GJ)

SOLO SPRING: **nabaneyaagad** *vii* there is a solo spring (as on a #6 conibear trap) (NJ)

TENSIONER SPRING: **oningwiiganaabik** *ni* side springs, tensioner springs (as on the sides of a conibear or leg-hold trap) (NJ)

TRAP ONE'S SELF: **dasoonidizo** *vai* trap oneself (RT, NJ, GJ)

TRAP TRIGGER: **niisiniweba'igan** *ni* trap trigger (on conibear trap); *pl* **niisiniweba'iganan** (NJ)

TREE NOOSE TRAP: **basaakobijigan** *ni* tree spring noose trap; *pl* **basaakobijiganan** (RT, NJ, GJ)

TRIGGER CLASP: **niisinigan** *ni* trigger clasp (as on a conibear trap); *pl* **niisiniganan** (NJ)

TRY TO ESCAPE: **wiikwaji'o** *vai* try to get away (as in from a trap) (RT, NJ, GJ)

TRAVEL:

FLOAT: **bimaasin** *vii* float, travel on the air or wind (RT)

TRAVEL: **babaamiwijigaade** *vii* be carried, taken around (RT)

TRAVEL WITH SOMEONE: **aadwaa'am** *vta* travel with s.o. (by boat or car) (GJ)

TREE:

BALSAM: **inaandag** *na* balsam; *pl* **inaandagoog** (AM); *also* **ininaandag** *na* balsam (KP), any evergreen (NJ); *pl* **ininaandagoog**; *also* **zhingob** *na* balsam, evergreen; *pl* **zhingobiig** (RT, NJ, GJ)

BE A CERTAIN WAY: **inaakwad** *vii* be in a certain way (s.t. stick-like) (RT, NJ, GJ)

BE A RAINFOREST: **gimiwanoowaakwaa** *vii* be a rainforest (RT)

BE DENSE BRUSH: **zagaakwaa** *vii* be dense, brushy woods, thick brush, thicket (ES, NJ) [*cultural note*: this term can be used as a metaphor for hard times; *example*: Da-zagaakwaa obimaadiziwin giishpin bizindawaasig ookomisan. = Her life will get hard if she doesn't listen to her grandmother.]

BE FORKED: **niingidowaakwad** *vii* forked, crotched (as in a tree) (GJ)

BE FORKED: **niingidowaakozi** *vai* forked, crotched (as in a tree) (GJ)

BE PLEASANT SOUND OF LEAVES: **minwewebagaasin** *vii* be a pleasant sound of wind in the tree leaves (NJ)

BE SMOOTH: **zhooshkwaakozi** *vai* be smooth (s.t. treelike) (RT, NJ, GJ)

BE STRAIGHT: **na'aakozi** *vai* be straight (treelike) (RT, NJ, GJ)

BECOME OAK: **mitigomizhiiwi** *vai* become an oak, turn into an oak tree (RT)

BIRCH BARK LODGE COVERING: **wiigwaasabakwaan** *ni* bark lodge covering; *pl* **wiigwaasabakwaanan** (RT, NJ, GJ)

BIRCH TREE SEED STRINGS: **wanimikoons** *ni* birch tree seed strings; *pl* **wanimikoonsan** (RT, NJ, GJ)

BLACK SPRUCE: **zesegaandag** *na* black spruce; *pl* **zesegaandagoog** (NJ); *also* **zhingob**; *pl* **zhingobiig** (AM)

CHERRY TREE: **ookweminaatig** *na* cherry tree; *pl* **ookweminaatigoog** (RT)

CONIFER SOUNDS PLEASANT IN WIND: **minweweyaandagaashi** *vai* pleasant sound of an evergreen tree in the wind (NJ)

DEAD TREE: **mishiiwaatigowi** *vai* be a dry (dead) tree (RT, NJ, GJ)

FEMALE TREE: **ikwewaatig** *na* female tree; *pl* **ikwewaatigoog** (RT, NJ, GJ)

HARVEST TREE CANDY: **ozibanike** *vai* harvest tree candy, peel the outer bark to eat the inner bark (typically of a poplar) (NJ) [*cultural note*: sweet, sticky substance in the inner bark (typically of poplar) was highly prized and consumed as a kind of candy]

HIGH IN TREES: **ishpaatigong** *pc* high in the trees (RT)

JACK PINE: **akikaandag** *na* jack pine; *pl* **akikaandagoog** (RT, GJ); *also* **okikaandag**; *pl* **okikaandagoog** (NJ)

LIMB BY CUTTING: **jiishaakwa'ige** *vai* cut limbs off a tree (GJ); *also* scrape a hide (NJ)

LIMB SAPLING: **jiishaandawe'ige** *vai* limb small trees (as in cleaning saplings for use as lodge poles) (NJ)

LIMB SOMEONE (SAPLING): **jiishaanda'wi** /**jiishaanda'w-**/ *vta* limb small tree (as in cleaning saplings for use as lodge poles) (NJ)

MAKE BASSWOOD STRING: **wiigobiike** *vai* make string from basswood fiber (RT, NJ, GJ)

MAKE BIRCH BARK LODGE COVERING: **wiigwaasabakwayike** *vai* make birch bark lodge coverings (RT, NJ, GJ)

MAKE SOMEONE SMOOTH BY CUTTING: **zhooshkwaakozhwi** /**zhooshkwaakozhw-**/ *vta* cut s.o. smooth using s.t. (knife), as in trimming the knots off a sapling, making it smooth (NJ)

MALE TREE: **ininiiwaatig** *na* male tree; *pl* **ininiiwaatigoog** (RT, NJ, GJ)

PINE NEEDLE: **zhingwaakwaandag** *na* pine needle; *pl* **zhingwaakwaandag** (RT, NJ)

PINECONE: **wazhashkwedowens** *na* pinecone; *pl* **wazhashkwedowensag** (RT, NJ, GJ)

PLEASANT SOUND OF CONIFER IN WIND: **minweweyaandagaasin** *vii* pleasant sound of evergreen boughs in the wind (NJ)

RAINFOREST: **gimiwanoowaakwaang** *pc* rainforest (RT)

ROTTEN TREE: **biigijiisagowi** *vai* be a decayed tree (standing) (GJ)

SHAKE TREE: **ishkwaakobijige** *vai* shake a tree (person or bear) (RT, NJ, GJ)

SHAKING TREE: **ishkwaakobijigan** *ni* tree or pole that is shaken; *pl* **ishkwaakobijiganan** (RT, NJ, GJ)

TREE BENT BY THE WIND: **neweyaak** *na* tree that is bent by the wind; *pl* **neweyaakoog** (GJ)

TREE BRANCH: **wadikwan** *ni* tree branch, wood knot; *pl* **wadikwanan**; *loc* **wadikwaning** [*example*: Wadikwaning izhi-boonii. = He lands on a limb.] (NJ, GJ); *also* **odikon**; *pl* **odikonan** (GJ)

TREE BURROW: **mitigwaazh** *ni* burrow or nest inside a tree (RT)

TREE CANDY: **oziban** *ni* tree candy, the consumable part of inner tree bark (NJ) [*cultural note*: sweet, sticky substance in the inner bark (typically of poplar) was highly prized and consumed as a kind of candy]

TREE FROG (BOREAL CHORUS FROG): **agoozimakakii** *na* boreal chorus frog (type of tree frog); *pl* **agoozimakakiig** (GJ, NJ)

TREE FROG (GRAY TREE FROG): **obiibaagimakakii**; gray tree frog; *pl* **obiibaagimakakiig** (NJ)

TREE MAKES PLEASANT SOUND OF LEAVES: **minwewebagaashi** *vai* tree makes a pleasant sound of leaves in the wind (NJ)

WHITE SPRUCE: **gaawaandag** *na* white spruce; *pl* **gaawaandagoog** (AM); *also* **mina'igwaandag**; *pl* **mina'igwaandagoog** (RT, NJ, GJ)

TREE: *see also* WOOD

TRICERATOPS: **neso-eshkaned** *vai-prt* triceratops; *pl* **neso-eshkanewaad** (NJ); *also* **nesweshkaned** *vai-prt* triceratops; *pl* **nesweshkanewaad** (NJ)

TRIGGER:

    TRAP TRIGGER: **niisiniweba'igan** *ni* trap trigger (on conibear trap); *pl* **niisiniweba'iganan** (NJ)

    TRIGGER CLASP: **niisinigan** *ni* trigger clasp (as on a conibear trap); *pl* **niisiniganan** (NJ)

TRILL: **gidaatabitaagozi** *vai* trill, fast sounding call (as in bird) (RT, NJ, GJ)

TROUT: **namegos** *na* trout; *pl* **namegosag** (RT, NJ, GJ)

TRUDGE THROUGH SAND: **bimidaawangii** *vai* trudge through sand (NJ, GJ)

TRY:

    MAKE BEST EFFORT: **inwaazo** *vai* make one's best effort (ES)

    TRY TO SPEAK: **goji-giigido** *vai* try to speak (RT, NJ, GJ)

TULABEE: **odoonibiins** *na* tulabee; *pl* **odoonibiinsag** (RT, NJ, GJ)

TUNDRA: **bapashkwaa** *vii* be tundra (RT); *also* **dootookikamigaa** (RT); *also* **mashkawikamigaa** (RT)

TUNNEL:

    DIG TUNNEL: **zhiibaa-waanike** *vai* dig a tunnel (RT)

    TUNNEL: **zhiibaa-waazh** *ni* tunnel; *pl* **zhiibaa-waazhiin** (RT)

TURKEY: **mizise** *na* turkey; *pl* **miziseg** (NJ, GJ); *also* **misise** (RT)

TURN:

    CROSS LINE: **gaashipoobizo** *vai* cross the line (as in driving out of lane), or miss a turnoff (as in driving) [*example*: Gigaashipoobizomin. = We missed the turn off.] (NJ, GJ)

    SPRINKLE WATER TURNING: **gweki-zaswebiiga'anjigaawan** *vii* sprinkle water while turning (as in a lawn sprinkler) (RT, NJ, GJ)

TURN SOMETHING DOWN: **waashaanzhe'an** *vti* dim, turn s.t. down (as in a kerosene lantern) (RT); *also* **waashaanzhenan** (NJ)

TURN UPRIGHT: **azhe-mayaawibidoon** *vti* turn s.t. upright, upright s.t. (RT, NJ, GJ)

UPRIGHT: **azhe-miinobijige** *vai* upright things, pull things straight (RT, NJ, GJ)

TWINE: **asabikaanaak** *ni* twine spindle; *pl* **asabikaanaakoon** (RT, NJ, GJ)

TWIST: WRING OUT TWISTING WITH STICK: **ziinikobiigaakwa'an** *vti* wring out twisting with stick (RT, NJ, GJ)

TWO: TIE TWO TOGETHER: **niizhoopizh** /**niizhoopiN-**/ *vta* tie two together (RT, NJ, GJ)

TWO: *see also* DOUBLE

TYPE OF LODGE: **dinawigamig** *pc* type of lodge (RT, NJ, GJ)

TYRANNOSAURAUS REX: **gegwaanisagizid** *vai-prt* tyrannosaurus rex; *pl* **gegwaanisagiziwaad** (NJ)

UNABLE TO MAKE FIRE: **bwaanawi-ishkodawe** *vai* be unable to make a fire (RT, NJ, GJ)

UNDECIDED: **wawaanendam** *vai* confused, undecided, unsure (RT, NJ, GJ)

UNDER:

ANCHOR POLE FOR NETTING UNDER ICE: **anaamizigoneyaatig** *ni* anchor pole for ice netting; *pl* **anaamizigoneyaatigoon** (RT, NJ, GJ)

PALM: **anaamininj** *pc* under the palm  (NJ)

POLE TO SET NET UNDER ICE: **anaamizigwaneyaatig** *ni* slider push-pole for setting net under ice; *pl* **anaamizigwaneyaatigoon** (RT, NJ, GJ)

PUT NET STRING UNDER ICE: **anaamizigoneyaabii** *vai* put net string under ice (RT, NJ, GJ)

SET NET UNDER ICE: **anaamizigosabii** *vai* set net under the ice (RT, NJ, GJ)

SOLE: **anaamizid** *pc* under the foot, underneath (RT, NJ, GJ)

STRING FOR NETTING UNDER ICE: **anaamizigoneyaab** *ni* ice netting string (with pole); *pl* **anaamizigoneyaabiin** (RT, NJ, GJ)

SWIM UNDERWATER: **bimakwazhiwe** *vai* paddling, swimming underwater (RT, NJ, GJ)

UNDER ICE: **anaamizigwam** *pc* under the ice (RT, NJ, GJ); *also* **anaamikwam** *pc* under the ice (RT, NJ, GJ)

UNDER LILY PADS: **anaamibag** *pc* under the lily pads (RT)

UNDER WATER: **anaamiindim** *pc* under water (RT, NJ, GJ)

UNDERGROUND: **anaamakamig** *pc* underground (RT)

UNDERNEATH: **anaamikaa** *vii* be underneath (RT)

UNICORN: **eshkani-bebezhigoganzhii** *na* unicorn; *pl* **eshkani-bebezhigoganzhiig** (RT, NJ, GJ)

UNLOAD:

UNLOAD AND BRING INLAND: **gopiwidaaso** *vai* unload and bring inland (NJ, GJ)

UNLOAD HARVEST AND BRING INLAND: **gopimine** *vai* unload harvest from canoe and bring inland (NJ, GJ)

UNSURE: **wawaanendam** *vai* confused, undecided, unsure (RT, NJ, GJ)

UP:

CAUGHT BY LEG: **zagigaadebizo** *vai* be flung up, caught by the leg (as a rabbit in a tree spring-noose trap) (NJ)

COME UP: **izhi-onde** *vii* it comes up in a certain way (as in lava) (GJ)

STICK UP FINS TO KILL: **michige'wi** /michige'w-/ *vta* stick up fins to kill s.o. (NJ); *also* **michigwe'o** /michigwe'w-/ (GJ)

UPRIGHT:

TURN UPRIGHT: **azhe-mayaawibidoon** *vti* turn s.t. upright, upright s.t. (RT, NJ, GJ)

UPRIGHT: **azhe-miinobijige** *vai* upright things, pull things straight (RT, NJ, GJ)

UPSTREAM: SWIM UPSTREAM: **ogiidaajiwane'o** *vai* swim upstream (GJ); *also* **ogiidaajiwanwe'o** (NJ); *also* **ogiidaajiwaneyaadagwe** (GJ); *also* **ogiidaajiwanweyaadagwe** (NJ)

URINATE: TICKLE UNTIL URINATION: **gizhigibizh** /gizhigiN-/ *vta* squeeze or tickle s.o. to urinate (RT, NJ, GJ)

USE:

BE USED: **inaabadad** *vii* be used in a certain way (RT, NJ, GJ)

MAKE USE, RELY: **aabajitamaagoowizi** *vai+o* rely upon things, make use of things (NJ)

USE AS HAMMER: **bakite'igaage** *vai+o* use s.t. for a hammer, use s.t. to hit [*example*: Waagaakwadoon bakite'igaagen. = Use the hatchet as a hammer.] (NJ)

USE AS UMBRELLA: **agawaate'odizo** *vai+o* shade one's self with s.t.[*example*: Babaamaajimoo-mazina'igan agawaate'odizon. = Shade youself with an umbrella.] (NJ)

USUALLY: **ishakonaa** *pc* usually (RT, NJ, GJ)

VACUUM WATER: **wiikwa'ibiise** *vii* suck, vacuum water out (RT, NJ, GJ)

VASE: **zhaabwaate-omooday** *ni* vase; *pl* **zhaabwaate-omoodayan** (RT, NJ, GJ)

VICE GRIP: **dakonjigaans** *ni* pliers, vice grip; *pl* **dakonjigaansan** (NJ, GJ); *also* **dakwanjigaans** (RT)

VINE: **bemiging** *vii-prt* vine, plant (as in one that grows along the ground); *pl* **bemigingin** (RT)

VINEGAR: **binigan** *ni* vinegar (RT)

VISION: *see* SEE

VOICE CARRIES: **jiingwe** *vai* voice carries long ways (RT, NJ, GJ)

WAG TAIL: **wewebaanoweni** *vai* wag one's tail (RT, NJ, GJ)

WAIT:
> LIE IN WAIT FOR SOMEONE: **akandamaw** *vta* lie in wait for s.o. (RT, NJ, GJ)
>
> WAIT FOR SOMEONE: **akamaw** *vta* wait for s.o., anticipate s.o. (RT, NJ, GJ)
>
> WAIT FOR SOMEONE TO COME: **akawaabam** *vta* wait for s.o. to come into view (apiichinaag) (RT, NJ, GJ)

WALK:
> WALK FAST: **dadaatabose** *vai* walk fast (RT, GJ); *also* **gidaatabose** *vai* walk fast (NJ)
>
> WALK PROPERLY: **wewenose** *vai* walk properly, walk cautiously (RT, NJ, GJ)

WALL: PIN SOMEONE AGAINST WALL: **ombishidaakogibinewen** *vta* pin s.o. against the wall off the ground (GJ)

WALLEYE:
> DORSAL FIN: **omichigan** *ni* dorsal fin; *pl* **omichiganan** (RT, NJ, GJ)
>
> WALLEYE: **ogaa** *na* walleye; *pl* **ogaawag** (RT, NJ, GJ)

WANE: **animaasige** *vai* wane (as in moon phase) (JC)

WANT:
> WANT: **andawendam** *vai* want, desire, wish (RT, NJ, GJ)
>
> WANTED: **andawendaagwad** *vii* be wanted (RT)

WARM:

DRESS WARMLY: **giizhookonaye** *vai* dress warmly, dress in warm clothes (RT, NJ, GJ)

WARM:

WARM SAND: **gizhidaawangide** *vii* be warm sand (NJ, GJ)

WARM WATER: **giizhoogami** *vii* be warm water (NJ)

WART: **jiichiigom** *na* wart; *pl* **jiichiigomag** (RT, NJ, GJ)

WATCH OVER: **ganawaabandamaazo** *vai* watch over, caretake things (RT, NJ, GJ)

WATER:

ARRIVES: **bagamijiwan** *vii* water arrives in a certain place (RT)

BAIL WATER: **iska'ibii** *vai* bail (RT, NJ, GJ)

BE A CERTAIN WAY: **inaagamin** *vii* be a certain way (as in a liquid) (RT)

BE A PUDDLE: **waanashkobaa** *vii* be a puddle (RT, NJ); *also* **waanishkobaa** (GJ); *also* **waanashkobiiyaa** (RT, NJ)

BE CLEAR WATER: **onaagamin** *vii* clear water (NJ, GJ)

BE HEARD COMING THROUGH WATER: **zaasibiibizo** *vai* heard coming through water (as in a motorboat) (GJ)

BE PLEASANT SOUND OF WATER FLOWING: **minwewejiwan** *vii* good sound of water flowing (NJ)

BE SALTY WATER: **zhiiwitaaganibiisin** *vii* be salty water (RT, NJ, GJ)

BLUE WATER: **ozhaawashkwaagamin** *vii* be blue (water) (NJ, GJ)

BOTTOM OF LAKE: **mitaamik** *pc* at the bottom of the lake (RT, NJ, GJ)

BREAK SURFACE: **bagaskibiigishin** *vai* break the surface of water (as a beaver hitting water with tail) (RT, NJ, GJ)

CAPSIZE FROM WIND: **gwanabaashi** *vai* capsize from wind (NJ, GJ)

CAPSIZE IN RAPIDS: **gwanabaabago** *vai* capsize in rapids (NJ, GJ)

CAPSIZE: **gwanabise** *vii* capsize (RT, NJ, GJ)

CLEAN WATER: **biinaagamin** *vii* be clean water (RT, NJ, GJ)

CLEAR WATER: **waakaagamin** *vii* be clear water, be a clear lake (RT, NJ, GJ)

CURRENT CUTS ICE: **bagonezigwaa** *vii* current cuts a hole in ice (RT, NJ, GJ); *also* **bagonezigojiwan** (GJ); *also* **bookizigwajiwan** (GJ)

DEEP WATER: **ginwiindimaa** *vii* be deep water (RT, NJ, GJ)

DIRTY WATER: **wiinaagamin** *vii* be dirty (as in a liquid) (RT, NJ, GJ)

DRAIN WATER OUT OF SOMETHING: **ziikoobiiginan** *vti* drain the water out of s.t. (NJ, GJ)

EMERGE FROM WATER: **mookibiise** *vii* emerge from water, suddenly pop out of water (NJ, GJ)

EMERGE FROM WATER: **mooshkamo** *vai* emerge from water (NJ, GJ)

FILL WITH WATER: **mooshkinebiise** *vii* fills with water (as in a canoe) (RT, NJ, GJ)

FLOAT OFF IN CURRENT: **maajiiyaabagonde** *vii* float off in current (GJ)

FLOOD: **mooshka'ogo** *vai* s.o. is flooding out (as in ice) (RT, NJ, GJ)

FLOW: **onjigaa** *vii* flow, run (as in water) (RT, NJ, GJ)

FLOW CERTAIN WAY: **izhijiwan** *vii* flow in a certain way (RT)

FLOW DOWN: **niisijiwan** *vii* flow down, roll down (as in water) (RT)

FORCE WATER: **iska'ibiise** *vii* water forced up and out (RT, NJ, GJ)

GET OFF WATER: **agwaaba'iwe** *vai* get off water and go to safety (NJ, GJ)

GET WATER FROM SOMEONE: **onzibii'** *vta* make s.o. water, get water from s.o. (NJ)

GET WATER SOMEWHERE: **onda'ibii** *vai* get water from a certain place (RT, NJ, GJ)

GLIDE THROUGH WATER: **gichiwibiishkaa** *vii* glide slowly through water (RT, NJ, GJ)

GO DOWNSTREAM ON TOP OF WATER: **niisaajiwaneweyaaboono** *vai* go downstream on top of the water (GJ); *also* **niisaajiwanweweyaabono** (NJ)

GROW TO SURFACE: **mookibiigin** *vii* grow to the surface (as in lily pads to the surface of the water) (RT)

HEAD STICKS OUT OF WATER FLOATING: **zaagikwegomo** *vai* head is sticking out of water while floating (NJ, GJ)

LEAP INTO WATER: **bakobiigwaashkwani** *vai* leap into the water (RT)

MUDDY WATER: **azhashkiiwaagamin** *vii* be murky water, be muddy water (RT, NJ, GJ)

PLUNGE DOWN: **gaanjiba'ibiise** *vii* water is pushed out, plunged down (NJ, GJ); *also* **gaanjwa'ibiise** (NJ, GJ)

POOL: **maawandoojiwan** *vii* pool (water); *also* waves come together (RT, NJ, GJ)

PUMP WATER: **ikwa'ige** *vai* pump water (RT, NJ, GJ)

REFLECT IN WATER: **mazinaatebiigishin** *vai* reflect in the water [*example*: Mazinaatebiigishin mitig. = The tree is reflecting in the water. *example*: Mazinaatebiigishin gaa-pimised bineshiinh. = The bird casts a reflection in the water flying.] (NJ, GJ)

RUNNY: **nibiiwaagamin** *vii* be runny (NJ)

SET NET IN DEEP WATER: **ginwiindimaasabii** *vai* set net in deep water (GJ, NJ)

SHOWER: **wenjijiwang** *vii-prt* shower; *pl* **wenjijiwangin** (NJ)

SKIP LAND: **detesabi-booniimagad** *vii* skip landing, land by bouncing on the water (as in duck or float plane) (RT, NJ, GJ)

SLAP TAIL ON WATER: **damoo'am** *vai* slap one's tail on the water (as in a beaver) (NJ)

SLIDE THROUGH WATER EASILY: **zhooshkobiise** *vii* slides through the water easily (RT, NJ, GJ)

SLUSH WATER: **biitooskobiig** *pc* slush water (RT, NJ, GJ)

SLUSH WATER: **biitooskobiigaaboo** *ni* slush water; *pl* **biitooshkobiigaaboon** (RT, NJ, GJ)

SLUSH WATER UNDER SNOW: **biitooskobiigaa** *vii* be water under snow, be slush (RT, NJ, GJ)

SNARLING WATER: **gichi-babiikwajiwan** *vii* the water is really snarling (RT, NJ, GJ)

SPLASH: **gwaakwaashkwebiise** *vii* splash (NJ)

SPRING MELT WATER: **zhwaaganib** *pc* spring melt water (NJ, GJ)

SPRINKLE WATER WHILE TURNING: **gweki-zaswebiiga'anjigaawan** *vii* sprinkle water while turning (as in a lawn sprinkler) (RT, NJ, GJ)

SPRINKLER: **nibegaaziigaasing** *vii-prt* sprinkler; *pl* **nibegaaziigaasingin** (NJ); *also* **zaswebiiga'anjigan** *ni* water sprinkler; *pl* **zaswebiiga'anjiganan** (RT, GJ); *also* **ziswebiiga'anjigan**; *pl* **ziswebiiga'anjiganan** (NJ)

STORE WATER: **na'inibii** *vai* store water (NJ, GJ)

STORE WATER: **na'inibiigin** *vii* store water (NJ)

STRAINER: **ziikoobiiginigan** *ni* filter, strainer (RT, NJ, GJ)

SUBMERGE: **gonzaabiishkoozo** *vai* be submerged (as in ice weighed down by water) (RT, NJ, GJ)

SURFACE: **mookii** *vai* surface (RT, NJ, GJ)

SWEET SOUND OF FLOWING WATER WOMAN: **Minwewejiwanook** *name* Sweet Sound of Flowing Water Woman (NJ)

SWIRLING WATER: **gizhibaajiwan** *vii* be swirling water (RT, NJ, GJ)

TAKE OFF IN CURRENT: **maajiiyaaboode** *vii* take off in a current (NJ, GJ)

TAKE OFF IN WATER: **maajiiyaabogo** *vai* go off into the water (as in fish eggs) (NJ, GJ)

TAKE OFF ON WATER IN CURRENT: **maajiiyaabagonde** *vii* take off on top of the water in a current (NJ, GJ)

THROW IN WATER AND TOUCH BOTTOM: **noondakiise** *vai* throw s.t. in the water that cannot touch bottom (NJ, GJ)

TOUCH LAND IN WATER: **mizhakiikozhiwe** *vai* make it from below to land in the water (NJ, GJ)

TRY TO REACH BOTTOM UNSUCCESSFULLY: **noondakiikozhiwe** *vai* try to reach the bottom unsuccessfully (NJ, GJ)

UNDER WATER: **anaamiindim** *pc* under water (RT, NJ, GJ)

VACUUM WATER: **wiikwa'ibiise** *vii* suck, vacuum water out (RT, NJ, GJ)

WARM WATER: **giizhoogami** *vii* be warm water (NJ)

WATER BAILER: **iska'ibaan** *ni* water bailer, sponge; *pl* **iska'ibaanan** (NJ, GJ)

WATER IS PUMPED: **ikwa'ibii** *vii* water is pumped (RT, NJ, GJ)

WATER LEVEL DROPS: **iskaabiise** *vii* water level drops (RT, NJ, GJ); *also* **iskatese** *vii* water level drops (RT, NJ, GJ)

WATER POOLS: **bagonebiiwan** *vii* there is a pool of water on the ice from a hole (NJ, GJ)

WATER PUMP: **ikwa'ibaan** *ni* water pump (RT, NJ, GJ)

WATER SKI: **ogijibiibizo** *vai* water ski (RT, NJ, GJ)

WATER SOURCE: **onjijiwan** *vii* water comes from somewhere, be a water source (NJ, RT)

WHITE WATER: **waabishkaagamin** *vii* be white (water) (NJ, GJ)

WIND CAUSES RIPPLE: **wiisigamaasin** *vii* wind causes small ripples on calm water (RT, NJ, GJ)

WRING BY HAND: **ziikoobiiginan** *vti* wring s.t. by hand, drain the water out of s.t. (NJ)

WRINGER: **ziinaakwa'igan** *ni* wringer (RT)

WATER: *see also* BOIL

WATER LILY: **makopinagaawanzh** *na* water lily plant; *pl* **makopinagaawanzhiig** (RT)

WATERMELON: **eshkandaming** *vii-prt* watermelon; **eshkandamingin** (RT, NJ, GJ)

WAVE:

MAKE WAVES: **ondaadigwe** *vai* make waves (as an animal or person in a boat) [*example*: Nashke iwidi ondaadigwe! = Look over there something is making waves.] (NJ, GJ)

PADDLE INTO WAVES: **onjishkawa'o** *vai* paddle straight into waves (NJ, GJ)

PADDLE WITH WIND AND WAVES: **naamiwana'o** *vai* paddle with the wind and waves at one's back (NJ)

PLEASANT SOUND OF WAVES: **minweweyaashkaa** *vii* good sound of waves (NJ)

PROPEL: **naamiwana'ogo** *vai* be propelled faster by wind and waves (in watercraft) (NJ)

SURF: **ogidaashkaabizo** *vai* surf (RT, NJ, GJ)

SWING SOMETHING: **wewebaakowebinan** *vti* wave, swing s.t. (as in s.t. stick-like) (NJ)

THERE MAKING WAVES: **ondaadigotoo** *vai* s.o. is there making the waves (NJ, GJ)

WAVE MOTION: **minawaashkaa** *vii* be the pleasant motion of the waves (NJ)

WAVE SOUND: **madweyaashkaa** *vii* waves make a sound (RT, NJ, GJ)

WAVES COME FROM SOMEWHERE: **ondaadigo'o** *vai* makes waves from a certain place (as in ripple from surfacing fish or muskrat) (RT, NJ, GJ); *also* **ondaadigoshin** *vai* (RT, NJ, GJ)

WAVES COME TOGETHER: **maawandoojiwan** *vii* pool (water); *also* waves come together (RT, NJ, GJ)

WAVES MOVE: **miziweyaashkaa** *vii* waves move all over (RT, NJ, GJ)

WAVES ROLL IN: **biidaashkaa** *vii* waves or tide roll in (RT, NJ, GJ)

WHITE CAP: **waasaashkaa** *vii* there are white caps (RT, NJ, GJ)

WAX: **biidaasige** *vai* wax (as in cycle of the moon) (JC)

WEAR:

WEAR MITTEN ON WRONG HAND: **aabitanakakezi** *vai* a mitten or glove is worn on the wrong hand (NJ) [*example*: Aabitanakakeziwag. = Two left-handed or right-handed gloves or mittens are worn.]; *also* **aapidanakakezi** (GJ)

WEAR SHOE ON WRONG FOOT: **aabitanakakeyaa** *vii* a shoe is worn on the wrong foot (NJ) [*example:* Aabitanakakeyaawan. = Two left-footed/right-footed shoes are worn.]; *also* **aapidanakakeyaa** (GJ)

WEAR SHOES ON WRONG FEET: **napaadakizine** *vai* wear shoes on wrong feet (GJ)

WEATHER:

AWARE OF WEATHER: **dadiibaabandamaazo** *vai* make sure one is aware of weather (NJ, GJ)

RELUCTANT BECAUSE OF WEATHER: **ginaabandamaa** *vai* don't want to go because of inclement weather (NJ, GJ)

STRANDED BY WIND: **ginaanimanishi** *vai* be wind-bound, be stranded because of high wind (NJ, GJ); *also* **ginisinaa'ago** *vai* be wind-bound, be stranded because of high wind (NJ, GJ)

WEAVE:

BE WOVEN: **zhaashaabwaabiiginigaade** *vii* be woven (RT, NJ, GJ)

WEAVE: **bimidaabiiga'ige** *vai* weave (NJ)

WOVEN ITEM: **zhaashaabwaabiiginigan** *ni* woven item; *pl* **zhaashaabwaabiiginigan** (RT, NJ, GJ)

WEB:

WEBBED FOOT: **miziweyiigizide** *vai* have webbed feet, as in a beaver or duck (NJ)

WEBBED WING: **miziweginingwiigwane** *vai* have webbed wings, as in a bat (NJ)

WORLD WIDE WEB: **giiwitaakamisab** *na* world wide web (RT, NJ, GJ)

WORLD WIDE WEB LINK: **aanikekonesesijigan** *ni* web link; *pl* **aanikekonesesijiganan** (NJ, GJ); *also* **aazhawikonesesijigan**; *pl* **aazhawikonesesijiganan** (RT, NJ, GJ)

WEED:

WEED: **bashkobijigaade** *vii* be pulled out, be weeded, be removed from somewhere (RT)

WEED: **bashkobijige** *vai* pull out plants, weed (RT)

WEEDY: **bizaakwaa** *vii* be weedy, full of sticks (GJ)

WEEK: **anama'ewi-giizhikwagad** *vii* be a week (RT)

WEIGHT:

> NET WEIGHT: **gitaamika'igan** *ni* anchor, weight for nets; *pl*
> **gitaamika'iganan** (RT, NJ, GJ); *also* **gonzaabiishkoojigan** *ni*
> net weight or sinker for drowning set (on trap for animals); *pl*
> **gonzaabiishkoojiganan** (RT, NJ, GJ)
>
> ROCK WEIGHT: **gonzaabiishkoojiganaabik** *na* rock weight; *pl*
> **gonzaabiishkoojiganaabikoog** (RT, NJ, GJ)
>
> WEIGH: **apiitani** *vai* weigh a certain amount, be a certain weight
> (NJ)

WET:

> DAMP: **dipaabaawe** *vii* get damp (RT, NJ, GJ)
>
> MOIST SOIL: **dipiiwikamigaa** *vii* be moist soil (RT)
>
> RUNNY: **nibiiwaagamin** *vii* be runny (NJ)
>
> WET: **dipiiwan** *vii* be wet, moist (RT)
>
> WET AND COLD: **dakibiigaji** *vai* be cold from being wet (rained
> on, sweaty) (NJ, GJ)
>
> WET LEAVES: **dipiiwibagaa** *vii* be wet leaves (RT)
>
> WET SAND: **nibiiwadaawangaa** *vii* be wet sand (NJ)

WHALE: **misaakig** *na* whale; *pl* **misaakigoog** (GJ)

WHEAT: **bakwezhiganashk** *ni* wheat; *pl* **bakwezhiganashkoon** (RT)

WHEEL: **detibiseg** *vii-prt* tires, wheels; *pl* **detibisegin** (RT, NJ, GJ)

WHISKER:

> ANIMAL WHISKER: **miishanowaan** *ni* animal whisker; *pl*
> **miishanowaanan** (RT); *also* **miishidoonaan**; *pl*
> **miishidoonaanan** (NJ)
>
> HAVE WHISKERS: **miishidoone** *vai* have whiskers (RT, NJ, GJ)

WHISPER: **gaaskanazomagad** *vii* whisper, sound softly (RT, NJ, GJ)

WHITE:

> WHITE CAP: **waasaashkaa** *vii* there are white caps (RT, NJ, GJ)
>
> WHITE CLAY: **waabaabigan** *na* white or gray clay (NJ)
>
> WHITE SIDE SHOWS: **waasiingwewebinige** *vai* the white side
> shows (RT, NJ, GJ)
>
> WHITE WATER: **waabishkaagamin** *vii* be white (water) (NJ, GJ)

WHOOPEE CUSHION: **boogidi-apikweshimon** *ni* whoopee cushion; *pl*
**boogidi-apikweshimonan** (NJ)

WIDE:

BE CERTAIN WIDTH: **ikowaaginigaa** *vii* be a certain width (RT, NJ, GJ)

BRUSH TRAIL WIDER: **mangadeyaakwa'ige** *vai* make trail wider (brush out) (NJ, GJ)

CUT WIDE STRIPS: **mangadezhigaade** *vii* cut in wide strips (RT, NJ, GJ)

LARGE: **mamaandido** *vai* be amazingly large (NJ)

MAKE TRAIL WIDER: **mamangideyaagoneshkige** *vai* make trail wider (in the snow) (GJ); *also* **mangadeyaagoneshkige** (NJ, GJ); *also* **mangademochige** (NJ, GJ)

STRIP WIDE: **mangadebidoon** *vti* strip s.t. into wide (as in bark) strips (RT, NJ, GJ)

WIDE TEETH: **mamaangaabide** *vai* have wide teeth (RT)

WIDTH: **apiitadezi** *vai* be a certain width, be a certain dimension of mesh (as in a net) (RT, NJ, GJ)

WIDE: *see also* BROAD *and* LARGE

WIGWAM LODGE: **wiigiwaam** *ni* wigwam lodge; *pl* **wiigiwaaman** (RT, NJ, GJ)

WILD: **bagwaji-** *pv* wild (RT)

WIND:

BE PLEASANT SOUND OF CHIMES: **minweweyaabikaasin** *vii* good sound of metal (as in wind chimes) [*example*: Minweweyaabikaasinoon. = The (wind chimes) sound good.] (NJ)

BE PLEASANT SOUND OF GRASS BLOWING: **minwewekosiwaagosin** *vii* be a pleasant sound of the grass blowing in the wind (NJ); *also* **minweweshkosiwagaasin** *vii* good sound of grass blowing in the wind (NJ)

BE PLEASANT SOUND OF LEAVES: **minwewebagaasin** *vii* be a pleasant sound of wind in the tree leaves (NJ)

BENT BY THE WIND: **naweyaashi** *vii* be bent by the wind (RT, NJ, GJ); *also* **zhagashkaashi** *vai* be bent by the wind (GJ)

BENT BY WIND: **zhagashkaasin** *vii* be bent from wind (GJ)

BREAK BY WIND: **bookwaashi** *vai* broken off half way up by the wind (NJ, GJ)

BREAK IN WIND: **bakweyaandagaasin** *vii* be broken off in the wind (as in a pine bough) (RT, NJ, GJ)

CAPSIZE FROM WIND: **gwanabaashi** *vai* capsize from wind (NJ, GJ)

COLD WIND: **dakaanimad** *vii* be a cold wind (RT, NJ, GJ)
CONIFER SOUNDS PLEASANT IN WIND: **minweweyaandagaashi**
*vai* pleasant sound of an evergreen tree in the wind (NJ)
FLOAT: **bimaasin** *vii* float, travel on the air or wind (RT)
GOOD WIND: **minwaasin** *vii* be good wind (as from a fan) (RT,
NJ, GJ)
GRASS BENDS PART-WAY TO GROUND: **zhamashkosiweyaasin**
*vii* grass bends part-way down to ground from the wind (GJ)
GRASS BENDS TO GROUND: **zhagashkosiweyaasin** *vii* grass
bends down to ground from the wind, the grass is dancing (NJ,
GJ); *also* **zhamashkosiweyaasin** (NJ)
GRASS BLOWING NICELY IN WIND: **minokosiwaagaasin** *vii* the
grass is blowing nicely in the wind (NJ); *also*
**minoshkosiiwagaasin** (GJ)
GRASS FLATTENS IN WIND: **nabashkweyaasin** *vii* grass flattens
in the wind (LM)
PADDLE WITH WIND: **naamiwana'o** *vai* paddle with the wind
(NJ)
PLEASANT SOUND OF CONIFER IN WIND: **minweweyaandagaasin**
*vii* pleasant sound of evergreen boughs in the wind (NJ)
PROPEL: **naamiwana'ogo** *vai* be propelled faster by wind and
waves (in watercraft) (NJ)
PULLED BY WIND: **bakwadaasin** *vii* be pulled up by the wind
(RT, NJ, GJ)
ROOF RIPPED BY WIND: **bakwadanabakweyaasin** *vii* roof ripped
off by the wind (of a house) (RT, NJ, GJ)
ROOF RIPPED BY WIND: **bakwadanabakweyaashi** *vai* have one's
roof ripped off by the wind (RT, NJ, GJ)
SAIL: **ningaasimoono** *vai* sail (NJ, GJ)
SOUND IN WIND: **inweweyaashi** *vai* have a certain sound in the
wind (RT, NJ, GJ)
STRANDED BY WIND: **ginaanimanishi** *vai* be wind-bound, be
stranded because of high wind (NJ, GJ); *also* **ginisinaa'ago** *vai*
be wind-bound, be stranded because of high wind (NJ, GJ)
STRONG BREEZE: **mashkawaanimad** *vii* wind blows hard, be a
strong breeze (as from fan) (RT, NJ, GJ)
SUFFICIENT WIND: **debaasin** *vii* be sufficient wind (as from a
fan) (RT, NJ, GJ)

TREE BENT BY THE WIND: **neweyaak** *na* tree that is bent by the wind; *pl* **neweyaakoog** (GJ)

TREE MAKES PLEASANT SOUND OF LEAVES: **minwewebagaashi** *vai* tree makes a pleasant sound of leaves in the wind (NJ)

WARM WIND: **aabawaanimad** *vii* be a warm wind (RT, NJ, GJ)

WIND ARRIVES: **bagamaanimad** *vii* wind comes up, gets windy (RT, NJ, GJ)

WIND BLOWS OUT: **animaanimad** *vii* wind goes onward, wind goes out (RT, NJ, GJ)

WIND CAUSES RIPPLE: **wiisigamaasin** *vii* wind causes small ripples on calm water (RT, NJ, GJ)

WIND STARTS INTERMITTENTLY: **mamaadaanimad** *vii* wind starts intermittently (RT)

WIND STOPS: **noogaanimad** *vii* wind stops (RT, NJ, GJ)

WING:

BROAD WINGS: **mamaanginingwiigwane** *vai* have broad wings (RT)

HAVE WINGS: **ningwiigane** *vai* have wings [*example*: Mii gaa-izhi-ningwiigwaned bapakwaanaajiinh. = A bat has wings like this. (NJ)

WEBBED WING: **miziwegiiningwiigwane** *vai* have webbed wings, as in a bat (NJ)

WINK: **ziibiskaabi** *vai* squint, wink (RT, NJ, GJ)

WINTER: SPEND WINTER SOMEWHERE: **biboonishi** *vai* spend the winter somewhere (RT)

WIPE:

WIPE MOUTH: **gaasiidoone'o** *vai* wipe one's mouth (RT, NJ, GJ)

WIPE OFF ON ROCK: **gaasiiyaabikishkan** *vti* wipe s.t. off of rocks with one's body (NJ, GJ)

WIPE OFF ROCK: **gaasiiyaamikishkige** *vai* wipe off rocks under water (NJ, GJ)

WIPE-OFF MARKER: **gaasi-adisibii'igan** *ni* wipe-off marker; *pl* **gaasi-adisibii'iganan** (RT, NJ, GJ)

WIRE: ANCHOR WIRE: **gitaakwa'iganeyaab** *ni* anchor wire (for a trap); *pl* **gitaakwa'iganeyaabiin** (RT, NJ, GJ)

WOLF: MALE DOG, HORSE, WOLF: **naabesim** *na* male dog, male horse, male wolf; *pl* **naabesimag** (RT, NJ, GJ)

WOMAN:

SWEET SOUND OF FLOWING WATER WOMAN:
**Minwewejiwanook** *name* Sweet Sound of Flowing Water
Woman (NJ)
TALK ABOUT WOMEN: **dazhimikwewe** *vai* talk about women
(RT, NJ, GJ)
WOOD:
BASSWOOD FIBER: **asigobaan** *ni* processed basswood fiber (RT,
NJ, GJ)
GLOWING ROTTEN WOOD: **waasakonejiisag** *ni* glowing rotten
wood (NJ, GJ)
GREEN WOOD (CHOPPED): **ishkaatig** *ni* green wood (chopped); *pl*
**ishkaatigoon** (GJ)
GREEN WOOD (STANDING): **ishkaatig** *na* green wood (as in
standing green trees); *pl* **ishkaatigoog** (GJ)
ROTTEN WOOD (STANDING): **biigijiisag** *na* rotten wood (still
standing); *pl* **biigijiisagoog** (GJ)
ROTTEN WOOD (DOWN): **biigijiisag** *ni* rotten wood (downed); *pl*
**biigijiisagoon** (GJ); *also* **biigijiisagaatig**; *pl* **biigijiisagaatigoon**
(GJ); *also* **biigijiisagwaatig**; *pl* **biigijiisagwaatigoon** (NJ)
WOOD KNOT: **wadikwan** *ni* tree branch, wood knot; *pl*
**wadikwanan**; *loc* **wadikwaning** [*example*: Wadikwaning izhi-
boonii. = He lands on a limb.] (NJ, GJ); *also* **odikon**; *pl*
**odikonan** (GJ)
WOOD: *see also* TREE
WOSELEY: **Biinjiboonaaganing** *place* the shoot between Three Mile and
Woseley Lake (in Quetico Park) (GJ)
WRING:
WRING BY HAND: **ziikoobiiginan** *vti* wring by hand, drain the
water out of s.t. (NJ)
WRING OUT CLOTH OR HIDE: **ziiniskobiiga'an** *vti* wring out cloth
or hide (RT, NJ, GJ)
WRING OUT TWISTING WITH STICK: **ziinikobiigaakwa'an** *vti*
wring out twisting with stick (RT, NJ, GJ); *also* **biimaakwa'ige**
(NJ, GJ)
WRINGER: **ziinaakwa'igan** *ni* wringer (RT)
WRIST: **aanikawigananinjaan** *ni* wrist; *pl* **aanikawiganinjaanan** (RT, NJ);
*also* **aanikawiganeninjaan** (GJ)
WRITE:

WRITE IN ALL CAPITAL LETTERS: **mangibii'ige** *vai* write in all capital letters (JC)

WRITE WELL: **minobii'ige** *vai* write well (RT, NJ, GJ)

WRONG:

FALL WRONG WAY: **napaadaakwese** *vai* fall in the wrong direction (GJ)

FOLD BACKWARDS: **napaajiiginan** *vti* fold backwards, wrong way (GJ)

PUT SHOES ON WRONG FEET: **nanepaadakizine** *vai* put one's shoes on the wrong foot (NJ, GJ)

WEAR SHOES ON WRONG FEET: **napaadakizine** *vai* wear shoes on wrong feet (GJ)

YEAR: BE A CERTAIN YEAR: **gikinoonowagad** *vii* be a certain year (as in telling specific date) (NJ)

YOUNG STICK: **oshkaatigoons** *ni* young stick; *pl* **oshkaatigoonsan** (GJ)

YOYO: **gagiizhibaayaabiigibijigan** *ni* yoyo; *pl* **gagiizhibaayaabiigibijiganan** (NJ, GJ)

ZEBRA: **bepeshizi-bebezhigooganzhii** *na* zebra; *pl* **bepeshizi-bebezhigooganzhiig** (NJ)

# APPENDICES

## Order of Fish Spawn

The authors of this dictionary shared a great deal of cultural information in the process of documenting vocabulary. We have tried to provide cultural notes and example sentences throughout the dictionary entries to provide more of that information directly in the book. A few notes will provide useful support and context for some of the entries. There was lots of substantive discussion about fish spawning. Anecdotal cultural information includes that gray tree frogs sound loud and numerous immediately before the onset of the sturgeon spawn and that the hatching of fish flies signals the start of the smallmouth bass spawn. Although there may some regional variation, the authors concurred that fish spawned in the following order:

1. NORTHERN PIKE: **ginoozhe** *na* northern pike; *pl* **ginoozheg** (RT, NJ, GJ)
2. SUCKER: **namebin** *na* sucker; *pl* **namebinag** (RT, NJ, GJ)
3. WALLEYE: **ogaa** *na* walleye; *pl* **ogaawag** (RT, NJ, GJ)
4. PERCH: **asaawens** *na* perch (fish); *pl* **asaawensag** (RT, NJ, GJ)
5. MUSKELLUNGE: **ozhaawashko-ginoozhe** *na* muskellunge; *pl* **ozhaawashko-ginoozheg** (NJ); *also* **mashkinoozhe** (AM); *pl* **mashkinoozheg**
6. CRAPPIE: **gidagwadaashi** *na* crappie (KP); *pl* **gidagwadaashiwag**; *also* **ezhegamoons** (GJ); *pl* **ezhegamoonsag**; *also* **odazhegamoons** (NJ); *pl* **odazhegamoonsag**
7. STURGEON: **name** *na* sturgeon; *pl* **namewag** (RT, NJ, GJ)
8. SMALLMOUTH BASS: **odazhegomoo** *na* smallmouth bass; *pl* **odazhegomoog**; *also* **noosa'owesi** *na* smallmouth bass; *pl* **noosa'owesiwag** (RT, NJ, GJ)
9. TROUT: **namegos** *na* trout; *pl* **namegosag** (RT, NJ, GJ)
10. WHITEFISH: **adikameg** *na* whitefish; *pl* **adikamegwag** (RT, NJ, GJ)

## Example Sentences

1. Meme bedowed dibaajimo wii-kimiwang. (NJ) = When the pilated woodpecker makes a low call, he tells of pending rain. [it sounds like he is saying "fix-it, fix-it"]

2. Meme gidaatabitaagozid dibaajimo wii-mino-giizhigak. (NJ) = When the pilated woodpecker makes a trill call, he is saying that it will be a nice day.
3. Ma'iingaans gii-kidaatabi-waawoonod dibaajimo wii-kichi-noodininig. = When a coyote makes a fast yelp, he is saying there will be a big wind.
4. Ma'iingaans gii-pejiwoonod owiikomaa' wiiji-ma'iingana' ji-bi-wiidoopamigod. = When a coyote makes a low howl, he is inviting his fellows to come and eat with him.
5. Maang gii-piibaagid wii-noodin ikido. = There will be a wind when the loon yells.
6. Aazha asaniiwag. = They are already dried up (as in tree bark past peeling time).
7. Akawe gidanweshimigom. = The weather is telling you to stay home and do your real work.
8. Baakibiise amikob. = The beaver pond breaks open.
9. Agoozimakakii gii-kidaatabwewed wii-niiskaadad. = When the boreal chorus frog (type of tree frog) has a trill call the weather will turn bad. (NJ)
10. Ningii-piinji-boodaadaan. = I blew into it.
11. Mishiiwaatigoonsan wii-poodaweng. = Dry wood (standing dead) for building a fire.
12. Gibinde'an ishkwaandem! = Close the (cloth) door!
13. Gigii-miizii-aanimi'aa. = You scared the crap out of him.
14. Obiibaagimakakii dibaajimo mii azhigwa wii-aamiwaad namewag. = When the gray tree frog calls, the sturgeon are going to spawn. (NJ)
15. Bimijizide-miikanaakeshimo, mii ezhichiged waabooz. = He dances sideways making the trail, this is what the rabbit does.
16. Apiigisin, gaawiin mizhishawi-ayaasinoon. = It lies as a layered covering, it is not a bare space (as in the nature of the reinforcement tabs on the end of a birch bark lodge covering).
17. Agokeni miishikaadens. = The [pollen] collects on the hairy legs [of bees].

18. Gego bapasangwaabamaaken awiiya! = Don't blink your eyes at someone!
19. Gaawiin maamashkawadinzinoon. = It doesn't freeze strong.
20. Ginwiindimaang izhi-bagida'waan! = Set the net in deep water!
21. Gego onzongeken! = Don't verbally attack based on what your child has come and told you!
22. Aabajitoon giwaagaakwad ani-zaagaakwaag gibimaadiziwin. = Use your hatchet when there are hard times (a thicket) in your life.
23. Zenibaan ezhinaagwakin mashkosiwan. = The grass which look like ribbons.
24. Bimoode ginebig. = The snake slithers along.
25. Wadikwaning izhi-boonii. = He lands on a limb.
26. Mazinaatebiigishin mitig. = The tree is reflecting in the water.
27. Mazinaatebiigishin gaa-pimised bineshiinh. = The bird casts a reflection in the water flying.
28. Gidandawendam wii-ani-wiijiwadwaa. = You want to go along with them. [*cultural note*: It is considered unadvisable to comment excessively about how beautiful the leaves look in autumn as the spirits may interpret the statements as a sign that one desires to accompany the falling leaves as they dress up to die.] (NJ, GJ)
29. Onzaam gizhide gaa-wii-onji-wi-nibaayang. = It's too warm, it makes us feel sleepy.
30. Wawiyazh ikido. = He is just saying it for fun.
31. Ningii-piinjiweba'ige. = I scored a point.
32. Gaawiin nindizhaasiin onzaam nindaakoz. = I'm not going because I'm sick.
33. Wiikaa ningii-koshkoz wenji-bezikaayaan. = I got up late that is why I am late.
34. Ningii-tajise ji-gii-andawaabandamaan. = I didn't have time to go pick it up.
35. Ningii-ondami'aa wenji-bezikaayaang. = I'm the reason we (exc.) are late.
36. Hay', onzaam gibezikaamin, aazha gii-kiba'igaade. = Darn, we're too late, it is already closed.

37. Nenibaawizh iidog! = It's about time!
38. Nenibaawizh iidog gigoshkoz! = It's about time you woke up!
39. Mii bijiinag gii-izhichigeyaan. = This is the first time I did this.
40. Mii bijiinag wii-wiisiniyaang. = We're going to eat just now.
    [Apologetic way of saying, because we were late in getting
    up, or delayed for some other reason]
41. Dedeb igo gaa-wiisiniyaan zhebaa! = It's a good thing I ate this
    morning!
42. Dedeb igo gaa-agwana'aman daa-gii-tipaabaawewan. = It is a
    good thing you covered them, they would have gotten
    damp.
43. Wiinge wiisagazheyaakizodog. = He must be really sunburned.
44. Aabaji'adwaaban. = What you should use. (GJ)
45. Nindoodenawing. = In my town (NJ) [*conjugation note*:
    uncommon locative formation]
46. /-aka-/ = occasionally glancing up while waiting [morpheme]
47. Edawayi'ii inaabide-ayaa. = It has teeth on either side. [In
    reference to a blade that has teeth angling out on each side,
    so the cut space is wider.]
48. Aadaagoneshin. = He's having hard going through snow.
    [Implicating a deep snowy winter to come. This can be
    predicted by observing the horizontal leveling of the stars
    that constitute Orion's Belt, more level meaning more
    snow.] (GJ)
49. Ganwaapo. = He eats too much of something and doesn't even
    want to look at it any more. (NJ)
50. Gii-wanii'ige mewinzha odoodaanaaming, gaawiin geyaabi
    noongom. = He used to trap long ago in his background,
    but not any more. (NJ)

Ogimaawigwanebiik (Nancy Jones) is a highly respected elder from Nigigoonsiminikaaning First Nation (Northwestern Ontario). She worked for many years as a teacher and cultural advisor for schools and tribal programs in Ontario, Minnesota, and Wisconsin. Her published works include *Aaniin Ekidong: Ojibwe Vocabulary Project* and *Awesiinyensag: Dibaajimowinan Ji-gikinoo'amaageng.*

Maajiigwaneyaash (Gordon Jourdain) is the Head Language Nest Teacher at Enweyang (University of Minnesota-Duluth). He is currently licensed to teach in Wisconsin and Minnesota. He has taught at Waadookodaading Ojibwe Immersion Charter School (Reserve, Wisconsin) and Lac Courte Oreilles Ojibwe Community College (Reserve, Wisconsin). He is co-author of *Aaniin Ekidong: Ojibwe Vocabulary Project.*

Zhaangweshi (Rose Tainter) is a longtime teacher and curriculum developer for Waadookodaading Ojibwe Immersion Charter School (Reserve, Wisconsin). She hails from Ponemah (Red Lake Reservation, Minnesota) and was featured in the acclaimed film *First Speakers: Restoring the Ojibwe Language.* Her published works include *Aaniin Ekidong: Ojibwe Vocabulary Project* and *Awesiinyensag: Dibaajimowinan Ji-gikinoo'amaageng.*

Waagosh (Anton Treuer) is professor of Ojibwe at Bemidji State University and editor of the *Oshkaabewis Native Journal.* His published works include *The Assassination of Hole in the Day*, *Ojibwe in Minnesota*, and several works on the Ojibwe language.

Waawaakeyaash (Keller Paap) is teacher and co-founder of Waadookodaading Ojibwe Immersion Charter School (Reserve, Wisconsin). His publications include *Aaniin Ekidong: Ojibwe Vocabulary Project, Awesiinyensag: Dibaajimowinan Ji-gikinoo'amaageng*, and several children's books in the Ojibwe language.

# THE ASSASSINATION OF HOLE IN THE DAY

### ANTON TREUER

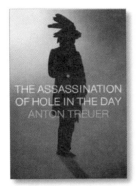

Explores the murder of the controversial Ojibwe chief who led his people through the first difficult years of dispossession by white invaders—and created a new kind of leadership for the Ojibwe.

On June 27, 1868, Hole in the Day (Bagone-giizhig) the Younger left Crow Wing, Minnesota, for Washington, DC, to fight the planned removal of the Mississippi Ojibwe to a reservation at White Earth. Several miles from his home, the self-styled leader of all the Ojibwe was stopped by at least twelve Ojibwe men and fatally shot.

Hole in the Day's death was national news, and rumors of its cause were many: personal jealousy, retribution for his claiming to be head chief of the Ojibwe, retaliation for the attacks he fomented in 1862, or reprisal for his attempts to keep mixed-blood Ojibwe off the White Earth Reservation. Still later, investigators found evidence of a more disturbing plot involving some of his closest colleagues: the business elite at Crow Wing.

While most historians concentrate on the Ojibwe relationship with whites to explain this story, Anton Treuer focuses on interactions with more than fifty elders to further explain the events leading up to the death of Hole in the Day. *The Assassination of Hole in the Day* is not only the biography of a powerful leader but an extraordinarily insightful analysis of a pivotal time in the history of the Ojibwe people.

"An essential study of nineteenth-century Ojibwe leadership and an important contribution to the field of American Indian Studies by an author of extraordinary knowledge and talent. Treuer's work is infused with a powerful command over Ojibwe culture and linguistics." —**Ned Blackhawk**, author of *Violence Over the Land: Indians and Empires in the Early American West*

**Anton Treuer**, professor of Ojibwe at Bemidji State University, is the author of *Ojibwe in Minnesota* and several books on the Ojibwe language. He is also the editor of **Oshkaabewis Native Journal**, the only academic journal of the Ojibwe language.

## NOW AVAILABLE

CLOTH • 304 PAGES • 6 X 9
30 B&W PHOTOGRAPHS, NOTES, INDEX, APPENDIX, BIBLIOGRAPHY
$25.95 • ISBN-13: 978-0-87351-779-9
E-BOOK: $20.95 • ISBN-13: 978-0-87351-801-7

## BOOKSTORES & RESELLERS

Borealis Books titles are available direct from the publisher or from wholesalers. Contact us for discount schedule and terms (800-647-7827 or Leslie.Rask@mnhs.org). Canadian resellers should contact Scholarly Book Services at 800-847-9736.

## ALSO OF INTEREST

**Ojibwe in Minnesota**
Anton Treuer
$14.95, Paper, ISBN-13: 978-0-87351-768-3
E-Book: $11.95 • ISBN-13: 978-0-87351-795-9

**Living Our Language: Ojibwe Tales and Oral Histories**
Anton Treuer
$19.95, Paper, ISBN-13: 978-0-87351-404-0
E-Book: $15.95 • ISBN-13: 978-0-87351-680-8

E-books are available from your favorite e-book vendors in a variety of formats.

### BOREALIS BOOKS
c/o Chicago Distribution Center
11030 South Langley Ave.
Chicago, IL 60628-3830
phone: 800-621-2736; fax: 800-621-8476

Name _____

Address _____

City _____ State _____ Zip _____

Phone _____

Check enclosed ___ VISA ___ MC ___ AmEx ___ Discover ___

Credit Card # _____ Exp. Date _____

Signature _____

| CODE | TITLE | QUANTITY | PRICE | TOTAL |
|------|-------|----------|-------|-------|
| 779-9 | The Assassination of Hole in the Day | | $25.95 | $ |
| 768-3 | Ojibwe in Minnesota | | $14.95 | $ |
| 404-0 | Living Our Language | | $19.95 | $ |

Subtotal $ _____

10% discount (MHS members) $ _____

State, county, or city sales tax* $ _____

Shipping ($5.00 + $1.00 per additional book) $ _____

TOTAL ENCLOSED $ _____

*Minnesota residents, 6.875%; Hennepin County residents, 7.275%; Minneapolis residents, 7.775%; St. Paul residents, 7.625%; Anoka, Dakota, and Washington county residents, 7.125%; Illinois residents, 10.25%.

# OJIBWE IN MINNESOTA

### ANTON TREUER

This compelling, highly anticipated narrative traces the history of the Ojibwe people in Minnesota, exploring cultural practices, challenges presented by more recent settlers, and modern-day discussions of sovereignty and identity.

With insight and candor, noted Ojibwe scholar Anton Treuer traces thousands of years of the complicated history of the Ojibwe people—their economy, culture, and clan system and how these have changed throughout time, perhaps most dramatically with the arrival of Europeans into Minnesota territory.

*Ojibwe in Minnesota* covers the fur trade, the Iroquois Wars, and Ojibwe-Dakota relations; the treaty process and creation of reservations; and the systematic push for assimilation as seen in missionary activity, government policy, and boarding schools.

Treuer also does not shy away from today's controversial topics, covering them frankly and with sensitivity—issues of sovereignty as they influence the running of casinos and land management; the need for reform in modern tribal government; poverty, unemployment, and drug abuse; and constitutional and educational reform. He also tackles the complicated issue of identity and details recent efforts and successes in cultural preservation and language revitalization.

A personal account from the state's first female Indian lawyer, Margaret Treuer, tells her firsthand experience of much change in the community and looks ahead with renewed cultural strength and hope for the first people of Minnesota.

**Anton Treuer** is professor of Ojibwe at Bemidji State University and editor of *Living Our Language: Ojibwe Tales and Oral Histories, Aaniin Ekidong: Ojibwe Vocabulary Project, Omaa Akiing,* and the *Oshkaabewis Native Journal,* the only academic journal of the Ojibwe language.

## AVAILABLE NOW
PAPER • 112 PAGES • 6 X 9
50 B&W ILLUSTRATIONS, 1 MAP, NOTES, INDEX,
BIBLIOGRAPHY
$14.95 • ISBN-13: 978-0-87351-768-3

## BOOKSTORES & RESELLERS
MHS Press titles are available direct from the publisher or from wholesalers. Contact us for discount schedule and terms (800-647-7827 or Leslie.Rask@mnhs.org). Canadian resellers should contact Scholarly Book Services at 800-847-9736.

## ALSO OF INTEREST
**Living Our Language**
Ojibwe Tales and Oral Histories
Anton Treuer
$19.95, Paper, ISBN-13: 978-0-87351-404-0
NATIVE VOICES

---

## MINNESOTA HISTORICAL SOCIETY PRESS
c/o Chicago Distribution Center
11030 South Langley Ave.
Chicago, IL 60628-3830
phone: 800-621-2736; fax: 800-621-8476

Name

Address

City                State        Zip

Phone

Check enclosed ___ VISA ___ MC ___ AmEx ___ Discover ___

Credit Card # _____ Exp. Date _____

| CODE | TITLE | QUANTITY | PRICE | TOTAL |
|------|-------|----------|-------|-------|
| 768-3 | Ojibwe in Minnesota | | $14.95 | $ |
| 404-0 | Living Our Language | | $19.95 | $ |

Subtotal $ _____

10% discount (MHS members) $ _____

State, county, or city sales tax* $ _____

Shipping ($5.00 + $1.00 per additional book) $ _____

TOTAL ENCLOSED $ _____

*Minnesota residents, 6.875%; Hennepin County residents, 7.275%; Minneapolis residents, 7.775%; St. Paul residents, 7.625%; Anoka, Dakota, and Washington county residents, 7.125%; Illinois residents, 10.25%.

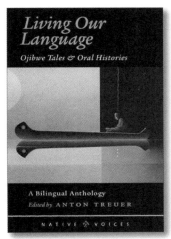

**NOW AVAILABLE**
LIVING OUR LANGUAGE:
OJIBWE TALES & ORAL HISTORIES
A BILINGUAL ANTHOLOGY

$19.95 PAPER 320 PAGES
ISBN: 978-0-87351-404-0
E-BOOK: $15.95 ISBN: 978-0-87351-680-8

## BOOKSTORES & RESELLERS

MHS Press titles are available direct from the publisher or from wholesalers. Contact us for discount schedule and terms (800-647-7827 or Leslie.Rask@mnhs.org). Canadian resellers should contact Scholarly Book Services at 800-847-9736.

E-books are available from your favorite e-book vendors in a variety of formats.

# LIVING OUR LANGUAGE

## ANTON TREUER

As fluent speakers of Ojibwe grow older, the community questions whether younger speakers know the language well enough to pass it on to the next generation. Young and old alike are making widespread efforts to preserve the Ojibwe language, and, as part of this campaign, Anton Treuer has collected stories from Anishinaabe elders living at Leech Lake (MN), White Earth (MN), Mille Lacs (MN), Red Lake (MN), and St. Croix (WI) reservations.

Based on interviews Treuer conducted with ten elders--Archie Mosay, Jim Clark, Melvin Eagle, Joe Auginaush, Collins Oakgrove, Emma Fisher, Scott Headbird, Susan Jackson, Hartley White, and Porky White--this anthology presents the elders' stories transcribed in Ojibwe with English translation on facing pages. These stories contain a wealth of information, including oral histories of the Anishinaabe people and personal reminiscences, educational tales, and humorous anecdotes.

'A rich and varied collection of tales from the Ojibwe (Chippewa) tradition . . . Drawn from printed and oral sources, the stories are meticulously and sensitively translated and anotated giving shape, form, and nuance to a fragile, almost extinct, civilization. This preservation project will be a vital addition to Native American lore." – *Library Journal*

'A major contribution to Anisbinaabe studies. Treuer's collection is particularly welcome as it brings in new voices to speak of the varied experiences of the Anishinaabeg of recent generations." - **John D. Nichols**, co-editor of *A Concise Dictionary of Minnesota Ojibwe*

**Anton Treuer** is professor of Ojibwe at Bemidji State University, and the author of *The Assassination of Hole in the Day* and *Ojibwe in Minnesota*. He is also the editor of *Oshkaabewis Native Journal*, the only academic journal of the Ojibwe language.

---

## MINNESOTA HISTORICAL SOCIETY PRESS

c/o Chicago Distribution Center
11030 South Langley Ave.
Chicago, IL 60628-3830
phone: 800-621-2736; fax: 800-621-8476

Name _____

Address _____

City _____ State _____ Zip _____

Phone _____

Check enclosed ___ VISA ___ MC ___ AmEx ___ Discover ___

Credit Card # _____ Exp. Date _____

| CODE | TITLE | QUANTITY | PRICE | TOTAL |
|------|-------|----------|-------|-------|
| 404-0 | Living Our Language | | $19.95 | $ |

Subtotal $ _____

10% discount (MHS members) $ _____

State, county, or city sales tax* $ _____

Shipping ($5.00 + $1.00 per additional book) $ _____

TOTAL ENCLOSED $ _____

*Minnesota residents, 6.875%; Hennepin County residents, 7.275%; Minneapolis residents, 7.775%; St. Paul residents, 7.625%; Anoka, Dakota, and Washington county residents, 7.125%; Illinois residents, 10.25%.

# MINNESOTA HUMANITIES CENTER

# AANIIN EKIDONG

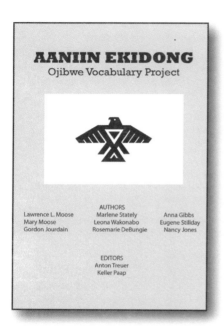

**AANIIN EKIDONG**
Ojibwe Vocabulary Project

AUTHORS
Lawrence L. Moose    Marlene Stately    Anna Gibbs
Mary Moose    Leona Wakonabo    Eugene Stillday
Gordon Jourdain    Rosemarie DeBungie    Nancy Jones

EDITORS
Anton Treuer
Keller Paap

For the Ojibwe language to live, it must be used for everything every day. While most Ojibwe people live in a modern world, dominated by computers, motors, science, mathematics, and global issues, the language that has grown to discuss these things is not often taught or thought about by most teachers and students of the language. A group of nine fluent elders representing several different dialects of Ojibwe gathered with teachers from Ojibwe immersion schools and university language programs to brainstorm and document less-well-known but critical modern Ojibwe terminology. Topics discussed include science, medicine, social studies, geography, mathematics, and punctuation. This book is the result of their labors.

## FREE DOWNLOAD

minnesotahumanities.org/aaniin

## PURCHASE

amazon.com
lulu.com
minnesotahumanities.org/aaniin

# First Speakers
## RESTORING THE OJIBWE LANGUAGE

This inspiring new documentary about ongoing efforts to revitalize the Ojibwe language was produced by Emmy-award winning producer John Whitehead. Major segments are devoted to the community of Ponemah on the Red Lake Reservation, the immersion schools in Bena, Minnesota, and Reserve, Wisconsin, and resource development at Bemidji State University.

## VIEW ONLINE OR DOWNLOAD

http://www.tpt.org/?a=productions&id=3 or

http://www.tpt.org and type in "First Speakers"

# Birchbark Books

By Kimberly Nelson
Illustrated by Clem May
Translation by
Earl Otchingwanigan
(Nyholm)
Audio by Anton Treuer

## I Will Remember: Inga-minjimendam

With these words the author introduces the young narrator who takes us through the everyday experiences that he most enjoys—a walk along the lakeshore or through the woods, "looking at all the little animals that are there," netting fish with his father, swimming, ice fishing, going to pow-wows. "But most of all," he says, "I like to listen to my grandfather tell stories. He tells all sorts of legends to me, and about all those things he did when he was small." The bilingual text— English and Ojibwe—is imaginatively and colorfully illustrated from the artist's own experiences living near the shores of Red Lake in northern Minnesota.

## ORDER ONLINE
http://www.birchbarkbooks.com

## VISIT
Birchbark Books
2115 West 21st Street
Minneapolis, MN 55405
612-374-4023

# Birchbark Books

## OMAA AKIING
### *Anton Treuer, Editor*

This monolingual anthology of Ojibwe stories by elders from Leech Lake will entertain and enlighten. Walter "Porky" White, Hartley White, Susan Jackson, Emma Fisher, and Charles "Scott" Headbird share numerous chilhood reminiscences, jokes, and stories in their first language.

## ORDER ONLINE
### http://www.birchbarkbooks.com

## VISIT
### Birchbark Books
### 2115 West 21st Street
### Minneapolis, MN 55405
### 612-374-4023

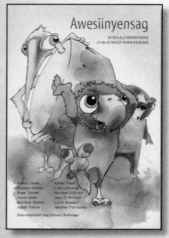

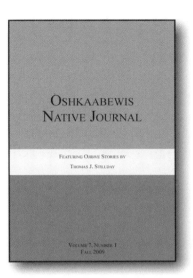